Data Processing Contracts

Other books by Dick H. Brandon

Management Standards for Data Processing
Management Planning for Data Processing
Project Control Standards
Data Processing Organization and Manpower Planning
Data Processing Management: Methods and Standards

Data Processing Contracts

Structure, Contents, and Negotiation

Second Edition

Dick H. Brandon

and

Sidney Segelstein, Esq.

Revised by
George Ian Brandon, Esq.

VNR Van Nostrand Reinhold Company
New York/Cincinnati/Toronto/London/Melbourne

Library of Congress Catalog Card Number: 83-5842
ISBN: 0-442-21034-5

Manufactured in the United States of America

Published by Van Nostrand Reinhold Company Inc.
135 West 50th Street
New York, New York 10020

Van Nostrand Reinhold Company Limited
Molly Millars Lane
Wokingham, Berkshire RG11 2PY, England

Van Nostrand Reinhold
480 Latrobe Street
Melbourne, Victoria 3000, Australia

Macmillan of Canada
Division of Gage Publishing Limited
164 Commander Boulevard
Agincourt, Ontario MIS 3C7, Canada

15 14 13 12 11 10 9 8 7 6 5 4 3 2 1

Library of Congress Cataloging in Publication Data

Brandon, Dick H.
  Data processing contracts.

  Includes index.
  1. Computer leases—United States. 2. Computers—
Specifications—United States. I. Segelstein, Sidney.
II. Brandon, George Ian. III. Title.
KF946.B73 1983   346.73'025   83-5842
ISBN 0-442-21034-5   347.30625

PREFACE
to the Second Edition

The authors of this book, my father and his best friend, died together in an airplane accident in September, 1981.

The book survives as an important and unique contribution both to lawyers and to their clients who are or will be data processing users. In recognition of the lasting nature of the book, the present revision seeks only to take account of developments in the law and, to a lesser extent, the industry which might be critical to the reader. Significantly, for example, there is now a "common law" of data processing contracts of which the reader must be aware—courts have now considered some of the issues about which the authors could only speculate when the book was first published.

The Second Edition, then, preserves the insight and approach of the authors while updating the book for reference in the "contracting environment" of today. Instrumental in this updating process was Andrew Plunkett, whose research and drafting assistance is gratefully acknowledged. Thanks are also due to Peggy Mulcahy, whose administrative and secretarial skills helped, as usual, to meet the "unmeetable" deadline.

Finally, mention must be made of the sadly prophetic closing sentence of the Preface to the First Edition. Dad, perhaps—but I would have preferred to have gotten it another way, and another day.

George Ian Brandon, Esq.

Port Washington, N.Y.

PREFACE
to the First Edition

This book is a reference book. It is designed to serve as a guide to management interested in obtaining one or more products or services supplied by the 'computer industry'—an amalgam of some 2,000 companies offering a bewildering variety of things, under an even greater variety of contractual arrangements—or sometimes none at all.

The book is designed as a cookbook. Part of it is devoted to discussion of the philosophical parameters of contracts but that is not its significance to the user. The major part of the book is a dull, indexed list of contract terms and clauses potentially usable by someone interested in constructing a specific contract. If your interest is in developing a software package contract, review the chapter on software packages, select those terms you consider necessary or important, and evaluate the alternative clauses given in the appendix.

This book is designed primarily for the data processing user, although it should be of help to vendors wishing to improve their contractual practices—or wishing to understand the reasons for their users' recalcitrance. It is not designed to be a legal form book; although it covers substantive points useful to corporate counsel. Most attorneys will wish to construct their own contracts, using their own language—in this case the book will identify the scope to be covered, and will suggest approaches to unusual problems.

The clauses provided herein are designed to be useful, and to provide ideas to the negotiator or his counsel. They are not optimized—there are hundreds of alternative ways of presenting a contractual element—we have simply selected one or more alternatives which we felt to be useful. It is therefore mandatory that the book be used intelligently, as a reference, with caution, and in all events *with the active participation of counsel.*

One can argue about the validity of the cookbook approach. However, the subject is so complicated and so intertwined that it is almost impossible to produce a book which would cover the subject completely and adequately. And, since the standard of contracting in the computer field (certainly as exemplified by the standard contracts in use) is totally inadequate, this book attempts to take an initial step, in covering at least the basic components of a vendor-user relationship. "In the land of the blind, one-eye is King" goes an old expression, and in this way we hope to make at least a contribution to the state-of-the art in this heretofore sadly neglected area.

No book is really the work of the authors alone. The authors wish to express their deep appreciation to the following vendors who contributed their standard contracts for partial inclusion in the Appendix, as part G of appropriate clauses. The vendors are listed in alphabetical sequence.

Applied Data Research, Inc.
Brandon Applied Systems, Inc.
Bunker-Ramo Corporation
Burroughs Corporation

Honeywell Information Systems, Inc.
IBM
ITEL
Leasco Division of Reliance Group
NCR
Univac Division of Sperry Rand.

For optimum illustrative purposes, the GSA contract with Honeywell was used, and our appreciation extends to the General Services Administration of the U.S. Government as well.

Our thanks must also go to our faithful secretaries, for typing above and beyond the call of duty, Miss Grace Helmers, Mrs. Nancy Mackin, and Miss Deborah Grice. Finally, our associates, partners, relatives and friends who bore with us through the production and development of this book deserve whatever they can get.

New York, N.Y.

Dick H. Brandon
Sidney Segelstein, Esq.

LIST OF ILLUSTRATIONS

LIST OF CONTRACT CLAUSES

*Page in right-hand column refers to entry in the Appendix.

INDEX TO CLAUSES BY RISK RATING

*Page in right-hand column refers to entry in the Appendix.

Risk Rating 4—No Impact (28 Clauses)

TABLE OF CASES

CONTENTS

1 THE CONTRACTING ENVIRONMENT

A. INTRODUCTION

Ten years ago, the vast majority of the purchase or rental of computer-related goods and services was obtained without the benefit of an adequate contract. Much of it is still obtained that way, or without any contract at all.

However, as the risk associated with the purchase of such goods and services has increased as the complexity of their uses has increased, so too have the resulting dissatisfaction and, inevitably, litigation increased. This will continue to be the case as user sophistication increases, and as the impact of computer-using activities reaches into higher and higher levels of management. As a result, it is expected that litigation will become to an even greater extent a routine part of life when using computers in the business environment.

In recognition of the maxim that an ounce of prevention is worth a pound of cure, and for the protection of all concerned, it is unassailably wise to prepare a comprehensive contract for the acquisition of the resources necessary in using computers. Thus, a relatively little amount of time spent on the careful preparation of a series of contracts covering resource acquisition should pay off one hundredfold during and after implementation of the computer installation.

B. CONTRACT OBJECTIVES

A contract for the acquisition of goods or services is a multiple purpose document. It will serve to define the relationship between the parties, and it should further serve to provide a clear indication of the potential difficulties inherent in the relationship,

A contract should be developed with the view that it should never be looked at again after it has been drawn and executed. It is clear that the implementation of the computer installation is a highly complex undertaking which must be governed by the good will and technical cooperation of the parties involved. If it becomes necessary to refer to the contract to enforce that relationship, it is probably too late to have a truly successful installation. There is no way of enforcing *good will:* one can only enforce the mechanical commitments defined in a contract. Thus, although a contract may be negotiated extremely energetically and although it may appear as if the contractual document is the most important document in the entire installation, it is probably a good practice to take the contractual document and lock it away somewhere in the hope that the relationship between the parties can be established so that no further reference to the contract is required. The objectives of both parties should converge to the point where they are solely interested in implementing the spirit of the agreement. The letter of the agreement should never have to be consulted or, worse, needed to enforce the agreement.

Notwithstanding this, the contract has significant value both prior to and during the implementation process. Key objectives of the contract are:

1. As protection against potential disaster, unanticipated at the time the relationship was initiated. These disasters can include business termination of the vendor, or potentially of the user; the reassignment of personnel whose relationships were vital to the implementation of the contract; or a natural disaster, act of God, strike, or other event which might disrupt the implementation of the computer installation activity.
2. A clear documentation of the agreement between the parties, and the commitments made by each party to the other. Time has a way of erasing memory of individuals involved in a contractual relationship. Thus, it is useful to commit to paper in one document the totality of commitment on both sides of an agreement.
3. To delineate clearly the responsibility of each party in the implementation process. It should be recognized that each party has responsibility for the performance of specific tasks which may affect the proper performance by the other party.
4. To provide *clear* technical and legal descriptions so that future participants in the process will be able to decipher the terms of the relationship.
5. To provide a point of reference in the event the relationship breaks down, without affecting the progress of the joint implementation activity.
6. To establish quantitative, mechanistic measures of performance where it is feasible to do so.
7. To alert management to the problems associated with computer implementation, and to increase their sophistication by providing a comprehensive document describing the relationship.
8. To overcome arrogance on the part of certain vendors in the industry, in part emanating from certain monopolistic practices which have become traditional in the computer industry.
9. To provide some means of recourse and some definition of remedies, if all else fails.

C. USES OF THE CONTRACT

The contract document itself should be of very little use, as already indicated. It can be used as a reference, to define the responsibilities of the parties in the implementation process. It should be used to resolve any disputes which might take place between the parties, and it is potentially useful as an enforcement document to ensure that the other party is aware of the agreements made and is responsible for performing accordingly.

Historically there have been few notably successful implementations of computers in industry and in government. In part this is due to the breakdown of the relationship between the vendor and the user involved. Some of the failures could have been prevented by more careful contracting practice; in fact, the actual development of a careful and comprehensive contract will result in highlighting those areas where particular care must be taken in implementation. The contracting process itself therefore can be of considerable assistance in planning the implementation process correctly.

Unfortunately, principal vendors in the computer field do not believe it desirable from their point of view to structure a comprehensive contract. This has resulted in a tradition of grossly inadequate contractual relationships, which provide very little protection for the user, and concomitantly provide little protection for the vendor as well. However, the vendor generally is in a much better position than the user, since the vendor is protected by sheer size, the difficulty of the litigation process, and the general ennui of the buying public. Moreover, the contract is normally on the vendor's form, drawn by its attorneys to protect him against the most obvious—and most frequently occurring—problems. The vendor-drawn contract also usually contains those "boiler-plate" clauses traditionally attempted by vendors, such as warranty disclaimers, all tending to avoidance of any liability. As a result, the development of a sophisticated contract primarily benefits the user, and this text is addressed to the user for that reason.

D. THE CONTENTS OF A CONTRACT

A properly written contract will minimize the hidden risks of the parties to it, by focusing upon the responsibilities of each to the extent that they can be foreseen. A good contract will deal comprehensively with the two substantive aspects of any transaction. The first aspect is that of describing the job to be done and the price to be paid; the second is to explore the contingencies.

The descriptive part of a contract is generally thought to be the easiest and most straightforward. On the contrary, it is the most difficult. The best example of good descriptive contracting is that utilized in the construction industry—the plans and specifications prepared by an architect and engineer and given by the builder to the general contractor as part of the construction contract. Properly prepared plans and specifications leave nothing to chance and cover all aspects of design, materials, workmanship and structure. In the data processing industry physical plans and specifications are of less consequence, since many items are standard in configuration. Most important are performance specifications and delivery criteria and these should be exhaustively dealt with.

An example will suffice. Here are two contracts for the purchase of the same article:

A. "One Horse—$100 C.O.D.—one year rental"
B. "One solid black, two-year-old stallion, with all his teeth, vaccinated within the last 30 days, complete with horseshoes, weight at least 1600 pounds, trained for the saddle, capable of running one mile in 2 minutes or under, in good health, otherwise as is. Delivery to X stable on or before January 1, 1976. $100 C.O.D. (cash only). Freight charges of $45 to be borne by Buyer, and risk of injury or death to Seller until received by Buyer at X stable. Price covers one year's rental. Buyer to return horse to Seller at end of year, freight prepaid.

Unfortunately, there are too many "one horse" contracts being signed daily in the computer field. Inadequate description of physical, performance and delivery criteria are the rule and suppliers have a great factual advantage over users when problems arise because of these descriptive inadequacies. The solution to the problem is to first think out what is expected from the resource purchase in the most comprehensive possible manner and incorporate that list in the contract. The thought processes involved will lead directly to the second substantive aspect, that of contingencies. This is the area that deals with answers to an infinite variety of questions starting with the words "What if?"

Reverting to the purchase of the horse, some thought reveals the following "what if" questions, among many others, and some possible contracting answers.

1. What if the horse goes lame within 30 days? Get some warranty extending into the future.
2. What if the horse goes lame within 30 days, but as a result of being improperly shod? Get the warranty to exclude misuse.
3. What if the horse is delivered, but a day late? Get a "liquidated damages" provision.
4. What if late delivery is a result of a strike or accident on the carrier? Determine who will bear the loss.
5. What if the horse turns out to be sterile? Get a warranty of virility extending for some future time period.
6. What if there are sales taxes payable on the rental of a horse? Fix responsibility for payment.
7. What if a horse cannot be moved between different states without a medical examination? Fix responsibility for this.
8. What if the horse dies within the year? Of natural causes? Of accident? Of abuse?
9. What if there is a dispute between Buyer and Seller on the contract? If they are located in different states, which law controls?

The potential list of "what ifs?" in any complex transaction is probably infinite, but the exercise is a very necessary one. The best contracts written are those that pay careful attention to contingencies. Lawyers sometimes try to categorize descriptive elements of a contract as "covenants" or "promises" and the "what if" elements as "representations" or "warranties." The distinctions are basically of little value. It is the thought processes that count. Some "what if" questions can be resolved by proper description of required performance and some descriptive elements of a contract; particularly those having to do with future events are best considered in the "what if" framework. The user staff which comprehensively thinks out and lists the performance criteria and the contingencies early in the procurement stage will make the role of management and of counsel considerably easier and will make the negotiating process much more straightforward. These thought processes, it might be added, are not simple, and assistance of counsel is urged at this stage, since lawyers are (ostensibly) trained to think this way.

E. THE GSA CONTRACT

There is one exception to the weak contracting practices in U.S. industry, and that is the contract negotiated annually by the General Services Administration of the U.S. Government. The GSA contract is a relatively comprehensive document, which provides for the acquisition of hardware and software on terms which cover a reasonable percentage of the totality of terms normally considered desirable. Unfortunately, the GSA negotiates a blanket contract, which must of necessity be generalized, since it will cover the procurement of anything from small systems to giant installations. Thus, the GSA contract cannot cover *specifics* in the relationship between a particular government installation and a particular vendor; only the general terms of the relationship relating to price, delivery, default and such can be covered in a blanket contract.

Notwithstanding this, the GSA contract is a highly useful document even for a nongovernment user, who can refer to it in examining the types of terms required and obtained by the largest user of computers in the world. Thus, the reader is advised to obtain a copy of the GSA contract signed by the particular vendor concerned with the reader's own requirements. This will provide a good initial base from which to construct a totally viable contract.

F. THE INDUSTRY

1. Nature of the Industry

In early 1975, there were some 140,000 computers installed in the United States, and an additional 120,000 in the rest of the world. In the United States, computer expenditures on an annual basis account for over 35 billion dollars, or somewhat over three percent of the gross national product! People employed in computer-related professions number well over 1.5 million, and people whose job functions are affected by computers in one way or another include over half the working population. Despite all this, the computer industry is a very young industry, and has only just celebrated its 25th anniversary. In 1965 there were less than 20,000 computers installed in the United States; thus the principal growth of the industry has been in the past ten years, and its traditions and practices have not yet been firmly established.

However, the impact of the computer is obviously highly significant. An annual expenditure of 30 billion dollars must indeed be justified on the basis of displacement of equivalent costs, or the generation of comparable benefits to industry and government. This phenomenal growth should not suggest that the industry has stabilized, and that the total number of computer installations has now reached a saturation level. Quite the contrary, it is forecast that by 1980 the United States will have a computer population of well over 300,000, and that total annual computer expenditures will be in excess of 90 billion dollars (in terms of 1975 dollars). This would be some 6% of the gross national product, and would involve the employment of somewhere over three million people in computer-related professions. The impact of this has to be significant. Not only will computers be used to perform all routine operational functions of business information processing and to improve the quality of engineering and product design, but they will be used in every process of managing all business and governmental organizations in the United States. This means an ever-increasing dependence by society on computers, which in turn means an ever-increasing risk if computer implementation or computer use should fail.

In 1965 the failure of a computer system for a week or more would simply have resulted in a reverting to manual replacement systems capable of performing substantially identical functions. The payroll would have been calculated by hand, and perhaps typed by hand, if computer processing were disrupted by some natural or unnatural disaster. In 1975, an equivalent failure would cause chaos in an organization; it would probably result in the implementation of various types of backup procedures, with potentially significant delays in the delivery of necessary operational materials to parts of the organization. However, even in 1975 the organization's survival would not be threatened by a significant computer failure. This will not be the case in 1985, when the computer itself will control the operation of much of the organization. Failure of the heart of the organization will indeed result in (possibly temporary) failure of the organization. It is entirely likely that a computer failure in 1985 will require a cessation of business for the period during which the computer is unavailable, with the result that it may be impossible to restart the organization if such failure persists for a long period of time.

This again serves to point out the increasing importance of a realistic relationship between vendor and user of computer goods and services. Users can see therefore that it is almost impossible to avoid being a pioneer in the computer field. There are no established traditions, there are no clear-cut practices of management, and certainly there are no established contractual practices.

2. Make Up of the Industry

The U.S. computer industry at the present time is made up of some 2,000 vendor organizations trying to provide a wide variety of goods and services to using organizations in industry and government. Vendors in the field can be generally classified as follows:

1. Principal Manufacturers of Large-Scale Computers. Eight of the largest manufacturers in this category, dominated in sales by IBM, are:
   IBM
   Digital Equipment Corporation
   Burroughs
   NCR
   Sperry
   Control Data Corporation
   Honeywell
   Amdahl
2. Principal Manufacturers of Small-Scale Computers. Computer applications are becoming more and more specialized. As a result, the industry is becoming increasingly fragmented with both large and small companies manufacturing specialized computers to fit a particular niche in the field. One major segment includes those companies manufacturing office systems and word processors. Wang, Xerox and Lanier are all in this category. One of the newest and fastest growing segments of the industry is the personal computer market. Apple, Commodore, and IBM are all manufacturers of low-priced personal computers.
3. Peripheral Manufacturers. In this category are the manufacturers that sup-

ply peripheral components used in conjunction with computers. These include tape drives, disc drives, memory extensions, printers, card readers, and a variety of other specialized equipment from companies such as Storage Technology, Textronix, Datapoint, and Xerox.

4. Terminal Suppliers. Terminals are generally treated separately, because terminals may be purchased and used totally independently, for example, using telephone hook-ups. Anyone can purchase a terminal, and it is not uncommon for students to use terminals at home for use in communicating with their school's computer. There are well over 100 manufacturers of terminals, ranging in size from AT&T to a host of smaller manufacturers producing a variety of terminals, including some that can be hooked up to home television receivers. Terminals include key-driven typewriter-like devices, such as produced by Texas Instruments or Xerox; cathode ray tube devices, such as produced by IBM, Datapoint, and Textronix; and remote job entry terminals, which provide for full-scale entry of batch processing data and generally have the capability to read punch cards or paper tape, and to produce output on a high-speed printing device.

5. Communications Equipment and Services. As data processing services begin to expand into every level of an organization, communication of data from geographically disparate components of the organization becomes vital. Thus the integration of data communication services and computing services will be the hallmark of the industry in this decade. Vendors supplying communication services include AT&T, IT&T, MCI, and a host of other manufacturers making modern equipment, communication control devices, multiplexers, and even satellite equipment. Additionally, due to recent changes in government regulation and antitrust enforcement policy, two industry giants, IBM and AT&T, can be expected to compete vigorously in this segment of the industry.

6. Supplies. In this category vendors can be classified as providing consumable and nonconsumable supplies. In the category of nonconsumable supplies are such items as disc packs, tape reels, or printer ribbons, and installation facility elements, such as tape library shelves, fireproof vaults, or transportation carts for equipment and supplies. Consumable supplies generally refer to items such as punched cards, printer forms, paper tape or optical scanning documents. There are hundreds of vendors in this category, which not only serve the computer field but also other office needs.

7. Machine-related Services. This category includes somewhat over 5,000 companies, providing services using equipment on their premises. This includes machine time brokerage organizations, service bureaus providing a wide variety of services, time-sharing services, or organizations providing the end result of processing, applications services of one type or another. Also considered in this category are banks and others prepared to perform payroll or other applications processing.

8. People-related Services. In the category of people-dependent services are systems engineering and programming services, consulting services, and other specialists who provide a range of services which may be purchased from outside or alternately may be provided from within the organization. There are at least 2,000 organizations providing this type of service.

9. Product-related Services. This category includes organizations providing data processing training services, publishing books or magazines in the computer field, and most importantly those organizations selling software packages, a special product born of the computer field.

10. Financial Organizations. The annual acquisition of billions of dollars worth of products and services often requires financial support. Thus, leasing and other financial companies may be used to finance the acquisition of equipment, of software, or to underwrite or insure the development of a system.
11. Used Equipment Vendors. It is not always necessary to purchase computers or computer components from the original manufacturer. Today there is a somewhat depressed used equipment market, capable of providing previously owned equipment of high quality at a significant reduction in cost, limited only by the rapid advance of technology, and resulting acceleration of obsolescence.

This classification is not intended to be exhaustive; it is used only to provide an illustration of the variety of products and services available in the computer industry, and the great variety of organizations which make these services or products available. Again the point is clear—a contractual relationship is necessary which clearly defines the responsibilities of both parties, and outlines the way in which the products or services will perform the functions for which they are sold.

G. THE STANDARD CONTRACT

The purchase of hardware represents by far the largest part of the total purchase of goods and services. Thus the hardware contract and the contractual relationships implied therein essentially dominate the contractual practices used in the acquisition of other goods and services. In hardware the manufacturer which dominates the market, IBM, in turn determines to a large extent what contractual practices will be considered as de facto standards.

Unfortunately the computer industry started as a rental industry, primarily because IBM until 1956 made its equipment available on a rental basis only. This lies at the root of the contractual problem in the industry; a rental contract is not a complex document, and since it is ostensibly terminable on short notice, it does not require that the obligations of the parties be spelled out in great detail. At least that was the philosophy which existed in 1956, when a consent decree signed by IBM required IBM thenceforth to make available its equipment for sale as well.

The contract in 1956 was a very simple Machine-Use Agreement, under which the user agreed to use the equipment and pay for it promptly and under which the vendor agreed to provide the machine and keep it "in good working order." If the user was dissatisfied the contract simply allowed termination with thirty days notice, without penalty. This type of "machine use" agreement provided the manufacturer with enormous flexibility, since it did not set forth any particular obligation for the performance of the equipment, for its acceptance on the user's site, or for the reliability implied by "good working order." Unfortunately, the 1956 contract continues to pervade the industry and the philosophy of contracting to this very day. After signing the consent decree in 1956, IBM was forced to provide for the sale of its equipment and it thereby constructed a purchase contract which was very similar to the previous rental contract. It provides basically for the passage of title from IBM to the user without any significant recourse from the user to IBM. Upon purchase, the user executes a maintenance contract, a separate document, cancelable on thirty days notice by either party, where again IBM undertakes to maintain the equipment in "good working order." If there is a complaint, it is quite possible to cancel the maintenance contract, even though the user has made a total commitment to the equipment by virtue of its purchase.

Recourse to the manufacturer at that point is very limited, and restricted by both the contract and the Uniform Commercial Code.

This then is the foundation of contracting practice in the computer industry, and all other manufacturers, recognizing the clear advantage of this practice, followed IBM's lead in establishing a standard contract which provides little protection for the user, and which provides for short term termination. Unfortunately significant problems are not solved by short-term termination. In the context of an equipment purchase, the problems of termination are extraordinary. The sale is absolute, and nonmaintenance does not void the obligation to pay for purchased hardware. The user's investment in planning, systems design, programming and general implementation of a computer system is so huge, that he is bound by this investment to use the system for a long period of time. Thus, although the contract for rental or maintenance is not a binding document, the practice and practicalities suggest that the user is inevitably bound; unfortunately the manufacturer is not and it is at this point that relationships can deteriorate and a more viable contract becomes highly desirable.

Similarly, standard contracts in other components of the industry have taken the hardware contract as their model. After all, it can be argued that if the acquisition of a million dollar computer is governed by a hardware contract of only one or two pages, the acquisition of a $100,000 software package certainly needs no more. Unfortunately the reverse is also true here, but traditions (even bad ones) appear hard to break.

The user should examine the standard contract with a great deal of skepticism. This skepticism should be focused on what the contract omits, rather than what the contract commits. The standard contract as such is not an acceptable document from the viewpoint of the user. Anyone who accepts the standard contract as the sole instrument defining the agreement between the parties in a computer acquisition had better recognize the motto "caveat emptor."

H. TYPES OF CONTRACTS

1. Resources of Data Processing

The resources used by data processing organizations are extensive (and expensive). The principal resource, in terms of its importance to the success of the installation, is the personnel of the installation: the management, analysts, programmers, operators, and various staff and support personnel. In this book, however, the prime resource is considered to be computer hardware, since it governs to a large extent the contractual practices in the field, and since it represents the majority of goods and services obtained from *outside* the organization. It is not the intention to slight the importance of personnel or organization in this text; it simply places the emphasis on the area of data processing where contractual relationships are most significant. A brief list of resources used in a data processing installation is significant, and points to the types of contracts to be considered by a manager interested in establishing an installation:

- Computer hardware
- Peripheral equipment
- Terminals
- Communications equipment
- Supplies

- Facility equipment, such as fire protecton equipment, alarms, intercoms, library material and the like
- Software
- Space
- Guard services
- Bureau services
- Programming services
- Training
- Consulting services
- Site preparation and construction
- Transportation of equipment
- Publications, books, and magazines
- Conversion services for programs, or data
- Equipment test time
- Backup and emergency services, etc, etc, etc.

2. Contract Form

It is possible to structure a contract in at least three different ways. Although form in data processing and all other contracts is secondary to substance, the industry has historically fallen into three patterns of contract form. First, most comprehensive and most rarely utilized is a complete master contract with a vendor, embodying all services and responsibilities of that vendor with regard to the installation. Thus, if one were to purchase a computer from a vendor, the master contract would include the purchase agreement, the maintenance agreement, software to be purchased or supplied with the computer, alterations to equipment, relocation or transportation of equipment, potential training services, and the like. This form of contract is most preferable, since it sets forth the relative responsibility of the two organizations and since it can clearly state that a failure of one component or element of the contract affects other elements of the contract.

An alternative is to separate the various contract elements into separate documents, which tends to dilute the responsibility of the vendor. This is the form preferred by most manufacturers, for precisely that reason. Failure of the maintenance contract should have no impact therefore on the responsibilities of the user in the purchase contract. This is generally to the disadvantage of the user and it is strongly recommended that the responsibilities of the parties be embodied in a single master contract where all obligations can be set forth explicitly.

The third practice which has become common in the computer industry is to sign the standard contract, and to amend that contract through use of a unilateral "side letter." This side letter ostensibly commits the vendor to perform additional services for the user. It is a unilateral document, but if it is signed by the proper authority within the vendor's organization, and if it is not excluded by a clause in the standard contract, then a side letter contemporaneous with or subsequent to the contract can usually be deemed a binding commitment on the part of the vendor. "Side letters" or proposals that antedate the signed contract are fraught with danger and cannot be relied upon. This is especially true where vendors utilize a "merger" provision, as in most standard contracts, to the effect that all *prior* representations and agreements are merged in the contract and are not enforceable unless contained or referred to therein.

Despite the short history of the industry, its practice is sufficiently ingrained so that most contractual relationships with a hardware vendor will be embodied in multiple contracts. Wherever possible and feasible, therefore, the contract should provide for specific contractual remedies if specific clauses are breached. Thus, if a vendor fails to provide a product or a service on time, it should perhaps pay some form of liquidated damages related to the length of the delay, or its impact. If the vendor fails to maintain equipment in good working order, perhaps it can be forced to supply substitute equipment. In any event, each clause should be examined to determine if specific remedies can be identified in the event the clause is not complied with by either party, to insure that contract enforcement is as simple as possible.

3. Liquidated Damages

It is often simple and effective to identify specific dollar damages whenever a contract provision is breached. This provides for easy enforcement and furnishes incentive for insuring compliance. It is difficult, however, to assess *realistic* liquidated damages, since failures in a computer environment can be rather severe, and since *consequential* damages are often exempted by reasonable people. Liquidated damages are an attempt to fix, by agreement, the amount of the loss suffered by a party, where the actual loss would be difficult to compute with exactness. As recently as five years ago, it was common practice to use liquidated damages of an even $100 per day for failure to deliver components which made it impossible to operate the computer. If one considers however that $100 a day, despite its onerous sound, is only $36,000 per annum, or the salary of one systems engineer or salesman, it may well be to the fiscal advantage of the vendor to *delay* delivery, rather than incur significant overtime costs to meet an arbitrary delivery date.

In addition, if a computer installation operates on a million dollar annual budget, and one vendor's failure to deliver delays the installation and places into limbo investments made in planning, siting, programming, testing and the like, then compensation of $100 a day is clearly insignificant by comparison. By the same token, it would be highly unreasonable to expect a computer vendor to sign a contract calling for delay liquidated damages of $20,000 per day, although that is a far more reasonable level of compensation from the viewpoint of the actual damages incurred by delivery delays. To date, no computer contract has been signed with liquidated damages in that range.

Liquidated damage provisions must always be realistic. A weak vendor may agree to an unreasonably high amount, and the user may never get the benefit. If a party agrees to but fails to pay liquidated damages, the only recourse of the other is to the courts. The courts will uniformly refuse to enforce the provision if it is unreasonable in amount, and will call it a "penalty" (See chapter 4).

4. Remedies at Law

If it is impossible to stipulate specific remedies within the contract, then breach of the contract automatically forces reliance upon legal remedies. This will be costly, in terms of time and money. Of course, so will the enforcement of a liquidated damage amount, if the vendor refuses to pay voluntarily. Obtaining judicial determination of true damages, however, will require considerable additional time and will require the presentation of convincing evidence, not only of breach, but of the actual damages sustained. This can be done through either arbitration or litigation, depending on whether the contract itself stipulated arbitration, or is silent. A more comprehensive discussion of remedies available at law is given in chapter 4.

I. USING THE BOOK

This is a *guide* to contracting in the computer field. It attempts to provide a framework for contract negotiations, to allow structuring of special contracts for goods and services used in computer installations. The book is comprised of ten narrative chapters, and an equal number of pages reflecting specific suggested contract clauses. The first three chapters identify the problems and define procedures for approaching them. Chapter 4 examines the law to date and indicates to the layman how the law can be used to his benefit in a contractual setting. It defines the law of contracts in terms of protection for both user and vendor.

The remaining chapters provide indexing to some contract clauses given in the appendix. For each type of contract, suggested clauses are discussed in the remaining six chapters. Chapter 5 identifies terms common to all contracts, and chapters 6 through 10 classify contracts by type and indicate which terms are suggested for each specialized contract. These chapters therefore identify *when and where* each term is to be used, and discuss the issues surrounding each major clause, with its advantages and disadvantages.

A user interested in signing a specific contract should read the introductory material, and then proceed to the appropriate chapter in which the contract in which he is interested is outlined. This will give him an index to desirable specific clauses in the contract he is attempting to develop. The user can then select those clauses which appear significant to him, augmenting them with clauses germane to the project. In addition, selected general terms outlined in chapter 5 should be appended to most contracts. Although these may not be significant in many cases, they are useful, and as the user's counsel will indicate, sound legal practice normally suggests that most of these should be considered.

At this point the user will have a list of clause numbers, obtained from chapters 5 through 10, with an understanding of the reasons why each clause might be useful. At this point the user can go to Appendix A of the book in which the clauses are outlined in a standard format, indexed in clause number sequence. For each clause the risk factor is indicated, the intent of the clause is shown, an optimal clause is identified, and various fall-back alternatives are highlighted, if appropriate. In addition, where feasible, remedies are given. For those clauses covered in the standard contract, the standard contract wording of selected vendors is also given. In those cases, the difference between the standard contract wording, and the wording identified as ideal, will be significant in reflecting the changes desirable in the standard contract.

As a shortcut, or as an alternate starting point accessible by specific type of data processing contract, Appendix B sets forth various checklists which contain many of the elements of common forms of data processing contracts.

Finally, it should be repeated that no contract should be constructed using this text without the benefit of counsel. Entering into computer contracts without legal advice is a practice which can only spell disaster, regardless of the contents of this text, and regardless of the intelligence of the user.

A. INTRODUCTION

1. Timing

The importance of contract negotiation and a viable contract is defined in chapter 1, and it is now assumed that the reader is committed to developing a realistic contract. It is important to recognize that the timing of the contract negotiation is of paramount significance. It does no good to negotiate a hardware maintenance contract after the hardware has been delivered, since the *leverage* which the user has over the vendor is insignificant at this point. At this point only the money associated with the maintenance contract provides leverage assuming that the purchase contract has been completed and the equipment paid for. Contract negotiation must be performed at a time when sufficient leverage is available to insure that fall-back positions and alternatives can be exercised. In hardware contracting, therefore, the best time to negotiate a contract is at the time that the vendor has just been selected in a competitive procurement, so that there is in fact a stand-by alternative, namely another vendor.

Once a commitment to a specific vendor has been made, the leverage of the user is reduced step by step. As each day passes, the user spends additional funds tailored to the specific vendor's equipment, thereby reducing leverage by an equivalent amount. If he were to terminate this vendor at each point, his cost would be increased by the amount he had invested in that particular vendor's equipment. Figure 2-1 indicates the cash flow incurred by both user and vendor in a typical computer implementation project. It clearly indicates that the time for negotiating a contract is at the point that a specific vendor has been selected and, in fact, prior to the notification of other vendors that a

2
COMPETITIVE SELECTION PROCESS

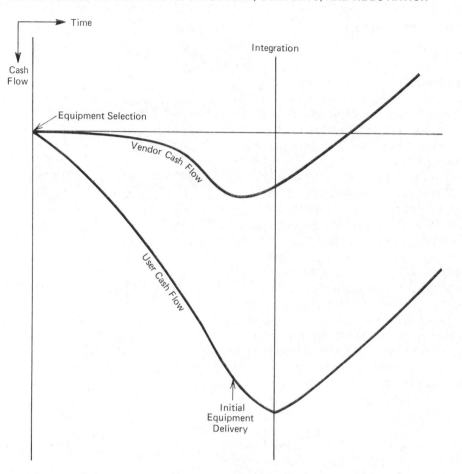

FIGURE 2-1. Relative Cash Flow of User and Vendor.

selection has been made. Selection in this context only means ranking of the vendors, and negotiating a contract with the highest-ranked one.

The negative cash flow of the user is comprised of site preparation, which is often targeted on a specific vendor's equipment, personnel training, systems design, programming, all of which will be specific to the vendor selected, and other resource acquisition steps, many of which will be governed by the characteristics of the selected equipment. As a result, it is desirable to insure that the terms of the contract are defined at the outset of the relationship, and it is often advantageous to delay the planning process until after a satisfactory contract has been negotiated.

Similar exposure exists in software development contracts, where progress payments are made which commit the user inexorably to the vendor. If the contract has not been signed prior to the start of the job, the user's leverage will decline as his progress payments are made, or as he develops specific plans to use the software in his installation, and commits funds for user training, for example, or for facility modification. Similarly, if the software contract in turn triggers a hardware contract, the failure to complete the software contract on time may result in penalty costs associated with the hardware contract.

2. Selection

Leverage is obtained by competition, and as indicated above, by proper timing. As a result a formal selection procedure is recommended below which will insure that competition and leverage exist. In the selection process it is desirable to insure that at least three vendors submit proposals to satisfy the requirements of the user. Even if it is decided in advance that a specific vendor has the best resources to satisfy the user's needs it is still a good idea to obtain proposals from three vendors. This will provide the necessary negotiating leverage with the preselected vendor.

A second reason for a formal selection process is to insure that the *acquisition method* is determined prior to finalizing the contract. It is important to determine whether equipment is to be rented or purchased, and whether or not software is to be purchased, rented or leased from a third party. This determination should be made at the completion of the selection, and will require inputs from the selection process itself.

The contract is a part of the selection process as well. The selection process ostensibly is designed to obtain the "best" vendor, i.e., that vendor which best satisfies the aggregate requirements of the user. These requirements can be broken down into a series of selection criteria, one of which is clearly the *willingness* of the vendor to enter into a rigorous contract. A vendor who is willing to enter into a complete contract is a better choice than one unwilling to execute anything but a standard contract. All other things being equal, therefore, the selection process would point to the vendor with the greater willingness to negotiate. This criterion will therefore have to be determined prior to final selection, so that the contracting process is inextricably interwoven with the selection process, as defined below and in chapter 3.

B. THE OVERALL IMPLEMENTATION PLANNING PROCESS

1. Introduction

The overall process of planning a computer installation is a complex undertaking, lasting from one and a half to four years, depending on scope, complexity, and experience of the parties involved. The process is one which can be divided into a number of steps; for purposes of this text, seven major planning steps are defined, of which only the first three are of particular interest here.

2. The Planning Steps

The seven planning steps are as follows:

1. *Feasibility Analysis.* The first stage in the planning process is a study to determine if a proposed information systems change is economically feasible and technically practical. This involves an examination of the information processing needs of the organization, and a determination whether or not a new form of systems methodology can meet these needs more effectively and more economically.

2. *Equipment Selection.* In the second phase, the necessary computer equipment is selected, provided of course, that this alternative is best. This involves the competitive selection process described below.

3. *Resource Planning.* The remaining resources necessary for the computer implementation process are assembled in this phase. This too may involve contractual negotiation, since these resources will include the site, personnel, software packages or software systems, standards, security systems, fire protection equipment, and the like.

4. *Systems Analysis and Design.* The new information system will require analysis and design, so that implementation on the selected equipment can take place. This stage is normally performed with in-house personnel, so that a contract is rare.

5. *Programming.* Translation of the solutions evolved in the preceding phase into actual machine language is the next stage of the implementation process. Again, at this stage internal personnel are most often used, although certain types of software packages may be employed.

6. *Systems Integration.* This is the complex step of integrating the new information system into the organization, installing the equipment, converting the data, determining that the system functions effectively, performing a total acceptance test on the system, and finally making the system operational on a permanent basis.

7. *Post-installation Management Audit.* In the final phase, management examines the implementation process and determines if the objectives established in the feasibility analysis have been met. Overall performance is evaluated, and defaults in performance are identified. To the extent that such defaults may be the responsibility of vendors, and may therefore be covered under contracts previously executed, this installation audit stage is important in following up compliance and in enforcing the ultimate contract.

As indicated above, only the first three steps are of principal interest and necessary to bring the contract negotiating process to a satisfactory conclusion.

C. THE FEASIBILITY ANALYSIS

The feasibility analysis sets the stage for the subsequent phase, and typically results in development of the functional specifications used as a basis for equipment selection and the contract. The contract will call for a computer system capable of performing certain functions, first identified in the feasibility study. These "performance criteria" are established as a part of an overall determination of the requirements of the organization in terms of information processing. The basic steps in a feasibility study are as follows:

1. *Definition of Objectives.* A statement of corporate and systems objectives which must be met to make the project viable.

2. *Identification of Areas of Information Processing.* Definition of the areas within the organization where information processing systems exist, and where the contemplated information system can be effective.

3. *Identification of Alternatives.* Determination of which information processing alternatives can technically meet the needs of the organization in the areas identified.

4. *Establishment of Needs.* The operational and management requirements of each of the areas being examined must be identified. This will lay the ground work for the development of functional specifications.

5. *Projection of Requirements or Needs.* The present needs of the organization will clearly not be satisfied by an information systems change which will take one and a half to three years to implement, and which will require perhaps three to five years to return its investment. As a result, the information needs must be projected a possible five to eight years into the future to evolve a set of functional specifications which will satisfy the requirements of the organization to a point where the system can become obsolete.

6. *Hypothetical Systems Design.* To ensure that the project is *technically* practical it is necessary to design a hypothetical system which will meet the requirements, using the alternatives given. This will demonstrate that it is possible to design a system which meets the functional needs for each alternative.

7. *Economic Analysis.* Each alternative must be examined to determine its economic impact, or, the development and operating cost. This will determine which alternative provides the lowest overall cost and still is technically practical and can meet the requirements of the organization five to eight years into the future.

8. *Intangibles Evaluation.* In addition to economic parameters, which are significant and affect the selection of an alternative, one must consider intangible factors which could be equally significant. These may include the improvement of accuracy of information processing, the establishment of better controls in the organization, the betterment of customer service, and the like. Notwithstanding these, however, economics has to be a prime consideration.

The output of the feasibility study is a report to management which indicates the functions which a new information system must be capable of performing some five to eight years in the future, and the cost constraints under which the system must operate. If the selected alternative is a computer system, this forms a principal basis on which computer performance characteristics can be defined in a comprehensive computer contract.

D. THE SELECTION PROCESS

1. Introduction

The global parameters of the selection process have already been defined. The feasibility study has resulted in the development of tangible functional specifications, economic constraints, and an examination of possible alternatives. It is now the responsibility of the selection process to select the "best" system to meet the identified requirements, and to conclude with a contract or series of contracts which cover the user in the rest of the implementation process.

2. Selection Steps

The steps generally followed in the equipment selection process are given below. To a large extent they are similar to the steps followed in software selection.

1. *Documentation of Functional Specifications.* The basic functional specifications developed in the feasibility study are augmented and expanded to become a full-fledged proposal request document. The normal practice is to

include in the specifications the details required for bidding, and the details required for proper proposal preparation. Primary to the specifications, however, are the statements of system needs given in the feasibility analysis.

2. *Selection Criteria.* The selection process will be carried out to obtain what is assumed to be the "best" system for the organization. "Best" is of course a composite of a significant number of criteria, each of which must be independently determined and weighted. Thus "best" will include such criteria as operating performance, cost, capacity, software quality and quantity, expansibility of the system, modularity, quality and facilities for maintenance services supplied, support and assistance supplied, vendor reputation, experience with specific application areas, reliability, willingness to negotiate a contract, and the like. These criteria, and such others as may be deemed to be of importance to the user, must be determined in advance so that they can be included in the specifications and made available to the vendors.

3. *Weighting of Criteria.* Each criterion does not have an equal impact on selection. As a result, relative weights should be assigned to insure that the selection process is impartial. Military installations may emphasize reliability over cost, whereas commercial installations might be more concerned with vendor support or vendor reputation. Accordingly, it is a useful practice for these weights to be determined by members of management concerned with the use of the equipment. These weights will definitely assist the contract negotiator in determining which contract clauses are important, which are critical, and which might have only a relatively minor impact. If, for example, reliability is given a heavy weight in the criteria evaluation, then clearly it must be given an equally heavy emphasis in the actual contract negotiation.

4. *Proposal Request Issuance.* It is recommended that at least three vendors be given requests to produce a proposal. This will take advantage of the necessary competition, provide a fall-back position in negotiation, and optimize the number of ideas which will be submitted to the organization by participating vendors. The proposal request issuance generally includes the specifications and documentation necessary to give the vendors a complete understanding of the requirements of the user. In addition, it is probably desirable to outline to the vendors what *type* of proposal they should prepare, its format, and the organization of the material within it.

Most important, the user's request should state that the proposal submitted will be incorporated as part of a contract. This final caveat is necessary to ensure that the proposal does not carry the disclaimers often found in such documents, and to further eliminate a great deal of "boiler plate" which is totally unnecessary, confusing to the user, and not binding on the vendor. It also tends to avoid careless, unspecific, and "glossy" proposals, and removes from the negotiations considerable "salestalk" from which vendors constantly retreat.

5. *Bidders Conference.* It is a useful practice to have a conference with the vendors at which ambiguities can be discussed and clarified. These questions and answer sessions often raise many useful "what if?" questions that have not been previously considered.

6. *Proposal Receipt and Evaluation.* The proposals received from the vendors are evaluated on the basis of each of the established criteria. For each criterion, the response of each vendor will be evaluated and defined on a comparative basis. Vendors are then ranked by criteria, resulting in a composite, weighted criteria matrix. This should point to the vendor that has supplied the "best" proposal.

7. *Contract Specifications.* The specifications for the contract should be drawn by the user, rather than the vendor. The first round of negotiation will then be based on the user's requirements rather than on departure from the standard contract. However, such specifications should not be issued until after the proposals have been received, to ensure that vendors are not frightened away by the extent and depth to which contracts are going to be required. (This is defined in detail in chapter 3.)

8. *Vendor Selection.* After receipt of a response to the contract specification, which provides an indication of the vendor's "willingness to negotiate a contract," the total criteria can be ranked, and the optimal vendor determined. The first-ranked vendor should be selected, subject to management approval and subject to the negotiation of a satisfactory contract.

9. *Analysis of Acquisition Method.* Finally, prior to negotiation of the contract, a determination should be made of whether the equipment should be purchased, rented, or leased through a third party. The difference among these methods can be significant and it can often affect user cost. The different methods can also result in different types of contracts between the parties, so that this determination must be made prior to final negotiation.

10. *Contract Negotiation.* The last step in the selection process, described in more detail in chapter 3, is contract negotiation. For this the contract specification will act as a base, tempered by the response of the vendor, and by the responses indicated in the original proposal document. At this point all of the information necessary to complete a satisfactory contract should be available. Also, the leverage is optimal, since, at this point, the second-ranked vendor has not yet been told that he has not been selected. Thus there is total fallback; it is possible to go to a totally different vendor to complete the negotiations, if for some reason the contract negotiating process breaks down. At the same time no investment has been made in a particular vendor's equipment, either through training of personnel, or site preparation. This then is the best time for the negotiating process to begin, prior to any further implementation.

E. ACQUISITION METHOD ANALYSIS

1. Introduction

The type of contract to be entered into can be a function of the acquisition method to be used. In order to simplify the contracting process, the vendor will insist that, if the system is to be rented, then a rental contract be required, augmented by the necessary maintenance, software usage or software package contracts. If, on the other hand, the equipment is to be purchased, then title will pass to the user, and a purchase contract is written, along with a maintenance contract and possibly supporting software contracts. The vendor's customary position is, however, a spurious one.

If a rental contract is to be used, it is clearly desirable to include a purchase option as part of that contract. In fact, most vendors do offer a purchase option agreement under which the user may purchase the equipment on his site at a discount determined as a function of the rent he has paid to some identified maximum. If the user has a future opportunity to purchase, and it is even remotely likely that he will exercise that option, then it becomes *mandatory* to prepare a purchase contract as an exhibit to the option agreement at the time of contract negotiation, when the leverage still exists. Once the machine has been rented, and is on site for a year or more, and the user decides to enter into a purchase contract, there is no further leverage. The vendor will simply decline to negotiate anything but a standard contract, since the user has no alternative except to purchase this system or to continue renting it. With a purchase option agreement, therefore, all of the clauses of the purchase contract must be considered at the time of contract negotiation!

The determination of acquisition method is important to the user, since it can mean a significant increase in cost if the wrong method is chosen. In addition, the contract negotiator should have a clear idea of the leverage associated with the contract in terms of cost components for which he will be negotiating. It is one thing to negotiate a rental contract for $10,000 per month, with a 30 day cancellation clause. It is another to negotiate a purchase contract for $500,000. Both represent the same value, but the psychology of negotiating a purchase contract generally provides greater weight from the viewpoint of the negotiator.

2. Cost Components

The contract negotiator should be aware of the components of cost being negotiated, which in part are a function of the acquisition method.

1. Purchase contract cost components include:
   - purchase price
   - cost of maintenance
   - cost of money
   - residual value or trade-in value
   - cost of insurance
   - investment tax credit
   - balance sheet effects
   - income statement effects of depreciation versus rental
2. Equipment rental cost components to be considered are:
   - equipment rental
   - overtime usage costs
   - investment tax credit pass-through
   - income statement effects of rental versus depreciation
3. Third part leasing cost components are:
   - lease discount
   - lease payment
   - investment tax credit pass-through
   - accounting treatment of finance leases as conditional purchase agreements

In addition, consideration must be given to the tax effect of lease, purchase, or rental, and to the possible effects on the user's balance sheet. A purchased item will appear as an asset, whereas a rented system will not appear at all, and some rental contracts may be treated as purchases for balance sheet and income statement purposes.

A. INTRODUCTION

It is recommended that the entire strategy of contract negotiation be designed to overpower the vendor in the negotiating process, and to retain the dominance and position of the user during the negotiation. This strategy should result in an optimal contract. The methodology is directed to insuring that the user's position is not compromised at any time.

This book is not intended as a text on negotiation. There are a number of very effective texts available which deal with the art of negotiation,[1] the psychology involved, and the optimal methodology for the actual *adversary proceeding* which negotiation represents. This text will concentrate principally on the subject matter to be negotiated, rather than the strategy of negotiation itself. However, the general methodology of contract negotiation, and the techniques which are most useful in defining a comprehensive contract are outlined in this chapter.

In general, the best posture to be adopted by the user is one of total self-confidence. The user must demonstrate total familiarity with contracting practice, and total awareness of and insistence on meeting his own requirements. The user must remain in total command of the situation. The methodology defined herein offers the user the opportunity to stay in command through the *competitive* selection process.

B. THE NEGOTIATING AND CONTRACT DEVELOPMENT PROCESS

There are a number of steps suggested in the process leading to the eventual

3
CONTRACT NEGOTIATING METHODOLOGY AND STRATEGY

---

[1]One of the best, from the standpoint of the user, is J. Auer & C. Harris, *Computer Contract Negotiations* (New York: Van Nostrand Reinhold, 1981).

completion of a viable contract. The steps require significant preparation, and careful selection of the contract clauses and terms desired. This preparation, however, should result in the development of a favorable and comprehensive contract, if the steps are followed, and if the vendor is prepared to cooperate. The steps are outlined below:

1. *Determine the Type of Contract Desired.* In the first chapter, the various types of contracts were defined, and the alternatives available to the user were established. The user must initially determine the best alternative among a master contract, separate contracts, or a side letter to the standard contract.

2. *Explore and List the Substantive Performance Criteria and the Contingencies to be Dealt With.* The plans and specifications of the user's project and the "what if?" contingencies to be focused upon are the skeleton and nervous system of the contractual organism. They will be fleshed out by the actual contract document.

3. *Select a List of Desirable Clauses.* At this point the user must display considerable care because the global contents of the contract will start to be defined. A contract can consist of a large number of clauses. This book, for example, lists over 250 possible clauses which could be included in a master contract for hardware and software. It is therefore one source for possible ideas of clauses to be contained in a master contract. However, it should not be the only source from which the user selects desired clauses. The standard contract supplied by the vendor, the requests issued by the user for bids, the proposals submitted by all vendors, suggestions from counsel to the organization, the specific technical requirements of the organization, and the ideas of the personnel involved in the selection process are all desirable sources for potential contract clauses. Finally, of course, the vendor itself may have some ideas, or requirements of specific terms to be included, and these should be recognized at this time as well.

4. *Construct the Contract Specification.* The initiative should remain with the user, as already indicated, and the contract specification is one way of forcefully establishing that initiative. The contract specification is a document which defines, for each of the potential clauses, an optimum position which the user intends to take. It is a document used to elicit a response from the vendor, and to provide the strongest statement of the user's requirements. The detailed contents and method of preparation is given in section C below.

5. *Issue the Contract Specification.* The contract specification document should be issued to *all* vendors still involved in the selection process. Each vendor which has met the requirements of the selection process, and has submitted a proposal with a response to all questions, should be issued a contract specification. This insures that an impartial evaluation will be made of each vendor's willingness to negotiate a contract, which in turn will serve as a factor in the overall selection methodology. It also insures that the spirit of competition is retained through the initial part of the negotiating process, when leverage is required.

   It has already been noted that the contract specification is a different document from the functional specifications used in obtaining proposals from the vendors. Only after satisfactory proposals have been received from the vendors, should a contract specification be issued.

6. *Evaluate Responses to the Specification.* The vendors are asked to respond to the contract specification by indicating their agreement, disagreement, or

comments. The responses of the vendors to the document must be evaluated, and the vendors ranked on their willingness to negotiate. This ranking should be added to the selection process criteria matrix in order to determine which vendor is "best" with respect to the criterion: "willingness to negotiate."

7. *Perform Exposure Analysis for Each Vendor.* The initial responses of the vendors will be used to determine the extent of the exposure which the organization faces if a contract is to be signed with a particular vendor, under the conditions agreed to at that time by that vendor. An analysis of these responses assists management in understanding the risks and exposure associated with each of the vendors at this point. In addition, such an analysis highlights the areas where further negotiation is highly desirable or manda- tory with particular vendors. This comparative analysis will result in a clear understanding of the concessions being offered by each vendor and will be of considerable assistance in using negotiating leverage to force deficient vendors into more acceptable positions. The detailed methodology as- sociated with exposure analysis is given in section D.

8. *Advise Vendors of their Deficiencies.* The exposure analysis points to the major areas where each vendor is deficient. As an *initial* step in the negotiat- ing process, before deciding which vendor is ranked first, it is desirable to publish a deficiency letter. This letter is a document which defines to each vendor the key areas where that vendor is deficient, and which contains an invitation to each vendor to correct deficiencies and to improve its position in the negotiating process. Use of a deficiency letter before ranking the vendors provides maximum leverage. A deficiency letter can be written by counsel, who probably provides the strongest authorship at this point in the negotiating process. The signature of counsel on such a letter will make clear to the vendor that the contract negotiation is to be conducted by legal as well as technical staff. This can also be established by transmitting the original specification under cover of a transmittal letter signed by counsel.

The deficiency letter normally merely identifies areas in which the vendor's response is considered totally unsatisfactory to the using organization. The vendor is requested to reconsider the response given in those cases where it is not acceptable to the user, and will result in disqualification of the vendor from further consideration if the position is not altered. The deficiency letter therefore should address only key areas, with a serious exposure factor. Do not identify minor points; these will emerge as part of the negotiat- ing process at a subsequent stage. The purpose of the deficiency letter is to force the vendor into improving key areas whose coverage is considered mandatory by the user.

9. *Select the Optimal Vendor.* The selection process should at this point have already disclosed the vendor considered "best" under the conditions given. (The deficiency letter response may or may not have been included.) The original response to the contract specification will normally be a suf- ficient indication of the vendor's "willingness to negotiate," to allow the entry of that criterion in the overall selection process. The response to the deficiency letter will be used in subsequent negotiation and need not necessarily be significant in influencing the selection of a particular vendor.

10. *Obtain Responses to Deficiency Letter.* At this time the responses to the deficiency letter should be obtained so that the total negotiating posture of the vendor is obvious, and to update the evaluations made earlier despite

the fact that the vendor has already been selected. The selected vendor will undoubtedly be deficient in areas, and a comparison of the other vendor responses will be helpful in the negotiation.

11. *Meet With the First-Ranked Vendor.* An initial meeting should be held with the first-ranked vendor, to advise that vendor of continuing deficiencies which exist in the contractual relationship. The vendor should be advised that he is first-ranked provided that key deficiencies can be cured. Once these deficiencies are settled, the actual negotiating process leading to the development of the *written* contract can begin.

    During this initial meeting, a date should be established for the first *negotiating* session, provided that the vendor has favorably responded to the deficiencies outlined at this meeting. Again, note that this is *another* opportunity for the user to obtain concessions from the vendor prior to actual identified negotiation. It is clear, of course, that this is a part of the negotiating process, despite its label. In effect, the user is asking the vendor to optimize the user's "going in" position, prior to the start of negotiation. By further setting an actual start date for the negotiation, the vendor is under considerable pressure to come up with realistic responses to the deficiencies outlined during this initial meeting.

12. *Start Negotiation.* The initial negotiating session is held after the final position of the vendor has been determined. The first session should be an introduction of both negotiating teams, the establishment of points of contact, and the determination of the administrative process to be followed in insuring that all agreements are properly recorded, and that the wording of the ultimate contract will reflect the substantive components agreed to during negotiation. Counsel for both sides should be introduced during this session, and the lead negotiator appointed by the user should be identified. This person should immediately take the lead in the statement of the positions which the user will take.

13. *Complete the Final Contract.* After the negotiating sessions are over, and basic substantive matters have been agreed to, the contract itself can be completed. This will involve significant negotiation itself, as there may be differences in wording, or specific nuances generated by wording, which must be altered. The draft contract is normally circulated to all parties involved, comments are collected by the lead negotiator, and changes are made as required by all parties. Ultimately, the final contract will emerge out of this process, even though a considerable amount of time may have passed.

The total time involved in contract negotiation can be fairly significant. The time lapse between a contract specification issuance and contract completion can be from two to four months. Some of this is overlapped with other processes which are a part of selection. The final part can be overlapped with the initiation of the remaining planning functions, although it is desirable of course to perform no planning functions which may be vendor-dependent until the contract is actually signed. To do otherwise reduces the ultimate user leverage in settling final issues. The total process of negotiating a contract including all 13 steps above can take from four to five months. Not more than six to eight weeks of this time is added to the total process of systems implementation, since the remainder can be overlapped with other stages of the process.

C. THE CONTRACT SPECIFICATION

1. Introduction

The contract specification is a vital document in the negotiating process. In addition, it is a document which may survive and have value beyond the contract. Specifications should be constructed carefully to have a psychological impact on the vendor, establishing the user as the dominant party in the overall negotiation. The contract specification is normally developed as a joint effort between the technical and legal personnel associated with the ultimate negotiation.

2. Purposes of the Contract Specification

There are a number of reasons for having an effective contract specification. The first and perhaps most important reason is that the issuance of such a comprehensive document clearly places the advantage with the user, through initiation, through boldness, and through the establishment of a total document which far exceeds that which the vendor may have had in mind as a viable contract between the parties. It sets the framework of the transaction from the viewpoint of the user and requires the vendor psychologically to tailor its needs within that framework.

A second reason for a comprehensive contract specification is that such a document may be used in future to show the *intent* of the parties. If the final contract is ambiguous or unclear in certain respects, it may be possible to refer to the specifications to clarify the meaning of the ultimate agreement.[2] Thus, the contract specification may serve as documentation of the initial intent of the parties and may become useful in subsequent arbitration or litigation.

A third reason for a good specification is to evaluate the vendor's willingness to negotiate. As has been observed, this will be a factor in the selection process, and will provide an evaluation of that criterion.

Another purpose of the contract specification is to provide an early insight into the vendor's position, and a focus upon weaknesses which need to be corrected. The position of other vendors included in the selection process but not selected is also helpful in the negotiation, and is obtained through the specification. Thus if it is known that vendor X is willing to concede a specific issue, it can be used by the negotiator in the actual negotiating sessions to induce vendor Y to concede that point. The contract specification, when issued to all vendors involved in the process will serve to generate valuable input to the negotiator.

An important purpose of the contract specification is to throw the vendor off balance. The vendor until this point has received only functional specifications from the user, with no indication that the contract will be anything but standard, or that the user has any specific contractual requirements. The contract specifications, if well done, will create an attitude change in the vendor. He may suddenly realize that he will be asked to make specific concessions in each area identified as part of the contract. The vendor, normally accustomed to taking an order on his printed form, will be thrown off his stride and will ultimately make the negotiating process a more realistic one from the user's viewpoint.

Finally, the contract specification will serve as a document to alert *top manage-*

---

[2]The possible dangers to the user of proceeding by standard vendor form, in this case accompanied by written proposals and following assurance letters, are illustrated in Teamsters Security Fund of Northern California, Inc. v. Sperry Rand Corp., 6 CLSR 951 (N.D. Cal. 1977) (user recovered on theory that integrated agreement included proposal and written assurances of vendor).

ment to the exposure associated with the proposed contract, and to set forth what type of contract would be considered ideal. This gives management an idea of possible losses associated with signing a contract with vendors who do not meet requirements of the specification. Thereby, the risks identified for each vendor can be clearly isolated for review by top management.

3. Contents of the Specification

The following Table of Contents is suggested for the contract specification.

a. The Letter of Transmittal
A contract specification should be introduced by or accompanied by a letter of transmittal, preferably written by counsel or by the appointed negotiator, and should identify the objectives of the specification, and the importance to the user of the establishment of a viable contract. The Letter of Transmittal should also indicate the responsibility assigned to the vendor, the response required, and the timing of the entire contract negotiating process. A typical Letter of Transmittal might read as follows:

"GENTLEMEN:
We are confident that you are aware of the importance of the installation of our new system to our organization. You and your associates have been heavily involved in providing us with information and a proposal.
If your organization should be selected, we will be negotiating a contract with you. Our review of the standard contract submitted by you as part of your proposal indicates that a more comprehensive contract is necessary for a project of the importance and magnitude of our new installation. As a result I am pleased to enclose a copy of our contract specification. We request that you respond to this specification as indicated, not later than (date), so that we can reassess the direction of our negotiation, and evaluate your responsiveness to our needs.
In your response please indicate whom you designate as the party responsible for negotiation. We can then make contact with this person, and initiate negotiating procedures, if and when your organization is selected as the initial vendor for purposes of negotiation.

Yours very truly,

[USER]"

b. Introduction to the Contract Specification
The second item of the specification will be an introduction, which identifies the principal objectives of the specification. Typical objectives include the evaluation of the vendor's willingness, and the definition of user requirements. There is no need to identify the other objectives of a contract specification listed in section C-2 above. The introduction will also identify the type of response which is required. Normally the vendor will be given a choice of the following types of responses:

1. *Assumed.* The user has already assumed that the identified clause in the contract specification is in fact acceptable to the vendor. This should normally refer to clauses with relatively minor impact, which might be considered standard, or which are included in the vendor's standard contract.
2. *Included in Proposal.* If the vendor has already agreed in his proposal to

provide a given concession or to meet a specific requirement, then a contract specification item marked "2," will already be included and will require no further negotiation, except possibly with regard to wording.

3. *Mandatory.* There may be certain clauses which are mandatory from the viewpoint of the vendor, or from the viewpoint of the user. These may not have been included in the standard contract or the proposal, but they are necessary nonetheless. These may arise out of the specific conditions underlying the procurement, or out of a policy decision made by management.

4. *Response Required.* A fourth category of clauses are those which are raised for the first time. They are not included in the standard contract or the proposal, and they are not necessarily mandatory. These are the negotiable clauses which the user desires. It is up to the vendor to respond to the particular clauses and to react to the words used in the specification.

It is now the vendor's prerogative to respond to these four categories. Theoretically, the vendor need only respond to the last category, as the only one that is still negotiable; the remainder is either assumed, already contained in the standard contract or proposal, or required by the user. However, the exact way in which the first three categories are worded may not be acceptable to the vendor, and it is likely that some comments will be generated even for these three categories. As a result, the contract specification should clearly state the role of the vendor, and the responsibility he has in identifying his position with respect to each item. Where a vendor accepts a clause as written, that clause should be capable of being transferred in those exact words to the final contract draft or side letter.

c. List of Clauses

The third segment of the contract specification is a table of contents, listing the clauses associated with the specification. Since this list may include upwards of 200 clauses, it is generally desirable to group these into categories. For purposes of this book the categories used in grouping contract clauses are functional, retaining like subjects in like groups. A table of contents to the contract specification is therefore generated by listing the clauses in the sequence in which they appear in the subsequent section.

d. Basic Position with Respect to Each Clause

For each clause the user defines the basic position to be taken. This can be done by either writing the clause in the exact words in which it is acceptable as a contract clause, or by identifying the objectives to be served by the clause. In general, it is desirable to identify the actual words of the clause wherever possible. In that case an idealized position can be taken by the user, which, if acceptable, can result in the transfer of the actual paragraph to the final contract document. In this section terms which are peculiar to the document, and whose definition is to be expanded, should be underlined, so that a separate *definition of terms* can be used as part of the contract specification.

e. Definitions

Since many terms in a contract will be unique to that contract, or will have a unique meaning therein, separate definitions of those terms should be made. This will simplify the contract specification and the ultimate contract. The term "component," for example, can have many meanings in a technical sense. By clearly defining it in the definition section of the contract specification, and by underlining it wherever it is used, it will be established as a uniform definition. This definition, if acceptable to both parties, will then be carried into and become part of the contract section titled "Definitions."

D. EXPOSURE ANALYSIS

1. Exposure Involved

The aggregate exposure involved in a data processing contract can be significant. It is necessary to assess it, and to assess the risk associated with a potential total failure. Once this has been done, the user can determine if a contract can be drawn to protect against each *item* of risk. Thus, exposure analysis is desirable to give user management an indication of the risks involved, and to point to key areas within the contract where protection is required.

The installation of a new system, whether hardware or software, is an expensive undertaking. If one is assuming that the life of a hardware or software system must be at least five years to return its investment cost, then the cost of such an installation must be summed over at least a five-year period. The aggregate costs can be significant. For example, an analysis of the installation of a one million dollar computer could show the following total costs:

(a) Initial Investment Costs

Initial planning	$25,000
Site preparation	5,000
Staff training	75,000
Systems analysis and design	400,000
Programming, testing and systems installation	300,000
Additional test time for program testing prior to installation	25,000
Initial supplies	50,000
Data conversion and parallel operation	200,000
Contingency	50,000
Total Investment Costs:	$1,130,000

The initial investment costs of a one million dollar computer are thus more than 110% of the acquisition cost of the computer itself.

(b) Operating Costs

The operating budget of a one million dollar computer installation on an annual basis might be as follows:

Rental, or amortization and maintenance	$240,000
Operating staff and data entry staff	350,000
Supplies	40,000
Overhead	100,000
Amortization of planning costs over five years	225,000
Cost of money associated with investment	140,000
Total	$1,095,000

This annual operating budget of $1,095,000 projected over five years, results in a cost in excess of five million dollars. A general rule of thumb is that the total cost associated with using a computer over a five-year period is approximately equal to five times the purchase cost, or the cost of approximately 250 months of rental. There is thus no such thing as a small computer contract; the cost implications of a computer contract are at least five times the value of the computer itself. This further suggests that the aggregate costs of the user, and the exposure of the user, are far more significant than the costs and exposure of the vendor.

(c) Risk

The best way to assess the risk associated with a contract of this magnitude is to assume that after two years of planning, when the system is about to be installed, the vendor defaults in total, and fails to deliver a system acceptable to the user. This is the *maximum exposure*, the risk associated with a total failure. The costs associated with a total failure include the investment costs for that specific computer, such as the cost of design, programming and planning. It also includes at least a part of the site costs, better than half the training costs, and the costs associated with test time, supplies and conversion. A minimum loss for the example above, would be in the order of $800,000. In addition the user has lost two years. If the user must restart, and reinvest an additional $800,000 to accomplish the same objectives, then he will not only require $800,000 but an additional two years. Therefore, the operating savings to be realized during those two years must be considered lost as well. If one assumes that an investment of 1.1 million dollars should have a pretax return of at least 20%, then the operating savings are at least $220,000 a year, and the losses associated with a two-year delay will be over $400,000. The total losses of this failure would be 1.5 million dollars, or about 25% more than the cost of the computer.

Similarly, if the vendor were to encounter a delay of a year for one reason or another, the costs of the delay can be identified as well. They would include the savings associated with a year of operation, previously assessed at $220,000 in the example. In addition, necessary systems maintenance will be required during the year to maintain and update the systems, which normally is in the order of 20% of the systems development cost. This cost was approximately $700,000 so annual maintenance would be $140,000. In addition, operating staff and overhead would have been obtained in anticipation of prompt delivery. These costs probably would be in the order of $200,000 per year, and would not be salvageable. Finally, there would be the cost of money on the investment deferred for one year. A charge of $140,000 would not be considered unreasonable. It can be seen that the total cost of a one-year delay is in the order of $700,000 or approximately half the total cost of aborting the system.

This analysis of total risk points the way toward an identification of potential indemnity, and the liability associated with the vendor's responsibility. Damages which can be identified in the contract should be keyed to the risk amounts identified in this sort of analysis.

2. Exposure Analysis

To further assess the impact of a contract, or the impact of not having coverage in areas where protection is desirable, a brief analysis of exposure can be made, in recognition of the risk, on an area by area basis.

The first step in this analysis is to divide the contract terms in the specification into categories of importance. These categories could be identified as follows:

- Key Contract Terms
- Significant Contract Terms

- Minor Contract Terms
- Terms with no Quantifiable Impact

(This is the categorization adopted in the remainder of this book.)

An alternative approach is to classify terms by the amount of risk associated with each term. In a small-scale contract, this might result in six categories as follows:

1. A risk of $0–$1,000
2. A risk of $1–$5,000
3. A risk of $5–$25,000
4. A risk of $25–$75,000
5. A risk of $75–$150,000
6. A risk of over $150,000

Regardless of the method of classification, the contract clauses can then be identified by category. It is then possible to assign weights to each category and to determine the total number of "points" associated with each weight. Figure 3-1 indicates what such a table might look like for a typical hardware contract, containing a total of 140 clauses. In this example seven categories are established on the basis of an assessment of the relative risk of each clause. The first category are clauses with no quantifiable impact. These have not been weighted, and are not considered. In each of the other categories, clauses are identified, and particular weights assigned. In this example, a clause with a risk of from $0 to $1,000 was given a weight of one, and a clause with risk in excess of $150,000 was given a weight of 40. By multiplying the number of clauses in each category by its weight, the total weight of that category can be determined and an aggregate score for the total contract can be determined. In this case the aggregate total of all weights is 1,142. If the total exposure is $1,200,000, then the value of each weighted point is approximately $1,000. By evaluating the responses of each vendor to each clause, a particular score is obtained. This allows an assessment of the responsiveness of the vendor and his willingness to negotiate. This is illustrated in Figure 3-2.

This illustration was taken from an actual procurement, in which an assessment was made of the risk of a particular hardware and software situation. In this case only three clause classifications were used: key, important, and minor. The key clauses, of which there are only four, were each weighted at a value of 29, the important clauses were weighted at a value of four, and the minor clauses were given a valuation of one. An assessment of the responses of the vendors to the initial contract specification indicated a range of responsiveness from 22.9% of the maximum

Category	Risk Range	Weight	No. of Clauses	Total Weight	% of Total Weight
1.	No quantifiable impact	0	42	0	0
2.	Risk of $0–$1000	1	27	27	2.4
3.	Risk of $1000–$5000	4	12	48	4.2
4.	Risk of $5000–$25,000	8	21	168	14.7
5.	Risk of $25,000–$75,000	16	14	224	19.6
6.	Risk of $75,000–$150,000	25	19	475	41.6
7.	Risk of over $150,000	40	5	200	17.5
	Total		140	1142	

FIGURE 3-1. Weighted Contract Clauses.

A. Weight Distribution

Clause Classification	No. of Clauses	Unit Weight	Total Weight	% of Total Weight
Key	4	29	116	42.1
Important	29	4	116	42.1
Minor	43	1	43	15.8
Total:	76		275	

B. Summary of Scores

Clause Classification	Maximum Possible	Burroughs	Honeywell	IBM	Univac	Standard Contract
Key	116	51	29	6	95	6
Important	116	73	55	33	90	0
Minor	43	32	29	24	35	4
Total:	275	156	113	63	220	10
% of Total Possible		56.7	41.1	22.9	80.0	3.6

SOURCE: Brandon Applied Systems, Inc., Client Study B309

FIGURE 3-2. Assessment of Vendor Responsiveness.

possible weights to 80.0%. It should be noted that the standard contract was evaluated as well, and it represented only a dismal 3.6% of the total. In this case, the risk associated with failure was assessed at a total of three million dollars. It is now possible to assess the exposure of each response by taking the difference between the ideal score and the actual score of each vendor and multiplying that difference by the average value of 1/275th of three million dollars. By dividing three million dollars by 275, each weight has a value of $10,900. A vendor which scores a total of 220 points has a continuing exposure of 55, the difference between 275 and 220. The monetary risk associated with signing a contract with this vendor is 55 times $10,900 or approximately $600,000. Similarly, signing the standard contract provides maximum exposure of 265 times $10,900 or approximately 2.9 million dollars. This type of analysis gives a good quantification of exposure, which can be useful.

It should be recognized that this is a mechanistic method of assessing the exposure of a contract and it may not be specific enough in certain areas. It is only a tool used to assess the contract and to identify areas where it can be improved. It should never be used as a sole basis for negotiation, since common sense obviously will override any mechanistic indications which this technique may provide. However, the technique is useful in giving an indication of the exposure associated with each vendor and, on a comparative basis, in providing an insight into the vendor's responsiveness. That is useful in assessing the vendor's willingness to negotiate, and it can provide the negotiator with added impetus for insuring that his negotiation is capable of obtaining the best deal with any vendor.

E. UNDERSTANDING THE ADVERSARY POSITION

In negotiating with a vendor it is important to clearly understand the position of the vendor, and the positions of the individuals participating in the negotiation. Negotiations are performed by human beings, with viewpoints which may differ

Negotiations are performed by human beings, with viewpoints which may differ from the corporate policy or viewpoint. Thus, it is important for the negotiator to have an understanding of the positon not only of the organizaticn, but of the human beings, their flexibility, their authority, their freedom, their motivating forces, and their relationship with the overall organization. Know your adversary!

1. The Vendor Cost Components

It is important initially to understand what the value of the contract is to the vendor. This indicates how much the vendor is willing to concede, since in no case will the vendor concede more. Note however that value may not only be economic; in addition to profits, the vendor must consider the public relations value of the contract, entry into a new industry, the breakthrough in establishing a new type of installation, or the prestige associated with the user's name. However, the economic values of a contract usually predominate and should be understood. Thus it is desirable for the user to forecast what the total value of this contract might be to the vendor. Cost components in a typical hardware situation are shown in Figure 3-3.

From this illustration it can be seen that the vendor might obtain profits ranging from 15 to 25% of the total purchase cost of the hardware. Similarly, the vendor's budget for marketing support and installation support is between 3 and 5% of the purchase cost of the machine. However, this installation support budget is assigned to the marketing organization on the basis of all machines being sold in a particular territory. Thus a branch office which is expected to sell 100 million dollars worth of equipment will have an installation support budget of between 3 and 5% of that total, which could all be theoretically assigned to a single user if the branch manager deemed that to be the best approach. It would be rare for a single user to get the entire installation support budget of a particular branch. However, it does suggest that negotiating strength will move installation support activities from users who do not negotiate to users who do.

In addition to the direct value of the hardware contract, which is partly determined on the basis of the profits it can generate, there are other values to the manufacturer which can be quantified. It is clear for example that a successful manufacturer will have a significant probability of selling additional equipment during the life of the contract for expansion purposes, or for improvements in systems architecture. In addition, that same vendor will have a better opportunity of ultimately supplying a

Approximate Distribution of Purchase Dollar
Received by Main-Frame Manufacturer

IBM	Cost Component	Other Manufacturers
21%	Hardware	25%
6%	Engineering	8%
7%	Software	11%
31%	Marketing Organization	30%
3%	Installation Support	5%
5%	Corporate Overhead	6%
27%	Profits	15%

SOURCE: Brandon Applied Systems, Inc., Study Project B-105

FIGURE 3-3. Cost Components of Hardware.

replacement machine when the system reaches the end of its useful life. This means that the probability of future profits can be assessed and perhaps quantified as well. In addition, the vendor will also supply software, supplies, and possibly manpower or education during the contract, with additional value in terms of additional profits. As a rule of thumb, therefore, it might be appropriate to assume that the vendor will derive a total profit equal to twice the profit in the initial purchase contract.

In addition to the value of obtaining a contract, there is also a psychological and financial impact associated with *not* getting the contract. The vendor has made an investment in the proposal in the order of $20,000 to $100,000 for proposal development, a possible benchmark, customer entertainment, and assigning manpower to assess the customer systems. This investment is lost if the contract is not obtained. There is also a psychological loss which is the converse of the public relations benefit of obtaining the contract. The absolute loss can be important; allowing another vendor to enter a heretofore protected market can be equally important. All of these factors, economic and psychological, can be tallied for negotiating purposes. It is clear that the negotiation will fail if the user negotiating team demands more than the value of the contract, or, the converse thereof, more than the losses associated with not obtaining it. Thus, the negotiating team should carefully balance demands with value, and recognize what is available for negotiating purposes.

2. The Human Element

At the same time it should be recognized that the negotiation is perfomed by individuals, whose values, gains and losses may be different from those of the vendor. To the salesperson, for example, this contract may be the most significant situation of the entire year. It may mean the difference between making quota or not making quota. It may mean a $20,000 commission, or potential promotion. The salesperson, on balance, has a great deal more to gain or lose from the contract than the vendor, on a relative basis. The salesperson is likely to be most oriented toward negotiating a contract favorable to the user, since the salesperson is interested in not losing the business, at *almost* any cost. The salesperson will get his or her commission irrespective of concessions which the vendor may make. Alas, the salesperson is often least able to commit the vendor to any significant concessions; he or she can, however, by knowing the vendor's internal organization, often bring about healthy negotiation within the vendor's organization.

Next in line in terms of interest in obtaining the order is the branch management. In many cases branch managers obtain an override over the sales commission, and in all cases branch managers are held responsible for selling their quota. Thus, the branch manager is equally interested in obtaining the order, although the phrase "at any cost" which might apply to the salesperson will not necessarily apply to the branch manager. Branch management is responsible for a budget, and must retain its total concessions with customers within a specified fraction of the total sales of the branch. Branch management however will still be on the side of the user, because branch management is interested in the sale first, and in the cost of the sale second.

Third in the sequence of interest in obtaining the order is probably regional or district management. This is still part of the vendor's marketing organization concerned with maximizing sales. However, profit responsibility at the region or district level is far more significant, and the regional or district manager or designee, when participating in contract negotiation, is likely to be much more conservative than branch management.

Finally, most removed from the interest of the user, and most difficult to deal with, is the vendor's legal representative. In most instances the legal representative has been established as a *protector* of the vendor, with the responsibility of insuring that the user does not obtain a contract more favorable than vendor policy permits, and further, that the sales organization does not "give away the store." Normally, the vendor organization has a very strong representative in its legal or contract negotiating representative. It is this person who will create the greatest difficulty in the negotiating process, and who should be isolated as quickly as possible as part of the negotiation. Whenever problems arise in the negotiating process, an appeal should be made to branch management, as the responsible organization most likely to be concerned with the user interest, and most likely to be hurt if the order is lost.

A final note in attempting to understand the position of the adversary in the negotiation relates to the personality of the individuals concerned. In addition to a check list of value items which the negotiator prepares, he should also prepare a short biographical synopsis of the individuals participating on the opposing side. Each synopsis should indicate the background of the individual, his or her current position, and personality traits. Important traits such as quickness to anger, willingness to compromise, and others should be identified where possible to insure that the negotiating team has a realistic understanding of the personalities of the participants, and can appeal to those personality characteristics most likely to result in negotiating advantages to the user.

3. Highly Leveraged Contracts

The preceding discussion emphasized the hardware contract, and the profit and values associated with hardware. Although million dollar contracts may be involved, the associated profits are only modest relative to the cost of making a proposal, doing a benchmark and otherwise participating in the negotiating process. There are a number of other types of contracts, referred to in other chapters, whose leverage is perhaps more significant. In these cases the user has a significant strategic advantage over the vendor. Such contracts are of two types: the contract in which the profit margin is major, since the costs have already been incurred; and the contract in which a very large organization deals with a small one.

In the first category of course, the most obvious type of contract involves software packages. By definition, a software package has already been developed by the organization, and the costs of development have been incurred, whether written off or not. A sale of a package to a user results in incremental profits, despite the fact that the marketing cost may be very high. The difference between gain and loss of a package contract to a selling organization is the difference between almost a 100% profit and none at the point of contract signing. This provides considerable leverage to the using organization, and this leverage can be used, within reason. However, although there is leverage, and most software package organizations are prepared to concede on issues which might otherwise not be considered prudent, it does not make sense to insist on a contract so onerous to the selling party that it ultimately results in business termination or other disaster. In that event the contract becomes totally worthless. Even where the vendor is not destroyed by a series of onerous contracts, there is a tendency to harbor resentments over "bad" deals, and these resentments can sometimes be acted out in the context of service, maintenance and upgrading. When such leverage exists, therefore, it should be used with caution.

The second case of high leverage comes about by virtue of the disparity of size of the two negotiating organizations. A large, Fortune 500 company, negotiating a service bureau contract with a small service organization, automatically has leverage born of size. In addition, the prestige of the large organization might add considerably to the prestige of the service organization. Again, however, excessive leverage should not be used to the disadvantage of the selling organization where such disadvantage can result in business disruption, vendor dissatisfaction, impossibility of proper performance, or business termination.

F. NEGOTIATING STRATEGY

As indicated, this is not a text on negotiating strategy, but some points will be mentioned to insure that the negotiating process is carried out in a reasonable manner.

1. *Don't Ask for Everything at Once.* It is not desirable to present the other side with an overwhelming series of requests at the beginning. The vendor has already received the contract specification, and has responded to it. The vendor is already aware of the fact that the user has requested a fairly significant change from the standard contract. The vendor therefore has already been placed on guard. Further demands might create a difficult situation, in which the vendor might decide to walk out rather than deal with a massive problem in the contract. If the vendor has made it to the negotiating table in spite of having seen the contract specification and having recognized its weight, then the vendor is prepared to negotiate and compromise. Accordingly, it is not desirable to overpower the vendor at the initial negotiating session. Group clauses to be discussed into categories so that all major ones are not discussed at the beginning. This suggests an analysis of the clauses, so that they can be discussed in a functional sequence to be determined prior to the start of the negotiation.

2. *Retain Command and Control of the Negotiating Process.* The user must stay in command of the negotiation and should therefore be responsible for initiating discussions of each topic, on a topic by topic basis. The user should take the minutes of the meetings, and use those minutes to express the agreements reached. It is not necessary for the user to perform the drafting of the contract, although this is probably desirable. If the user takes and publishes the minutes of each meeting, then the user retains control over the agreements reached, and retains some control over the wording. Whether or not the user drafts the contract is a decision of counsel for the user.

   The negotiating process should be *dominated* by the user. To do this, a single leader of the negotiating team should be appointed, capable of exercising control over his team, capable of redirecting discussions, and capable of resuscitating issues when they need to be discussed again.

3. *Optimize the Rank of Participants.* The negotiating process should include high-level managers from the user organization. First of all, this will give rise to the vendor's own need to obtain equally highly ranking personnel from within his organization. And since such high-ranking vendor personnel will normally be interested in not impeding progress of the local sales organizations, they will be interested in accelerating the contract negotiating process by making

concessions on minor points. In addition they have decision-making capability without recourse to other organization elements, and they would normally consider minor points to be of such insignificance that they are prepared to make ready concessions in those areas. A disadvantage of using high-ranking personnel is that in the case of major points they may withhold decisions or be quite negative. However, this is probably not a significant disadvantage, since resolution of major issues requires referral to a fairly high level in the organization in any case.

High-ranking user managers who participate in the negotiating process will also add to the prestige of the using organization in other ways. They can emphasize the importance of the contract, and their own fears of the potential exposure. As a result, their participation will help beyond their experience, which should also be considerable.

4. *Provide a "Good Guy" and a "Bad Guy."* Negotiation is an adversary process, with at least two sides. Since it is an *adversary* process, the leading negotiator will eventually be regarded as a "bad guy" by the vendor's personnel, and will not be a useful person in future relationships. At the same time, a "good guy" will have to be present at the negotiation to mediate, and to slow down the real or feigned anger which may erupt from time to time. In other words, if the negotiator becomes too involved and/or too negative, whether on purpose or not, it becomes necessary for someone within the user organization to provide breaks, and to protect the then fragile relationship between the user and the vendor. Police officers who use a variation of this technique in interrogating criminal suspects call it the "Mutt and Jeff" routine.

5. *Alternate Between Storm and Sunshine.* A negotiating session will have a varying number of moods. It will be difficult during periods of argument and acrimony. Those periods should be alternated with periods of attention to clauses or agreements which are considered reasonable by both parties so that there is the opportunity to establish a friendly relationship at certain points during the negotiation, even though there is acrimony at other points. The alternation of these periods in a regular manner insures that neither party walks out of the negotiation without just cause.

6. *Use Trade-offs.* A negotiating session of necessity is comprised of give-and-take. These trade-offs should be used very carefully. When the negotiator decides that he is prepared to accede to a request from the vendor, or when he realizes that he has no choice but to accede because the vendor is intractable on a point, and the negotiator is prepared to give in on that point, then the negotiator should use the trade-off capability. He might at that point go back to a clause which had been suspended for which no agreement has been reached and indicate that he will accede to the point in question *if* the vendor will agree to accede to the previous point.

7. *Be Prepared to Drop Issues.* If it is impossible to reach an agreement on a particular issue, the user should be prepared to drop that issue and suspend it until the next session. It is possible that in subsequent discussion the issue might become moot; alternately a resolution or alternative may be found if time passes. The issue should simply be placed in abeyance, and the negotiator should in the next negotiating session determine if either party is prepared to move from the position taken during the preceding negotiating session. Resuscitation of these issues might take place as part of a trade-off or a give-up of another issue.

8. *Always Have a Fall-back Position.* It is desirable to always have a second position for each issue under discussion, and for the negotiation as a whole. A fall-back position for a specific clause might simply be a softening of that clause, or preparedness to accept an inferior position. This can be brought out when the vendor is unprepared to accept the clause as written. If the vendor offers an alternative, then the fall-back position can be tried if it is better for the user than the offered alternative, or if it can be made to appear as a reasonable compromise between the vendor's position and the user's. If the vendor is totally intractable then the fall-back position can be brought out as a compromise between the user requirements and the vendor's unwillingness to provide any kind of response.

In addition to the fall-back in each clause there must be an overall fall-back position. There is a second-ranked vendor, who may or may not be a good alternative. It should be remembered that the vendors were selected on the basis of the commitments they were prepared to make either in the proposal, or as a result of separate discussions. If the prime vendor becomes unwilling to make such commitments in a written contract, then perhaps the selection of this vendor was an error in the first place, and the second-ranked vendor would be the better choice. If at any time the vendor declines to meet its previous commitments, or if the negotiating position of the vendor is so intractable as to render a potential contract meaningless, it may be desirable to actually switch the negotiation to the second-ranked vendor.

In any event, the negotiator should be authorized to break off negotiation and to resume negotiation with the seond-ranked vendor. He will not normally do this without consultation with the team, and in fact will only do so under the most extreme circumstances. The authority and the knowledge that he is able to shift to another vendor will make him a far more effective negotiator, even if he never exercises this option.

Should the negotiations break down totally and the option exercised to start negotiation with the second-ranked vendor, this should not prevent the resumption of negotiation if the prime vendor decides to change his position. It is sometimes necessary to convince a vendor that the user is serious by initiating negotiation with another organization. At that point, if the vendor is unwilling to resume negotiations it is a clear indication that the second vendor will be a better choice. If the vendor is willing to resume negotiations on a better basis, it will result in a far more effective contract.

9. *Provide Exit Opportunities.* There may be occasions during the negotiation when it is better to stop all further discussion rather than generate continuing acrimony. If the negotiations have broken down or there is considerable disagreement, and no apparent resolution is in sight, there should be some exit opportunities during which the situation can be reconsidered. At this point the vendor and user personnel should separate, and perhaps discuss among themselves the approaches to be taken. It is at this point for example that the vendor salesperson or sales manager might convince the vendor negotiator to soften his position. Thus, opportunities to break and separate for lunch, for coffee, or just to regroup are desirable in any negotiating session.

Additional techniques for negotiating can be obtained from a number of other sources. Among these, reference 1 provides interesting insights into negotiating postures.

A. GENERAL CONTRACT LAW

4
CONTRACT LAW: GENERALLY, AND IN THE COMPUTER FIELD

A contract in law is generally defined as a legally enforceable understanding. The law of contracts therefore embraces virtually every form of human interaction from the simplest purchase to the most complicated corporate reorganization.

The purpose of this chapter is to expose the reader to some elementary concepts in the law of contracts and to present specific statutory provisions that for some computer transactions define the rights and obligations of the contracting parties. An awareness of how the judicial system interprets, modifies, amplifies, and detracts from attempts by contracting parties to articulate their agreement will highlight the need for careful, complete, and comprehensible contract drafting. Recently, the courts have reached issues peculiar to parties who are contracting with respect to computers, and these early attempts at keeping the law in pace with technology are especially interesting.

In this chapter, words of caution are in order. Treatises on the law of contracts often run volumes; what follows is the broadest of overviews. Bearing in mind the ancient adage about "a little knowledge," the reader should read on for background purposes, but in any contractual transaction should make use of legal counsel.

Lawyers are expensive, contentious and often slow-moving. The temptation on the part of a businessman is great to avoid needless expense and delay. Unfortunately, transactions in the data processing field often falsely appear insignificant in dollar values. As noted earlier, a $10,000 monthly rental on a 90-day cancellable equipment lease represents, superficially, a mere $30,000 exposure. Experience invariably establishes, however, that such an installation is rarely removed at the end of three months, and generally cannot be economically canceled in less than 5 years. Moreover, the ancillary costs attendant to a $10,000 per month equipment installation for planning, training, software, housing and other resources are generally at least double the equipment rental cost. Very few data processing contracts are therefore insignificant.

It is thus wise to treat data processing related agreements the way management treats long-term real estate leases, each of which, although involving small current costs, represents a serious long-term contingent liability, entails substantial related expenses and, most important, is legally, physically and financially difficult of extrication. Such arrangements always involve complex and sophisticated legal concepts, *and require legal assistance.*

There is another important reason for the use of counsel. The personnel involved in data processing are generally technical staff and management personnel. Technical people, all too frequently, tend to become immersed in the technical aspects of their work, to speak in shorthand and to take any number of matters for granted. Counsel, on the other hand, is generally not proficient in either the technology or the jargon of the various technical functions within the company. One of the most reliable methods of self-education in a subject (including a proposed transaction) involves the attempt to explain it to an intelligent, uninvolved layman. Hopefully, counsel meets those specifications. The very simple questions raised in the mind of a lay lawyer, subjected to such a discourse, are often those that have been ignored or taken for granted by technical personnel and are usually the ones that will be most troublesome in the contracting framework. From a wholly selfish point of view, technical personnel ought to undergo the articulation process involved in educating a lawyer with respect to a given data processing transaction, since mistakes also must be rationalized before a management similarly unfamiliar with the technicalities of data processing.

B. APPLICABLE LAW

The general common law of contracts will govern the rights and obligations of parties to a computer transaction unless the state has legislatively provided otherwise. Article Two of the Uniform Commercial Code (the "U.C.C." or the "Code") is a collection of statutory provisions that codify the common law with respect to transactions in goods.[1] Where the Code applies, parties have recourse to a uniform body of law that encompasses all aspects of commercial transactions, including formation, revocation, rescission, breach of contract, warranties, delivery, parol evidence, and damages. Because Article Two of the U.C.C. has been adopted in every state but Louisiana, commercial transactions subject to its provisions are assured some uniform treatment. However, not all commercial transactions come under the Code's scrutiny. Excluded from coverage in the sales provisions are, generally, leasing arrangements and secured transactions

---

[1]The U.C.C. was drafted under the joint sponsorship of the American Law Institute and the National Conference of Commissioners on Uniform State Laws. Originally approved in 1952, the Code is periodically revised to account for new legal developments. References in this book to the U.C.C. are to the 1977 revised edition.

The scope of the U.C.C. is expansive, encompassing many types of transactions from bank deposits to secured transactions. In this book, only a few of the sales provisions of Article Two of the Code are considered. The most readable and yet comprehensive analysis of the important Articles of the Code is White and Summers, HANDBOOK OF THE LAW UNDER THE UNIFORM COMMERCIAL CODE (2d ed. 1980).

as well as transactions for services as opposed to transactions for goods.[2] Unfortunately, to date courts have not consistently decided what types of computer transactions are subject to the U.C.C.

Most lawyers would agree that a straight sale of computer hardware is a sale of goods within the scope of the U.C.C. However, the typical computer transaction involves more than simply hardware. Instead of procuring separately the many components of a working data processing system, most customers acquire the entire package in one transaction; software, customer education, and installation and maintenance services are among the many components involved. Although separate agreements might be involved for some of the components, courts will often view the agreements as part of a single transaction to acquire a data processing system.[3] Fortunately, courts have interpreted "goods" broadly and generally have found that computer transactions are governed by the sale of goods provisions of the U.C.C. whenever hardware is a significant element of the transaction. An integrated "turnkey" computer system has been deemed "goods" for the purposes of the U.C.C.[4], as have entire transactions where software and services provided for in the contract were "incidental" to the hardware component.[5] However, a transaction solely for services, or a mixed transaction where the hardware component is insignificant as compared with the service component, may fall outside the scope of the U.C.C.[6] Further, the status of software under the U.C.C. is a confused area that has yet to be resolved by the courts. It seems safe to say that most procurements of complete data processing systems are likely to be characterized as transactions in goods subject to the provisions of Article Two of the Code.

Not only must there be a transaction in goods for the U.C.C. to apply, but the transaction must also be a sale, as opposed to a lease or security arrangement. Here again, courts have expanded the coverage of the Code, and thus will often treat a leasing arrangement as the economic (and legal) equivalent of a sale. For instance, in *Chatlos Systems, Inc.* v. *National Cash Register Corp.*[7], a federal district court was confronted with a financing plan commonly used in computer procurements. The customer in *Chatlos* executed a contract with a computer vendor to obtain a small business computer system. Because the customer's credit was not approved, the vendor sold the system to a bank which in turn leased it back to the customer. Going directly to the essence of the transaction, the court decided to apply the U.C.C. "notwithstanding the incidental ser-

---

[2]"Goods" are defined in U.C.C. § 2-105 as "all things (including specially manufactured goods) which are movable at the time of identification to the contract for sale. . . ."

[3]*See, e.g.*, Triangle Underwriters, Inc. v. Honeywell, Inc., 457 F. Supp. 765 (E.D.N.Y. 1978), *aff'd in part, rev'd in part*, 604 F.2d 737 (2d Cir. 1979).

[4]*See, e.g.*, Chatlos Systems, Inc. v. National Cash Register Corp., 479 F. Supp. 738 (D.N.J. 1979), *aff'd in part, rev'd in part*, 635 F.2d 1081 (3d Cir. 1980) (several agreements, including one solely for services, held part of the entire transaction for a sale of goods).

[5]*See, e.g.*, Carl Beasley Ford, Inc. v. Burroughs Corp., 361 F. Supp. 325 (E.D. Pa. 1973), *aff'd*, 493 F.2d 1400 (3d Cir. 1974) (written agreement for sale of hardware coupled with an oral agreement to provide software held jointly to involve a sale of goods).

[6]Courts are likely to scrutinize carefully contracts where the service component dominates the transaction. *See, e.g.*, North American Leisure Corp. v. A & B Duplicators, Ltd., 468 F.2d 695 (2d Cir. 1972) (transaction not for goods where the essence of the agreement was the vendor's obligation to reproduce magnetic tape); Computer Servicenters, Inc. v. Beacon Mfg. Co., 328 F. Supp. 653, 655 (D.S.C. 1970), *aff'd*, 443 F.2d 906 (4th Cir. 1971) (transaction not for goods where the contract price was for "analysis, collection storage, and reporting of data" supplied by one party to the other).

[7]479 F. Supp. 738 (D.N.J. 1979), *aff'd in part, rev'd in part*, 635 F.2d 1081 (3d Cir. 1980).

vice aspects and the lease arrangement."[8] The court was quick to recognize that the economic effect of the lease was no different than an installment sale, and thus would not permit the form of the transaction to disguise what was in substance a sale.[9]

Whether any given computer transaction that includes some kind of lease arrangement will bring to bear the provisions of the U.C.C. will depend upon several factors in addition to the express intent of the parties, among them: the term of the lease, the presence of an option to purchase, and the circumstances surrounding the transaction.[10] The trend of most courts to construe liberally the coverage provisions of the U.C.C. should result in an increasing number of computer "leasing" arrangements being treated as sales within the purview of the U.C.C. Moreover, even in those cases where the U.C.C. does not apply, courts will often refer to its provisions for theoretical guidance. Careful planning and drafting of computer contracts can help insure that disputes will be resolved under the U.C.C. and not under the less specialized common law of contracts.

C. UNDERSTANDINGS NOT LEGALLY ENFORCEABLE

A contract is an understanding that is legally enforceable. An understanding need not necessarily be reduced to writing to constitute an enforceable contract, nor does written evidence of an understanding necessarily exclude unwritten agreements from an enforceable contract. But for there to be a contract, there must at a minimum be an understanding.

The most common arrangement that is not a contract is what lawyers call an agreement to agree. If A agrees to buy from B all of A's requirements for punch cards during the next year at "prices and terms to be negotiated from time to time," the parties have really not entered into any understanding at all. Courts will not enforce such an agreement to agree notwithstanding that B may have bought a plant and inventory to meet what he anticipates are A's requirements nor will they enforce it against B even if A finds himself without a substitute supply of cards.

Some kinds of understanding do not rise to the dignity of a contract because they lack a material element known as "consideration." Consideration has become a very sophisticated concept, but its elementary aspects are readily understandable. A vendor's promise to deliver merchandise will not bind him unless supported by consideration, consisting normally of the buyer's promise to pay. Consideration problems rarely arise in the world of commerce, and there are many exceptions to the rules requiring consideration.

There are many types of understandings that fulfill both the layman's notion of a contract and the legal requirements, but are for public policy reasons not deemed enforceable. Some examples are:

(a) Illegal Contracts. You may not sue to collect a promised bribe nor, if you are the briber, to recover a bribe already paid. The law generally treats the parties to an illegal agreement by leaving them alone, in whatever position they find themselves.

---

[8]479 F. Supp. at 742.

[9]*See also* Earman Oil Co., Inc. v. Burroughs Corp., 625 F.2d 1291, 1297 (5th Cir. 1980) ("the real economic effect of the transaction," where Earman ordered a computer from Burroughs which was then sold to a third party and leased to Earman, "was a sale direct from Burroughs to Earman").

[10]*See* Bernacchi, Davidson and Grogan, COMPUTER SYSTEM PROCUREMENT, 30 Emory L. J. 395, 400 (1981).

(b) Contracts which Violate Particular Public Policies. The law generally does not enforce promises to marry. The courts in many jurisdictions will not permit a Nevada casino to sue elsewhere upon a gambling debt, notwithstanding that such debt is valid and enforceable in Nevada.

(c) Contracts which Violate the Statute of Frauds. Because courts have traditionally experienced difficulty in the resolution of disputes involving oral understandings, where one party either denies the existence of an agreement or where the parties differ on its substance, a body of law has developed which refuses enforcement of many types of oral understandings. That body of law is known as the Statute of Frauds.

(d) Penalties. The ancient legal maxim "The law abhors a penalty" has developed into a legal doctrine that prohibits contracts (or portions of contracts) the purpose of which is simply to penalize a party. If A promises to pay his employer $10,000 if A fails to get to work on time, the law will not enforce such an agreement, notwithstanding A's reputation for being unable to get to work at the duly appointed hour and the disruption and anguish caused his employer by such failure.

(e) Unconscionable Contracts. In line with historical precedents involving extortionate contracts, courts and legislatures have recently expanded the concept of "unconscionability" to protect the ignorant and the impoverished (and those persons whose relative economic strength is minuscule compared to persons with whom they are contracting). As a result, unconscionability claims arising from computer contract disputes have burgeoned in recent years. Computer failures are common and often devastating to an unsuspecting user. In some instances, the customer is saddled with losses that far exceed the price paid to the vendor under the contract. But the standard vendor-supplied contract will usually restrict severely the customer's remedy in the event the vendor has breached the contract. As a result, some customers have tried to rely upon the doctrine of unconscionability to avoid the impact of such onerous contract terms.

However, courts are not receptive to unconscionability claims arising from commercial transactions. Transactions to acquire data processing systems are no exception.[11] A rare case where a computer customer successfully advanced an unconscionability claim was *The Glovatorium, Inc. v. National Cash Register Corp.*[12] The customer in *Glovatorium* was a first-time computer user faced with substantial losses resulting from a computer that failed to perform as expected. The contract with the vendor disclaimed warranties and excluded the vendor's liability for consequential damages. Finding no solace in the contract, the customer pressed his claim in court, successfully arguing that the liability limitations in the contract should not be enforced because they were unconscionable. '

As computers become more integrated into society and as businessmen become more sophisticated with data processing, courts will expect a greater degree of responsibility from computer customers. For example, in *Loveright Diamond Co. v. Nixdorf Computer Corp.*[13], a computer user sued to

---

[11]*See* Note, *U.C.C.* § *2-719 As Applied to Computer Contracts—Unconscionable Exclusions of Remedy?*, 14 Conn. L. Rev. 71 (1981).

[12]No. C-79-3393 (N.D. Cal., May 1, 1981), *aff'd on other grounds*, 684 F.2d 658 (9th Cir. 1982). *See also* Chesapeake Petroleum and Supply Co., Inc. v. Burroughs Corp., 6 CLSR 768 (1977), *aff'd on other grounds*, 384 A.2d 734 (Md. App. 1978) (waiver of damages provision held unconscionable).

[13]No. 78-4585, slip op. (S.D.N.Y. Oct. 9, 1979).

recover losses incurred as the result of a defective computer, arguing in part that certain contract terms were unconscionable. The unsympathetic court reasoned that the likelihood of unconscionability did not exist where, prior to signing the contract, the customer had retained an independent computer consultant to help him to select an appropriate computer.

In the vast majority of cases, terms in computer contracts that limit the obligations or restrict the remedies of a party will be enforced by the courts. Even where there is a great disparity in technological sophistication between the vendor and the user, it is unlikely that a court will stray far from the general rule that a commercial contract negotiated between substantial business concerns is presumably not unconscionable.[14] Because most vendor-supplied contracts contain terms that in some situations could work harshly, it is important for the prospective customer to understand exactly what it is the vendor is obligated to provide and how limited the customer's remedy will be in the event the vendor fails to perform.

There are other areas where the application of legal doctrines interferes with the validity and enforcement of presumably complete and valid understandings. Most of these are based upon policy considerations in areas of antitrust, labor, health, safety, consumer protection and like areas where society has decided to interfere with the otherwise free right of parties to contract. Some of these governmental policies may impinge on contracts in the data processing field.

Further, the policies described may sometimes apply to and render illegal particular terms of parts of an agreement, thus affecting the rest of the arrangement, without destroying it. Conventionally, particularly in printed-form contracts, there is a "partial invalidity" provision which provides that if a portion of the agreement is found to violate any law, the balance of the agreement will not be affected (See Clause 5-20). Such a provision can cause disastrous results to A, who pays B substantial consideration for territorial or product exclusivity as a distributor, and then finds, because of prevailing antitrust attitudes, that he can neither stop B from violating that exclusivity nor get his money back.

D. LEGALLY ENFORCEABLE UNDERSTANDINGS

One of the most difficult problems in contract law is defining the scope of a legally enforceable understanding. The law has developed many doctrines to help courts tackle this problem. Some doctrines serve to deny legal effect to portions of an understanding and others work to expand or amplify understandings. Many of these doctrines have been codified in the U.C.C. The underlying principle is that the law will give effect only to matters upon which the parties have in fact agreed.

Problems arise when a written contract does not contain everything that one contracting party believed was included in the basic understanding. B's salesman arrives at A's purchasing agent with a glossy brochure about B's equipment. B's salesman engages A's purchasing agent with additional statements about the characteristics, capability and performance of the equipment. B then signs a purchase order for the equipment on a form provided by B's salesman. Buried in the "fine print," among other things, are (a) disclaimers of warranties; and (b) a sen-

---

[14]*See, e.g.*, Chatlos Systems, Inc. v. National Cash Register Corp., 479 F. Supp. 738, *aff'd in part*, *rev'd in part*, 635 F.2d 1081, 1087 (3d Cir. 1980) (clause excluding vendor's liability for consequential damages not unconscionable because "the claim is for commercial loss and the adversaries are substantial business concerns").

tence stating that the purchase order constitutes the entire agreement and that all prior negotiations, discussions, representations, and understandings are merged in the purchase order and are of no effect unless expressly set forth therein. When the machine fails to operate according to the glossy brochure or the salesman's statements, A consults his counsel and discovers, to his dismay, the serious likelihood that everything that preceded the purchase order was mere "talk" and that A may not have any recourse.

Legal doctrines that supplement, detract from, or modify understandings are particularly significant in computer contract disputes. The standard computer contract is surprisingly short document, considering the costs, complexities, and risks involved in acquiring a data processing system. The standard contract is often couched in very general terms and usually defines the rights and obligations of the parties without reference to the specific goods and services passing under the contract. In contrast are the negotiations that typically precede the signing of the contract, where the vendor and the customer have discussed in great detail the capability and reliability of the computer system. If during the negotiations the vendor orally represents to the customer that the computer will be "up and running" within six months, but the contract makes no mention of timetables, has the vendor breached the agreement when the computer has yet to function one year after delivery? If a customer negotiates to acquire a data processing system and signs three separate agreements, one each for software, hardware, and service, does the vendor's breach of any one agreement confer further rights to the customer under all three? Careful contract drafting can often prevent questions like these from arising. The following discussion sets forth some basic principles of contract interpretation.

1. The Parol Evidence Rule

Courts try hard to limit contracts to the contents of the documents which articulate the understandings. Courts do so for a variety of reasons, primarily to promote certainty by refusing to hear conflicting oral testimony as to what else the parties had in mind.

There is a similar problem that virtually every businessman has encountered: a particularly offensive clause in a written contract is pointed out to B's salesman, who urges A to leave the clause in because it is (a) a peccadillo of B's board chairman or B's house counsel, or (b) meaningless and, in any event, will not be enforced. An ancient rule of law, known as the Parol Evidence Rule, permits courts to hear oral testimony even with respect to a written agreement only in circumstances where the testimony will amplify or explain an incomplete or ambiguous provision. Under no circumstances, however, will a court permit any testimony regarding oral representations or understandings whose import is to vary or contradict the terms of a written document. The rule's application often leads to a morass of conflicting testimony.

Oral testimony concerning a written contract often serves only to establish the absence of any specific additional oral understandings. For instance, a salesman, admitting to certain statements, may declare that the statements were unintentional, mere "talk," or even a joke. One element, however, of contract law is that an enforceable promise or representation must be intentional and made with a view to be bound. Some jokes may be taken very seriously by the listener.

The point is that oral communications are not as trustworthy as those that have been reduced to writing, even when parties are both totally honest. Recollections vary: spoken words, even if recollected, are often ambiguous and capable of a variety of interpretations based on circumstances, atmosphere and even tone of voice. Intention on the part of parties to be bound must be established by the oral statements, which may become still another matter of proof in addition to proving that the statements themselves were made.

Too often customers enter into written agreements to procure computer equipment based on the vendor's representations, explanations, and demonstrations made during the course of the negotiations without considering whether these pre-contractual statements are legally enforceable. The negotiations preceding the acquisition of a data processing system are often long and involved. During the process, vendor personnel will discuss with the customer the hardware, software, service, and support aspects of the proposed acquisition. The customer is usually supplied with detailed specifications and performance statistics. Time-tables for installation and availability will also be discussed. Throughout this process, the vendor freely makes representations with respect to the computer's capabilities and reliability and the vendor's ability to deliver, install, and "fine tune" the computer to the customer's satisfaction.

In limited situations, it is possible for these pre-contractual representations to become part of the contract. Under the U.C.C., a seller creates express warranties by "[a]ny affirmation of fact or promise . . . which relates to the goods and becomes part of the basis of the bargain . . ." Express warranties are also created where the seller provides a "description of the goods which is made part of the basis of the bargain . . ."[15] An express warranty is legally enforceable and a buyer has a cause of action against the seller for breach of warranty in the event that the goods do not conform.

Before a customer takes comfort in the vendor's express warranties, it must be understood that they rarely come into play in computer transactions. There are two reasons for this. First, computer vendors invariably include in their standard form contracts terms known as "merger" or "integration" clauses which purport to wrap up the written agreement as the entire understanding of the parties and to exclude all other non-written agreements and understandings. Second, the Parol Evidence Rule prevents a customer from introducing evidence that would contradict the written agreement.

The Parol Evidence Rule is reflected in Section 2-202 of the U.C.C. Terms with respect to which parties agree and intend as a final expression of their agreement cannot be contradicted by evidence of prior oral agreements or oral agreements made when the contract was executed. In most cases it will be difficult to prevail on a claim that an executed standard computer contract was not intended as a final agreement, and for this reason parol representations by either parties will not be considered part of such a contract. In *Investors Premium Corp.* v. *Burroughs Corp.*[16], an insurance company leased a computer upon alleged representations by the vendor that the computer was capable of handling the company's present business needs without requiring additional personnel. After testing the computer for over six months, the company decided to convert the lease into an outright purchase. The sale was memorialized in a written agreement that contained a merger clause excluding most understandings, agreements, representations, and warranties. When the insurance company later sued the vendor alleging breach of warranty, the court held that the writing was one which "set out the

---

[15]U.C.C. § 2-313(1).
[16]389 F. Supp. 39 (D.S.C. 1974).

entire agreement between the parties and by a separate conspicuous paragraph all outside matters are excluded."[17] Because the vendor's prior representation that the computer would handle the company's needs failed to appear in the written contract, it did not enter into the enforceable agreement.

As noted above, the Parol Evidence Rule has another side, one that permits evidence to be heard so that agreed upon terms may be explained or supplemented. For instance, the Parol Evidence Rule may permit a customer to establish the existence of a prior oral agreement to provide programming services where the written agreement to procure a computer is silent on that point. In *Carl Beasley Ford, Inc.* v. *Burroughs Corp.*[18], the court reasoned that because a computer is useless without the programs necessary to operate it, and because the contract at issue failed to consider the subject of programming, the customer should be permitted to introduce evidence establishing a prior oral agreement to provide programming services. Thus, where the writing itself or other direct evidence suggests that a written agreement is not intended as a complete and exclusive statement, evidence may be admitted to establish additional consistent terms.

At the risk of redundancy, it should be stressed that where the written contract provides that its contents constitute the entire agreement between the parties, it is difficult, and frequently impossible, to introduce into evidence the background and the verbal agreements and representations, if any, that were involved in the transaction as a whole. On the other hand, even where a document declares itself to be the entirety of the agreement, a court will sometimes receive oral testimony if the document is ambiguous or incomprehensible.

The Parol Evidence Rule teaches two lessons. First, it is important to reduce the *entirety* of an understanding to writing. Second, it is necessary to articulate the understanding clearly and comprehensibly. The utilization of legal counsel and of some nontechnical staff personnel, such as a contracting agent, somewhat removed from the transaction and not immersed in its technical aspects, can be a useful approach, if only to review the document for clarity and comprehensiveness.

2. Judicial Gap-Filling and Implied Provisions

Often, courts face the problem of the interpretation of written (or even oral) contracts involving the total absence of agreement on some particular aspect. Where contracting parties have agreed on enough to make the agreement legally binding (and this is often a subjective determination) but have failed to consider and agree upon a material element, courts have developed techniques to fill in the missing aspects. For instance, consider the situation where a written agreement otherwise complete on its face lacks a provision to cover the time of delivery of purchased equipment and the parties, in fact, never agreed on a delivery date. Courts will normally, of their own volition, add a delivery date by determining what a "reasonable" time is, in light of all of the prevailing circumstances. The test of "reasonableness" has been utilized by courts to add a variety of missing provisions to agreements. To determine what is "reasonable," courts again will resort to oral testimony about customs and usage in an industry, general commercial practices, background discussions, and generalized notions of fairness.

The concept of "reasonableness" has been widely utilized and is a good one; its

---

[17]Id. at 44.
[18]361 F. Supp. 325 (E.D. Pa. 1973), *aff'd mem.*, 493 F.2d 1400 (3d Cir. 1974).

application to litigation in the world of commerce (as well as to virtually every other area of Western law) has served to promote stability in the world of commerce, to assist imperfect legal draftsmen, and to assure, in general terms, that undue advantages are not taken in the universe of contractual arrangements.

It should be stressed, however, that such gap-filling by judges may work substantial unfairness to a particular litigant in a given case. All too frequently what is generally considered reasonable may be totally unfair in a particular contracting environment. While attaching notions of reasonableness to a particular aspect of a contract, a court may not take into account that the particular element really warrants an unreasonable interpretation. If A pays a premium because he wants early delivery, but neglects to get specific agreemtn on the time of delivery, a "reasonable" time concept will be unfair to A.

The statement by A to B's salesman that A needs delivery within three months and B's response advising A to sign the order and "I'll see what I can do about it" may give rise to the legal conclusion that the parties did not agree on delivery and that delivery, accordingly, is due within a reasonable time. A court may, to A's chagrin, determine in the case of a main-frame, that current delivery schedules published by the major computer manufacturers set the framework of what is a "reasonable" delivery time. Since these vary widely, the test may have unpredictable results.

The U.C.C. offers some assistance in this area by providing that an agreement must be interpreted in light of the party's course of dealing[19] and course of performance[20], and in consideration of applicable usages of trade.[21] In addition, the U.C.C. offers an array of gap-filler provisions that operate when an agreement is silent with respect to certain essential terms. For instance, if an agreement fails to provide delivery terms, the time of delivery is a "reasonable time,"[22] at a reasonable hour.[23] And where the contract is otherwise silent, delivery shall be made at the seller's place of business.[24] The U.C.C. also provides payment terms and price terms. Generally, the buyer must tender payment when and where the seller tenders goods.[25] The Code's other provisions on payment are worthy of detailed inspection by the reader, as, for example, it is possible to conclude a valid contract for the sale of goods under the Code without stating an agreement on price. Here again, the appropriate measure is a "reasonable price."[26]

---

[19]A course of dealing is defined in U.C.C. §1-205(1) as follows:

A course of dealing is a sequence of previous conduct between the parties to a particular transaction which is fairly to be regarded as establishing a common basis of understanding for interpreting their expressions and other conduct.

[20]A course of performance is defined in U.C.C. §2-208(1) as follows:

Where the contract for sale involves repeated occasions for performance by either party with knowledge of the nature of the performance and opportunity for objection to it by the other, any course of performance accepted or acquiesced in without objection shall be relevant to determine the meaning of the agreement.

[21]A usage of trade is defined in U.C.C. §1-205(2) as:

A usage of trade is any practice or method of dealing having such regularity of observance in a place, vocation or trade as to justify an expectation that it will be observed with respect to the transaction in question.

[22]U.C.C. §2-309(1).
[23]U.C.C. §2-503(1)(a).
[24]U.C.C. §2-308(a).
[25]See U.C.C. §2-511 comment 2.
[26]U.C.C. §2-305.

Although courts are thus willing to fill contractual gaps where absolutely necessary, it should not be assumed that courts will cure or even deal with enough omissions to turn a skeletal agreement into a completely fleshed-out understanding. Quite to the contrary, many dreadful problems not considered by one or both parties will be ignored by courts, often with disastrous consequences even though a properly thought-out agreement should have covered these eventualities. This should be carefully considered in light of the fact that industry "standard" contracts have many earmarks of a skeletal agreement.

For instance, although courts will ordinarily supply missing provisions relative to time or place of delivery, they will refuse without express agreement to insert a missing clause to cover a buyer's complaint that a piece of equipment, when delivered, turned out to be too big to be moved into his premises through existing accessways. A court will normally leave the purchaser to solve that access problem on his own, in spite of his protest that the seller visited the premises and saw all the access routes.

More seriously, in the absence of an understanding a court will not help a purchaser of software complaining that new equipment will not operate on his system because of lack of capacity or incompatibility. Similarly, it is quite likely that the law would give no aid to a purchaser of a software package that performs its intended function but does so outrageously slowly, unless the agreement expressed or implied time performance specifications!

In addition to sometimes dealing with confusions and omissions in contracts, Western law has developed, and continues to develop, accretions or implied provisions, which, like mollusks to whales, attach themselves unseen and unconsidered to contractual arrangements. Many such implied terms attach to contracts even if the parties expressly intend otherwise, generally because of public policy considerations. For the most part, however, these accretions by implication can be negated by express treatment in a properly drafted contract.

Many such implied contract terms are applicable to virtually any kind of contract. Some examples are:

(a) Apparent Authority. In most instances, a person signing a contract on behalf of his employer who gives the appearance of authority will be deemed to have authority to bind his employer whether or not he has such authority in fact. Accordingly, a company may find itself bound to an agreement signed by a data processing manager, because the company, as an emolument, gave him the title "Vice President-Data Processing." Worse still, that manager could sign a single letter which expressly, or by its import, creates (or radically modifies) a contract. For this reason many companies do not permit any correspondence by officers, divisional officers or managers to be mailed without review by a central authority.

(b) There are implied contract provisions concerning the effect of communications or notices in the operation of contracts. Certain communications, absent a specific contractual provision dealing with communications and notices, may be deemed effective when sent. A party may, thus, find itself bound by a notice sent by the other party and never received. This problem can, of course, be dealt with by proper contract draftsmanship (see clause 5-24).

(c) Except in unusual circumstances, the law does not give effect to representations relating to pure matters of law. A vendor's incorrect representation that a particular installation will not violate applicable zoning laws, may leave the purchaser with no remedy. The law implies that such representations are merely nonbinding opinions. This is, of course, an oversimplification. In the example discussed, if the purchaser were to obtain the zoning resolution and have the vendor make specific representations as to the factual elements that make up the zoning requirements, the vendor would probably be legally responsible. Courts, incidentally, are now tending to hold sellers liable for representations even when they impinge upon matters of law *if the vendors are experts* and the buyers are ignorant and rely upon the vendors. This has arisen, in part, because of increased consumer orientation, and commercial enterprises should take no comfort from this recent tendency. In all events, problems in this area can be solved by proper contract drafting.

(d) The law sometimes will add an implied provision to a contract in order to avert an unforeseen, unconscionable result. Assume A agrees to groom B's horse for 20 years, in exchange for which B agrees to pay A $500 a year, and the horse dies at the end of the third year. Notwithstanding that the parties neglected to consider the eventuality of the horse's death, it is likely that a court will terminate B's obligation when the horse dies. There are, however, many cases where a court will not extinguish a contractual liability even where the result appears mildly absurd. Unless otherwise expressly provided, A's liability under a contract to pay for public relations or consulting services over a fixed time period will probably continue after A has sold his business and no longer needs the services. Foresight and attention to contingencies such as these can avoid such unanticipated occurrences.

There are many other implied provisions that attach themselves to contracts absent specific arrangements or understandings to the contrary. The law creates implications with respect to whether contracts are assignable and concerning the nature and extent of performance required in order to fulfill the contract's obligations.

In addition to these judicially developed implied terms, the U.C.C. provides mandatory terms which may not be disclaimed or varied by agreement of the parties. Most fundamental is that parties may not disclaim their Code obligations of good faith, diligence, reasonableness, and care.[27]

3. Implied Warranties and Representations

Early in the development of civilized law in the Western World, it became obvious that most transactions, however simple or silent, involved a variety of implications, most of which did not even occur to the parties. Since these implications, by and large, reflected elementary societal mores and were necessary for the preservation of public order and the development of commerce, they were soon recognized by courts and given legal effect.

As an example, let us consider the simplest commercial transaction, and assume that the transaction takes place wholly in silence. A goes to the corner store and buys a steak from B, paying by check in an amount exactly equal to the price of the steak. Without a word, jurisprudence tells us, B has represented to A, among other

---

[27]U.C.C. §1-102(3); *see also* U.C.C. §1-203 ("Every contract or duty within this Act imposes an obligation of good faith in its performance or enforcement").

things, that the steak is edible; that it is not rancid; that it weighs the amount set forth on the label; that B is the owner of the steak; that it contains no noxious or harmful substances (meaning poisons, not cholesterol); that the steak has not been mortgaged to B's creditors. A, too, has made silent implied representations to B that A's balance is sufficient to cover the price of the steak; that A will have no claims against B if A unsuccessfully makes use of the steak for some unusual purpose, such as to treat a black eye; and, that A has not pocketed any additional merchandise without paying for it. Wall Street lawyers could make both lists much longer. Most of the implied warranties and representations developed in the law arose to limit the old doctrine of *caveat emptor* and to protect the buyer against those failings or insufficiencies of the purchased product or service that any normal purchaser now expects without asking. For instance, the law may also imply the concept that where a commercial sale is made through the use of a sample, the product sold must conform to the sample. Similarly, where goods are advertised by description, the goods shipped must conform to the description. This, of course, is interesting to computer users who select equipment based on a benchmark.

The two most deservedly famous and all-encompassing implied warranties are those commonly called the Warranty of Merchantability and the Warranty of Fitness for a Particular Purpose. Section 2-314 of the U.C.C. codifies the former and writes such a warranty into a contract for sale if the seller is a "merchant" of the goods sold.[28]

The Warranty of Merchantability imposes a minimum obligation on the merchant computer vendor to provide goods that are "merchantable." To be merchantable, the goods must be, *inter alia*, "at least such as pass without objection in the trade" and "fit for the ordinary purposes of which such goods are used."[29]

Of perhaps greater importance to the computer user is the implied Warranty of Fitness for a Particular Purpose. As discussed earlier, vendors and their customers typically engage in extensive discussions prior to executing a contract. During these discussions the vendor's sales representatives and hardware and software specialists will often conduct site surveys, prepare installation plans, and ascertain from the user the intended use of the computer. Under the U.C.C., an implied Warranty of Fitness for a Particular Purpose arises where "the seller at the time of contracting has reason to know any particular purpose for which the goods are required and that the buyer is relying on the seller's skill or judgment to select or furnish suitable goods."[30] As it is normally the computer vendor's *job* to determine the user's particular needs and requirements in order to recommend a suitable computer, this implied warranty may impose on the vendor an obligation to ensure that the computer to be provided is not only merchantable but fit for the particular purpose of this user. The principal difference between the two major implied warranties is thus that the Warranty of Merchantability covers uses to which goods are customarily put whereas the Warranty of Fitness for a Particular Purpose covers specific uses of a buyer that are peculiar to his business.[31]

---

[28]Almost every computer procurement will be from a merchant, defined in U.C.C. §2-104(1) as a person "who deals in goods of the kind or otherwise holds himself out as having knowledge or skill peculiar to the practices or goods involved in the transaction . . ."

[29]U.C.C. §2-314(2).

[30]U.C.C. §2-315.

[31]U.C.C. §2-315, comment 2.

Because the user generally relies heavily upon the superior skill and expertise of the vendor, and because the vendor is generally well aware of the particular needs of the user, the agreement between the two parties will routinely involve a Warranty of Fitness for a Particular Purpose.[32] However, this theoretical creation of implied warranties is greatly diminished by the presence in most vendor form contracts of clauses which explicitly exclude implied warranties. The Warranty of Merchantability can be effectively disclaimed by an explicit and conspicuous writing that states that the implied Warranty of Merchantability is excluded. The Warranty of Fitness for a Particular Purpose can be excluded by a conspicuous writing to that effect.[33] Examine any vendor's standard contract and you are sure to find a paragraph, in boldface print, that meets the above criteria exactly. As exclusionary language in the vendor's contract will usually be given effect by courts,[34] it is the goal of every user's lawyer to get the vendor to delete the disclaimer; the two implied warranties are important and useful, although not sufficient by themselves.

The two major implied warranties nevertheless have great utility, and may conceivably need no supplementing, in the case of purchases of peanuts, bolts of cloth, and even light bulbs, cars and office furniture. Their utility is primarily dependent upon two variables. The most important variable is the universe of discourse that exists about the products sold; the more common and widely used the product, the more dependable these warranties are. With widely-used, established products, there is common agreement about what constitutes a commercially satisfactory specimen. The second variable upon which the utility of these implied warranties depends is the simplicity of the product. It is far easier to judge what is a commercially acceptable sofa or shirt than it is to obtain agreement on what is a commercially acceptable computer, chemical cracking plant or steamship.

The exploration of the basic protections afforded by implied warranties is intended to display that the law does try to afford minimal protections and to set basic commercial standards. The goal of the other chapters of this book is to see that these minimal standards are improved upon to the extent care and human imagination can permit. The goal of the responsible businessman should be to attempt to articulate as clearly and as thoroughly as possible his specific demands and requirements, whether in terms of physical specifications, character, quality, performance, reliability, utility, length of life, speed, efficiency, payment, nonperformance, damages, etc.

It is also important to remember that the Uniform Commercial Code may not cover any number of transactions within the data processing field. Although, in some instances, it may be that many of the same legal implications may attach, it is by no means clear what implications will apply to purchases by data processing users of services such as consultation, software, systems design and development, service bureau services, key punching services, hardware maintenance agreements, or time-sharing arrangements.

---

[32]*See, e.g.,* Sperry Rand Corp. v. Industrial Supply Corp., 337 F.2d 363, 369-70 (5th Cir. 1964); Chatlos Systems, Inc. v. National Cash Register Corp., 479 F. Supp. 738, 743 (D.N.J. 1979).

[33]U.C.C. §2-316(2).

[34]*See* Bernacchi, Davidson and Grogan, COMPUTER SYSTEMS PROCUREMENT, 30 Emory L.J. 395, 414-18 (1981).

4. The Nonlitigative Utilization of Contracts

Prior to an examination of the consequences of broken promises, misrepresentations and the like, a brief reiteration of the role to be played by a contract is in order. From a lawyer's point of view, a contract is a sword or shield to be used in that arena of civilized combat known as litigation. That ultimate, and ultimately most important, purpose should be kept in mind during the negotiation and preparation of agreements. The less drastic, more immediate purposes of the contracting process are at least equally significant.

It can be safely assumed that most businessmen desire to live up to their obligations and that, within the strictures of human frailty and imperfection, most businessmen substantially do so. The prime purpose of a contract, then, is to expose and articulate the various matters that are to be accomplished and to focus responsibility on the party whose obligation it is to accomplish each. Most contract litigation arises when the parties have failed to consider some potential problem, and have therefore neglected to determine in the contract where responsibility will lie. Sometimes, a party is aware of a particular focus of responsibility or potential problem, but assumes that the solution is properly the obligation of the other party and therefore, says nothing.

Thus, either by failure to consider, or by inadvertent neglect to mention, a purchaser buying a computer "fully installed" may find himself in court with his vendor in an attempt to determine which of them should properly pay for particular wiring or floor supports. In a similar vein, it is the proper purpose of a contract to define and articulate the characteristics, both quantitative and qualitative, of the items to be purchased. These characteristics can be designed on a result-oriented basis. The parties should negotiate, agree upon and articulate how, when, how quickly and with what degree of exactitude or margin for error, the purchased item will perform.

This book is not an argument for "tough" contracts; it is a plea for well thought-out, clearly articulated and exhaustive contracts. If the duties, obligations and expectations of each party are expressed, negotiated, agreed to (with an understanding of their implications) and clearly set forth in a written document, the chances that both parties will be satisfied with the performance of the contract are increased immensely. The reasons are obvious. The more fully a party understands the allocation of responsibility down to the remotest of contingencies, the more properly he can evaluate the price to be paid or received. Similarly, the more fully he can direct his energies to the avoidance of contingent problems that are his own responsibility, the less opportunity there is for subsequent backbiting, and the less necessity there is for the negotiation or litigation.

5. Litigation

The last resort, of course, is litigation. It is by no means a satisfying process. What most contracting parties want most—to get the other party to do what he promised to do—is generally most difficult to obtain in litigation. Generally speaking, the only form of satisfaction that courts award is monetary satisfaction. Even in those rare instances where a court will do more than award money, the award comes too late to be meaningful.

(a) *Damages as Primary Remedy—Credit Problems.* Another constant source of unhappiness to litigants is the fact that courts merely decree the payment of damages. The collection of damages is often a futile process.

Judgment debtors, as unsuccessful litigants are often called, all too frequently are insolvent, bankrupt or financially irresponsible. Many simply disappear. Except for major original equipment manufacturers, the data processing industry is replete with vendors of goods and services who are seriously undercapitalized or financially irresponsible. To the extent possible, purchasers in these areas should seek reasonable vendors. It is remarkable, although somewhat understandable, how frequently purchasers of data processing goods and services fail to verify the reliability of their vendors, where the same purchasers are quite careful about their own customers' credit. It is characteristic of the data processing field that purchases of hardware and software entail long-term arrangements and that large sums of money are rapidly paid to vendors, without substantial holdbacks to secure future performance. *It is wise to think of these arrangements as involving an extension of credit by the user to the vendor, so that appropriate credit checks can be made.*

(b) *The Concept of Breach or Default.* A contract is breached when a promise is not kept or a representation or warranty is or becomes untrue. There is much legal lore on the difference between a promise (or covenant) and a representation (or warranty). The distinction, although very clear at its extremes, is of little practical importance. In the absence of fraud or other special circumstances, the aggrieved contracting party does not care whether the breach is a result of a broken promise ("I will deliver your equipment on Monday at 3:00 P.M.") or a misrepresentation ("The equipment will run at 3000 lpm."). For the purposes of this discussion, then, we will speak of a broken contract, a default, or a breach, however arising.

There are essentially two categories of breach although, as with all categories in the law, the lines of demarcation between them become very unclear in specific applications. One type goes to the heart of the understanding and renders the entire contract void. An extreme example would be that of the manufacturer who agrees to deliver a system consisting of a main-frame, tape drives, disc drives, systems and applications programming and a set of tools. In a properly drawn agreement, and probably even in an improperly drafted agreement, a vendor who delivered only the tools would be deemed to have broken the contract in its entirety. The purchaser would have no obligation to keep or pay for the tools and would have recourse to the seller for losses occasioned by the seller's failure to perform the entire contract.

The other types of breaches are those which do not go to the heart of the agreement, but which subject the defaulting party to pay damages for a portion of the contract that he has failed to fulfill. An example would be the failure to deliver promised tools or manuals for an equipment installation. Some defaults are so insubstantial that there may not even be compensation available in damages. Short delays in delivery of items, *without actual loss to the customer*, are often found not to give rise to monetary damages.

The U.C.C. codifies the rights and obligations of parties to a computer contract in the event of default. A customer can reject the delivery of a computer that does not conform to contract specifications within a reasonable time.[35] Of course, a defect which the vendor can correct is likely not

---

[35]U.C.C. §2-601. *See* Carl Beasley Ford, Inc. v. Burroughs Corp., 361 F. Supp. 325, 330-31 (E.D. Pa. 1973), *aff'd*, 493 F.2d 1400 (3d Cir. 1974).

a justifiable reason to reject the computer.[36] By accepting a nonconforming delivery, the customer does not necessarily waive an action for damages against the vendor. If the vendor provides assurances that the defect will be cured or if the defect is not readily apparent from the computer upon delivery, the customer retains the right to revoke his acceptance and sue for recovery of the price paid together with damages provided the defect "substantially impairs" the value of the equipment.[37]

Some of the most hotly contested lawsuits involve differing opinions between contracting parties on where to draw the line between breaches of such materiality as to permit a termination of the agreement and breaches which are of lesser substance. A properly drafted agreement can delineate between major and minor defaults and delays. Such delineations are easiest in areas involving nondelivery, delivery delays, hours of down-time in a given period of elapsed time, etc. More difficult, but still capable of delineation, are standards for performance, speed, number of errors, and other quantifiable measures.

(c) *Trial by Jury.* Before discussing the legal remedies available to contracting parties, let us consider the arenas in which such remedies may be sought. Absent specific agreement to the contrary, a litigant will have recourse only to the established courts. Incidentally, most contract lawsuits involve the constitutional right of either party to have his case tried by a jury. This constitutional right, like many others, can be waived by a provision in the agreement and it is prudent to consider in most sophisticated data processing arrangements whether to eliminate by contract the right to jury trial. However, this may depend on the nature of the user. A perceived "little guy" may meet with more than usual success before a jury when his adversary is an enormous vendor like IBM.[38] On the other hand, it will frequently be difficult and time-consuming for the lawyers to educate a jury with respect to the language, technology and other complexities attendant to the utilization of data processing resources. Although educating a judge will probably be equally as difficult, a properly drawn contract will, hopefully, articulate the understanding and the points of dispute in reasonably nontechnical terms. Most judges are well trained and experienced in dealing with contractual provisions.

(d) *Selection of Forum.* The law also provides complex rules to determine which court in what state is the proper forum to hear dispute. Agreements between a New York vendor and a California customer, may, under certain circumstances, be incapable of litigation in the courts of either state. Contracts can and should provide where litigation can be brought and what law will govern. (Clause 5-26)

(e) *Litigation vs. Arbitration.* If the parties agree, they can be required to resort not to the courtroom but to arbitration. Most contracts with arbitration clauses provide for arbitration by and under the prevailing rules of the American Arbitration Association. It is permissible, however, for contracting parties to agree to any other mutually satisfactory method of arbitration of their disputes, however formal or informal, subject only to certain minimal

---

[36]U.C.C. §2-508.

[37]U.C.C. §2-608.

[38]*See, e.g.,* Catamore Enterprises, Inc. v. International Business Machines Corp., 548 F.2d 1065 (1st Cir. 1976), *cert. denied,* 431 U.S. 960 (1977) (jury verdict of $11,400,000 did not survive appeal).

legal requirements. Whether or not to include an arbitration provision in any or all of a company's contracts is a determination that should be made at top management levels with the assistance of counsel. Some considerations involved are as follows:

(i) Arbitration proceedings are generally thought to be informal and directed toward nontechnical considerations of fairness. Courtroom litigation is thought of as rigid and technical, with more attention paid to documentation than to the impressions of the parties. These public conceptions have never been empirically verified. Since some elements of any contract, looked at by themselves, are likely to appear unfair to one party or another because they were bargained for by giving the other contracting party an equally unfair advantage in some other area, it cannot safely be assumed that arbitrators will necessarily arrive at a just result in the context of a particular dispute. On the other hand, it may be that considerations of fairness, rather than a technical approach, are of the utmost importance in the resolution of disputes.

(ii) Arbitrators can sometimes be selected who are expert in the technology and who, thereby, will require little or no background education. This would seem to militate in favor of arbitration. On the other hand, arbitrators who are experts sometimes bring to a dispute their biases developed over years. Sometimes they have a particular point of view based upon their own past victimizations, real or imagined, and simply by taking too much for granted fail to give ear to a particular problem.

(iii) Arbitration is generally a far more rapid process than courtroom litigation. There have been instances, however, of protracted arbitration, taking place over a period of years, largely because arbitrators are businessmen or lawyers occupied with their own affairs and incapable of attendance at proceedings for more than a small fraction of their working hours. By contrast, most judges, once they begin to hear a case, will go on without interruption until the trial is over.

(iv) An award in arbitration is generally final, and not appealable except for outrageous errors. Judge's mistakes are appealable, often both as to factual determinations and legal conclusions.

(v) Arbitration helps the financially weaker party. Superficially, it is probably true that sympathy for the underdog prevails equally in both courthouse and arbitration panel. Arbitration also further tends to favor the weaker party by permitting him to assert his rights *at a far lower expense* and with the expectation of a more rapid determination than in litigation. The fear of significant legal costs and great delays in achieving satisfaction have often made weaker parties more compromising, less aggressive in claiming legal rights and perhaps more accommodating to their powerful customers than they should be, in order to get their money or to avoid the additional expense of litigation.

(vi) Arbitration is generally cheaper.

(vii) Since arbitration is informal, it is generally less fearsome to the employees of the parties to be called as witnesses.

(viii) Arbitration is often thought of as conducive to quick, amicable settlements of disputes, both because of its relative informality and because there appears historically to be a propensity on the part of arbitrators to bring about mediated settlements. Arbitrators, like most people, prefer settlements to disputes and avoid decision-making. The same propensities, incidentally, exist in judges and are enhanced by crowded court calendars. Some people believe that judges tend to compromise cases with dollar settlements, whereas arbitrators seem to be more skillful at mediating disputes and restoring communication and performance between disputants.

6. The Doctrine of Waiver (See Clause 5–23)

Before turning to a survey of the remedies available for contractual breaches, a word is in order about the doctrine of waiver. Absent specific contract terms, and sometimes even in the face of such provisions, the law has recognized that a party's conduct may modify his prior agreement. Where the conduct of the parties after signing the agreement clearly indicates that certain provisions were not given effect by the parties, courts will frequently treat such provisions as inoperative. *Very often, waivers arise in law by reason of the inaction of a party.* An agreement may call for delivery to a customer of processed data within 24 hours after receipt of the raw data by the service bureau, but if over a period of months or years the actual delivery practice has been 72 hours, judges can be led to the conclusion that the time requirements set forth in the agreement were not really important and were waived by the practice of the parties.

As has been stated, many agreements in the field of data processing require continuing performance over an extended time period. Inaction, even if occasioned by mere lack of attention on the part of a party, can have disastrous effects upon a clear and unequivocal agreement. The service bureau customer who has the right to compel delivery within 24 hours, but never does so for lack of any particular need under normal circumstances, may find that when the need finally does arise, the right to the required performance may have disappeared.

Properly drawn agreements in every industry generally provide that waivers may only be claimed if reduced to writing and signed by the party to be charged with the waiver, that there will be no waivers implied by action or inaction and that the waiver of a single breach shall not be deemed a waiver of any subsequent similar breach.

7. The Process of Litigation

The process of litigation, historically, grew up not so much as an attempt to do justice between disputants as to simply quiet disputes and maintain public order. The judicial arm of most governments is generally the smallest in size and budget. Courts rarely seek out litigants, but must be approached by them.

Civil litigation is conducted under some surprisingly severe restraints. The court brings nothing except the most common denominator of human knowledge to a dispute. All else must be supplied by the parties. The party who fails to bring to the attention of the court all of the material evidence necessary to a favorable disposition of his case, including expert guidance, records or testimony from uninterested third parties and even guidance as to the applicable propositions of law, stands to lose his case. The judicial role is fundamentally passive. Hundreds of thousands of jurors have sat on juries and never asked a question of litigants; many judges take the same approach.

Good record keeping on the part of clients is important to their lawyers. The merest glimmer of an anticipated lawsuit should cause the businessman to contact his counsel with a view toward preparation for eventual "combat." The complicated and restrictive rules of evidence prevailing in most courts often will not coincide with the businessman's conception of how logically to prepare for litigation.

Because of the passive, noninterfering approach that courts follow, the common award to aggrieved litigants has been money to compensate for economic loss occasioned by other parties' defaults. This form of compensation is called damages.

8. Damages

An ancient legal maxim, still in good standing today, declares that there can be no damages awarded where no injury has been shown. By injury, the courts mean, in commercial transactions, an economic loss. If the service bureau customer cannot prove a direct economic loss arising from late receipt of processed data, a court will not award the customer a penny. The customer may, of course, find that continual late deliveries will stand as a valid defense when the service bureau sues the customer to collect its lost profits on the canceled contract. In other words, a *material* breach by the vendor may permit the buyer to cancel the contract, even without proof of economic loss, but damages will not be awarded to the buyer without such proof.

The measure of recovery upon default by a party to computer contract is defined in part by the contract, and in part by general contract law. Where it applies, the U.C.C. provides the exclusive remedies for actions based on contracts. There is a rapidly expanding body of case law applying the U.C.C. to damage disputes arising out of computer transactions. An exhaustive analysis of these cases is beyond the scope of this book. However, a computer case which is illustrative of the complexities of damage calculation under the Code is *Chatlos Systems, Inc.* v. *National Cash Register Corp.*[39] Chatlos was a small business concern that procured a computer from NCR at a cost of about $75,000 upon the salesman's representations that the computer would solve inventory problems and reduce labor costs. The underlying contract warranted the computer against defects "in material, workmanship and operational failure from ordinary use," and limited Chatlos's remedy in the event of default to "correcting any error in any program as appears within sixty days."[40] The contract expressly relieved NCR from liability for consequential damages.

From the date of delivery, the computer supplied to Chatlos failed to perform as warranted. Chatlos cooperated with NCR for over twenty months in an effort to correct the bugs that prevented the computer from performing various essential functions. Despite their joint efforts, the computer was never fully operational. In the end, Chatlos had the machine removed and then sued NCR to recover damages for breach of warranty.

To digress for a moment, the reader should understand that recoverable damages fall into two broad categories: direct and consequential damages. The former includes generally the price paid for purchase of a nonconforming computer or, if the nonconforming computer were accepted by the purchaser, the difference between the value of the computer as accepted and the value of the machine had it conformed to contract specifications. Consequential damages are defined by the U.C.C. to include "any loss resulting from general or particular requirements and needs of which the seller at the time of contracting had reason to know."[41] Indirect or consequential damage questions, unfortunately, arise frequently in

---

[39]479 F. Supp. 738 (D.N.J. 1979), *aff'd in part, rev'd in part and remanded*, 635 F.2d 1081 (3d Cir. 1980), *aff'd as modified*, 670 F.2d 1304 (3d Cir.), *cert. denied*, 102 S.Ct. 2918 (1982).
[40]479 F. Supp. at 743–745.
[41]U.C.C. §2-715(2).

the data processing field. When a computer fails to perform as warranted, the shock waves can disrupt an entire business. If the company loses customers as a consequence of interrupted service due to a malfunctioning computer, can the company recover the lost profits it would have earned had the customers stayed? There is little legal authority on the subject of how far liability for consequential damages extends in the data processing field. This is primarily the result of a fairly universal practice on the part of suppliers of data processing goods and services: to disclaim expressly in their contracts liability for "indirect," "special," or other consequential damages.

In *Chatlos*, the trial court determined that NCR had breached both express and implied warranties with respect to the computer delivered to and accepted by Chatlos. Although the contract purported to limit Chatlos's remedy to repair, the court concluded that Chatlos was entitled to damages because NCR was unable to correct the defects in the computer.[42] For breach of warranty with respect to accepted goods, the U.C.C. provides for direct damages measured by "the difference . . . between the value of the goods a accepted and the value they would have had if they had been as warranted."[43] Applying this formula to the facts before it, the trial court determined the value of the computer accepted by Chatlos to be approximately $6,000. The trial court looked to the amount Chatlos had indebted itself to obtain the computer, about $75,000, to affix a value to the computer had it been as warranted. The difference, $57,152 (after several adjustments), was awarded to Chatlos. Despite the contract term excluding NCR's liability for consequential damages, the trial court went on to award Chatlos additional damages totalling $63,558, including the cost of employees' and executives' time, the cost of floor space occupied by the computer, and the cost of excess inventory.

It is important to note that the dividing line between foreseeable, recoverable consequential loss and nonforeseeable, nonrecoverable loss is very uncertain.[44] For this reason, disappointed users should assess and document early on all types of damage incurred as a result of a malfunctioning computer. Courts can be liberal in their definition of consequential damages although most are wary of including lost profits as an element of recoverable loss.[45]

Both Chatlos and NCR appealed from the trial court, contesting the damage award. The court of appeals reversed the award of consequential damages, holding that the contract specifically excluded recovery of this type of loss and that Chatlos had failed to show that the exclusionary language was unconscionable.[46] The appellate court reasoned that at the time of contracting, it was reasonably foreseeable to Chatlos that a defect in the computer would disrupt normal business routines, require additional employee time, and impair efficiency. Nevertheless, Chatlos signed a contract that excluded recovery of these types of losses and the court found "nothing in the formation of the contract or the circumstances

---

[42]Because NCR was unable to fix the computer, the contract's limited remedy of repair "failed of its essential purpose" under U.C.C. §2-719(2). *See* 479 F. Supp. at 745.

[43]U.C.C. §2-714.

[44]*See, e.g.*, Applied Data Processing, Inc. v. Burroughs Corp., 394 F. Supp. 504, 508-11 (D. Conn. 1975); Carl Beasley Ford, Inc. v. Burroughs Corp., 361 F. Supp. 325, 333-35 (E.D. Pa. 1973), *aff'd*, 493 F.2d 1400 (3d Cir. 1974).

[45]*See* Fredonia Broadcasting Corp. v. RCA Corp., 569 F.2d 251, 259 (5th Cir.), *cert. denied*, 439 U.S. 859 (1978).

[46]635 F.2d at 1087. Chatlos would have had to show that the exclusion of consequential damages was unconscionable under U.C.C. §2-719(3).

resulting in failure of performance that makes it unconscionable to enforce the parties' allocation of risk."[47]

After closing the door on Chatlos's claim for consequential damages, the court of appeals turned to the question of direct damages. The trial court was again reversed: in affixing a value to the computer had it been as warranted, that court had failed to take into account the market value of the equipment. The U.C.C. does not use the term *market value*, but the appellate court reasoned that to ignore the market value would deny a buyer the true benefit of a good bargain. Accordingly, the case was sent back to the trial court for a new determination of the damages.

There, the trial court recalculated Chatlos's direct damages under the benefit of the bargain theory approved by the appellate court. Chatlos offered truly expert testimony, in the person of one of the authors of this book, to estimate the value of a computer system that would perform the functions the NCR machine had been warranted to perform. Based on this testimony, the trial court concluded that the fair market value of the computer system Chatlos contracted for was $207,826. This sum, less the value of the computer delivered to Chatlos, $6,000, resulted in an award of $201,826, a dramatic increase over the original award.

Apparently undaunted, NCR again appealed. In a split decision, the appellate court approved the damage award. The lone dissenting judge (amazingly!) questioned the accuracy of the expert's testimony, finding it difficult to believe that NCR would agree to sell a computer for less than $100,000 when such a computer purportedly had a fair market value in excess of $200,000.[48]

From a vendor's point of view, then, the immensely expensive consequences of a defective part, defective software, or a sloppy installation make it fair—indeed necessary—to place limitations on a vendor's liability for indirect, consequential damages. Vendors are understandably obstinate on this subject; these exculpations from liability are generally nonnegotiable. If a vendor does agree, he will usually insist upon some absolute dollar limitation on his exposure.

On the other side, wary computer users should take every practical precaution to avoid indirect losses, including duplication of data and the use of backup systems and products. As noted above, it will be extremely difficult to obtain a vendor's commitment to remain liable for indirect damages. Similarly, it will be difficult to convince a court that the astronomical losses resulting from a defective computer were foreseeable to the vendor at the time of contracting. The goal of each party to a computer contract should be to reduce the monetary risk involved through carefully crafted contract provisions.

One last category of damages deserving of attention is the area know as liquidated damages. As was stated, there can be no damages awarded without proof of an economic loss. Sometimes it is difficult, if not impossible, for an aggrieved party to prove the dollar amount thereof. Courts, recognizing that difficulty, have permitted parties to contract for liquidated damages. Contractual liquidated damage provisions generally recite that they have been included because of the difficulty of ascertainment of actual damages. In proper cases, courts will enforce agreed-to liquidated damage amounts without requiring proof of the existence or extent of a loss. The courts, however, look very carefully into agreements providing for liquidated damages, since the law will refuse to enforce any provision which it deems a penalty. A penalty, simply defined, is a punishment that does

[47]635 F.2d at 1087.
[48]670 F.2d at 1311.

not fit the crime. *Liquidated damage provisions should, accordingly, attempt to establish a fair approximation of what actual damages would have been, had the tortuous process of establishing them been carried out.*

9. Judicially Compelled Performance of Contracts

What about all of those things that the vendor has promised but failed to do? Except under the most extreme and unusual circumstances, if a vendor promises to do something, you cannot compel him to do so. You can merely sue for a refund of any sums paid for the excess cost of having someone else do it. You cannot force an equipment dealer to replace defective equipment, even if the contract requires him to do so; you can sell the defective equipment for scrap, buy a substitute piece of equipment and sue the dealer for the difference.

There are some situations, of rare application in the data processing field, where courts will exert themselves to require something more of the unsuccessful litigant than the mere payment of money. Where a person contracts to buy a specific parcel of land, and the vendor refuses to convey it, courts, for peculiar historical reasons which deem every parcel of land unique, will compel the seller to deliver a deed. In a curious search for consistency, courts will also compel the buyer, who has defaulted on his contract to buy the land, to accept a deed and pay for the land rather than require the seller to sell the land to someone else and sue the buyer for any financial loss on the resale. In a few other areas, generally involving unique goods, courts will occasionally compel parties to perform contracts rather than pay damages.

In the data processing field, a court might use its coercive powers to force a party in possession of another party's property, such as files, tapes or other processed material, to return it to its rightful owner. Very few other examples can be imagined where courts will compel performance of an act, rather than payment of damages.

10. Injunctive Relief: Restrictive Covenants

There is a slightly more liberal attitude on the part of the courts toward stopping or preventing people from doing things which might injure others. Injunctions, in the data processing field, as in other fields, often involve contractual elements known as restrictive covenants. Restrictive covenants are agreements, or portions of agreements, where a party has contracted not to engage in a particular activity. Before a party can get an injunction, he must prove that the injury he will sustain if the act is carried out cannot be adequately compensated by money, that he will be irreparably harmed if the action is not prohibited and that he has no other remedy. For example, a person who sells a software business and agrees not to solicit or do business with the existing customers of the business being sold, will be enjoined from violating that agreement. The release of genuine trade secrets, in the face of an agreement not to do so, will conventionally be enjoined. If a particular program is developed by a software consultant as a proprietary product for his customer, and if, in the face of a contractual prohibition, the consultant makes a copy of the program and proceeds to try to sell the same program to others, the courts will normally enjoin him from doing so.

In order for restrictive covenants to be enforcible by injunction, they must be carefully drafted. Covenants that are overly broad, inadequately particularized, or unduly restrictive of free commerce will not be enforced by the judicial system.

Restrictive covenants, when contracted for, are often of critical importance in a transaction and often involve matters in which monetary damages are inadequate. Accordingly, restrictive covenants should be drafted with great care.

11. Defenses in Contract Litigation

Litigation is a two-sided affair. The party being sued can raise any number of defenses to excuse his claimed breach and can deny that he violated the contract. The party being sued will often counterclaim against his opponent and seek damages for the latter's claimed default. A discussion of available defenses in contract litigation is outside the scope of this book. The defense based upon the doctrine of waiver has already been touched upon.

Only one other area of defense will be mentioned, the default of the other party. That area is probably the most common defense used as an excuse for nonperformance of an agreement. A user cannot successfuly sue a vendor for nondelivery if the contract required the user to pay in advance of delivery and the user did not pay. The ramifications of that elementary example are far-reaching. The law recognizes that certain promises or conditions are dependent upon others, and that some sequence is often either expressed or implied in an agreement. If party A drops out of a sequence, party B may be excused from his obligation to carry out the next steps in the chain of performance. This defense is of fairly widespread application in the data processing field since most contracts in that field involve elements of sequential performance. Vendors frequently claim that their failure or delay in delivery of goods or services was based not on their own default but on the fact that the user had failed to supply needed preliminary data or physical materials. Great care should be given to structuring these sequences. The contract should protect each party against delays by the other in any interdependent chain of events. Where a failure on the part of one party to meet a particular element in the sequence is considered not to be material to the rest of the sequential performance of the agreement, that fact should be noted in the contract so as to prohibit the other party from treating such nonperformance as an excuse to stop working.

12. A Good Contract Is Worth More than a Thousand Legal Principles

Hopefully, the preceding overview has provided some insight into the basics of the law of contracts. The elementary point that should be retained is that legal principles are of less significance to a party than a complete and precisely articulated agreement. There follows a discussion of particular legal issues (other than those arising specifically from the law of contracts) and their areas of specific application in the data processing field.

E. SOME LEGAL ISSUES PECULIAR TO OR IMPORTANT IN THE CONTEXT OF COMPUTER CONTRACTS

No book devoted to legal and contractual problems in the data processing industry would be complete without reference to several problems that turn up with perplexing regularity, most frequently because they have not been thought through in the contracting process. The concepts discussed below are not entirely peculiar to the data processing industry, but it is a fair statement that no other single industry shares all of them. Alas, it is also fair to state that these issues are particularly vexatious in the data processing field, both because of the immense financial impact of data processing on the economy as a whole, and because of the lack of any well-established business or legal custom and usage in the computer field.

The issues discussed below are being highlighted primarily to awaken the reader's interest in their existence. Many potential ramifications of these issues have not come into being and can only be speculated about. Unfortunately, where ramifications are unclear and not fully exposed, perfect solutions cannot be designed. An awareness of the problems, however, can assist the user in designing some attack upon them in a properly drawn agreement, so that responsibility and liability can be focused upon at least to the extent that such responsibility and liability can be reasonably foreseen.

1. Proprietary Rights Over Intellectual and Other Property

No area of the law surrounding computer technology is more confused than the area involving the proprietary rights of creators or innovators in the field. The area of patents on machinery and other hardware is fairly simple and not dissimilar from patent problems generally. All other creative and innovative areas in the industry are more difficult to outline. Normally, the problems attendant to the protection of creativity are those of the vendor and are of little interest to the user provided that the user is protected contractually by the vendor against the vendor's infringement upon the rights of others.

It should be interesting, however, for the user to become familiar with the reasons why most software and service contracts are replete with provisions designed by vendors in an attempt to protect the proprietary rights that vendors claim in their products or processes. On a less academic basis, there is good reason for the user to become familiar with the concept of proprietary property since in many data processing contexts, the user may find that he and his business, data, methods, customers and other information, may suddenly be exposed or even come into the possession of others.

To reduce the issues of manageable proportions, it is necessary to divide the proprietary information area into two categories. Below, under the heading "Privacy, Security and Confidential Information," we will discuss the issues of major importance to the average user, those dealing with the protection of the information within the confines of the user's computer. The current section will concern itself with the legal problems inherent in the protection of proprietary material directly involved in the data processing function itself, which normally erupt when an imaginative individual involved in the area of data processing makes a discovery or an invention.

   (a) *Patent Rights.* If the innovation takes the form of a particular item of equipment or a physical process, there is normally no problem since such an invention if new and useful[49] is readily patentable, thus providing a legal monopoly on its use.[50]

   If, however, the innovation is an intellectual one, i.e., a program, a system, an approach, a shortcut, an idea, a logical design, or any other form of software not tangible in and of itself, the innovator may have a problem in secur-

---

[49]35 U.S.C. §101.

[50]*See, e.g.,* The Telephone Cases, 126 U.S. 1 (1888) (telephone patentable as unique use of electricity for the transmission of sound).

ing patent protection. The Supreme Court is to date badly confused over the patentability of computer programs and the like, and sufficiently so that no rule has emerged by which persons in the data processing field can be generally guided. If pressed for an overly simplistic statement of what might be the combined holdings of the recent Supreme Court decisions[51] in the area, we would advise that a computer program alone remains unpatentable, but its use in conjunction with a computer in a novel process may be.

(b) *Copyright.* The copyright laws may, on the other hand, permit the copyrighting of some software, but obtaining a copyright will usually injure rather than protect the innovator. A copyright does not protect the idea, but only the immediate expression thereof.

The concept of "protectibility" under copyrights is a difficult one to grasp. Some irrelevant examples may help. For instance, in a dictionary, the precise words in a definition are protected against copying, but the definitional ideas belong to no one. Pythagoras, when he discovered the principle governing relationships in a right triangle, commonly expressed as "$A^2 + B^2 = C^2$," could have copyrighted those precise words. But he would have been unable to stop anyone from writing a text containing the same idea expressed in different words, such as "side one multiplied by itself plus side two multiplied by itself equals the hypotenuse of the triangle multiplied by itself." Thus, the copyrighter of a computer program can obtain protection for the particular articulation of his idea or method, but will expose, for appropriation by others, the logic, the structure, the method and the organization of the program.

Disgraceful as this may seem, there is a rational reason for it. Being eminently practical, early lawyers and legislators (to the extent they are ever different) determined to give patent and copyright protection only to tangible creations and to leave the realm of ideas relatively free and open. This made for some problems later on[52] with respect to the protection of computer software which can be (but is not always) tangible, but which is always the expression of an idea. Not only does copyright protection for software remain unsatisfactory, but it also remains incomplete and thus sometimes unavailable. For example, two recent decisions have considered the question of the copyrightability of object codes, or programs, in "read-only memory" form. One concluded that copyright protection was available against unloading and duplicating a ROM;[53] the other held that it was not.[54]

Recently, Congress has sought to remedy the problems inherent in offering copyright protection for software.[55] Nevertheless, until the law catches

---

[51]*E.g.*, Gottschalk v. Benson, 409 U.S. 63 (1972) (program unpatentable where mere algorithmic mathematical formula); Dann v. Johnston, 425 U.S. 219 (1976) (machine system to sort banking transactions not patentable as obvious); Parker v. Flook, 437 U.S. 584 (1978) (program unpatentable where mere mathematical process to compute alarm limits in catalytic conversion); Diamond v. Diehr, 450 U.S. 175 (1981) (process for rubber-curing including a program held patentable).

[52]*See generally* Final Report of the National Commission on New Technological Uses of Copyrighted Works (1978).

[53]Tandy Corporation v. Personal Micro Computers, Inc., 524 F. Supp. 171 (N.D. Cal. 1981); *see also* Williams Electronics, Inc. v. Artic International, Inc., 685 F.2d 870 (3d Cir. 1982).

[54]Data Cash Systems, Inc. v. JS&A Group, Inc., 480 F. Supp. 1063 (N.D. Ill. 1979), *aff'd on other grounds*, 628 F.2d 1038 (7th Cir. 1980).

[55]*See* Computer Software Copyright Act, Pub. L. No. 96-517, §§10(a) and 10(b), 94 Stat. 3028 (1980), amending 17 U.S.C. §§101 and 117.

up even further with the technology involved,[56] users will be subject to fairly severe (and possibly costly) uncertainty in this area.

(c) *Trade Secret Protection.* Perhaps the most satisfactory way of protecting proprietary data processing innovations such as packaged programs is by means of this body of law, which may vary from state to state and generally only offers protection as between contracting parties. The basic theory protects the innovator's use of his novel idea, method or process while allowing him to offer it to others, by contract, on a limited basis.

As a result, as is discussed elsewhere, vendors of proprietary packages go to great lengths in an attempt to secure the proprietary aspects of their product by imposing restrictions upon the user. These are directed toward prohibiting the user from disclosing, reproducing and making unauthorized uses of the proprietary information.

The significance of the concept of trade secret protection, in the context of the creation of data processing ideas, is twofold. The user must understand the reasons for the vendor's insistence upon a variety of onerous restrictions and must be prepared to accede to most. The user must also maintain an awareness of the potential liabilities if he violates these restrictions. Since the proprietary information being licensed by the vendor is his stock-in-trade and since the loss of its secrecy may render it valueless to him, the careless, disorganized or malicious user may find itself faced with a lawsuit of monstrous proportions by reason of its unauthorized disclosure.

Several contracting guidelines become apparent. The user should negotiate a limitation on its liability for unauthorized disclosure. The character and the amount of liability should differ depending upon the circumstances of the disclosure. If the user's disclosure is willful, malicious or grossly negligent, it might not be unfair for the vendor to seek damages without limitation as to amount. At the other end of the scale, if the user has adhered to all the contractual restrictions designed to protect against disclosure including, say, the obtaining of a signed nondisclosure agreement from all its employees, the user should probably incur no liability by reason of the theft of proprietary material by a disgruntled employee. Under such circumstances, the user should, of course, agree to assign to the vendor all of the rights available to the user for injunctive and other relief against the thief. Between the two extremes, in areas such as ordinary lack of care, thefts by outsiders of the proprietary data while in the user's possession and the like, mutually satisfactory solutions are more difficult to achieve.

The second reason for user interest in the concept of trade secret protection of proprietary material involves the area of software development. On those occasions when a user contracts with a consulting or other service company for the creation of customized programs or systems, generally at great expense to the user, it is not unreasonable for the user to find itself displaying "proprietary" emotions about the products of such a project. The expenditure of large sums of money by the user for a particular system is normally embarked upon in order to obtain a competitive advantage. Since an automobile company which engages a software consultant to design

---

[56]Efforts are under way all over the world. For example, a Committee of Governmental Experts on Problems Arising from the Use of Computers for Access to or the Creation of Works, of the World Intellectual Property Organization, meets annually in Western Europe.

a program to automate its assembly line operations would not want the consultant to market that program to other auto companies, the contract should provide that the program, when developed, is the company's own and sole proprietary property. Since the automobile manufacturer cannot protect itself against competitve development of an idea such as a method of automating an assembly line function, it can at least try to make it equally costly for the next manufacturer to do so. The customer, thus, should require the consultant to deliver all elements of the program and retain no copies. That approach, however, does not deprive the consultant of the know-how and information stored in his or her head. Thus, in a development project of any novelty or magnitude, the automobile manufacturer might reasonably demand that the consultant sign a restrictive covenant, agreeing not to design or develop a similar or comparable program for any competitor for a defined period of time, and to keep what he knows of the user's program secret.

2. Privacy, Security and Confidential Information

In virtually every modern business, the user is in possession of information, the confidentiality of which is important to the user, both directly and because of potential liabilities to others. Much of this information can be found in the confines of the user's computer. The user should assume that in any data processing related transaction, this information will, to a lesser or greater extent, be exposed. This potential for exposure is most obvious in the context of arrangements with a service bureau or in software development. The exposure, however, exists in the context of a potential purchase or lease of hardware, where the vendor's marketing and technical specialists can often be found familiarizing themselves with the customer's problems through an inspection of its data.

The potential injury to the user itself, or to others who may make claims against him, by reason of the theft, misuse, misappropriation or disclosure of information in the user's possession cannot be overstated. The user will generally be in possession of some or all of the following kinds of data, the exposure of which may have serious consequences:

Proprietary know-how, including but certainly not limited to data processing know-how, often developed at great expense
Lists of customers
Mailing lists
Internal financial data and projections
Product development data
Market surveys and analyses
Research
Pricing, marketing, and inventory data and projections

On a different level, the user may also have assembled a variety of information which has certain fiduciary aspects to it, such as:

Personal data concerning its employees
Reports received from franchisees or licensees
Confidential information concerning customers

Some types of users will have in their possession information relating to others that is strictly confidential. Banks, insurance companies, hospitals, schools, and governmental agencies will normally have in their possession vast amounts of very personal information, the disclosure of which could subject them to serious legal penalties.[57]

Accordingly, it is of the utmost necessity that user secrecy be respected by appropriate contractual arrangements. In addition to contractual safeguards, all companies should develop an operational approach to the safeguarding of secrets both from insiders and outsiders, preferably on a "need to know" basis. Confidentiality and the security of the user's information are important for at least two reasons. The first is protection of the property rights of the user in its own business data, know-how and all of the other elements that make up the good will of a business concern, and whose loss or disclosure may directly injure or destroy the user. The second is protection of data which relates to others, which has come into the user's possession for specific and restricted purposes or which has been entrusted to the user as confidential information. The loss or exposure of such data will cause the user to be attacked from outside for the abuse of the privacy and property rights of others.

The most vexatious area involving proprietary information, privacy and security involves service bureau arrangements. It is imperative that a proper service bureau contract contain provisions protecting the customer against the misappropriation, misuse, disclosure and loss of valuable data. Elsewhere in this volume, several approaches to these controls are discussed. In the service bureau context, the loss, destruction or erasure of information can be disastrous. Unfortunately, no adequate contractual solution is available, and the sole meaningful approach is preventive, by duplication of materials. Duplication of vital information is probably advisable under any circumstances even where information is in the possession of the user itself.

3. Liabilities to Third Parties for Unauthorized Disclosures

The loss by a user of its own data creates no legal (as opposed to business) problems. On the other hand, the loss, misuse or disclosure of information in the possession of the user concerning others can have serious legal implications. Most of these implications have not been particularly refined by experience in the law. Some ramifications have been codified in recent consumer protection legislation, particularly legislation regulating consumer credit reporting agencies.[58] This volume will not attempt even a summary of the law surrounding the circulation or disclosure of defamatory information or the violation of rights of privacy of individuals. Defamation and privacy cases, however, are sometimes costly since juries can readily put themselves into the place of the injured party.

4. Other Liabilities to Third Parties

The utilization of computers can subject the user to a variety of exposures, in addition to those arising out of misuse or disclosure of confidential data. These problems arise from either human or machine error and are not dissimilar to liabilities

---

[57]*See* subsection 3 below with respect to such liability to third parties.

[58]15 U.S.C. §§1681 *et seq.*

which have existed in the world of commerce prior to the computer age. At one extreme is liability like that of the automobile credit company which repossesses a car belonging to one of its customers for nonpayment of notes, notwithstanding the fact that the customer is not in default. The credit company will be found to be liable to the customer for the wrongful repossession, in spite of its claims that the failure to record the customer's payment was due to computer error. At the other extreme is the liability that would probably be imposed on a tire manufacturer whose computerized and automated manufacturing plant produced a defective and unsafe tire. It is interesting to note that in both cases the liability would be exactly the same whether or not computers were involved in the process.

Except in certain extreme situations, either involving dangerous instrumentalities or those regulated by statute (such as credit agencies), liability to third parties generally depends upon a finding of negligence. Negligence is generally found where the information involved is under the company's control and if it had been properly processed (mechanically or by people), the injury to the third party would not have occurred.

It is fairly certain that no user will be able to negotiate any meaningful assumption of liability on the part of a hardware vendor to third persons as a result of the vendor's negligence or defects in the vendor's products. In special circumstances, a user should press to obtain such vendor's assumption of liability; an instance might be a hospital acquiring a computer for monitoring life signs of critically ill patients.

In some cases, the vendor will be liable directly to third parties for his negligence or defective computer; these instances generally involve areas of inherent danger to human life. Although the authors know of no reported cases, it can be hypothesized that the manufacturer of a computer device for air traffic control might be declared liable in an air crash occasioned by a defect in the computer equipment or by its negligent manufacture. Legal responsibility for dangerous instrumentalities is governed by legal concepts which normally operate for the benefit of consumers irrespective of contractual provisions.

There is one last subtle danger of exposure to third party liability that should be mentioned. Manufacturers and other vendors in the computer field generally insist upon exculpation from any liability for consequential damages. Some, however, go further. The authors have seen contracts prepared by vendors which seek to have the *user indemnify* the vendor against liabilities to third parties arising out of the use of the equipment or software sold. Language purporting to indemnify the vendor should be stricken by user's counsel. The legal propositions involved can be summarized as follows: If a vendor is found liable to a third party, it is because of the vendor's fault or neglect, not that of the user; if the user then indemnifies the vendor against such liabilities, the net effect is that the user is protecting the vendor against his own negligence. There is no legal or economic justification for such a practice.

5. Compatibility, Modularity and Continuing Support

The discussion that follows is not exactly legal discourse. The reason for its inclusion here is that it is normally not considered by laymen, but is often a subject of disputes in court, in the absence of governing provisions in contracts. Even where the concepts are in the minds of the businessmen negotiating a computer transaction, their articulation of them is often difficult and sophisticated legal help will be necessary.

(a) *Compatibility.* Compatibility, in lay terms, generally involves the vendor's assurance that the purchased equipment or software will be "compatible" with the user's present or contemplated equipment or software. In the case of a speaker-phone to be attached to a telephone handset, the concept is normally very simple; compatibility in that case means that the speaker-phone can be connected to the handset and when connected will operate. Unfortunately, the ability of an item to be physically connected by an interface to another item, in the context of data processing, is merely one adjunct of the concept of compatibility. Meaningful compatibility must also be measured in terms of speed, efficiency, interference, loss of power, and other aspects of a mechanical and electronic interrelationship. The first job of a user's negotiator is to get an assurance of compatibility from his vendors; the second job is to get a comprehensive definition of compatibility. To rely only on a statement that the purchased equipment or software will be compatible with other equipment may be grossly inadequate in the context of litigation. An item of peripheral equipment capable of being plugged in to a mainframe and which will operate in some fashion may be deemed by a judge to satisfy a warranty of mere "compatibility" even where it operates very slowly or in such a manner as to use an undue amount of the computer's time or circuitry.

No discussion of compatibility should be concluded without mentioning the desirability of obtaining a *continuous* compatibility warranty. A 360 user, in the 370 era, could often get the vendor of an expensive software package to warrant that the package would be compatible with either series of computer.

(b) *Modularity.* The concept of modularity is well known to computer users, particularly because vendors make modularity an important selling concept. Modularity, simply stated, means the ability of the system to be horizontally expanded in a number of directions. Here too, specific contractual provisions ought to be constructed. No mere statement of "modularity" will be a workable definition. Furthermore, the concept of modularity is not infinitely stretchable. All modular systems do have limits, either physical, electronic, mechanical or operational. The user should define his projected requirements to the extent possible, and obtain from the vendor assurances of modularity within those requirements.

(c) *Availability of Continuing Support.* The concept of modularity leads directly to the concept of the availability of future support. A well-drafted data processing agreement must take into account the rather sorry state of the law. The law, for good and sufficient reason, rarely penalizes companies for going out of business; moreover, the law does not normally, absent a specific agreement, prohibit a company from dropping a product line. Although the law will enforce warranties that remain in force even after a company has discontinued a product line, if the warranty has expired, the law does not require a manufacturer to offer maintenance or furnish spare parts or items previously offered as modules of a discontinued product line. There are innumerable users of machinery who are keeping their equipment running through the use of hairpins, imagination and other field expedients because of the unavailability of spare parts.

A properly drafted agreement, which requires the vendor to carry spare parts and offer repair services for some finite period of time, can help solve the problem; if the vendor discontinues a line, his obligation to furnish parts or service will survive. If the vendor fails to furnish them, in spite of his agreement to do so, the law will permit the user to have the necessary parts custom made, if they are not otherwise available, and to charge the vendor with the cost thereof. No solution, of course, is a perfect solution; even the best agreement cannot stop the vendor from going out of business. Although a well-drafted agreement will give rise to a claim in bankruptcy, creditors of a bankrupt company rarely get more than a minuscule fraction of their claims.

The ultimate solution to the problem of maintaining a steady source of parts, service and supplies, even in the event of bankruptcy of the vendor, is to provide in the agreement for the vendor to supply the user with plans, specifications, manuals and all other technical data concerning the acquired equipment or software. The availability of these materials to the user will, at least, assure that if the vendor is no longer in existence, the purchaser will have the wherewithal (albeit at great cost), to have the necessary parts, services and supplies obtained elsewhere.

6. Finance-Leases and "Holder in Due Course" Problems

One last "legal" problem left for discussion is the "holder in due course" problem. It generally involves an attempt on the part of the vendor to make a "divisible" contract at the peril of the user.

A contract which provides for the user to make deferred payments tempts the vendor to take the contract to a bank and sell it or borrow against those future payments. Banks, however, do not treat such contracts as accounts receivable (capable of being readily purchased or financed) if they contain any continuing obligations on the vendor's part; that is so because banks do not want to be involved in disputes which could delay or hinder collection based upon a user's claim of nonperformance by the vendor. As a result, the concepts of the "finance-lease" or "finance-purchase" have arisen. These concepts have been most notoriously used, to the detriment of consumers, in the areas of food freezer plans, home improvements and appliance purchases. In the classic case, the contract provides that the seller intends to assign the future rentals or purchase price installments accruing to a bank (or other financial institution); that the bank will not be responsible for any warranties or other performance obligations of the vendor; that the user agrees to pay the bank or other assignee of the contract the full amount of the payments to be made in the future, without offset, defense or other claim; and that the user will look *only to the vendor* for recourse in the event of breach of any warranty or other failure of performance. The net effect of such provisions is obvious. The user is required to pay absolutely to the bank and does not have the economic leverage of holding back payments in order to enforce the vendor's obligations.

There are vendors who insist that they cannot or will not do business with users on any other basis than this except, of course, for outright cash purchases. In the case of an outright cash purchase, the user is in the same predicament, since it has paid the vendor in full and similarly has no economic leverage against the vendor.

The more insistent the vendor, the more cautious the user should be. The implication of either the finance-lease or the cash sale approach is, after all, that the vendor does not have sufficient working capital to finance the continuation of his own business and must depend upon the user's credit or cash to stay alive. Some vendors try to rationalize their approach by complaining that the user's credit is not adequate. That argument is illogical. If the user's credit were inadequate, the bank would not finance the vendor based on the user's contract.

Throughout this book, the user has been urged to provide for hold-backs of money in adequate amounts for limited periods of time in order to secure the continuing performance of the vendor. A normal lease arrangement satisfies this requirement. In the case of an outright purchase, even if the user is not concerned about the vendor's financial responsibility, the concept of a hold-back is still of great practical importance, since it provides economic incentive to the vendor to perform, so that he can collect the hold-back. In the case of weakly financed vendors, the hold-back protects the user against the vendor's discontinuance of business, to the extent the vendor has not performed.

7. High Technology Export Controls

While it is outside the scope of this volume to do any more than mention this subject, vendors and multinational users should be aware that certain forms of technology may not be exported to certain countries, or that export licenses may be required.[59] As a result, contracts involving the sale or lease of such technology for whatever use should provide appropriate representations (or prohibitions) with respect to compliance with existing export control and licensing requirements.

F. CONCLUSION

The aim of this chapter has been to convince the user that courts, by their very nature, are bound to resolve particular disputes by application of extremely broad principles of generalized application. Thus, where parties are in a dispute as to which they have no agreement, the law will attempt to resolve their dispute by reference to broadly based principles of justice or uniform statutes which, in a particular case, may not make very much sense or do effective justice. Where parties have a contract, the courts will resolve disputes based upon the terms of the agreement. Where the agreement is grossly inadequate or incomplete, the courts may attempt to lend assistance outside the agreement, but, again, their assistance will be based on legal doctrines which may have no precise bearing upon the issues before them.

The goal, then, is to draft contracts that leave no subject open to dispute. The *perfect* contract would define the focus of responsibility and liability for any conceivable potential problem or contingency. The courts would still be necessary for enforcement of the resolutions decreed by the contract, if the party in default were to refuse to pay or perform.

Moreover, a good contract generally keeps the parties out of court. It is generally the case that parties whose responsibilities are *clear* rarely refuse to perform. Most litigation arises not because of a refusal to honor an obligation, but because of differing opinions as to legal responsibility for a particular problem. Alas, perfection is rarely if ever attainable. To attempt perfection, however, is both noble and generally rewarding.

---

[59]*See* 50 U.S.C. App. §§2401 *et seq.*

A. INTRODUCTION

5
GENERAL TERMS

There are a number of terms applicable to any type of contract, regardless of whether it is for the procurement of hardware, software, services, or even facilities. These terms are referred to as general or common terms, and should be considered applicable to any contract. Thus, if a master contract is drawn to cover the entire relationship between a vendor and user, these terms have to be included in that master contract. If, however, the contract is divided into three separate contracts, then it becomes necessary to consider the inclusion of each of these terms in each contract. It should be noted that a hardware purchase contract, for example, completes upon the payment for and transfer of title of the purchased item. Any clauses relating to confidentiality in the purchase contract would not necessarily be applicable to the maintenance contract, unless there is a cross-reference, or unless such confidentiality clauses survive the completion of the purchase contract by its terms. It should be noted further that each separate contract normally stands on its own, and often contains a clause providing that it constitutes the entire agreement relative to its subject matter. The mere attachment of one contract to another may not solve this problem unless there are specific cross-references.

The terms covered in this chapter have been arbitrarily divided into four groups. The first group of "substantive" terms deals with the substance of the contract. The second group of "financial" terms relates to those clauses which have financial or economic implications. Third are terms relating to disclosure, and fourth are those deemed mechanical, whose presence is required to insure the legality of other terms.

It is the responsibility of the user or user counsel to determine which of these terms are desirable, to which contract they apply, and how they should be applied. Based on the information in this chapter, the user should make a list of these terms by contract, and then obtain suggested wording from Appendix A.

B. SUBSTANTIVE TERMS

5-01   Arbitration

It is desirable to have a clause referring disputes to binding arbitration in most contracts. The typical clause refers all disputes under the contract to binding arbitration under the rules of the American Arbitration Association, whose headquarters is located at 140 West 51st Street, New York, N.Y., 10019. Arbitration is desirable as an alternative to litigation, because in most cases it is far faster and considerably cheaper than litigation (see Chapter 4). Arbitration can be accomplished in a matter of months rather than years, at a fraction of the legal fees associated with litigation. In addition, arbitration is a relatively informal procedure and therefore has the advantage of providing an opportunity for *mediation* as much as strictly technical litigation. Whereas the decision of the judge in litigation may be black or white, it is not uncommon for a decision by an arbitrator to be a more compromising one, which covers the gray areas more effectively.

An alternative to arbitration of all disputes is to restrict arbitration only to those disputes which fall below a certain amount of money, thus making sure that litigation is used for disputes involving a sufficient amount of money to make it worthwhile to undertake the time and expense of litigating. In this case an amount between $50,000 and $200,000 would be realistic.

Arbitration is also desirable if the user organization is lethargic, and unwilling to litigate because of potential public relations problems or other difficulties. It is very common for organizations not to pursue legitimate disputes through litigation simply because it is too much effort, or because it has unfavorable implications. In this eventuality the arbitration process can be used without publicity and without generating extensive public records, and produce a reasonable solution to a dispute between two parties.

Notwithstanding this, arbitration may not be advisable for the user who is in a strong position relative to the vendor. Thus, if the vendor is a small software or services supplier, whose own resources would not normally be sufficient to litigate extensively, litigation might well be to the advantage of the user who is capable of waiting out the vendor and obtaining a settlement in his favor. The resources of hardware manufacturers, however, tend to outstrip the user, or at the very least, are sufficient to engage in lengthy litigation.

5-02   Business Termination

It is in the interest of the user to protect himself against untimely termination of business by the vendor. Business termination can have many causes, ranging from the bankruptcy of a financially troubled vendor to the decision on the part of a major vendor to leave a particular line of business. Everyone in the field of data processing is aware of the several major American corporations which have decided over the years to leave the business after incurring losses in the hundreds of millions of dollars. Their computer business was terminated as surely as if they had gone bankrupt, and their users had to find other alternatives. In two of these publicized cases alternative vendors immediately assumed responsibility, so that user damage was relatively low.

Particularly in the case of smaller companies, or poorly financed companies, business termination provisions should probably call for some remedies to be included in the event the vendor decides to leave the business. In this case, rights and title in the property, the software, the programs associated with a service center operation, and the like can be included as part of the business termination provision. Separate business termination clauses are provided for specific contractual obligations of hardware, software, and service organizations.

5-03   Most Favored Nations

It has traditionally been the policy of most vendors in the computer field to pass on decreases in price to all users, much as price increases are passed on. In some cases this takes the form of the "most favored nations" clause, which essentially states that if any better terms are offered to any other customer of the vendor then such terms in the future shall be passed on to the user. This means that future benefits given to customers will *automatically* be given to the user. It has a disadvantage, however, in that it will normally constrain the vendor from giving too many clearly identifiable benefits, which might trigger "most favored nations" clauses in other contracts. It is not uncommon for IBM, for example, to provide a "most favored nations" clause in its contracts or its side letters. By virtue of having done this in many other user contracts, IBM restricts itself from giving any readily identifiable benefits, which might force it to give similar benefits to thousands of other users. By structuring and identifying the contract as a special one by reason of the uniqueness of the application, the site or location, the configuration, or any combination thereof, it may be possible to avoid this problem and thereby exempt it from being classed as similar to other contracts, which could trigger the "favored nations" clauses in those.

5-04   Assignment by User

In general the contract should be assignable by the user to any affiliated organization, or to one with common interests. Any subsidiary, parent company, related company, or a company with common shareholders or common interests, should be capable of undertaking the obligations of the contract, especially if the liability of the original user remains. The contract should be assignable on a sublease basis without restriction, provided that the obligations are guaranteed by the original contracting organization. The right to assign, then, should be given to the user on an unrestricted basis to any related company, and on a sublet basis to an unrelated company.

There may be procurements where the user desires a right to assign if his plans change and if he can find a suitable substitute. It is sometimes possible to negotiate a release of liability from the vendor, if a suitable replacement is obtained, with the consent of the vendor. The contract should thus provide that such consent cannot be withheld unreasonably.

5-05 Assignment by Vendor

In general the right of contract assignment by the vendor should not be granted as easily. If the vendor were to assign the contract, the responsibilities might still remain with that vendor, but the performance of the contract would no longer be in the hands of the same people, and the quality of performance might suffer. It may be impossible to control qualitatively the commitments to be met by the vendor's assignee, despite guarantees that might exist. Thus the right of the vendor to assign the contract should be constrained, and restricted solely to assignment to a parent or other related company.

A particularly troublesome clause that appears frequently in standard vendors' contracts deals with the vendor's right to assign the payments receivable to a lending institution. Typically, a lease for an item of peripheral equipment will provide (1) that the vendor may assign the lease to a bank, which will enjoy the status of a "holder in due course," (2) that the rental obligation to the assignee will be absolute, without offset, and (3) that the lessee can look only to the vendor for performance of maintenance or other lease obligations. Without such a clause, most vendors cannot finance their leases or time-sales. It is urged that, except when dealing with an extremely financially strong vendor, this type of clause be excised from the deal. If it remains in the contract, the classic result is that the vendor goes bankrupt, the machine breaks down and the user is required to continue to pay the bank assignee, notwithstanding the fact that the user is getting no benefit from the leased equipment and cannot have it repaired. A clause of this type is included in Appendix A, to illustrate the problem.

C. FINANCIAL

5-06 Cross-Guarantees

It is desirable to obtain cross-guarantees from a parent, when the vendor is a subsidiary of a larger organization with greater resources. This is especially desirable when using a service organization which is a subsidiary of a very large company. Several major American organizations have established subsidiaries specifically for the sale of services or software packages. In major contracts, it is desirable to get the guarantee of the parent company to help insure that its resources, which were probably used in the marketing of the services, do in fact stand behind the products to be delivered. This will also prevent loss through possible bankruptcy of the subsidiary, or the transfer of assets from the subsidiary to the parent without protection of the user organization.

5-07 Indemnification Inclusions

Whenever indemnities are included in a contract, whether against infringements, as specific remedies, or against activities or actions by individuals, the scope of such indemnification should be defined. Indemnification should always include all costs associated with the exercise of the remedy, such as counsel fees, court costs and the like. These should be explicitly defined in the contract so that liquidation of damages elsewhere in the contract will incorporate these without further reference.

Remember, also, that a properly drafted indemnity must protect against claims whether or not successful. A defense by a user of an unsuccessful infringement suit costs just as much as the defense of a successful one. One way around this is to get the vendor to commit himself, in the first instance, to defend. A specimen clause is provided to that end.

5-08 Limitation of Liability—User

The user will consider it desirable to establish an absolute limit to his liability, in the event of a breach of contract. In no event should the user's liability exceed the amount to be paid had the contract been satisfactorily completed. The contract liability should be limited to the smaller of that amount or provable damages which the vendor incurred. The latter typically should be no more than the profits which the vendor could have obtained from the contract. It is desirable to specifically indicate what that amount should be. If it is assumed that the vendor's profit percentage on the contract is 20%, and the total contract amount is for one million dollars, the maximum liability of the user in any event is all of the vendor's nonsalvageable costs plus 20% of the contract amount, as imputed profit, in the event of a complete breach by the user. However, this is already fairly generous, and a lower limitation of liability can probably be negotiated, typically to reimburse all vendor costs plus some small penalty, limited in any event to the maximum of the amount to be paid under the contract.

5-09 Liability Limit—Vendor

The vendor will probably want a similar limitation of liability, although there should be exceptions from the viewpoint of the user. For example, if there is a problem in the establishment of clear title to the product being sold, or there is an infringement of a patent or other right by the vendor, then the limitation of liability should not apply. Other than that, a reasonable amount of liability might be the actual amount of the contract, unless some greater amount is reasonably foreseeable in the context of the transaction, in which event that greater amount should be established as the maximum.

5-10 Consequential Damages

Vendors traditionally seek to avoid liability for consequential damages. It may be possible to convince a vendor to accept liability (see clauses 5-08 and 5-09) for possible consequential damages, especially where such damages are caused by negligence (or gross negligence) on the part of the vendor, or as a result of a major or willful breach by the vendor. In this event it might be reasonable to limit such consequential damages to the amount of actual 'cash' damage suffered by the user, plus the other costs included in any indemnification. Where negligence or defined breaches are used as the trigger for potential consequential damages, it may be possible for the vendor to obtain insurance for this liability, with some maximum, and perhaps with a significant deductible. However, it should be recognized that a computer system, whether hardware or software, when *improperly* installed, can create significant problems for the user organization. Such problems could result in major losses, which in turn could result in the destruction of the using organization. As a result, a consequential damage clause might be desirable as an element in significant data processing contracts. There will be great vendor resistance.

5-11 Rights Upon Orderly Termination

Any contract terminates eventually, even though that eventuality may be a number of years away. At the time of such termination, certain take-over practices may be necessary, and should be spelled out in any contract. The rights of the using organization at termination of the contract with respect to specific elements of the contract should be clearly defined. In addition there may need to be a specific definition of an orderly take-over in each of the different types of contracts. Renewal provisions also may have to be considered as part of this factor, although renewal provisions of a contract generally will be covered independently.

5-12 Force Majeure

This clause covers events beyond the control of either party, and suspends the contract if such an event causes an inadvertent breach. Many events are normally covered in a force majeure clause. Civil disorders, natural disasters, and hijackings or other criminal acts often depend on geographical location or particular parameters relating to the installation. Hurricanes occur in parts of the country, tornadoes in other parts, and earthquakes elsewhere. These could be covered under a blanket "act of God" exemption, as could acts of war, civilian uprisings, riots and the like. Strikes are normally considered *force majeure*, but this could be decided in each case, since the likelihood of a strike in a software organization is substantially lower than that in a manufacturing establishment. The structure of a force majeure clause will vary, and counsel for the using organization can structure an effective one. It should be noted, however, that in the standard contract, the force majeure clause exempts nuclear reaction as a potential cause, where it is caused by the using organization. An electric utility, with a nuclear power plant that failed, would not be able to use that failure as a contract exemption, if the standard contract were to be signed.

D. DISCLOSURE PROVISIONS

There are a number of provisions which need to be included on nondisclosure of information when two parties establish a relationship. Each party has the opportunity to learn something about the business practices, trade secrets, products and personnel capabilities of the other. Cross-agreements are therefore included to prevent disclosure of such information to outside parties for the life of the contract, and beyond.

5-13 Confidentiality

When two parties are in a close relationship, both should execute agreements not to disclose confidential information about the other. These should extend in time at least to the end of the contract, and probably beyond completion of the contract as defined in clause 5-15. However, any time that information is disclosed to the public by its owner, confidentiality terminates with respect to that information. Confidentiality should apply to business practices, to information about employees, products, and contractual relationships with other parties. It can be applied on a blanket basis without constraint, provided that when such information reaches the public domain it shall no longer be covered by the nondisclosure agreement. If certain data are known to be critically confidential, such as a proprietary mailing list, they should be specifically mentioned in the clause in addition to the blanket provisions.

5-14   Agreements with Employees

To enforce the confidentiality provision of a contract, each organization must have independent agreements with all its employees with regard to nondisclosure. Each party then certifies to the other that it has executed nondisclosure agreements with employees, and can then agree to give the other party the benefit of those employee agreements in order to enforce confidentiality against an employee. This approach is preferable to the guarantee by each company of the obligations of its employees. The authors' preference is for the cost of enforcement against nonofficer employees to be borne by the party whose secrets have been stolen. An employee agreement typically should cover the rights of the employer with respect to new ideas or inventions, since these rights in turn may be extended either to the using or vending organization in the contractual relationship, as defined in clause 5-17.

5-15   Survival Beyond Completion

Contracts normally terminate on the basis of their stated term, or on the basis of the occurrence of a specific event. When a contract involves the purchase of a product, payment for the product and its attendant delivery or transfer of title normally results in implied or expressed completion of the contract. Notwithstanding this, a nondisclosure provision of a contract needs to survive beyond the completion of the contract. Similarly, it is wise for a user to insist that the representations and warranties survive. In this case the contract should speak to that point and identify the length of time that the contract survives beyond its normal completion, or that specific contract terms survive beyond completion of the performance of the contract. Confidentiality is certainly one such term of a master contract; so are most warranties; there may be others as well, such as the constraint on hiring each other's employees, covered in clause 5-16.

5-16   Agreement Not to Hire Employees

Because of the relationship that will usually be established between two organizations, opportunities will arise for potential hiring-away of employees. This should be prevented where possible, or at least constrained unless approved in writing by the other party. This clause protects each from having his employees hired away by the other. Normally, such a provision carries its own remedies to prevent breach of the entire contract. A simple form of remedy is liquidated damages equal to a number of months of salary to be paid by the offending party. Normally this constraint also is bounded in time and in

geography; it is common for example, to restrict this to employees encountered in the performance of the contract, and not necessarily to all employees
world-wide of each organization. It is also possible to exempt unsolicited approaches made by employees, or approaches made by employees as a result of
direct advertising, provided that in such cases notice is given by the employee or
the prospective employer to the present employer. In any case, it is desirable to
have a mutually equitable clause, since both parties will be bound equally and
since damage to both parties can be equally severe.

5-17   Rights to New Ideas and Inventions

It is possible that as a result of the contractual relationship between the parties
new ideas or inventions will emerge, which will not clearly be owned by either
party. It is desirable to have in the contract a clause which assigns such new
ideas or inventions to one or the other party. Normally the using organization,
as the organization paying for services or products, is the organization which
obtains the benefits of any new ideas or inventions generated as part of its
contract. However, under certain conditions, such as in the case of a proprietary
software package or a proprietary hardware alteration, the rights to the invention or the idea might belong to the vending organization. This is a negotiable
point whose results would have to be assessed as part of the negotiation, probably by counsel for both parties.

E. MECHANICAL CLAUSES

There are a number of clauses which are necessary to make a contract complete, and thus to deal with common, nagging problems applicable to all commercial transactions. Some of these conventional clauses are listed below.

5-18   Headings Not Controlling

It is common practice in drafting a contract to head each clause or term with a
one- or two-word description, as in this text. These headings are for information purposes only, and are designed primarily to increase the rapidity with
which one can find related terms in a complex contract. As a result of their
presence, however, some confusion might exist in the mind of someone attempting to determine the intent of the parties. It is easiest therefore to eliminate headings from consideration by stating in the contract that headings are
placed there solely for the convenience of the parties and have nothing to do
with the substance of the contract. This is purely a mechanical clause, as can
be seen, but it is desirable to eliminate confusion where an actual heading
might in some ways conflict with the content of the clause which follows.

5-19   Entire Agreement

Vendors frequently insist on a clause stating in substance that the document
constitutes the entire agreement between the parties and supersedes all previous discussions, representations and agreements. The clause is a good one,
provided that the contract in question is, in fact, comprehensive and complete.
This clause is included in most contracts, and rightly so, since it eliminates any

commitments that might have existed previously in correspondence, older contracts, and perhaps even in conversations. It is therefore of benefit, in eliminating confusion where conflicts might exist between old contracts or commitments and the definitive final agreement. It is also a *dangerous* limitation, in that it eliminates all previous agreements, so that the negotiator must be fully confident that he has documented in the new contract all necessary constraints and commitments which existed in any previous relationship.

5-20 Partial Invalidity

Counsel's review of a contract normally assures that its provisions are legal. Unforeseen legal problems sometimes arise, however, particularly in areas involving governmental regulation, such as antitrust, health and safety and the like. It is therefore desirable for the contract to state that any provisions found to be illegal shall be stricken and the contract shall remain in full force and effect, as if the offending provision had never been in the contract in the first place. This prevents a party from trying to seek the total avoidance of a contract if some minor clause is found to violate the law.

5-21 Compliance with all United States Standards

The American National Standards Institute (ANSI) publishes a set of U.S. standards for various activities or products which could fall under the contract. It is desirable to include in the contract a provision which states that the contract, and the products to be delivered under the contract, comply with the standards established by ANSI, and by such other organizations as may have applicable standards. Underwriters Laboratories, for example, publishes electrical standards which might be appropriate for hardware, and reference to these could be included in a contract without any difficulty.

5-22 Amendments in Writing

It is important to specify that amendments to the contract be made only in writing. Oral amendments or additions to a written contract are often valid and their existence can be troublesome. In working conferences during implementation of a contract, a representative of a party may make a statement which the other party relies upon as a contract modification. To avoid this problem and the host of other problems attendant to oral understandings, the contract should specifically provide that no modifications will be enforceable unless in writing and signed by the party to be charged thereunder.

5-23 Waiver of Breach

On occasion, a party to the contract may be forced to breach a provision of the contract, which may be consented to by the other party. In such cases it is desirable to note that a consent to a breach is not necessarily a waiver of any subsequent breach, similar or dissimilar, nor does it represent a waiver of any other rights or of any other clauses of the contract. It is desirable to point this out so that the waiving of a single breach does not establish a precedent under which other or subsequent breaches are excused. A well-drafted clause of this type will also provide that a waiver of any breach must be in writing and that mere inaction by a party in the face of a breach does not constitute a waiver.

5-24   Notices

To insure that each party is given proper notice, and to insure that such notice reaches the party involved, specific notice addresses should be given in the contract, preferably with a backup address for copies of same, or the address of counsel where copies are to be sent. In addition, the manner in which effective notice must be given should be defined. This could be either registered or certified mail, return receipt requested. It should be noted that there have been cases where notices were sent which were never received by the intended recipient. In most states, notice is deemed given upon mailing, and actual receipt is not required, unless the contract provides otherwise. To protect potential recipients, therefore, a return receipt acknowledgement is a desirable adjunct to the contract, and multiple addresses should also be given in case of problems. The clause should provide that addresses for notice can be changed, by similar notice.

5-25   Authority

Most often a contract is signed by two individuals, on behalf of their respective organizations. It is desirable in the contract to state that each of these individuals is *authorized* to sign on behalf of the contracting organization, and furthermore that the individual personally has read each of the contract clauses, understands their implications and the responsibilities associated therewith, concurs in these clauses and has signed his name in evidence thereof. This may help prevent the claim that the person signing the contract is not authorized to execute it, and may prevent a further claim that the person signed but did not understand parts of the contract. Neither vendor nor user should rely entirely on the statement of authority in the contract, however. A contract of any magnitude should be accepted only if signed by a corporate officer of at least vice-presidential rank.

5-26   Governing Law

Contracts are made under the laws of a state, province or country. In the United States, contracts are normally made under the laws of the state. The selection of the state is relatively simple, since it is normally the one where either the user or the vendor has its headquarters operation. Selection of the governing law should be made on a logical basis, as opposed to a choice based upon the feelings of comfort of a party with the laws of his own home state. It is normally best to use the state of the *using* organization, since that is usually the state where the contract will be performed. If the user is a multistate operation, the state selected should be the one in which the contract is to be performed.

The selection of governing law does not imply that litigation can be brought in the state selected. Where lawsuits can be brought depends on a complex set of standards of legal jurisdiction, which are generally influenced by where the contract was made, where it is to be performed, and where the parties reside. A powerful user can sometimes get a vendor to agree in the contract to submit itself to the courts (or arbitration agencies) of a given state in the event of dispute. By being able to select a governing forum, a user can sometimes avoid unnecessary travel and expense in litigation with an out-of-state vendor, and force the vendor to bear such expense. The use of a pre-selected forum does not answer all of the problems, however. A judgment in New York will only reach assets located there; if the losing party is an out-of-state company without seizable assets in New York, it may be necessary to sue on the New York judgment in the debtor's home state. There is no way to solve that problem by contract, short of having each party deposit a large sum of money in escrow to secure against default—a most unlikely and unpalatable prospect.

5-27 UCC Applicability

The Uniform Commercial Code presents a method of insuring that a purchaser of goods is reasonably protected from abuses by a vendor (see Chapter 4). The Code, as enforced in 49 of the 50 states, can be referred to in any contract constructed for the data processing industry. The U.C.C. is normally applicable to any contract involving the purchase of goods. It is difficult to establish a software package as "goods," but the provision of certain types of services almost always involves the transfer of some "goods," such as documentation, source decks, and the like, which makes it likely that the U.C.C. is applicable. It is probably difficult to write all provisions of the Code into all types of contracts. It is normally simpler to state that "it is the intent of the parties to incorporate all appropriate provisions of the Uniform Commercial Code in this contract."

5-28 Patent Indemnity (also see clause 7-30.)

Indemnification is necessary for possible infringement of patents inherent in the use of equipment. It is equally applicable to software and is covered in detail in clause 7-30. The vendor must stipulate that he will hold the user harmless against any infringement of patents or copyrights which the use of the equipment may cause, and that he will defend the user in any actions arising therefrom.

5-29 Statute of Limitations

The statute of limitations defines the time period within which aggrieved parties may take action with respect to defaults under the contract. The limitations period for contract actions is typically provided by statute. In those states that have adopted the U.C.C., parties have up to four years[1] after a breach of contract or breach of warranty has occurred[2] to bring an action on the contract. However, the U.C.C. permits parties in their contract to reduce the limitations period to not less than one year. At the same time, the Code forbids an agreement to extend the four-year period. Vendors' standard form contracts often

---

[1]U.C.C. §2-725(1).
[2]*See* U.C.C. §2-725(2).

reduce the limitations period to one year and customers should be wary of accepting this provision.[3]

Because not all computer contracts involve "transactions in goods," the limitations period provided by the U.C.C. will not govern in all cases.[4] If the U.C.C. does not apply to a particular transaction, resort may be had to the general statute of limitations for contract actions in effect in the jurisdiction. To avoid uncertainty, it is desirable to state in the contract a three- to four-year limitations period. This covers both parties adequately in the event someone decides after many years to bring an action with respect to a contract that may have expired.

---

[3] *See* County of Milwaukee v. Northrup Data Systems, Inc., 602 F.2d 767 (7th Cir. 1979) (one-year statute of limitations specified in the contract bars customer's breach of contract action); I.B.M. v. Catamore Enterprises, Inc., 548 F.2d 1065 (1st Cir. 1976), *cert. denied*, 431 U.S. 960 (1977) (one-year statute of limitations specified in contract for all claims but nonpayment bars customer's breach of contract action but not vendor's action for nonpayment).

[4] In some jurisdictions the statute of limitations for contracts not covered by the U.C.C. is longer than four years. In Triangle Underwriters, Inc. v. Honeywell, Inc., 604 F.2d 737, 741 (2d Cir. 1979), a customer unsuccessfully argued that its purchase of a data processing system from Honeywell was not a "transaction in goods" subject to the U.C.C. The aggrieved customer had hoped to take advantage of a statutory six-year limitations period for contracts not within the purview of the U.C.C.

6
HARDWARE CONTRACTS

A. INTRODUCTION

Hardware contracts generally represent the most significant cash outlays in data processing, and the most complex contracts, although not necessarily the most dangerous. A hardware contract will very often include a requirement to deliver software packages; it may include the supply of staff, provisions for maintenance, and can require the supply of services. Thus, the hardware contract may embody provisions of most of the other contracts as well. This chapter covers only a pure hardware contract. The user will have to refer to other chapters to assemble a contract which embodies software packages, services, or other nonhardware elements.

A good hardware contract stipulates the *results* to be achieved with the hardware rather than merely describing the hardware itself. The contract should therefore be goal-oriented, defining operations and required outputs where possible. Hardware specifications are necessary to insure that the delivered product complies with the anticipated purchase. However, of greater importance is the definition of system performance in terms of expected *functions*. The contract elements defined in this chapter have been grouped into eight major categories:

B. Systems specifications, which include all specifications needed in the contract.

C. Services and supplies, which defines all attendant services and supplies to be provided by the vendor.

D. Costs and charges, which cover methods for charging and price protection.

E. Reliability and acceptance, which deals with methods of assuring that performance meets reliability and operational standards.

F. Maintenance which may be a

separate contract, governing all maintenance contract components.

G. Delivery, which gives alternate delivery plans.

H. Rights and options, which creates user options and rights.

I.   Damages, which attempts to define specific damages where appropriate.

In general, hardware vendors are more substantial than software vendors. This reduces the risk of business termination or bankruptcy, which can be a major consideration in dealing with a software or services vendor. However, if a small hardware vendor is used, or if there is a possibility that the hardware vendor could terminate its computer-related activities, it is desirable to examine the business termination clauses and concepts defined in chapters 7 and 8.

The primary risks in a hardware contract are delivery failure, or a failure of the hardware to perform as specified or as anticipated by the user. In either case the user cannot provide the services to his organization which were anticipated when the hardware was ordered. In both cases the hardware should be returned, and all user costs refunded. This may be awkward, since it is difficult to compensate the user for loss of time or for cancellation of a two-year development project. Reference is made to chapter 3 for the exposure analysis which should be made prior to contract signing.

Software to be delivered as a part of a hardware contract is treated as a hardware component for purposes of simpler contract development. Software components are treated as hardware components, and their delivery schedule is matched to the delivery schedule of the hardware. It is desirable to review chapters 7 and 8 to determine if any clauses in that chapter are applicable to a hardware contract as well.

The general discussion and structure of clauses which follow assume the purchase of new computers from original equipment manufacturers. However, it is possible to purchase a used computer, either from a used equipment vendor, from an original equipment manufacturer, or from another user. In this case the contractual relationship may be different, although the concepts, the goals and the results are intended to be the same. When purchasing a used computer, many of the clauses appropriate to a new computer are applicable. Systems specifications and guarantees may well be necessary, although a warranty of good operation and a reliability specification is of greater importance. In addition, reconditioning may be necessary, together with an agreement for continuity of maintenance. It is also wise to insure that all services provided by the original vendor to the first user will be available to the second user. The special structure of a used computer contract is outlined in chapter 10.

B. SYSTEMS SPECIFICATIONS

The delivery of an equipment system usually involves not only hardware but software as well. As a result, the system specification must include specifications for both. Each hardware or software component must be individually specified, and its operating characteristics defined. More importantly, hardware components and software components must be grouped, and group specifications stated as well. Finally, a specification is developed for the entire system, to evaluate if the functions to be performed by the system can be met upon systems delivery.

6-01 Hardware Component Specifications

The first specification in a hardware contract is normally the specification of each hardware component. It defines the operating performance and the physical characteristics of each component, and is normally made available by the manufacturer. Most manufacturers have detailed specification sheets for each component showing dimensions, weight, electrical characteristics and operating characteristics and ranges. These can be attached to the contract as schedules, or incorporated by reference in a specification clause.

6-02 Software Specification

A software component, for purposes of a hardware contract, can be treated in the same way as a hardware component. It has a set of characteristics which can be described in an equally detailed specification. Software is often delivered simultaneously with hardware in an operating *group* which functionally meets certain user requirements. The software component specification, although not always readily available from the manufacturer, will perform a similar function in the contract. In this case it is not necessary to describe physical characteristics; for software only the functional and performance characteristics are needed as part of the component specification. The software specification should include functional descriptions of the software, end products produced by the software, machine utilization, and machine operating constraints.

6-03 Hardware Configuration

The hardware components are combined into a group or configuration whose parameters must be defined. Normally this is simply a listing of the components to be delivered, quantities of each subcomponent, and a brief description of the component. In addition, the basic price of each component is often shown as part of the configuration, to provide a basis for dividing the total contractual commitment into its component parts, in the event components are substituted or upgraded in the future.

6-04 Software Configuration

Similarly, all software components will be listed in separate groups, with a brief description for each. This will define the total software requirement. If certain software components are to be delivered with the hardware because effective hardware operation is dependent on the components, and other components are to be delivered later for future use, then the software configuration is divided into these two groups. A delay in delivery of the initial group will be more serious, in terms of hardware payments, than a delay in delivery of the second software grouping. By grouping the software and hardware, reference in future parts of the contract will be simplified.

6-05 Systems Performance

It is assumed that a benchmark or other test of operating characteristics has been performed on the equipment prior to selection and contract signing. This benchmark provides a description of the operating characteristics and timing of the system as the user expects it to perform after delivery. This description of systems performance can serve as the standard to be met by the system when delivered. In the event that no benchmark is available, it is desirable to develop characteristics of systems performance which the vendor is willing to place in the contract. A statement that the system, when installed, will be capable of producing the entire payroll for 10,000 employees in an elapsed time of three hours would be sufficient, if this is a realistic test of the performance of the equipment. The principal need for a systems performance clause is to provide a basis for the final acceptance test of the system when delivered.

6-06   Inclusion of the Proposal

In the selection process the vendor has been warned that the proposal he submits in competition will be appended to or included in the contract. This clause serves this purpose, and should be included wherever feasible. The statements made in the proposal are embodied in the contract, so that if proposal errors are discovered the vendor may have to upgrade the system to meet vendor commitments.

6-07   Inclusion of Hardware Manuals

As in clause 6-06, it is desirable to include hardware manuals by reference in the contract. The manuals, on which the user has relied in making his selection, are an integral part of the specifications of the equipment. Inclusion will be helpful in insuring that vendor commitments are met by the delivered equipment. This is especially important if the equipment is "one of a kind," or is a new machine which, at the time of contract signing, is not demonstrable. In that event, the vendor may not even know whether the physical component specifications can be met, and the inclusion of all manuals and proposals as a part of the contract will insure that the user's rights are fully protected in the event that this material turns out to be misleading.

6-08   Inclusion of Software Manuals

It is perhaps even more important for software manuals to be included, principally because software is a less tangible and measurable product. It is easy to determine that a hardware component, such as a card reader, operates at 600 cards per minute, or that it is capable of operating in an ambient temperature range of 60 to 80 degrees Fahrenheit. It is more difficult to determine that a particular component of a major software system performs in accordance with its particular specifications. The more software material that can be included as a part of the contract by reference therein, the better it will be in ultimately insuring that the user will have some recourse if the software fails to meet its basic operating characteristics.

6-09   Guarantees of Compatibility

In the event that the user has assumed, on the basis of representations of the manufacturer, that the system will be in some way compatible with predecessor or future systems, then such compatibility should be warranted by the manufacturer. System compatibility to a predecessor system normally has been determined as part of a benchmark test. However, for the sake of safety, since a benchmark test will not include all possible operating conditions, the vendor should be requested to include a simple guarantee that this system is totally data and/or program compatibile with the predecessor system. Data compatibility is defined to mean the ability to read and write files generated by and for the predecessor system without adaptation. Program compatibility is defined as the capability to operate a program written and compiled for the predecessor system on the new system without change in the program or in the hardware configuration, and presumably vice versa. In the event the vendor has stated that the system being delivered is "upwardly" compatible with a future system, or with a different model in the line, then again data and program compatibility must be guaranteed if the user possibly intends to order this system as a future replacement. At the point of ordering the replacement system, it is too late to determine that the investment in the programs or data is lost.

6-10   Guarantees of Interface

It is often desirable or necessary to couple a delivered system to equipment of other manufacturers. This is especially true if data communications are a part of the system, since at least one component of the system is then coupled to (interfaced with) equipment belonging to a telephone company. However, the equipment could also interface with terminals of other manufacturers, or with expansion components or peripheral equipment of other vendors. As a result there is a need for interface data, which will allow coupling without further reliance on the principal manufacturer. This interface data can either be supplied as a part of the contract, or the vendor can warrant its availability. In addition, the vendor should warrant that this equipment can be coupled to and is compatible with industry standard equipment and industry standard interfaces for data communications and peripheral equipment.

Vendors do not always consider it desirable to attach "foreign" equipment to their own. However, most realize that this is a requirement of doing business in today's computer industry, where a variety of components are made by specialized peripheral equipment manufacturers, and where data communications interfaces are common. As a result, most vendors will agree to provide interface data, and will warrant that their equipment is capable of being interfaced on a compatible basis with the equipment of most manufacturers. If specific interface requirements of the system are known at the time the contract is being drafted, then such linkages should be included as part of the systems specifications above. Thus if the user already knows that a particular brand of terminal is being connected to the system, then a guarantee that this terminal can be connected without hardware or software modifications would be helpful in the contract.

6-11   Ability to Modify Equipment in the Field

Certain types of hardware components have characteristics which allow upgrading to higher speeds or greater capacities. Thus, a tape drive which operates at 120,000 characters per second can be modified to 240,000 characters per second, at an increase in value and cost to the user. In a rental contract, such upgrading is often done willingly by the manufacturer after installation, since it obviously means significant additional rental revenue. In a purchase contract the user should obtain a guarantee that the vendor is willing to perform such field upgrading at charges then in effect. This will insure that the "purchase" customer can obtain field modifications to this equipment, rather than be forced to buy new equipment which meets the increase in specifications. Rather than upgrading or modifying the system in the field, vendors occasionally have insisted that the system be exchanged for a new one, with a trade-in allowance given for the old components. This practice discriminates against the purchase customer in favor of the rental customer. To insure that this practice will not occur, a contract clause can be formulated to give the user the right to obtain all field modifications at prevailing charges, for components which can be so modified (Also see clause 6-65, section 6-F, Engineering Changes).

C. SERVICES AND SUPPLIES

In most hardware contracts, the vendor delivers hardware and software, and also services and supplies. The hardware vendor normally is capable of providing a full range of supplies necesary to operate the equipment, such as cards, tapes, disks, forms, printer ribbons, tape cleaning fluids, and the like. In addition, in the course of competition for the sale, the vendor may have committed himself to provide support services to assist the user in the installation of the system. This may range from assistance in the physical installation, to programming help, software support services, training, free machine time prior to delivery for test purposes, education, documentation materials and the like. These services and supplies must be specified, and the time and manner in which they are to be supplied must be defined in the contract so that these commitments can be adhered to and monitored.

6-12 Supply Requirements

It is necessary to define in the contract exactly what supplies the system needs for operating purposes. This insures that there are no surprises, no special components or other expensive elements that need to be purchased to make the system operate. The system should be delivered in an operational mode, and the user should know which supplies are required. A list of the replenishable supplies, such as ribbons for printing devices, print trains, tapes, cards, and disk packs should be contained in the contract.

6-13 Supply Specification

In many cases supplies can be purchased from vendors other than the hardware vendor. These supplies should meet the specifications defined by the original equipment manufacturer, which should be supplied in the contract to prevent the manufacturer from blaming inferior supplies for system failures. This is especially important where the hardware vendor provides these supplies, and where they are available at lower costs from competing vendors. The vendor should supply detailed specifications for each item required by the system, so that these items can be purchased independently and without fear of potential malfunction. Specifications for supplies should be readily available since the hardware vendor will have developed them for internal purposes, and in most cases these specifications can be readily appended to the contract.

6-14 Acceptable Supply Vendors

If there is any fear on the part of the user that the hardware manufacturer will object to the purchase of supplies from other vendors, this issue can be resolved prior to contract signing. The vendor can list other vendors which make comparable acceptable supplies. If the list is used to obtain the requisite supplies, the hardware manufacturer will have no complaint. It may be difficult to ask a vendor to provide a list of competitors; if this is not feasible, it is possible to develop such a list and ask the vendor to agree to incorporate it in the contract on the basis that the vendors make supplies for other users of the same hardware.

6-15 Guaranteed Supply Availability

It is sometimes the case that a required supply is not in the public domain, and is provided solely by the original equipment manufacturer. In that case, the hardware manufacturer could be said to have a monopoly on that particular element necessary for the satisfactory operation of the system. Such a monopoly could result in abuse if the relationship between the vendor and the user deteriorates for any reason. Abuse could include unwillingness by the vendor to provide the item, or a rapid, dramatic increase in its price. When dealing with a monopoly, it is good to insure that the monopoly will continue to supply the material as long as the equipment is in use, at prices now in effect, reasonably adjusted only to account for increases in manufacturing costs. This is protection for the user if there is only one source for a particular element necessary to maintain the system in working order. If, for example, the printer ribbon was a highly specialized one, made only by the original equipment manufacturer, and the vendor decided to increase its price arbitrarily by ten thousand percent, the user would have no recourse, unless a reasonable price adjustment clause and a guarantee of availability of such ribbons were incorporated in the contract.

6-16 Power Requirements and Specifications

One of the prerequisites of operating a computer system is power, normally supplied by a third party, the local utility. The power requirements of the system should be clearly stated in the contract and the variability in power supply allowed by the system should be defined. Power outages, brown-outs, voltage drops and the like are often blamed by manufacturers for equipment failure, and often they are indeed causal. To insure that they are not blamed unreasonably, it is desirable to establish a specific set of detailed power requirements and specifications, which indicate the operating ranges under which the equipment will not malfunction. Power input can then be monitored with a simple recording device, and the vendor can be held responsible for equipment malfunctions that are indeed its responsibility. If it is determined that power supplied by the power company cannot realistically meet the specifications defined, then it is possible to rectify the situation by adding equipment which can insure that power supply is satisfactory. It is desirable to know this in advance.

6-17 Specifications of the Ambient Environment

Computers are temperamental. Some computers are more temperamental than others, requiring a more rigorously controlled environment. It is the responsibility of the vendor to specify the ambient environment, and to indicate what is desirable for effective operation. These specifications should be included in the contract, again to prevent the vendor from using inadequate environment as a defense in a failure to meet reliability standards. It also protects the vendor from difficult operating conditions, under which he may find it impossible to maintain the equipment in good working order. Ambient environment requirements to be specified in the contract include temperature, humidity, any requirements for dust or smoke control, air conditioning necessary to meet the temperature and humidity requirements in the particular location, and the space necessary for each component, so that access is unhampered and electrical interference does not exist among components. In addition, if there are special problems with the site, such as proximity of a radio station, radar equipment, or other magnetic interference, then the vendor should insure prior to contract signing that the site is satisfactory. A warranty of satisfactory site selection is desirable for inclusion as part of this clause, especially if there are potential external magnetic fields which could interfere with the equipment. The vendor's engineers can perform the necessary magnetic sweeps to determine that the interference is not sufficient to damage equipment operation.

6-18 Cabling Requirements

It is normal practice for the equipment vendor to supply all cabling to connect components of the system. However, it is usual also for such cabling to be restricted in length. Certain types of components cannot be separated by more than a certain number of feet, because the timing characteristics of electrical signals passed across greater distances would interfere with the effective synchronization. When this is the case it should be defined in the contract, and all cabling restrictions specified. It is a good idea to attach to the contract a proposed equipment layout, with locations and distances shown, with an indication that this layout is satisfactory and that all cable connections can be made without further charge to the user. This is the simplest way of insuring that no charges for extra cables or boosting equipment will suddenly appear on vendor invoices.

6-19 Support Supplied by Type and Amount

If the vendor has agreed to supply assistance of any kind, it should be catalogued and defined by type and amount to be supplied. A timetable is a necessary part of the contract, since having vendor personnel available at a time when they are not usable is unacceptable. Integration of vendor and user personnel as part of the total development process must be done in accordance with a rigorously controlled schedule, amendable by the user, but not the vendor. The contract should include a list of staff types, assistance which they are supposed to render, the number of person-months or person-years of such assistance, and the period over which the assistance is to be supplied. Included in the staff categories are personnel to assist in:

- systems design
- programming
- software support
- software modification
- data base design
- data conversion
- site planning
- physical installation
- education
- public relations
- management orientation
- project management
- overall project review

In each of these cases it is possible for the vendor to supply assistance, either at no cost or at a predefined charge. Charges for each class of personnel to be supplied must be defined as well.

6-20 Staff Caliber

The caliber of the staff to be supplied under clause 6-19 must be clearly specified. For each category defined, the job description of the individual to be supplied should be added to the contract, with a statement of experience level of the personnel involved. (See clause 8-17 for greater detail, when such staff is supplied on a purchased basis in software development contracts.) The following clauses should also be incorporated in the contract for all support staff:

8-18 Full-time Employees
8-19 Accessibility of Staff in the Event of Business or Contract Termination
8-20 Noncompetition
8-21 Staff Insurance
8-22 Compliance with Security Regulations

In addition, all clauses of section 5-D (clauses 5-13 through 5-17), should be embodied in this contract.

6-21 Educational Curriculum

Most vendors provide a significant number of courses, either free or on a fee basis, for education of user staff, management and project personnel. This educational curriculum should be put down in the contract, and the availability and applicability of each course indicated. There should be a brief course description, its length, and its method of operation, i.e., seminar, workshop, video, programmed instruction.

6-22 Educational Availability

It is normal for some vendors to supply educational courses at no charge, up to a specific allotment, and thereafter to make certain charges to users of their equipment. This is clearly an instrument of marketing policy, and in some cases it is a negotiable one. As a result, the total allotment of free courses should be stipulated in the contract, and related to the educational curriculum of clause 6-21. It can also be done as number of course days available, leaving it to the user to choose courses which will provide greatest benefit. If these courses are available on a charge basis when the allotment is exceeded, this should be noted in the contract.

6-23 Continued Availability of Educational Courses

The user will find it necessary to train or retrain staff in programming, systems techniques, and operations as long as he uses the hardware system being delivered under the contract. Educational courses should be made available for as long as the system is installed. This requires a statement of continued availability by the vendor. In the event that the vendor is unwilling to guarantee continued availability of educational courses, clauses 6-24, 6-25 and 6-27 should be used as well.

6-24 Availability of Instructors

If necessary educational courses cannot be obtained on a public basis because the vendor has decided to discontinue them, the user may wish to have these courses taught on an internal basis to groups of user personnel. The vendor should agree to make available instructors qualified to teach these courses at charges in effect for such personnel at the time. The caliber of these instructors should be specified, or at least a statement included in the contract that such instructors shall have taught a specified number of the same or similar courses, which makes them qualified to perform such services for the user in the future.

6-25 Availability of Educational Materials

To teach courses internally it is necessary that educational materials be available as well, including the necessary student texts, syllabi, tests, and such instructional material as may be necessary for the teacher, such as a teachers' guide, audio-visual aids, and the like. The rights to this material should be made available to the user, whether the user intends to use it by employing the vendor's instructors or by teaching this course using his own staff, as defined in clause 6-27.

6-26 Rights to Future Courses

From time to time vendors may develop new courses which differ from courses presently available, and which may be applicable to the user. The user should have unlimited rights to access such courses, on the same basis that these courses are made available to all other users of the vendor. This will prevent potential unreasonable charges for future services.

6-27 Rights to Teach Courses Internally

Whether or not instructors are available from the vendor, or public courses are still offered by the vendor, the user should have the right to teach any course from the vendor's curriculum on an internal basis with user staff as instructors, and with vendor materials possibly reproduced by the user as course material. This changes to a requirement if the vendor no longer continues to offer the course or instructors on a public basis. As the system becomes obsolete and the general interest in these courses disappears, the need becomes greater. At that point it becomes meaningful for the user to provide its own training programs for its staff, using its own qualified instructors and copies of material used in the past by the vendor. Rights to do this must be granted by the vendor.

6-28 Test Time Availability

With the installation of a new machine it is common practice for the vendor to make available access to a comparable configuration of the new machine for purposes of testing user programs prior to installation of the machine on the user site. This will insure that productivity of the user in the early days of the installation is maximized, since the initial compilation and testing of programs will be completed through use of this test time. The basic allotment of this time is free, and the hours, their method of measurement, and schedule should be defined in the contract. The contract should stipulate when these hours will be available; it is highly undesirable to have all the hours on a continuous basis. It is equally undesirable to have all test time during the midnight shift, since user staff may not appreciate the idea of working odd hours. Finally, the site location should be stipulated, since considerable expense can be incurred by sending staff halfway across the world to obtain free test time. It is in the interest of the vendor to provide this time on a convenient schedule at a convenient location. However, if the relationship between the vendor and the user has deteriorated, this is another method by which the vendor can make life more difficult than necessary for the user. The contract should stipulate availability of test time, the schedule under which it is made available, and the site. In addition, if the user elects to use test time in excess of the free allotment, then charges for such additional time must be stipulated, normally as part of section D, Costs and Charges.

6-29 Availability of Documentation

Another service which the vendor must supply, important in terms of user need, is systems documentation, which includes hardware manuals, software manuals, and various types of training materials. These manuals together can add up to a significant library, reference to which is required by programmers, systems analysts, operational personnel, and others concerned with optimization of computer use. Documentation should be made available, without restriction, either on a no-charge basis, or at whatever reasonable charge the vendor has decided to make for it. The continued availability of this documentation, and the rights to use it on an unrestricted basis, should be defined in the contract.

6-30 Rights to Future Documentation

As new documentation is developed, the user should be given copies on an unrestricted basis. This can be a significant benefit, since manufacturers do produce large amounts of documentation. A clause in the contract should state that the manufacturer will routinely provide the user announcements of all new documentation produced and published and that the user will have the right to request copies of such material at any time thereafter.

6-31 Rights to Reproduce Documentation

Documentation is normally copyrighted by the manufacturer, who will normally charge for significant numbers of additional copies of any document. It may be cheaper for the user to reproduce such documentation, especially where it is used in training of new staff, or for tests. The user should have the right to reproduce this documentation, which can be granted by the contract, rather than after contract signing.

D. COSTS AND CHARGES

The vendor is obviously entitled to be paid, whether such payments are made exclusively for hardware, or for each component or element of the service supplied. Each and every charge to be made should be made known at the beginning, so that there are no surprises in invoices supplied by the vendor. Invoice surprises are often cause for disagreement, and contractual relations, like marital relations, most often break down as a result of financial disagreements. The contract should recite all conceivable charges and costs which can be incurred and to which the vendor is entitled. The contract should further provide that no charges other than those recited can be levied by the vendor unless approved in advance by the user.

6-32 Term of Agreement

The length of time during which the agreement survives, and during which charges are applicable, must be defined in the contract. A purchase contract presumably is complete upon delivery and payment for the product. Any provisions, such as warranties, which are intended to survive, must be spelled out. A maintenance contract expires in some finite period, perhaps three, five, or seven years from the initial installation of the system. Contracts under which software or services are supplied expire in some finite period also, to insure that prices can be renegotiated upon expiration. Price protection is generally limited by the term of the agreement, and price adjustments can only be made as indicated in the agreement, upon expiration of a specific portion of the agreement or when a new agreement is negotiated.

6-33 Payment

Invoices should normally be rendered on a monthly basis, in arrears. Invoices are due when rendered, but should be permitted to be paid in accordance with *normal business practices* of the user, which presumably implies something in the order of "net 30." Payment method, regardless of what is agreed, should be stipulated in the contract to avoid future controversy.

6-34 Hold-backs of Payments

Under certain conditions it may be useful to include a clause which provides for holding back certain monies due to insure contract compliance. Payment for hardware may be held up until the software is delivered. Payment for maintenance may be held up, pending rectification of reliability problems, and payment for other charges may be delayed depending on performance characteristics associated with the services so rendered. The user should carefully determine the products to be delivered at each stage by the vendor, the value of those products if the contract were to be aborted immediately thereafter, and the amount of money the user is willing to commit to the vendor at this stage. Other monies due should be held back pending completion of the remaining parts of the contract. This, however, may depend on the financial viability of the vendor: a strong vendor is capable of making restitution of funds paid in advance for services ultimately not delivered, whether such restitution is obtained by agreement, litigation, or arbitration. Hold-backs, even with strong vendors, have another potential salutary effect: they motivate the vendor to continue performance.

6-35 Tax Applicability

A hardware contract may be a complex arrangement providing for services, supplies, hardware components and software components. A variety of taxes may be applicable: sales taxes, use taxes, property taxes, gross receipts taxes, rental or occupancy taxes, income taxes, franchise taxes and the like. To the extent that the user is responsible for paying any of these taxes, their applicability should be stipulated, and the user should be held harmless from payment of any other taxes. It would be unfair to hold the user responsible for the incidental levying of a gross receipts tax in a location totally foreign to the user, where the vendor happens to have an operating activity. It would be equally unfair to superimpose ex post facto taxes on the user, if provision for tax payments are not in the original contract. A blanket clause which holds the user responsible for all taxes levied is unacceptable, and should not be allowed. A clause which stipulates exactly which taxes are applicable is realistic and provides sufficient warning to the user of his total obligations under the contract.

6-36 Warranty of New Equipment

Investment tax credit provisions of federal law in the United States and in the United Kingdom provide for tax credits in the event capital is invested in *new* equipment. The newness of such equipment must, however, be warranted by the manufacturer. The manufacturer should provide a certificate to the user that the equipment delivered is new and of original manufacture. Investment tax credits apply normally only to purchased equipment. However, on rented or leased equipment, such tax credits are normally granted to the owner, who can then agree to pass these on to the user (see clause 6-37). A warranty of newness is thus necessary in this case also.

6-37 Pass-through of Investment Tax Credits

If the equipment is rented, and it is new, then the equipment manufacturer who owns the equipment will be entitled to all or part of the investment tax credit, depending on the manufacturer's depreciation policy. It is then possible for the manufacturer to pass through the investment tax credit to the lessee. A stipulation in the contract of the vendor's willingness to pass through the credit, and a guarantee that the equipment is new (see clause 6-36) are necessary to insure that the user can make application to the authorities for the appropriate credit. This clause should be extended to cover additional equipment leased under this contract at a future time, the acquisition of a replacement component, and other materials which may be qualified under investment tax credit legislation.

6-38   Method of Charging and Charging Types

The relationship between the vendor and the user includes a variety of charges which the vendor will make for hardware, software, and services. These charges should be enumerated by type, the amount applicable by unit, and methods of determining amounts due. Charges and their characteristics should be stipulated for each of the following categories:

- Basic hardware charges, and the usage entitlement for such charges, in number of hours per month, or on an unlimited basis.
- Basic software charges, and their allowable use in terms of hardware elements where such software is to be used. When multiple computers are in use at the organization, multiple software charges may be different.
- Overtime charges, for overtime use of equipment or software, and the method under which overtime shall be measured and substantiated to the user.
- Holiday use of equipment or software, and appropriate charges for maintenance associated with such holiday use.
- Maintenance charges, maintenance overtime, on-call maintenance, holiday maintenance, and all other charges associated with a maintenance contract.
- Transportation charges, for delivering the machine both from and to the manufacturer, if rented.
- Basic installation charges, and charges associated with unpacking, uncrating, and installation, if any.
- Supply charges, charges for cabling, for disks, tapes, cards, ribbons, and other supply components.
- Spare parts charges, and whether or not such parts are available under a maintenance contract, or may be obtained on a direct basis.
- Charges for service, for training in excess of some free allotment, for extra documentation copies, for test time, and for person-power supplied under support activities, when such charges exceed the amounts committed at no charge.

In addition, methods for substantiation of these charges, for measurement, and for receipting should be defined, so that invoicing methodology is clear, and so that when an invoice is delivered there can be no question of its applicability.

6-39   Credits for Malfunctions or Other Failures

When charges are levied for successful use, there may be occasions when credits for such charges are given when malfunctions occur for which the vendor is responsible. Failures under which credits are applicable should be defined in the contract. They normally include hardware malfunction, vendor supplied software malfunction, or costly errors made by vendor personnel working for the user. In these cases a credit is given to the user, and the contract should stipulate the credit amount, and its determination. Normally the credit should be supplied for the time lost due to the malfunction, and for all the time necessary to rerun activities disrupted by the malfunction. It is up to the user to find substantiation methodology to insure that credits are properly taken, and to provide notification to the vendor of a malfunction which may result in a credit.

6-40 Price Protection Prior to Delivery

The contract is signed a number of months prior to delivery of the hardware and software components. During the period before delivery, prices defined in the contract should clearly be protected. There can be no basis for contract adherence if prices are adjusted prior to actual delivery of the goods. It is perhaps possible to provide a clause under which prices may be adjusted prior to delivery, in which event the user is entitled to cancel the contract, in exchange for a penalty payment by the vendor which compensates the user for the costs incurred in preparation, net of any gains which the user might have in transferring to another vendor's equipment. This is a difficult provision, however. It is normally simpler to provide that charges in the contract are protected at least until hardware is delivered.

6-41 Price Protection During Contract Term

In a rental contract, or in continuing charges associated with a purchase contract for maintenance, services and supplies, some price protection is desirable during the term of the contract. This can be handled by keeping the term of the contract short, which gives the vendor an opportunity to adjust prices upon expiration and provides a certain amount of flexibility to the user as well. However, a short-term contract is rarely to the advantage of the user, since it is up to the user to replace the services either from another vendor or his own staff, which will require time and investment, often greater than the investment in the equipment. Thus the user is committed to a long term in any event, and the vendor should probably have a similar commitment, to insure fairness. Thus it is useful to have a long-term agreement with the vendor for maintenance on a purchased machine.

A long-term hardware rental contract may be useful, provided that the length of term of the agreement provides benefits to the user. Such benefits are primarily in the form of price protection, during the term of the contract. In the event that the vendor is unwilling to provide price protection during the term of the contract, it may be possible to negotiate a "ceiling" clause, which will prevent the vendor from raising prices more than a stipulated amount. Prices could be tied to a "cost of living index," such as the one published by the United States Bureau of Labor Statistics. In any event, the user must carefully consider the method under which he is protected from arbitrary increases in price during the term of the agreement.

6-42 Price Protection for Expansion Equipment

One of the great advantages of computer systems built today is that they are modular, and expansible in small stages as the user's requirements increase. This allows a user to start with a smaller system, and expand it by adding additional storage, peripheral equipment, or terminals, as the need arises, or as the user expands his business activities. Unfortunately, when it is necessary to obtain such expansion equipment, there is typically only one vendor capable of supplying it, the original equipment vendor. Another vendor's expansion equipment might be more expensive to interface or cause excessive staff training costs. The vendor may be in a monopoly position, therefore, and it is desirable for the user to provide protection for the price of expansion equipment. The original contract should list available expansion equipment and its current prices and should provide for its availability at those prices or at later prevailing prices, subject to outside limits, such as a maximum of 15% per annum, or the increase in the cost of living index, whichever is larger. Clearly, reasonableness is all that is needed in this case; it is not necessary to make it uneconomical for the vendor to provide such expansion equipment, nor is it necessary to protect the user from all price increases. The only protection the user requires is from arbitrary price increases which may force him to purchase components at totally unrealistic prices.

6-43 Price Protection for Supplies and Services

The vendor is potentially in a monopoly position when providing supplies and services to the user, although it may be possible to find other vendors who can meet established specifications. It is not very significant to provide for price protection in these areas, since the amounts involved are normally substantially smaller, and since the inconvenience associated with using another vendor's supplies or services is not as great as in obtaining incompatible hardware from another vendor. However, where feasible it is useful to incorporate a reasonable price protection clause which limits increases on a rational basis. Such increases can be limited to some annual increment such as 15%, or the increase in the cost of living index, whichever is larger.

6-44 Price Protection for Maintenance Services

Maintenance personnel and spare parts are a basic requirement for user survival. It is often not feasible to use another vendor to provide maintenance services, although there are several independent service organizations which do provide maintenance in competition with some of the manufacturers, but whose facilities are not always available in all geographic locations. In the area of maintenance the vendor finds himself in perhaps the most monopolistic position of all, and it is in this area that the user has the greatest need for realistic price protection.

The first stage in such protection is the development of a long-term contract, which might provide for a base term of three to five years, with user options for renewal to a maximum term of perhaps eight to ten years based upon a realistic appraisal of the potential life of the equipment. Charges for the initial period should be held firm, with the possible exception of increases corresponding to increases in vendor labor costs. Charges in subsequent periods should be realistically adjusted according to some annual increment or the cost of living index. An alternative to maintenance price protection may be to provide maintenance internally, which a few installations have successfully achieved. This is covered in greater detail in the clauses covering the maintenance contract under section F.

E. RELIABILITY AND ACCEPTANCE

A vital ingredient of systems performance is the reliability of the system. The system must be capable of satisfying operational requirements of the user, provide the functions which the user expects it to perform, and be available on a relatively uninterrupted basis. Failures caused by software or hardware malfunctions should not occur frequently, because they may disrupt user activities significantly, and they may interfere with the operation of on-line systems to the point where end users are affected, or data is lost in transit. These kinds of failures are significant, and will be increasingly significant as systems and applications' complexity increases. Thus, it is necessary to improve reliability of hardware and software systems to a point where the safety of a user's system is insured under all conditions. Much of this can be accomplished by careful design of application systems which take failures into account. However, continued disruption and its expense will require consideration in the contract.

A second part of this problem is that of accepting the system when it is delivered. Acceptance testing includes a determination that the system can operate functionally and reliably. For this purpose, for continually monitoring the reliability of the system and the effectiveness of the maintenance supplied by the manufacturer, reliability standards must be established in the contract.

Reliability standards are defined individually for each of the components, and for the system as a whole. A component may break down without affecting the ability of the user to continue operations. An entire system breakdown does have a direct impact on the user's ability to continue operation. A series of component breakdowns may *curtail* the ability of the user to operate, so that an inconvenience factor has to be recognized. Separate reliability parameters must be defined for each case.

6-45   Reliability Parameters

The initial clause governing reliability should define what is meant by reliability. This implies a definition of the parameters of reliability, which include the frequency and duration of failure, whether such failure be component or system failure. For each of these, it is necessary to stipulate a reasonable mean time between failure (MTBF), which describes the frequency of occurrence, and a reasonable mean time to repair, which indicates the duration of down-time. Down-time *percentages* can be computed by taking the total working hours anticipated in the installation, and dividing them into the total of all down-time occurrences. Thus, when it is necessary to establish a *guarantee* of reliability it can be done both as a percentage of down-time, or its reciprocal, up-time, or it can be done by a maximum number of instances and a maximum aggregate duration. Either method is acceptable for establishing a basic set of parameters against which to measure the reliability of the system.

6-46   Guarantees of Performance

Reasonable parameters of reliability can be established in the contract, but vendors are often unwilling to guarantee performance to those reasonable standards. However, most vendors are willing to provide *some* guarantees of performance, and to provide remedies in the event such guarantees are not met across a realistic period of time. Thus a guarantee might be stated as follows:

> "The system shall be available for use not less than 90% in any 24-hour period, not less than 94% in any 7-day period, not less than 96% in any 30-day period."

A statement of this type provides a guarantee, which, if violated, can trigger various remedies.

Thus a remedial statement (see clause 6-48) could indicate that if such failure persists for more than two instances, that is more than two days below 90%, or more than 2 weeks below 94%, or more than 2 months below 96%, or any combination of these, then the user has the right to replace the failing components, to suspend payment of maintenance, to force the vendor to improve the quality of maintenance by replacing maintenance personnel, or all of the above. In other words, the user is capable of establishing required remedial action in the event significant failures occur, either in terms of frequency or percentage of down-time, across various periods of measurement.

Not all vendors are willing to provide guarantees of this type because they may be considered too inflexible or because they may affect the ability of the vendor to provide effective maintenance services. In that event it may be possible to get the vendor to *recognize the reasonability* of a set of standards defined by component and for the system as a whole. The vendor may agree to use his best efforts to maintain the system in good working order, where the achievement of the standards defined by the user is considered an indication of good working order.

6-47   Warranty

On most purchased systems the vendor will provide a warranty, comparable to those supplied by manufacturers of television sets, radios, and automobiles. Repairs with respect to labor and parts for an initial period will be performed at no cost to the user, if such repairs are necessitated by defects in the components. There should be no maintenance charges during an initial warranty period, which varies from 90 days to a year. The maintenance contract (if any) should start at the completion of this warranty period, and no maintenance cost should accrue during the warranty period. If the contract is negotiated on a rental basis, the rental should be reduced by the equivalent of the maintenance charge for the warranty period. In equity, a rental customer should not have to pay for maintenance, which is normally included in the rental charge, during the period when a purchase customer would not be required to pay for it. It may be useful to separate in a rental contract charges for equipment rental from charges for maintenance. This is the practice of some of the vendors at this time, which should be encouraged in the contract, if the warranty period is to be included on a rental basis.

6-48   Right to Replace Components (Lemon Clause)

Any manufacturer will occasionally produce a component which is so bad that its operating performance is totally unacceptable, and its characteristics are such that no matter how much maintenance is supplied, the components simply cannot be improved to operate at a level considered acceptable by the user. This component might be deemed to be a "lemon" in the terminology of the automobile marketplace. When a "lemon" is obtained by a user, the user should have the unilateral right to require the vendor to replace this component, regardless of whether it is purchased or rented. In a short-term rental contract such replacement is relatively easy to achieve; it is possible to cancel the offending component and to reorder a similar component as its replacement. This can only be done at the end of term of a rental contract, and if a long-term rental contract is used it is necessary to have a separate lemon clause. The lemon clause basically protects the user against a component that fails to meet the reliability standards defined over a considerable period of time, or that in the short run, fails to meet the reliability standards by a wide margin. 40% up-time for a component, whether it is for a week, a month, or three months, is just not an acceptable level of operation with which a user can make effective use of this component. When a component operates at that low a level, it should not be incurring any charges for the user, and the user should have, after giving the vendor the opportunity to remedy the situation, the opportunity to replace the component on a unilateral basis. Vendors often try to resist the inclusion of such a contract clause by referring to their standard "repair or replace" clause. The customary vendor-supplied clause, however, gives the *vendor* the option whether to repair or replace. This is not satisfactory and the option must be the *user's*, since it is possible for the vendor to attempt to remedy a severely malfunctioning component through increasing amounts of maintenance, which may be to no avail if there is something structurally wrong with the component.

6-49 Backup Availability

In the event of significant failure, as a result of an unreliable system, the vendor should provide arrangements under which backup is available to the user. Such backup may be at a local vendor installation, or an another user's installation in which equipment of comparable configuration is available for use under emergency conditions. If the requirement for backup is caused by malfunction of the vendor's equipment or software, and such malfunctions cannot be remedied on a short-term basis, the cost of such backup equipment should be borne by the vendor. Backup should be available on 12- to 24-hour notice, depending on the user's operations, and at a reasonable location, perhaps within a 50 mile radius, or within one to two hours travel time. The configuration of the backup equipment should match that necessary for operation of the user's most critical system, which should be spelled out as part of the backup clause.

6-50 Disaster Availability

It is possible that a disaster might occur which would disable the equipment for a long period of time, if not permanently. This disaster could be caused by a failure of a major component, for which a replacement is not available locally, and for which a replacement might require a week or more for installation. A disaster might be caused by an act of God, a fire, flood, or major electrical failure. In any event, the term "disaster" connotes that the machine will not be available for a long period of time, during which backup availability (see clause 6-49) may not be sufficient to satisfy the user's requirements. If a disaster permanently disables the equipment, and replacement equipment is required, or equipment is unavailable for long periods of time, the vendor should provide for alternative sources of hardware supply. If equipment replacement is necessary, a guarantee by the vendor that such replacement shall be made available within a defined period is useful. In addition, the vendor should provide for emergency backup facilities, which may be the use of a machine scheduled for delivery to another installation currently in final testing at the vendor's assembly plant. This alternative is normally available, although it might not be convenient. In the event of a disaster, any alternative which is provided is helpful. A contractual stipulation of the obligation of the vendor to assist the user in the event of disaster is necessary.

6-51 Acceptance Testing

The equipment is delivered, installed, and the vendor provides certification to the user that the equipment is now ready for use and that it is capable of performing all of the functions to specifications. At this point it is the user's responsibility to insure that the equipment does meet the specifications defined in the original proposal, and those defined in the contract under clauses 6-01, 6-02, 6-05, 6-09, 6-10, and 6-46. In other words, it is necessary to insure the following:

a. That the system's hardware components operate as specified, and that the individual operating characteristics are as indicated in the hardware component specifications.
b. That the system's software components operate as specified, and that the software fulfills the functions within the constraints defined, as indicated in the specifications.
c. That the system's performance matches the performance as indicated in the original benchmark tests, or as specified in clause 6-05.
d. That the system is compatible with respect to data and programs with a predecessor system, as defined in clause 6-09, with a potential future system, as defined in clause 6-09, and that the system can indeed interface with terminals and communications equipment as defined in clause 6-10.
e. That the system is capable of operating on the basis of reliability as defined in clause 6-46.

Acceptance tests must be designed to satisfy these five requirements, and these tests should be incorporated as part of the contract. Vendor agreement to these tests must be obtained before signing the contract, so that if these tests are not met, the contract can be deemed to be breached. Normally, though, the vendor should be given at least one opportunity to correct the configuration or its operation to insure that the specifications will be met in a subsequent test.

In addition to stipulating the acceptance test methodology to be followed, the contract should provide for the time period within which the test may be performed, and timing and procedures for notices of deficiency and vendor opportunity to correct defects. Hold-backs of payment pending final acceptance should also be set forth.

Parts a and b of the acceptance test can be run in relatively short periods by simply exercising the different components and insuring that they do in fact perform at rated speeds and at rated operating conditions. Part c should normally be performed in one or two days as well, since this is simply a rerunning of an existing benchmark test, which presumably did not take more than a few hours to perform. If these tests are performed satisfactorily, partial payment could be made. Part d, compatibility and interface testing, should likewise be capable of completion in a few days, although a more comprehensive test might be designed with respect to various communications interfaces.

The only part which will take a considerable amount of time is part e, which governs the operating reliability conditions over time. In this event, 30 days is probably the minimum period in which reliability of operations can be assessed. If during the 30-day period minimum standards are not met, the reliability period should be extended to a second 30-day period, since during the equipment "shake-down period" it is likely that more errors will occur than later on. The same is true for software, which during its initial operation will probably have a greater incidence of errors than after debugging.

Payment methods should be controlled by the ability of the equipment to pass all acceptance tests. These are negotiable, obviously, and will vary from contract to contract depending on previous experience with the vendor, whether or not the system has been installed successfully in other installations, and the importance of reliability to the user.

F. MAINTENANCE

The provision of maintenance is normally the responsibility of the vendor who has manufactured the equipment, although it may be governed under a totally separate contract. In any event, it covers a variety of clauses which make sure that repairs are made promptly and effectively or that continuing failures to make repairs effectively can be remedied in accordance with contractual provisions. The maintenance contract also should permit the user to perform his own maintenance or to transfer maintenance responsibility to another vendor. Reference is also made to clauses in section 8-E, which relate to staff caliber and staff constraints. These clauses (8-17, 8-18, 8-19, 8-20, 8-21, and 8-22) should be included in a maintenance contract, with respect to maintenance personnel who may from time to time be working in the user installation.

6-52 Available Maintenance Types

It is useful to stipulate in the contract the types of maintenance which can be obtained from the vendor, and the conditions under which these types are made available. It has been traditional in the industry to obtain maintenance on a fixed price basis, in which an "insurance" fee is paid to the vendor, for which all maintenance and spare parts are provided. This method of maintenance is the most secure. It may also be the most expensive method.

It may be possible (after obtaining reasonable experience with the system), to go into a maintenance contract on a time and materials basis. Here, the vendor charges for each call, and for spare parts necessary as replacements. This is a gamble, of course. If a significant number of maintenance calls and spares or expensive parts are required, the aggregate costs of maintenance may well exceed those under a fixed price contract. The user should have the opportunity of electing this method of maintenance at any time during the maintenance contract, however, and especially after expiration of the warranty period, when the user will have some experience with the effectiveness and costs of maintenance. The maintenance availability clause stipulates the types of maintenance available, and the charges thereunder. The contract can then set out the method selected by the user on a preliminary basis and the user's right to convert from one to another at any time. It is often difficult to obtain vendor agreement to a clause permitting the user to revert to "full" maintenance after any period of "time and materials" maintenance. In most situations, vendors can inspect the equipment and, at *user* cost, make such repairs as are necessary to bring the equipment up to standard maintenance levels.

6-53   On-site Maintenance

In a large installation, with considerable amounts of equipment, it is highly desirable to contract for on-site maintenance, where full-time vendor personnel are assigned to the site to perform maintenance functions.

In smaller installations, on-site personnel are highly desirable during the early days of a computer installation, when the machine is still going through a "shake-down" period. In both cases a stipulation should be included in the contract that the vendor will supply full-time on-site personnel for maintenance purposes during the designated period, and that such personnel shall remain on-site as long as the reliability standards are not met. After the reliability standards have been met for a period of 30 days, for example, and the system has been accepted, it may be possible to terminate on-site maintenance although this will depend on the nature of the installation. On-site maintenance should be resumed if reliability standards have not been met for a designated period; that is one form of remedy for failure to meet reliability standards. It is not good practice to keep on-site personnel available if they are not being used effectively, and they are simply sitting around. This type of usage tends to make vendor maintenance staff ineffective, and limits their experience, which can hurt in the case of a major failure.

6-54   Response Time for Off-site Maintenance

In the event that on-site maintenance is not provided, maintenance is made available to the user on an off-site basis. This means that the maintenance personnel will have to be summoned in the case of a failure, probably by telephone or by two-way radio. One measure of the effectiveness of maintenance is the response time, the period between the time that maintenance assistance is requested and the time that maintenance personnel appear on-site. This period of time can be significant, and can contribute to the duration of failure, since it is entirely possible that the system may not be operational during this period. Most vendors are prepared to provide a maximum response guarantee, on the order of two hours or less, depending on geographic location, traffic conditions, and weather conditions. In any event, it is useful to negotiate a response time maximum, and to include in that some form of liquidation in the event that the response time maximum is not met. The vendor might make a payment, or suspend maintenance payments if he fails to respond within the stated time. Another alternative would be for the vendor to be required to provide on-site maintenance if he has failed to respond in time more than once. A third alternative might be to allow the user to obtain assistance from a competing vendor at the expense of the original vendor. Of course, the contract should state that, once maintenance personnel have arrived, they will proceed diligently and remain on the job until completion of the repair.

6-55 Access Requirements

In order to perform effective maintenance, whether preventive or unscheduled, the maintenance personnel will require access to the equipment on a reasonable basis. It is recommended that reasonable access be provided, if such access can be given without extensive disruption to the user's normal business processing. If the machine malfunctions, and the system is not operating, presumably access will be made available immediately. However, if a component malfunctions, and the maintenance personnel require the use of the entire machine to validate the malfunctioning characteristics of the component, then such access should be restricted to the convenience of the user, or with some notice on the part of the vendor, so the user can prepare to disrupt his operation in an orderly manner. (Also note clause 6-66, Rights to Schedule Preventive Maintenance.)

6-56 Spare Parts

The availability of spare parts for repair purposes is normally the responsibility of the vendor, under a maintenance contract in which the vendor has agreed to supply all necessary spares. However, it is impossible for the vendor to have a sufficient supply of parts of all types and varieties at or near each individual installation. Thus, the vendor typically will have spare parts depots in various parts of the country, and may obtain a particular part from a remote location, if that part is used infrequently. It is to the user's advantage to know exactly where spare parts for his equipment will come from. This will allow him to plan and know the extent of the duration of down-time in the event of a significant failure. The contract should contain a list of all spare parts to be stored on the user's site, spare parts located at a local office, and parts that are obtained from a distance, which will require additional time. One way to list these parts is by amount of time required to obtain them, rather than by distance. If a part is obtained from a different part of the country, the flying time and schedule should be taken into consideration in the time required to obtain the part from that location.

6-57 Space and Facilities

Maintenance personnel require facilities at the user's site in order to operate effectively. They also require storage space for their equipment and for a supply of spare parts which is necessary for rapid repair. This is desirable from the viewpoint of the user, to make it as convenient as possible for vendor staff to provide effective maintenance for the system. The user should provide the facilities, storage space, and working space for maintenance personnel of the vendor. These facilities may include such equipment as a refrigerator for cold storage of parts, work benches, and storage cabinets. The exact requirements of maintenance personnel for the user's facility should be defined in the contract so that proper site planning can be performed by the user.

6-58   Continuity and Maintenance Renewal Rights

In general, a maintenance contract should survive, or be capable of renewal, for as long as the equipment is installed in the user's site, or possibly for as long as the equipment is installed in any user's site. If a user wishes to resell equipment which he owns, such equipment can only be realistically sold if the purchaser can be assured of obtaining maintenance for the equipment at a reasonable rate. The maintenance contract should be assignable in the event of equipment sale, and should carry the right to extend it for a finite period of time, at prices then in effect for all users. (Again, price protection should be covered, and reference should be made to clause 6-44). The principal objective of this clause is to provide continuity, a guarantee by the vendor that the vendor will continue to provide maintenance to the system for, say, eight to ten years (which can reasonably be expected to be the life of the system) during which the user or any other user will have the right to renew the contract at prices then in effect, subject to price protection.

6-59   Reconditioning on Resale

In the event the user intends to resell the equipment to another user, it is practical at the sale to provide a warranty by the vendor that the equipment is in good working order. Such a warranty is normally provided by the vendor, if the vendor has supplied the necessary maintenance on a continuing basis. In other words, if the vendor has been responsible for maintaining the equipment in good working order then the vendor should be willing to provide a certificate of good working order to a purchaser of the system. However, it is possible that the purchaser may require equipment reconditioning, to provide operating characteristics comparable to new equipment, or to replace components with significant wear and tear which probably would be replaced within the next 12 months under a normal maintenance program. Such reconditioning should be agreed to in advance, and a price for it established for each period in the future when the user might anticipate sale of the system. The vendor should agree (a) to provide a certificate of good working order, (b) to provide reconditioning of the system upon request at any time, and (c) to provide such reconditioning at prices stated in advance.

6-60   Rights to Training of Own Maintenance Staff

If the maintenance contract expires, and the vendor's renewal terms are onerous, or if the user decides, for any other reason, that it is more effective to provide his own maintenance, the user is dependent on the vendor for obtaining the necessary technology. This will include the necessary blueprints, circuit diagrams, and other informational material describing construction of the equipment. It will also require the training of personnel to perform maintenance. Under the contract the user should have the right to obtain training programs from the manufacturer sufficient to provide effective training in the maintenance of the installed equipment. These training programs can be defined by reference to the vendor's own training programs for his own maintenance personnel. These programs or instructors should be made available, on site, and all necessary training materials should be included. For reference to means of insuring continuity of this type of education, clauses 6-23, 6-24, 6-25, 6-26 and 6-27 should be reviewed as well. The maintenance training requirements can be incorporated as part of the total educational program in those clauses, or can be separated as part of a maintenance contract.

6-61 Rights to Purchase Spare Parts

Another requirement for performing maintenance directly is the availability of spare parts, which are normally manufactured by the vendor. To the extent such parts are available publicly or available from competing vendors, their specifications are on the vendor blueprints, and should therefore be accessible to the user. However, in most instances the spare parts, subassemblies, or components are manufactured directly by the vendor and are available only from the vendor. In this event the user should be given the right to purchase spares, and have price protection for these spares in accordance with terms defined in clause 6-44, or in accordance with a separate set of terms which govern the acquisition of spare parts. In any event, the right to purchase them is important if the user decides to perform his own maintenance at some time in the future.

6-62 Rebates for Failures Not Corrected Promptly

If the maintenance contract is a separate document, or if maintenance charges are stated separately, it is desirable to incorporate rebates of such charges in the event that failures have been corrected improperly, or in the event failures have not been corrected promptly. Any repair delay in excess of some minimum, such as an hour, probably should be subject to some rebate consideration, since the user's costs of such failures are far higher than any maintenance charges which may have been incurred. Also refer to Credits for Malfunction in section B, clause 6-39.

6-63 Malfunction and Correction Reporting

The contract should stipulate that it is the vendor's responsibility to provide the user with specific reports of malfunctions occurring in the system, their correction, and the amount of time lost as a result. The user in turn should summarize his malfunction activities, and the costs associated with the time lost. This provides a valuable protection record for future arguments, when reliability is questioned by the user, or when rebates are sought. Vendor malfunction reports should be stipulated by the contract, should identify the time of occurrence, the response time, the time of restoring of the system to full operation, the cause of the malfunction, and the components or parts replaced. This information will provide a significant log, especially if it is found afterwards that the malfunction was not properly corrected and it reoccurs. It will also provide an insight into the quality and caliber of maintenance staff, and into the amount of spare parts required in the maintenance function. If at some point in the future it is desired to go to a time and materials contract, or it is desired to perform one's own maintenance, a maintenance log of this type, properly filled in by the vendor, will provide valuable insight into the total costs involved.

6-64 Subcontract Restriction

The maintenance function is an important one, and the vendor should not have the right to subcontract it to any other organization. As a fall-back position, it can be stated that if the vendor elects to do so, the user should have the first opportunity to provide the subcontract service: in other words the user should have the right to terminate the maintenance contract and provide maintenance on his own or through his own contractors with all necessary support and assistance from the vendor, including spare parts access and training as indicated in clauses 6-60 and 6-61. Thus, the vendor's desire to subcontract can be dealt with on a basis which provides for termination by the user, and for the user taking over the maintenance function.

6-65 Engineering Changes

Most equipment, especially during its early life, is subjected to a fair number of engineering changes made by the manufacturer at his headquarters. In most cases such engineering changes are made for improvement in maintenance capability, for improvements in performance, or to correct defects. The user should have the absolute right to obtain all engineering changes at no cost, to assure that his equipment meets upgraded manufacturer standards. This right should be unconditional, regardless of disputes which the parties may have had, regardless of whether the system is purchased or rented, and regardless of whether the system is maintained by the user, the vendor, or a third party. Engineering changes should be made available to the user at no charge, and should be installed on the user's equipment in a proper operating fashion, immediately after their announcement.

6-66 Rights to Schedule Preventive Maintenance

Machines require periodic preventive maintenance, including cleaning, lubricating, or periodic inspection. The user should have the right to schedule this maintenance at a time convenient to its normal business operation, so that it does not interfere with the use of the equipment. Preventive maintenance should be performed by the vendor outside of the hours of normal operation, at a time agreed to by the user. In addition, the user should have the right to suspend preventive maintenance if the user feels that the time can be used more profitably by him if the user is prepared to accept the risk of increased unscheduled failure as a result of lack of preventive maintenance. The user should not exercise this option unless he is reasonably sure that the suspension of preventive maintenance will not significantly interfere with his normal operation. However, the right to suspend this maintenance function is one which the user should have. The vendor will usually insist on exculpation if the user's suspension of preventive maintenance causes machine malfunction.

6-67 User Right to Perform Maintenance Functions on Rental Contracts

In a purchase contract, maintenance is normally an on-going function subject to a separate contract or certainly subject to separate charges which can be clearly identified. The user can cancel this contract for nonperformance, or upon termination can undertake to maintain the equipment himself, which may result in economic benefits, or which may result in an improvement of the quality of maintenance. The user who rents equipment should have comparable rights to maintain his own equipment. Since rental normally includes maintenance charges, the user who elects to perform his own maintenance on a rental contract should be given a credit for the maintenance charges included in the rental. This should be contractually specified, and the maintenance charges credited in the event of such user election should be clearly delineated. In addition, the user should have the rights under clauses 6-60 and 6-61.

G. DELIVERY

Especially with new equipment, vendors have occasionally had difficulties in delivering components or entire systems. Thus the contract should provide some recourse for the user in the event the vendor fails to deliver one or more components of the system, fails to deliver the entire system, or fails to deliver a properly operating system. A functional approach is best since the vendor may deliver all but one component of a group without which the group may remain functionally useless. As a result, the stipulation of delivery dates should indicate which groups should be delivered together, which components are necessary to make a group operational, and for which components a delay in delivery will not be disruptive.

6-68   Delivery Dates by Component or Group

The list of hardware and software components is defined in clause 6-01. Attached to this list should be specific delivery dates. Delivery dates should normally be given within a range of, perhaps, ten days, since exact delivery dates are difficult to pinpoint and may depend on transportation availability and the like. In addition to defining hardware and software delivery by components, when components are used together in related groups, delivery dates of the entire group should be shown and the relationship established. If a group cannot function without specific components, these components should be isolated and their interdependency shown in the contract. If the group, for except one critical component, has been delivered, the entire group can be considered undelivered, because it will be functionally useless until complete.

6-69   Option for Early Delivery

In the event it is feasible and the user elects it, he may need an option to take early delivery of all or some of the components of a group to allow him to test. If early delivery is provided, the user should pay for those components, or pay at least the equivalent costs for the productive use obtained from such components. Early delivery of some components of a group for testing purposes may not constitute productive use. However, early delivery of a group used in a particular application will, and payment for those components should be made when they become functionally useful. In any case, the provisions for acceptance testing of the groups and the entire system should apply, so that if the vendor fails to deliver the remaining components of the system, the entire contract can be canceled and any payments made for early delivery can be refunded.

6-70 Right to Delay or Postpone Delivery

The user should have the unconditional right to delay delivery of all components for a definite period, such as 30 or 60 days, if for some reason he is not prepared to accept delivery on the stipulated date. In addition, the user should have the right to postpone the delivery of certain components or certain groups for a longer period. These rights should be defined based on the user's anticipated readiness, and on the length of time between contract signing and delivery. The longer that delivery takes, the longer should be the right of the user to postpone delivery.

6-71 Notice of Pending Delivery

The contract should stipulate that the vendor will give notice to the user of a pending shipment of components or of the entire system not later than 30 days before shipment, and on the day of shipment. In the case of the latter, such notice should carry inclusion of waybill numbers and transportation method, so that the user can anticipate delivery at his loading dock.

6-72 Irreparable Delays

A failure to deliver on the part of the vendor can be significant, if it extends for a long period of time. A delay of perhaps 30 days might not be significant, if the installation is not critical. However, under certain conditions a 30-day delay can be significant, while under other conditions a six-month delay might not be. As a result it is desirable to state in the contract when a delay gives rise to user damages and when a delivery delay becomes irreparable. Up to a point, the user can be compensated in liquidated damages for vendor delivery delay; after that point the user should have a cancellation option, with attendant damages.

6-73 Site Preparation Responsibility

The user is normally responsible for preparing a site for the installation which meets the requirements defined by the vendor. These requirements are partially defined in clauses 6-16, 6-17 and 6-18 in terms of power, ambient environment and cabling needs of the system. In addition, the site probably will require a false floor for cable connections and may require additional facilities, shelving, library equipment, safety equipment, fire protection equipment, entry control devices, other security elements, and the like. It is appropriate to identify the site responsibility of the user and to stipulate what must be done, and when. This will prevent the vendor from claiming that the user has prepared the site improperly, as an excuse for a delay in delivery.

6-74 Installation Responsibility

The equipment arrives at the user's receiving platform crated and packed in various forms. The equipment needs to be moved to the site, located properly, unpacked, uncrated, assembled, and brought up to operating condition. This must be the responsibility of the vendor, and if the vendor charges for this service, such charges should be stipulated as in clause 6-38. The responsibility and the time required for commissioning the equipment from receipt to turnover ready for use should be stated in the contract. Also note "Acceptance Testing," clause 6-51.

6-75 Risk of Loss Prior to Installation

Normally the vendor carries insurance on the equipment until it reaches the user's site. If it is a purchase transaction, the user is responsible for carrying such insurance as is necessary to guard its property. Most contracts will provide, however, that title to the equipment does not pass to the user until payment is made. As a result, there may be a period when the system is uninsured. If the contract is silent, some legal doctrines state that the user, as possessor under a contract to buy, will be responsible for loss or damage to the equipment; moreover, absent specific arrangements, the user's insurer may decline liability for loss based on nonownership. Risk of loss during this period must, thus, be covered by the contract and should be placed on the vendor, who can extend his insurance coverage in the installation period, prior to payment and title transfer. A basic clause will place the loss risk with the holder of title, which is the vendor until completion of the final acceptance test.

6-76 Right to Cancel Components Prior to Delivery

The user should have the right to cancel components until some point prior to delivery. Typically that is the point at which first notification of shipment is made by the vendor, which may be from 30 to 90 days prior to delivery. Prior to this notification the user should have the right to cancel components, if the user deems, in its sole discretion, that these components are not required to satisfy his functional needs. The vendor, of course, will usually seek contractual protection against user use of this release clause to escape from the entire contract.

6-77 Substitution of Components Prior to Delivery

As in clause 6-76, the user should have rights to substitute components prior to delivery, if the user determines that a substitute component is better suited to satisfy his needs. The right of substitution should be available to the user to the point of shipment. In a purchase contract though, a possible delay in delivery of the substituted component may have to be tolerated. To protect the vendor, substitution may have to include a provision which states that the substituted component shall be substantially equivalent in value, function, or capability.

H. RIGHTS AND OPTIONS

There are a variety of rights and options which can be extended to the user in a hardware purchase or rental contract. One condition of a rental contract normally is a purchase option, covered below. However, when a purchase option is exercised by a rental contract user, all terms of a purchase contract must come into being. The terms in a rental contract which do not apply in a purchase contract are the purchase option, the amount of rental credit appropriate thereto, and the protection of the purchase price, covered in clauses 6-86, 6-87 and 6-88.

6-78   Unrestricted Use and Function

The user is purchasing or renting a machine for his own use. The user should thus have the absolutely unrestricted right to use that machine for any function he deems appropriate. This function may be irregular or illegal, but in no event should the vendor have the right to control it. The user, by implication, holds the vendor harmless from any machine function which contravenes public policy, laws, or common morality.

The user may further elect to use the equipment in direct competition with the vendor, selling machine time, or selling the machine or its components to other users without restriction, regardless of whether such sales are made at cost, below cost or above cost, and regardless of whether such sales are made with the intention of making a profit or with the intention of competing with the vendor. In other words the user should contract for the absolute right to use his property for his own purposes, however he may define those purposes.

6-79   Unrestricted Location

In addition to unrestricted use (clause 6-78), the user should also have the right to have his equipment at any location he deems desirable. If this location is far removed from an appropriate vendor maintenance facility, the vendor response time for maintenance must be lengthened. However, the user may elect to transfer his machine to a division, branch, or subsidiary located in a foreign country, for example. In this event, a revision of the maintenance contract may also be needed, since maintenance rates in different locations sometimes differ.

6-80   The Right to Make Changes and Attachments

The user is the owner of the equipment, even though the vendor has the responsibility for its maintenance. This means that the user should have the right to make changes and attachments, subject to the vendor's right to object *only* if such changes and attachments will prevent the vendor from carrying out his responsibility in maintaining the equipment in good working order, to the reliability standards. If the equipment is rented, title to the system belongs to the vendor and not to the user. In this case, any changes and attachments probably will require the user to replace or correct any changes prior to returning the system to its rightful owner, the vendor. Most vendors provide policy statements or documentation on allowable changes and attachments. If such rights are documented, they should be appended to the contract or incorporated by reference.

6-81   Interface with Equipment of Other Manufacturers

Clause 6-10 defines interface specifications and the ability of the system to connect known components of other manufacturers, and known data communications equipment. The right to make this connection is granted in a separate clause. The user should have the right to connect his equipment to equipment of other manufacturers or supplied by a recognized telephone or data communications company, without restriction, and the vendor should agree to make available the interface specifications defined in clause 6-10.

6-82   Right to Upgrade Hardware

If it is possible to alter or change hardware during the term of the contract, the user should have the right to upgrade, at defined values. If, for example, it is possible to change from a low-speed to a high-speed printer by paying the difference, the vendor should grant the user the right to do so, at the price difference then in effect. This right should be bargained for both in terms of purchased and leased equipment. In case of a short-term rental system this is no problem, since at the expiration of the term any component can be canceled, and new components delivered to coincide with such cancellation. In a purchased system the component may not be capable of modification in the field (see clause 6-11), in which case a new component may have to be purchased. In this event, trade-in values for the old component, or a differential price for the new component, should be stated in the contract.

6-83   Software Upgrade

Upgrading software is somewhat more difficult than upgrading hardware. For one thing, the user should have the right to acquire all upgrades made by the vendor, at prices in effect for such upgrades. If the software is supplied free, then any enhancement made to that software should be supplied at no further charge to the user, for the life of the system. If the software is charged on a rental basis, then the user should have the right to substitute when enhanced software becomes available, or when the user decides to upgrade or downgrade software requirements as a result of experience or analysis. If the software has been paid for in a lump sum, and a perpetual license for its use has been granted, then the user should have the right to obtain revised or enhanced versions for a differential cost. In this case, trade-in value is a moot point since no physical property is worn out; a differential price should be established for any upgrade, which can be done by crediting any payments made to the cost at which the software is made available to other customers at that point in time.

6-84   Hardware Trade-in

If the user upgrades the machine and obtains a new system from the vendor, it is highly desirable to trade-in the old equipment against the purchase of the new equipment. This is potentially negotiable when the new equipment is selected. There is leverage at trade-in time which allows the user to negotiate a high trade-in value with the vendor of his choice. However, when upgrading the system, the installed vendor has an advantage, and may have a partial "lock" on the user installation. This "lock" includes the cost of conversion of the programs, which may not be necessary except for competitive vendors. As a result, the leverage for negotiating trade-in values is reduced if the original vendor considers himself in a privileged situation. It is therefore recommended that trade-in values be established at the time of initial contract signing, when a trade-in schedule can be established and included as a part of the contracting document. Nothing in the contract will prevent the user from increasing this trade-in value by negotiation, if appropriate at the time of trade-in.

The user should also attempt to negotiate an absolute right to resell the equipment to the vendor at scheduled prices. If the user decides to sell his equipment, whether upgrading it or not, this clause assures him that the equipment can be sold to the vendor. Such assurance can be helpful in calculating depreciation rates, in determining book values, and in doing an acquisition method analysis at the time of purchase. It is also helpful in negotiating the sale of the equipment to a third party, if the user decides to sell it on the used equipment market. It is similar to the "blue-book" value used for previously-owned automobiles, which provides a wholesale price at which an automobile can be sold. Obviously, the repurchase values will be lower than the trade-in values. Vendor resistance will be greater to a repurchase obligation than to a trade-in deal.

6-85   Title Transfer

In a purchase contract, completion of the contract is established by the completion of the purchase transaction, the delivery of the goods, and the transfer of funds, after which title passes. Title transfer in a computer purchase should pass *upon acceptance* by the user, that is, upon satisfactory performance of the acceptance test defined in clause 6-51. The contract should define the point when title passes, because some rights and responsibility of ownership pass with title, and the insurance responsibilities devolve upon the user at that time.

6-86   Purchase Option

This clause applies strictly to a rental contract in which a vendor often gives the user the right to purchase the installed system within a given period of time. This right seems to give the user an opportunity to try the system prior to committing himself to purchase. The choice between a long-term lease and a purchase, in fact, is generally based on financial statement and cost of money considerations. No lease of substantial hardware, with a purchase option, should be thought of as a trial period since the investment associated with installing the equipment is so high that even in a trial failure the minimum period during which the system has to be retained would run several years. If the user executes a rental contract with a purchase option, the terms under which the purchase option can be exercised, the time period for which it extends, and the method of exercise of the option can be defined in the contract.

6-87   Rental Credit

If a purchase option is exercised (clause 6-86), the user should obtain the benefit of a partial rebate or reduction of the purchase price as a result of rental payments made to the date of exercise of the purchase option. The amount of purchase price credit for each rental payment should be stipulated in the contract. Payment of the difference constitutes the purchase of the system and its title transfer. All other provisions of a carefully drawn purchase contract must be included in a purchase option including trade-in, separate maintenance provisions, and the like, and must be negotiated prior to signing the original rental contract.

6-88   Protection of Purchase Price Under Purchase Option

The purchase option to be exercised should provide for a purchase price, equal to the original purchase price minus any rental credits obtained. The purchase price should be firm and not subject to escalation, since the system is already installed. Thus, the purchase price should be equal to the price in effect on the *date of installation or the date of contract signing*, and not the price in effect on the date of exercise of the purchase option, unless that price is lower.

6-89   Availability of Expansion Units

If the user decides to expand his system by adding components, peripheral equipment, or subassemblies, the user should have the right to acquire those expansion units from the vendor from which he purchased the original system. This means that the vendor must undertake to continue to manufacture such expansion units. This provision should probably be limited in time, or by the vendor's capability to undertake continuing manufacture of expansion components or to provide them from equipment returned by other users. The user's right to obtain expansion equipment should be defined in the contract, at prices protected as indicated in clause 6-42.

6-90   Alternate Sources of Supply

If the vendor is unwilling to guarantee the availability of expansion units, or if the expansion units are available for only a short period of time, it may be desirable to include in the contract a list of acceptable alternate sources of supply for such components, peripheral units, or spares. As to sources of supply, the vendor should represent that they furnish an acceptable product which meets the specifications of the vendor and which can act as equivalent substitution components for those manufactured by the vendor, if the vendor elects to stop manufacturing them. Of course, the vendor cannot guarantee that these alternate sources will not dry up; the user, accordingly, should make his own investigation.

I.   DAMAGES

Aside from contractual remedies defined in Appendix A for breach of specific clauses, in a hardware contract it is probably desirable to identify the damages which the user will suffer if the contract is not completed on schedule, or not at all. This will require a summary of the user's costs, the loss of savings incurred as a result of a delay, and the alternate costs which the user may have to incur to change his source of supply of the equipment included in the contract. Damages clauses are traditionally the most difficult to negotiate.

6-91   Damages Incurred if Contract Terminated Prior to Delivery

If the contract is terminated prior to scheduled delivery, whether by breach, by user dissatisfaction or other circumstances, the user will have incurred costs related to the time elapsed since the signing of the contract, and presumably proportionate to the effort involved in completion of the development activities. In addition, the user may have lost savings proportionate to the amount of time elapsed from the point of contract signing to its termination.

In general it is possible to reasonably estimate the magnitude of these costs and losses and to provide a clause in the contract which states that if the contract is terminated through breach on the part of the vendor, then the user shall be entitled to recover specific damages. These can be defined as a certain amount for each month that the user was engaged in developing materials for the use of this equipment, and a specific amount relative to the loss of time which incurred a loss of saving.

6-92   Failure to Deliver

In the event the vendor fails to meet the scheduled delivery date, by failing to deliver components of the system when scheduled or needed, the damages caused may be more significant. In this case the user has probably completed his development efforts, and is prepared to begin operation using the new equipment. The user will have obtained operational personnel, and operation facility, space, and supplies, all of which may involve continuing losses from the scheduled delivery date until the system, or a substitute system, is put into operation. Thus a delay beyond the scheduled delivery period includes the user's costs in preparation, and the loss of savings proportionate to the amount of time lost and the costs of operational staff and provisions obtained in anticipation of delivery.

6-93   Liquidation of Damages

As an alternative to termination, it may be possible to assess specific liquidated damages for delays. These amounts can be established by negotiation, but should be sufficiently significant to provide an incentive for the vendor not to fail, and to provide compensation to the user if a problem does occur. If the vendor is not financially responsible, or his financial statement does not provide sufficient reassurance, such liquidated damage provisions can be supported by the posting of a performance bond, which is properly guaranteed by an insurance company, or by a parent company of a subsidiary vendor.

6-94   User Costs

To support claims for specific liquidated damages in court, in arbitration, or simply in negotiation with the vendor, it is probably desirable to delineate in the contract all user costs. This delineation should be done irrespective of whether specific damages are assessed, since it will serve to identify the costs incurred by the user in completing his contract responsibility. These are costs of development, programming, site preparation, testing, installation, systems integration, and potential user savings. This provides a point of departure for negotiation, in the event of a contractual breach or termination, where specific damages have not been agreed to. Where they have, the delineation can be important in a courtroom in order to convince a judge that the liquidated damages agreed to were not a "penalty" (which the law will not enforce) but a reasonable estimate of the user's loss under circumstances where the actual precise dollar loss is difficult to compute exactly. See chapter 4 for a discussion of the difference between penalties and liquidated damages.

7
SOFTWARE PACKAGE CONTRACTS

A. INTRODUCTION

The sale of software packages represents one of the most rapidly growing sectors of the computer industry market place, and involves the sale of essentially "intangible" assets. The "hard" products involved—paper, tape, or metal—are insignificant to the transaction; the significance attaches to the ideas, methods and processes embodied in the package. Conceptually, a software package sale is a license from one party to another to use a secret, proprietary process. Transactions like this are rare in commercial contracting history. There is also no tradition which governs the manner in which the transfer of a software package from one party to another should be performed, or implies certain types of quality or quantity standards. As a result a software package contract must be a tightly drawn, often unique document, which insures that both parties are reasonably protected.

Furthermore, software packages are often sold by small undercapitalized organizations. They often have a significant investment of scarce capital in the development of the package, without knowing whether or not they will earn a significant return on it. Thus they may be inherently unstable organizations, which will not attain economic stability until they reach the "critical mass" of sales for their package. Caution must be taken in contracting with undercapitalized organizations because the risks of bankruptcy or business termination are perhaps more significant than with hardware manufacturers. Even where business termination does not occur, the user may find itself unable to enforce warranties and obligations on the part of the vendor to service, maintain and upgrade the program because of the vendor's lack of funds.

A software package is generally not truly sold, since a sale involves a transfer of title. Therefore a software package normally is licensed for use. If it is on a rental basis, a charge is made for each month that the package is in use. An alternate method of procurement of the package is on the basis of a single payment, for which a *perpetual* (or a fixed term) license to use the package is issued. In either case, however, the user winds up with the rights to use the package, and not with title or ownership. This, as well as the fact that the package may not qualify as "goods", makes applicability of the Uniform Commercial Code a questionable factor, although UCC compliance can be written into the contract.

Software is also made available by hardware vendors, and it is often necessary to sign a software package agreement with a hardware vendor, who may be financially more substantial than an independent software vendor. In that case, some of the terms outlined below may not be necessary, or may be covered as part of a separate hardware contract. As an alternative, a master contract is drawn with the vendor, which provides for the procurement of software packages and hardware components. To insure the broadest possible coverage in this text, it is assumed that a software package is obtained from an *independent* vendor, whose resources may not be sufficient at all times to cover the contract.

The "sale" of a package represents incremental profits to the vendor selling it. In other words, there is no additional "manufacturing" cost. As a result the vendor's willingness to negotiate may be greater than the vendor of a hardware product, which still requires manufacturing after the contract is signed. This leverage should be used with caution, since it can backfire. However, the contract terms given below are not onerous in most cases.

Major risks inherent in a software package contract are as follows:

1. Nonperformance. If the package fails to meet its specifications, fails to perform effectively, uses far more hardware facility than anticipated, absorbs more run time than expected, or has any results other than those which the user expected, the package may not be usable. In that case the contract should provide for termination, since only successful results should be considered acceptable performance.

2. Cost of modification or integration. It is sometimes not possible to use a package instantly in the form in which it is provided. In many cases modification is required to adapt it to the requirements of the organization, or to the peculiarities inherent in the business. A payroll package may have to be adapted to take care of local taxation or special deductions which the company may encourage. A banking package may have to be modified to include the different service charges which the bank makes. Such modification can be quite costly and sometimes difficult to integrate into an unfamiliar package. As a result, some provision in the contract should be made for assistance with such modification at reasonable, established rates.

3. Bankruptcy of the vendor. The undercapitalization of the typical independent software organization does suggest from time to time that business termination is a possibility. This has been demonstrated in previous recessions, when the fallout of software companies was significant. As a result some provision for continuing possession, right to maintain and right to modify should be included in any software contract, all of which should accede to the user in the event of business termination, without penalties, charges or obligation.

4. Infringement. It is sometimes difficult to trace the title of a software package, since such titles are not recorded anywhere. The original ownership of a package is not always clear, and the source from which the package has

been derived is not always identified. Accordingly, some guarantee has to be given of ownership, and a comprehensive infringement indemnification must be provided to the user.

The pertinent clauses associated with a software package contract have been divided into four categories: performance, financial, installation support, and warranties.

B. PERFORMANCE

7-01   Specifications

Clearly one of the most important clauses in a software contract specifies the package in terms of functions and capabilities. These specifications can be drawn by the user, but more than likely they will be extracted entirely from the publications and sales literature of the vendor organization. It is the information supplied by the vendor which has attracted the user, and it is the information defined in sales or technical literature which has caused the selection of this package. It is these specifications which must be incorporated as part of the contract. This can be done by incorporating by reference the manuals, requisite documentation and sales literature associated with the package, or by writing a separate set of specifications which intrinsically meet the user's requirements. Compatibility with the user's systems is important as well.

In some cases the package has to be modified prior to its actual operation. In that case a clear statement must be made in the specifications that upon modification, whether such modification is performed by the user or vendor, the package will perform in accordance with the specifications and will meet the functional requirements of the user as stated. It is extremely important that the software package meet the user's need. Failure to meet user need should be a breach of contract.

7-02   Definition of Documentation

The total documentation to be supplied by the vendor to the user must be defined, so that the user can perform the necessary acceptance tests, not only on the package but on the documentation as well. It is generally a good idea to regard documentation as an integral part of the package, so that a definition of the documentation is a part of the specification of the total package.

7-03   Availability of Future Documentation

Documentation is changed, upgraded, improved, or added to a package, without changing the basic functions of the package. In some cases, as the package becomes more successful, the form of the documentation is improved to make it more saleable and more readable. In other cases documentation may be expanded as a function of requirements indicated by a growing body of users. In any event, the future documentation should be as available to the user of a software package as the documentation in existence at the time the package is transferred, regardless of whether the user has made a single payment or is making continuing payments for the package. Thus, this requires a statement in the contract that future documentation will be available whenever it is made available to other users of the package.

7-04   The Right to Reproduce Documentation

In most cases documentation for the package is copyrighted, and therefore reproduction is prohibited. A user who has paid a license fee for the use of the package should be entitled to reproduce the documentation, provided that the documentation is not used outside his organization, of course. As a result, a right to reproduce the documentation exclusively for use within the organization is a reasonable clause to include in a typical software package contract; it is often tempered by a limitation on the number of copies that can be made. Incidentally, many software packages are licensed not on a company-wide basis, but on an installation-by-installation basis. If a user wants the right to use such a package on all his computer installations, he will find himself involved in complex price negotiations.

7-05   Rights to Future Options

In essence, some form of "most favored nations" clause is required. In this case a "favored nations" clause must relate the right to purchase or obtain future options or changes to the package at the same price as future users. A distinction is made here between options and potential enhancements or upgrades, which may not affect the function of the package but only improve its performance. When an enhancement is made which affects the function of the package, by expanding it or by providing additional options, a charge is probably made, and that charge should be equal to the one charged all users. If, however, a package is upgraded to improve the efficiency of its operation without changing the function, then a charge should not be made, nor should a charge be made when an error is corrected (see clause 7-02). An inefficient operation is normally deemed to be similar to an error, and upgrades of this type should be provided by the vendor without cost. These are covered under separate clauses, however.

7-06   Run Time

It is important that a constraint be placed on the amount of machine time usurped by the package. It is reasonable to indicate in a specification that a package will provide certain functions, such as a payroll, or a utility function such as a sort. However, if the package performance usurps the entire machine for 24 hours a day, it is clearly not an effective or usable package, and it is clearly not in the interest of the user to purchase it, given this fact. To insure that the user is protected from a package which usurps excessive machine costs, a statement should be included in the contract that the total run time to perform the functions at stated volumes will not exceed a given amount. The contract can be canceled if the package fails to live up to this part of its performance specification.

7-07   Facility Requirements

Time is not the only variable which a package can usurp. Software uses other facilities, and constraints on these must likewise be established. These include input preparation needs, and constraints on core size or peripheral equipment usage. It is clear that if a package required a five million character core storage machine, a user with only a half million character machine would not be capable of using the package efficiently, if at all. The user should again be protected if facility usage exceeds expectations, as defined in a solid contract.

7-08 Error Correction

Software does contain programming errors, which will be discovered gradually through extensive use. It is not uncommon to detect errors in a software system two to three years after its initial use. This is due to the fact that unusual combinations of circumstances in the input data might occur infrequently. Some might only occur once a year, or once every two years, and when they do occur, errors may emerge. It is the responsibility of the supplier of the software package to correct such errors. If an other using organization finds an error, it is equally the responsibility of the supplying organization to disseminate the "fix" made to the package to all users of that package, so that the same problem will not reoccur.

7-09 Upgrades

Corrections are made to the package to improve the quality or efficiency of its performance. Such corrections should be made available to all users at no further cost. See the discussion under clause 7-05 above.

7-10 Source Availability and Access

A software package is delivered in machine language for ease of installation and use. Normally the software supplier has developed the package in a source language different from the object machine language. This source language is used for maintenance purposes, and is also needed for significant modifications to the package. Most software suppliers are reluctant to make this source language program available to users, because they could then make changes to the source which would affect the object programs in use. This would make it extraordinarily difficult for the supplying organization to maintain the programs. If a correction were made by the vendor to fix an error, and that portion of the program had been significantly amended by one user, that user might not be able to readily incorporate the correction into his program. In this case the using organization might try to hold the vendor responsible despite the fact that it was user access to the source which caused this problem. As a result, the source programs are normally kept by the vendor and given to the user only after the warranties expire or are waived by the user. The contract should provide for the availability of the source after the warranty has expired.

7-11 Escrow of Source Programs

The contract clause (7-10) which provides availability of source programs when warranties are terminated is an acceptable clause, unless the software organization goes bankrupt prior to the expiration of the warranty. In that event the creditors might well seize the assets of the vendor, including the source which could prevent the using organization from obtaining it when they are entitled to it. One solution developed by an inventive software specialist (Larry

Welke) is to provide an escrow account, where source programs are retained by an independent escrow agent, who will release them at a designated point in time, upon the bankruptcy of the vendor, or after some other designated event.

Currently, International Computer Programs Inc., of Indianapolis, Indiana will act as an escrow agent for any software seller. This arrangement could be highly practicable and will provide a guarantee of access to the source data from the viewpoint of the user, in any eventuality. If there is a dispute, the escrow agent holding the source may agree to act as an arbitrator in the dispute and determine whether or not the source should be released.

7-12   The Right to Modify

The user has paid for a software package, and to all intents and purposes it is his to do with as he pleases, provided that he does not resell it in competition with the vendor or violate the vendor's requirements of secrecy. This right of use should extend to the right to modify the package, although in that event the vendor may well insist on a waiver of maintenance. The vendor cannot be expected to maintain a package that has been modified by the user. On the other hand, the vendor may be willing to agree to continue maintenance of the package provided that any additional costs incurred in integrating main-tenance changes with the modifications made by the user shall be done at the expense of the user. This is a fair way to compensate a vendor for any additional costs incurred as a result of modifications made by the user. However, the user should have the absolute right to modify the package without constraint above that.

7-13   Compliance with Standards

In chapter 5 a contract clause was set forth which required compliance with standards established by ANSI, or by such organizations as Underwriter Laboratories (clause 5-21). In addition, there are installation standards to be complied with in data processing for software packages or development projects. The installation may have standards relating to programming lan-guage, to installation or operating practices, or to good programming practices. It is desirable to provide the vending organization with a copy of the user stan-dards manual so that the vendor can determine whether or not the software package generally complies with user standards. If it does, a statement of com-pliance with installation standards should be included in the contract, because it also protects the user with respect to future changes. If the package does not comply then it is desirable to identify the extent that it does, and to list those areas where noncompliance exists. Alternatively, if the vendor has a standards manual which has been used in the construction of the package, it can be incorporated by reference, and given to the user as well.

C. FINANCIAL

Since the financial responsibility of software organizations can be questioned at times, financial terms in the contract relate to the user's responsibility to make payments, to the financial responsibility of the software organization, and its ability to stand behind its performance commitments. The following clauses are suggested:

7-14   Charges by Type

All charges incurred by the user should be defined in a single location in the contract. The most obvious charge is the cost of the package, or the monthly license fee. However, there could be other charges which might be incurred, including support, machine time necessary for the vending organization to test and install the system, and/or expenses incurred for travel, subsistence or reproduction of documentation. The clause which defines these charges should limit them to those identified within the clause. Thus, no special charges, taxes or other burdens can be imposed on the user by a software organization in connection with the sale of a package, unless those charges have been identified at the beginning, and are incorporated in the contract.

7-15   Payment Terms

The timing of payments made for a software package has to be fairly carefully constructed. If the package is complete and ready to be installed, then payment of a part of the purchase price can be made at the time that a copy of the package programs and their documentation is delivered to the organization. The remainder can be paid after a successful installation and acceptance, with perhaps a small hold-back during the warranty period. Thus a suggested payment schedule might be:

25% upon delivery of the documentation and a copy of the package
25% upon installation and successful operation on the user's site
25% upon acceptance by the user, or not later than 30 days after installation
and the remainder after expiration of the warranty period or the expiration of the free maintenance.

Normally it is not desirable to make any advance payments to a software organization, unless these payments are collateralized by some product or deliverable.

If the package has not yet been completed, however, and delivery is scheduled into the future, some small down payment is desirable to bind the contract and to provide consideration for its execution. This should not be a large amount, since if the software organization fails to deliver the package on time, or goes out of business as a result of underestimating the cost of package development, this advance payment probably will not be recoverable. If that is indeed anticipated, it may be desirable to make advance payments to an escrow account for release to the software organization after package delivery, or for return to the user if the package is not delivered within 30 days from the scheduled date.

If payment terms are carefully drafted it may not be necessary to write a separate damage clause for failure to deliver. This assumes, of course, that the user has not incurred damages as a result of the failure to deliver. Whether or not the user will incur measurable damages from nondelivery, it is wise to have a liquidated damages provision covering nondelivery, to avoid the necessity of proving damages. The liquidated amount should be negotiated based on the foreseeable loss. If no specific loss can be foreseen, a liquidated damages clause calling for 10 to 15% of the contract price will probably be held reasonable.

7-16   Term of License

A software package may be obtained in perpetuity, which is equivalent to an outright purchase of the use of the package. If the package is rented, however, then the term must be stipulated, and renewal provisions defined. An initial term may be for a minimum of one or two years, in consideration of monthly rental payments. Upon expiration of the initial term, the user may have the right to renew it—possibly in perpetuity, or perhaps for one year at a time. Alternatively there may be a three-month trial period, during which the user is entitled to use the package on a monthly rental basis, after which he must elect to purchase it in perpetuity or for a long-term license. The variety of alternative terms of licenses is enormous, and bounded only by the imagination of the user. In a rental contract, consideration should also be given to credits for rental payments against a future purchase.

If the term of the license is for a finite period, beware of automatic renewal provisions. The contract should provide that the vendor must give notice of impending renewal so that the user can then decide whether or not to renew. Some states have made automatic renewal provisions unenforceable against users, unless the vendor gives prior notice to the user that renewal is coming up, so that the user can avail itself of the right to elect not to renew.

7-17   Nontaxable as Property

There have been a fair number of controversies in the data processing industry with regard to personal property taxation of software packages. The user should protect himself from eventual taxation, by noting in the contract that the package will not be subject to property taxes, or if it is ultimately subject to property taxes, that such taxes shall be borne by the rightful owner, the vendor. In part this is self-serving in that it suggests nontaxability by agreement, which of course is not necessarily acceptable to the taxing authorities. In all events, the contract can define who will pay the taxes, if imposed.

7-18   Quiet Enjoyment

Much as the lessee of an apartment is protected from adverse interests through the use of a "quiet enjoyment" clause, so should the use of a software package be protected by a similar clause. The clause is merely a shorthand representation to the user that, so long as the user performs his side of the bargain, the vendor will protect the user against any adverse claims by others.

7-19   Rights Upon Business Termination

The *general* rights which a user should have in the event of termination of business by a vendor have been defined in chapter 5 (clause 5-02). In the event that a software package seller terminates business, it is desirable to negotiate perpetual use of the package without further obligation on the part of the user. If a vendor goes bankrupt, or commits an act of bankruptcy, from that point forward the user should have unlimited rights to use the package without further payment. The argument in favor of such a concept is that the user will be deprived of support and service by reason of the vendor's business cessation, and that since the vendor's receiver or bankruptcy trustee will not be in a position to furnish such support, all future payments should cease. If business termination occurs during a warranty period, the user's obligation to make a final payment should be proportional to the amount of time that the user has enjoyed the protection of the warranty, and a further hold-back might be considered as well, to provide for the cost of correcting future errors. It should not be difficult to negotiate extensive user rights in the event of bankruptcy or business termination, since presumably the vendor will care little about what happens thereafter. The user should be well protected from this eventuality, which has occurred altogether too often in the data processing industry.

7-20   Price Protection on License Fee

If the licensing fee is paid on a regular basis, and the contract is renewable, it is probably desirable (and equitable) to establish price protection for that fee for future renewal. After all, the development costs of the package have already been incurred, so that increases in cost need not be passed on to the end user. It is not unreasonable therefore to insure that the license fee declines or stays at the same level in perpetuity upon renewal. A purchase option credit might be included as well, to reduce future payments.

7-21   Price Protection on Other Charges

The vendor is entitled to charge for maintenance services after the warranty period, and potentially also for future enhancements or options. Some form of price protection is desirable for both categories if feasible.

It is possible to establish a maintenance rate which is equitable, and which can be held constant in perpetuity, or adjusted by no more than the annual increase in the cost of living index, as published by the Bureau of Labor Statistics. Alternatively, an annual maintenance rate can be established with an annual percentage increase deemed to be reasonable by both parties. In either case, a constraint is desirable to prevent monopolistic increases by a vendor who alone is capable of providing the necessary maintenance.

Price protection on other charges which the vendor may make is somewhat more difficult to establish. Package enhancements cannot be defined in advance, and future options cannot be priced at the present. As a result, price protection in these categories should be restricted only to a "favored nations" statement; that is, charges made to the user will not be more than charges made to other users for similar services.

Charges made for personnel for installation support or modification can be protected, by including them in the contract at the time of signing. Since these services will be performed within a reasonable time after the date of contract signing, there is no reason to provide for escalation of their prices.

7-22   Availability of Financial Statements

It is very often possible to determine the financial responsibility of the software package supplying organization through an examination of their financial statements, or through access to their Dun and Bradstreet rating. Financial statements give a good indication of the financial structure of the organization. A statement in the contract that quarterly corporate financial statements will be provided to the user organization is highly desirable, if feasible. If the software organization is public, it should not be difficult. If the software organization is private then it will be somewhat more difficult and subject to negotiation. In any event, it is probably desirable to append a copy of the *current* financial statement to the contract coupled with vendor's representation of its veracity. If the vendor, in the short-term, becomes financially insecure, the user may have the opportunity to hold back money on the basis (if correct) that the vendor misrepresented its financial condition. Moreover, seeing the financial statement will provide insight into the present financial status of the software organization and will thus provide the necessary information to enable the user to properly negotiate payment schedules against delivery of partial products.

D. INSTALLATION AND SUPPORT

A software package is rarely usable directly from the vendor, without the benefit of assistance in installation. Assistance will help in making the necessary modifications to fit the user's unique environment, or to adapt the package to operating system or peripheral equipment differences. Alternatively, minor changes may be required in the software package simply because of potential timing differences, or because of user operating practices. In any event, it is a good idea to always obtain a certain amount of installation assistance from the software package vendor, prior to acceptance of and full payment for the package.

7-23   Delivery

If the package is ready and in operation in another installation, which may well have been a criterion for selection, then there should be little problem in obtaining delivery of the package at a given time. In that event the user should attempt to have the contract provide that the vendor will install at any time the purchaser requests, upon 30 days notice. The user can then select the time when he is capable of providing the necessary manpower for the package installation or modification and vendor will have sufficient notice to enable him to properly schedule his personnel requirements. If, however, the package has recently been developed, and this is one of the initial installations, the delivery parameters will have to be more carefully defined. In this event it is perhaps better to treat the contract as a software development contract, and to adapt clauses taken from chapter 8.

7-24   Delivery Failure

If the contract has been correctly constructed with regard to payment terms (see clause 7-15), then the vendor's failure to deliver will not normally affect the user in a direct cash sense. In some instances, however, failure to deliver a package can cause a delay in implementation of other user systems elements, and could therefore be damaging. If such damages can be identified, and if there is a likelihood that delivery of the package could be delayed for any reasons other than force majeure (see clause 5-12), then some form of liquidated damage might be desirable as a remedy against delivery failure. A per day charge might be applied to a delay in delivery, which might be based upon the impact on the user's resource availability for installation.

7-25   Installation and Modification Assistance

The vendor should supply installation assistance to the point where the user is capable of operating the package on a self-sufficient basis. If it is a stand-alone package which operates without modification, then the installation assistance can be limited to including the package on the user's library system, and insuring that the package works effectively in the user's operating environment.

However, many packages are sold as packages but still require substantial modification to be adapted to the user's environment. This is especially true of applications packages, because of the varying business environments in which they are used. In these cases it is not uncommon to ask the vendor, who has the greatest experience with the package, to make the necessary modifications. If significant, these modifications can be treated as a software development contract, and detailed specifications for such modifications can be drawn. In this event, clauses 8-01 through 8-07 should be reviewed, for the preparation of detailed specifications and the establishment of a fixed price for the development activity. If the installation and modification is minor, however, it could be performed on a time and materials or per diem basis, in which case a rather simple statement of objectives could suffice, coupled with an agreed limitation on the assistance either in terms of number of days or number of dollars.

7-26   Support Requirements

There are some packages which will require on-going support from the vendor to make changes necessary as part of the routine operation of the package. Such support requirements should be rigorously defined, and either limited to a number of days or dollars, or done on a fixed price retainer or annual maintenance charge. The terms under which the support requirements are to be performed, the support objectives, and the method of payment should all be included within the contract and price protection for such additional efforts should be included as well (see clause 7-21). It should be noted, however, that business termination on the part of the vendor would deprive the user of on-going support requirements. Some contractual provision should be sought to protect against this eventuality (See 7-19).

User self-sufficiency is a desirable goal to be achieved, if there is any possibility that the vendor might not be available to continue its support assistance. Again the provision of financial statements (see clause 7-22) would be desirable in signaling early the possibility of financial troubles within the vendor organization. Another aid to self-sufficiency will be the availability of source code to the user (See 7-10).

7-27   Acceptance

The delivery of a software package is a one-time occurrence, after which the vendor is going to be interested in receiving full payment for that package, or in initiating the continuity of licensing payments. It is thus necessary to provide for *acceptance* of the package, insure that its installation has been properly performed, and that the results achieved from the package meet the requirements originally defined.

This requires an acceptance test. Normally, the parameters of an acceptance test are defined as part of the selection procedure under which the package was obtained. That is, certain selection criteria were established and the fact that the package met those criteria, at least in terms of stated specifications and sales literature, was the key factor in selection. The specifications should be attached to the contract so that acceptance can be measured against them.

Three questions must be answered by an appropriate acceptance test:

A. Does the package work according to the specifications, and is the documentation supplied exactly that which is defined as part of the specifications?
B. Does the package meet the requirements of the user, and does it meet the expectations established during selection?
C. Does the package work in the user environment, on user equipment, and in accordance with user standards and operating practices?

An acceptance test must be built which provides the answers to these questions. This test should be defined in the contract, and agreement of the vendor to the test must be obtained prior to signing of the contract. It should be noted that most vendors are interested only in answering the first question. However, a package that meets the specifications but does not perform in accordance with the user's expectations is useless, and a package that doesn't work (or works far too slowly) in the user's operating environment is equally useless. All three parts of the acceptance test must be defined in the contract and must be agreed to by both parties (See also clause 7-31 for performance guarantees).

7-28   Destruction on Termination

A package which is leased for a finite period of time does not belong to the user. It is the property of the vendor, and on expiration of the lease it must be returned to the vendor. Vendors generally insist on a contract clause stipulating that the user will return all copies of the package and its documentation to the vendor, *or* that the user has the right to certify to the vendor that all copies of the documentation and the package have been destroyed. This is for the protection of the vendor to insure that the package does not continue in use without appropriate lease payments, and to insure that the package does not wind up in the hands of an unauthorized user. It is wise for the user to abide by these agreements. If, by reason of the user's fault or negligence, the package should fall into the hands of an unauthorized user, or, worse, of a competitor, the liabilities could be severe. As a result, it is desirable to include this obligation in the contract. Although in a perpetual license there is generally no obligation to return the package, vendors will generally insist upon clauses protecting the package from unauthorized use or disclosure.

E.   WARRANTIES

There are certain warranties which the vendor must make to the user:

7-29   Guarantee of Ownership

Perhaps the most important warranty which a vendor of a software package must make is that he is in fact the owner of the package, that it has been developed or obtained by him, and that he has the absolute right to lease that package to the user. In addition, this clause would normally contain a "hold harmless" provision, indemnifying the user from any responsibility to third parties in the event there is a problem with respect to ownership of the package. An indemnity unfortunately is only as good as the indemnitor. If the package in fact is owned by someone other than the vendor, the user will be liable to the owner, even if the user is innocent. The vendor must reimburse the user for whatever the user has been forced to pay. If the vendor is bankrupt or financially unable to make good, the user will face a net loss. This is still another reason for carefully inspecting the financial responsibility of the vendor.

In structuring a "hold harmless" clause it is desirable to include an obligation on the part of the vendor to defend all actions, so that the user does not have the responsibility of first defending himself from attack, and later attempting to recover damages from the vendor under the "hold harmless" provision. The vendor is thus made responsible for defending all actions which in some way attack the ownership of the package, and in fact the vendor is the person in the best position to defend against such attack.

Perhaps the best form of protection against claims of infringement of ownership rights is a determination by the user of the origin of the package. If it can be determined that the package was developed by the vendor, and that, as a result, no one else has rights to that package, this will provide the best assurance that no outside attack on ownership will take place. If the vendor has obtained this package from a third party on some basis, it is desirable to examine the contractual relationship between the vendor and the third party to insure that the vendor does have the right and authority to license the user on a continuing basis.

7-30 Copyright, Patent or Proprietary Right Infringement

Much as the user must protect against potential questions relating to the title of the package (see clause 7-29), equal protection must be sought for the potential of copyright or patent infringement, implied through the *use* of the package. Under present copyright and patent law, the user of an infringing device is in many instances liable (with the manufacturer) for the infringement, and it is therefore possible for a copyright or patent owner to sue all of the users and the manufacturers. As a result, it is necessary for the user to obtain an indemnification or provision which guards against the possibility of copyright, trade secret or patent infringement. This again is a "hold harmless" clause which provides for defense in all actions, and which insures that the user is relatively free from worry in the event the package inadvertently infringes some patent, copyright or other proprietary right.

In any event, as the means of legal protection for software become more certain (see chapter 4), user uncertainty in this area should decrease.

7-31 Guarantee of Operation

The vendor should warrant that the package will perform in accordance with the specification for a period of time and on the user's installation, provided it is used in accordance with those specifications. This is the period of time during which the package is warranted unconditionally, and any corrections required to make the package operational in the user's installation, regardless of the cost, must be made by the vendor at no charge to the user.

7-32   Free Maintenance

During the period of warranty, the vendor should agree that all maintenance to be supplied will be at no charge, since the period of free maintenance and the period of warranty of continued operation are coterminous. After all, it is only logical in the context of a guarantee of operation that maintenance will be included. The performance warranty and free maintenance period should be long enough to allow the package to have been utilized under most normal operating conditions. The warranty period should commence after the acceptance test is completed.

7-33   Rescission Rights During Warranty

The contract should include the right to rescind it at any time during the warranty period if the package fails to perform. This extends the acceptance test period to cover the entire warranty period, and allows the user to reject the package at any time during that period. This may be a harsh provision from the viewpoint of the vendor, but if the package is relatively new and untried, it is probably desirable to negotiate the inclusion of this clause. It provides the user with considerable flexibility, if the user is capable of rescinding the agreement and obtaining recovery of all funds paid to that point. Normally, no other damages should be due to either party, since both have incurred expenses associated with the aborted installation, and neither have gained any benefit.

A rescission provision is highly desirable, but becomes practically inoperative in the event of business termination of the vendor. Although the contract can be rescinded both by agreement and under bankruptcy law, recovery of the funds is a more difficult problem, unless they have been placed in escrow in the first place. It is unlikely that a vendor would be willing to escrow *all* funds paid for a package until the expiration of a significant warranty period. Examination of the financials supplied by the organization selling the package (see clause 7-22) will determine how important the need is for an escrow.

7-34   Freedom of Use

The rights to use the package are usually restricted so that the user will not have the right to use it in installations other than his own, and possibly only in a single site, even though he may have multiple computer installations in his organization. This restriction is a logical one, since essentially a royalty payment is being made for use of the package, and this royalty payment would normally vary depending on the number of installations in which the package is used. As a result, user rights to the package are restricted, and the user is incapable of giving it to any other user, or selling it to any possible purchaser. These restrictions are normal and acceptable when licensing a software package. However, no other restrictions with respect to the user of the package should be considered acceptable. The package should be usable in any way that the user sees fit, whether or not the *output* of the package is sold, the package is used in conjunction with other packages or other systems belonging to the user, or the use is for some purpose of which the vendor disapproves. The use of the package should be unrestricted within the user's organization, on any application, in any manner desired by the user, at any time of day or night. Such unrestricted use should be defined in the contract, so that the vending organization has no opportunity to prevent the use of this package in any manner which the user deems desirable.

8
SOFTWARE DEVELOPMENT CONTRACTS

A. INTRODUCTION

The development of a series of programs by a vendor for a user can create perhaps more significant problems than those involved in the sale of software packages (see chapter 7). On a contractual basis, it is necessary to attempt to define exactly what is being purchased, even though perhaps neither buyer nor seller knows. In addition, it is necessary to define levels of quality in an area where quality standards have not been established, payment terms when it is difficult to define what costs are going to be incurred, and a variety of other constraints which may not be determined until halfway through the development process. As a result, a software development contract becomes an extremely difficult document to construct where judgment factors sometimes outweigh the actual constraints which can be placed in the contract.

Again, comments can be made about the viability of vendors in the computer field. Risks similar to those involved with software package vendors must indeed be considered in the selection of a vendor to develop software. Thus, caution is the watchword of the contract negotiator in dealing with a vendor whose financial strength or capability and experience is not well defined.

Software development covers a wide range of services, from the conception all the way to installation and implementation of a working system. Thus it involves activities covering systems analysis, programming and systems implementation. It may also involve data, media or file conversion, and, in some instances, the conversion of existing computer programs to a new system or new environment. Thus, software development projects can vary widely in terms of the nature of the project itself and in terms of the scope, type and extent of the outside services to be utilized. It, therefore, behooves the user to carefully define the process, the responsibilities of both parties in the process, and the product "deliverables" at each stage in the process.

The risks to be considered in the development of a software system are similar to those risks considered in chapter 7, and to some extent are more extensive:

1. Vendor Bankruptcy. The risks associated with vendor bankruptcy are comparable to those associated with bankruptcy of software package vendors (See chapter 7), but the consequences of vendor bankruptcy in the case of a software development program are somewhat more significant. Progress payments will probably have been made to the vendor, against deliverables of questionable value. In addition, the user is generally seriously in need of the system being developed since it is being tailored for him. In most cases the time frame of development is longer, so that the time loss associated with an untimely termination of the contract is perhaps far greater.

2. Progress Payments. The loss of progress payments is a possibility if a dispute develops in the course of the contract, or if the vendor terminates business in the course of the contract. Since progress payments can be significant during the contract, and since the size of software development contracts can be large, a fair amount of money is at risk against a questionable product, parts of which may be delivered from time to time.

3. Material Schedule Delay. Perhaps more so than in any other field, the development of software has been underestimated, both in terms of cost and in terms of time. If a fixed price software development contract is entered into, cost underestimation will not normally hurt the user, unless it happens to bankrupt the vendor. A poor schedule estimate will hurt the user in any event. A major risk associated with a software development contract is, therefore, a delay in delivery, and delivery delays have been common in software development contracts.

4. Excessive Resource Usage. In most development contracts part of the resources used are purchased by or belong to the user. The user may agree to supply machine time, for example, and the vendor through inexperience or underestimation may abuse this resource to an extent where it disrupts the user operation or creates excessive costs. Similarly, other resources may be supplied by the user, such as data entry personnel, additional programming staff, staff associated with conversion, test data preparation, and the like. All of these can be misused unless the contract includes a significant constraint on their use.

5. Quality of Product. It is difficult to establish quality standards for a system being developed. This is true whether the system is developed internally or externally. Unsatisfactory product quality will result in an ineffective operation. This is difficult to cover in a contract; it is possible only by defining standards of performance, and by defining methodological standards to be followed in the construction of the system and the programs. This is not necessarily a satisfactory solution, although an effort must be made to establish realistic quality standards if the contract is to have meaning.

6. Staffing. A combination of the above factors leads to an examination of project staffing as a potential risk. Employees of the software developing organization should be full-time, and should be assigned on a full-time basis to the project. The caliber and quality of staff should be known, and the staff should execute some form of nondisclosure and noncompetition agreements. Resumes should be provided for members of the staff and in case of vendor business termination, staff should be available to assist in the take-over of the project by user personnel.

7. Retaining Economic Advantage. The user, in a software development frame-work, is sometimes seeking to obtain a significant advantage in efficiency or automation over his competitors. For example, an industrial user who can automate a manufacturing process can achieve an impressive competitive cost advantage over his nonautomated competitors; so can, say, the first department store chain that uses cash register terminals to maintain constant inventory figures or the first bank to offer bank statements showing sequentially numbered checks. Systems like those can be enormously expensive to design and put into practice. If the first user does not protect itself, the independent software developer can install the same system for a competitor, at a far lower cost by "piggy-backing" on the experience gained in the first development project. This problem is not solved by contractual provisions declaring that the developed system is the sole property of the user, nor even by requiring the developer to turn over all documentation in its possession to the user—the know-how and field experience gained by the developer stays with it, even outside the documentation. Appropriate development can be reestablished for a competitor at a far lower price.

The only solution is to negotiate a restrictive covenant prohibiting the vendor and its staff from taking on a development project of a similar character with any competitor for a specified period of time. A quite different solution is sometimes arrived at generally when the software developed is not highly proprietary and involves only elements of data processing efficiency. In this case, the vendor is permitted to develop and market similar products to others (either including or excluding direct competitors) on a joint venture or royalty basis at an agreed division of receipts or profits. Normally, it will be quite easy for a user to obtain vendor agreement to one or another of these restrictions, since vendors in soft-ware development are generally in great need of business and are willing to agree to most anything in order to get a big contract.

A number of clauses from chapter 7 apply to the software development contract, and are not repeated in this chapter. The user is responsible for reviewing the following clauses relating to software development and determining which are appropriate for inclusion and to what extent modifications may be required.

The following clauses are applicable, and have been modified and included separately in chapter 8 as well:

7-01 Specifications (clauses 8-01, 8-05)
7-13 Compliance with Installation Standards (clauses 8-03, 8-08)
7-14 Charges (clause 8-10)
7-15 Payment Terms (clause 8-11)
7-19 Business Termination Rights (clause 8-19)
7-27 Acceptance Method (clause 8-14)

The following clauses could be adopted directly and should be reviewed for their applicability:

7-02 Definition of Documentation
7-06 Run Time Requirements of the Finished Product
7-07 Facility Requirements of the Finished Product
7-08 Fixes and Error Correction
7-12 Rights to Modify
7-17 Nontaxable as Property
7-18 Quiet Enjoyment
7-21 Price Protection on Maintenance and Enhancements

B. PERFORMANCE

A key risk in having a software system developed by an independent contractor is the risk associated with getting a product which does not satisfy the requirements of the user. In this event, the contractor has spent considerable effort and money, and it is impossible to simply rescind the agreement and obtain a refund. In the case of a product, such as a software package, a money-back guarantee is feasible, and can be incorporated in the contract, since the product is not custom-made.

In the case of a custom-made product, acceptance becomes a more difficult problem, because complete rejection is generally unfair to the contractor and almost always impossible. Thus *the entire process* associated with software development must be monitored carefully, and the performance characteristics of the product checked carefully at each intermediate stage as well as at completion. This process will insure that rejection, if necessary, will come at the earliest possible moment.

8-01 Definition of Project Stages

As a first step in developing a quality standard, and a framework under which the development is to take place, the stages of the development process should be clearly defined. It is recommended that in the contract the actual phases of the systems development process be stated, and that each phase be further divided into appropriate tasks or steps. This allows agreement on the exact stages of the project, and allows both parties the opportunity to review the project at each stage, to determine the extent of its completion, to evaluate the quality of the product to that point, and to terminate the project if that quality is unacceptable. Figure 8-1 provides an example of a phase and task list of a software development project.

8-02 Project Deliverables

A software development project may require months or years to complete. During that period, the software vendor normally requires progress payments, if only to fund his payroll costs and other expenses. It is therefore desirable for the user to receive some evidence of continuing effort, and to obtain work products which could be used in the event of contract termination. Thus it is suggested that if progress payments are to be made in a software development contract that they be *exchanged* for work product which represents comparable value at each stage of the contract.

Phase and Task I.D.	Phase/Task Description	Product	% Completion
Preliminary	1. Develop preliminary project plan and schedule for Phase I 2. Management review and approval 3. Assign staff, review plan and schedule		
A.	Problem Analysis and Definition		
1.	Schedule and perform initial data gathering —interviews —observation of operations —documentation collection —questionnaires —research		
2.	Perform initial data analysis —identify and verify problems —determine organizations' information and data needs —determine scope or requirements, limitations and constraints		
3.	Prepare Design Requirements Statement (DRS).	Design Requirements Statement	
4.	Presentation of DRS to Management		
5.	Management review and direction/approval		
6.	Identify alternative approaches and complete feasibility analysis for each.		
7.	Prepare Design Proposal.	Design Proposal	
8.	Presentation to Management		
9.	Management review and decision		
10.	Prepare expanded Project Plan and Schedule (PPS) for the alternative approach authorized by Management.	Project Plan and Schedule	
B.	Data Gathering		
1.	Schedule and perform expanded data gathering in areas identified by initial data gathering.		
2.	Organize data and identify to facilitate analysis.		
3.	Complete Data Element Description Sheet for each data element identified.	Data Element Description Sheet	
4.	Collect information on requirements for decision-making, operational directives, and reports (both formal and informal).		
5.	Prepare Inventory of Existing Data Elements.	Inventory of Existing Data Elements	
6.	Prepare Inventory of Existing Reporting Requirements	Inventory of Existing Reporting Requirements	
7.	Perform supplemental data gathering as needed.		
8.	Present inventories to Management for review.		
9.	Management review and direction/approval.		

Figure 8-1 continues

Phase and Task I.D.	Phase/Task Description	Product	% Completion
C.	Data Analysis		

1.	Working with the inventories of elements and reports and using classification analysis work sheets classify each individual data element by
	  —type: controlling, reporting, supporting,
	  —use: generic grouping, i.e., descriptive, computational, quantitative,
	    —reports: managerial, operational, recordkeeping,
	    —timeliness: operational, transitory, archival, historical,
	  —system requirements: size, data retention, updating, maintenance, response requirements, security,
	  —logical/functional relationships with other data,
	  —current format and media, and
	  —name, synonym, definitions.		

2.	Prepare Master Classification Lists of the data elements.	Master Classification Lists	
3.	Prepare Performance Requirements and Characteristics Lists.	Performance Requirements and Characteristics Lists	
4.	Review findings with management.		
5.	Management direction/approval.		
D.	Development and Implementation of Standards		
1.	Identify and organize the contents of the standards manual.		
2.	Define and incorporate the Administrative and Environmental Standards.	Administrative and Environmental Standards	
3.	Develop and incorporate the method standards for the Data Definition Control System (DDCS).	Data Definition Control System	
4.	Assemble current data element definitions in a Corporate Glossary.	Corporate Glossary	
5.	Review Glossary and DDCS with Management.		
6.	Management direction/approval.		
7.	Train all users in Standards, DDCS, Corporate Glossary.		
8.	Implement DDCS, Corporate Glossary, CDB Standards.		
9.	Continue to improve and complete Corporate Glossary.	Corporate Glossary	
E.	Development and Implementation of the Data Integrity and Quality Assurance Program		
1.	Determine organizational or functional component responsible		

Figure 8-1 continues

Phase and Task I.D.	Phase/Task Description	Product	% Completion
	for the integrity and contents of every data element.		
2.	Establish program, plan and schedule for cleaning up all currently existing files.		
3.	Develop Methods for Auditing Data Element Contents and Quality.	Methods for Auditing Data Element Contents and Quality	
4.	Functional management establishes reliability parameters for each data element.		
5.	Establish data audit management report requirements.		
6.	Present program to all affected managers and top management.		
7.	Management review and direction/ approval.		
8.	Institute program and commence cleanups and audits.		
F.	Preliminary Design		
1.	Develop logical design alternatives based upon data classifications.		
2.	Develop logical design alternatives based upon system and functional requirements.		
3.	Develop physical design alternatives based upon —file structures, —access methods, —available hardware, and —available software.		
4.	Perform trade-off analysis between various design alternatives.		
5.	Prepare Trade-off Analysis Report.	Trade-off Analysis Report	
6.	Management review, decision and direction.		
7.	Prepare Detailed Design Project Plan and Schedule.	Detailed Design Project Plan and Schedule	
8.	Management review and direction/ approval.		
G.	Detailed Design and Testing		
1.	Prepare the detailed Design Specifications for the optimum design approved by Management in the previous Phase.	Design Specifications	
2.	Management review and direction/ approval of the detailed design.		
3.	Prepare Test Plan and necessary Test Data to test specifications and processes.	Test Plan and Test Data	
4.	Management review and direction/ approval of test plan.		
5.	Perform test and evaluate results.		
6.	Management review and direction/ approval of test results.		
7.	Modify design and retest as necessary. Repeat Task 6.		

Figure 8-1 continues

Phase and Task I.D.	Phase/Task Description	Product	% Completion
H.	Data Conversion and Implementation		
1.	Develop Conversion Plan and Schedule.	Conversion Pan and Schedule	
2.	Management review and direction/ approval.		
3.	Conduct training as necessary.		
4.	Convert data and establish new data base.		
5.	Maintain converted data.		
6.	When data conversion is complete, implement operations.		
7.	Management review, direction/ approval of conversion and implementation.		
I.	Post-Implementation Evaluation		
1.	Plan and staff for the Post- Implementation Evaluation study.		
2.	Conduct the study.		
3.	Prepare the Study Report and present Study Report to Management.		
4.	Management review and direction.		
5.	Development phase terminates. Routine maintenance and support begins.		

FIGURE 8-1. Basic Phase and Task List (Courtesy, Brandon Applied Systems, Inc.)

The project has been divided into a series of phases and tasks. Associated with some of these tasks and most of the phases are specific deliverables to be produced to meet the quality standards established for the product. At the end of the systems development activity, a systems design will have to be produced which undoubtedly will have to be approved by the user prior to continuing effort. At the end of the coding task, computer program listings will be available in source language on an untested basis. Certain types of documentation will be produced as well at each stage of the process. It is desirable to stipulate these products exactly, and to state that the user will obtain copies at each stage of the process.

Figure 8-1 also provides an indication of the types of output to be produced by each phase and stage. The vendor can be required by contract to submit acceptable documentation and products at each stage. If the products at any point are not acceptable, the contract should be terminable at that point, and the user is presumably capable of using the work products to continue the project on his own.

8-03 Documentation and Documentation Standards

The deliverables have been defined in clause 8-02, and some of these may be documentation. In addition, a clear statement should be made of all documentation to be produced, and the standards which that documentation must meet. Documentation standards can be defined, and should be at least as rigorous as those used in the user's installation for internal projects.

Documentation has multiple purposes. As defined in clause 8-02, documentation is evidence of progress to a certain point, and evidence of the quality of that progress. In addition, documentation is necessary for historical purposes, for proper systems operation, for an understanding of how to use the system, and for proper systems maintenance. These last objectives are not satisfied by the documentation requirements of clause 8-02, so that a separate provision must be made in the contract defining specifically what type of documentation is to be produced for each program, for each system, and for user *and* operating personnel. Documentation standards must be comparable to those used in the installation, or must be the standards in use by the vendor, provided that those standards are appended to the contract, and are acceptable to the user.

8-04   Project Scope

The *nature* of the products to be delivered has been defined, and it is now necessary to define the scope and boundaries of the system. Prior to the execution of a contract, a systems concept document should be produced as shown in figure 8-1. This document defines the scope and boundary of the system, defining it as an inventory system or a payroll system, for example. This scope definition will establish a basic identification of the activities associated with the project. This scope definition becomes more important if the project is to be done on a fixed price basis, since the funding is constrained and a scope constraint must be established as well.

8-05   Specifications by Stage

When purchasing a software package, it is entirely possible to attach to a contract the program specifications in great detail, since they are normally complete and the program is in operation. When describing an undeveloped package, it is far more difficult to attach detailed specifications. The only specifications which can be defined at the outset are those defined as systems scope (clause 8-04). It is almost impossible at the conception of the project to define specifications for the systems design, or actual program specifications. These can be defined in only very broad terms at this stage, and detailed specifications will have to wait until completion of each succeeding phase. Thus, the contract will have to carry a stipulation that specifications are to be produced at each stage which will define performance characteristics, run time characteristics, input and output requirements of the system and its subordinate elements, and the like. The contract can only stipulate the need to produce these specifications. Upon completion of each specification, the approval cycle defined under acceptance will have to be followed. If the follow-up specifications are approved, they will act as an addendum to the contract, which will have to be complied with in subsequent performance.

8-06   Constraints on Facility Usage

Clause 7-06 provides facility requirements for a software package, which in effect defines the minimum facility necessary to run that package. It is probably impossible to establish such detailed requirements at the inception of a software *development* project. It is therefore reasonable to state these requirements in the form of constraints, limiting factors established by the user, prior to entering into the contract. The clause would normally stipulate memory maxima, peripheral equipment maxima, and might also stipulate run time maxima as targets to be used in the design of the system. There are risks associated with this, in that these constraints may hamper the effective operation of the system. However, this is a decision which can be made by data processing management prior to entering into the contract, and will depend on the nature and type of software system being developed.

8-07   Constraint on Resource Usage by Vendor

It is not at all uncommon for the vendor to require participative resources supplied by the user. At a minimum these resources will be the participation of staff in the design concept and during the approval cycle. In addition it is quite common for the user organization to supply machine time for testing, machine time for installation, data entry resources, and perhaps additional resources to assist in programming, design, or user training. It is thus necessary to stipulate exactly what types of resources will be supplied by the user at each stage, the amounts of those resources required, and absolute maxima for which the user is responsible. If these maxima are exceeded by the vendor, resources should be made available only on a charge basis. This will insure that abuse of resources will be kept to a minimum by the vending organization.

In certain situations, it is possible for the vendor to work at the using organization. In that event, additional resources are required, such as facilities, space, furniture and the like. Again, the extent to which these facilities are required and their schedule must be defined in the contract prior to its execution.

Whenever vendor personnel use resources belonging to the user, provisions should be made for the execution of the necessary security documents, and for compliance with all security procedures. This will be covered in a separate clause, but should be noted at this point.

8-08   Compliance with Installation Standards

Data processing standards are not uniformly established, and in most installations are sadly lacking. Nonetheless, most using organizations have some established standards relating to language use, to operating practices, and to programming or systems design methodology. These are normally embodied in a standards manual, and are mandatory for compliance by user personnel developing systems and programs.

When systems or programs are developed by personnel external to the organization, they too should comply with all established user standards. These should be appended to the contract, and the vendor should agree that systems and programs developed thereunder will comply with the standards. In many cases software organizations have their own standards, which may be more comprehensive than those of the user. It is then possible to attach a set of standards belonging to the software organization, provided that the user is in agreement with these standards and is prepared to accept them intact. Alternately, it may be possible to arrive at a compatible subset of both standards in use, whether they be language standards, programming standards, systems design standards, or documentation standards, and to append these as project standards to the contract. A set of standards needs to be attached to the contract to define the total methodology under which the project is to be conducted.

8-09   Guarantee of Original Development

Clause 7-29 provides a guarantee of ownership with respect to a software package being sold. When a software system is being developed, it should be guaranteed to be of original design, and it should be defined to contain no material which might belong to, or infringe upon, anyone else. If software elements are used which belong to the vendor organization, or if software packages are incorporated as part of the development effort, then vendor guarantees of ownership for these components should be excepted, and rights to the unlimited use of these components should be obtained by the vendor for use in the development contract only. The user should be held harmless from any infringement possibilities, as in clause 7-29, and should be given a guarantee that all material is original and will ultimately belong to the user outright upon completion, acceptance and final payment. (See also clauses 8-13 and 8-20).

C. FINANCIAL

8-10   Charges

The total fees for development, whether time and material or fixed price, are to be defined in the contract and must include charges for all personnel associated with the project, for expenses to be incurred, for external purchases, software, machine time, or other resource requirements, and charges for maintenance, installation support, training, documentation and the like. In effect the user must be advised of all costs to be incurred, with a proviso in the contract that there will be no other charges except as specifically defined. A fixed fee contract is most desirable, but may not be feasibly established until halfway down the list of tasks, when the project definition is more firm. In the absence of a fixed fee contract, a time and materials contract will be necessary until the specification is firm. A time and materials contract should stipulate exactly what the charges are for and cancellation rights in the event that charges are excessive. The time and materials contract should also have an upper limit for each phase of the contract.

8-11   Progress Payments

It is common in a software development contract to have progress payments made as the contract proceeds. This is necessary because this type of project may extend for years, and it is unlikely that any software organization would be willing or able to wait that long for a contribution to its costs. In the contract, progress payments should be tied to product deliverables. Each product should be defined as in clause 8-02, and for each stage the percentage of the contract to be paid, or the amount of billing authority granted thereby, should be clearly established. Regardless of the billing authority generated by product deliverables, a certain percentage of the payments should be held back by the user, to guarantee ultimate completion of the contract. In effect, the user's interim payments should equal the costs incurred by the vendor, but not his profits. This suggests that if the contract is terminated by unsatisfactory performance of the vendor at any stage, or by business termination of the vendor, the user's cost would not have exceeded those costs which the user itself might have incurred in doing similar development work, and the user would have received value for money with the product to the extent developed. If that philosophy can be embodied in the contract, the user will have maximum protection from disaster during the contract, and will be shielded from surprises in project scope, project costs or excessive project schedules.

Progress payment provisions relating directly to product deliverables have to be carefully constructed to insure that the balance of funds flowing to the vendor is approximately equal to the value flowing back to the user, so that project termination at any time will not create a hardship for either party. All profits on the contract should be held back until final completion, at which time the vendor is entitled to payment of the funds held back.

D. INSTALLATION

8-12 Progress Reports

It is highly desirable to have a contract clause in which the vendor is required to make periodic progress reports, detailing the specific accomplishments made in the preceding period, and those anticipated in the ensuing period. The task descriptions used in these reports should conform to the phase and task list established in clause 8-01.

The progress report submitted by the vendor should be a formal one, preferably signed by a senior officer of the vending organization. It represents a statement of contractual completion, which, together with a specific deliverable product, will induce the user to make a defined progress payment. If it is treated in this manner, and a progress report turns out to be untruthful, then it may be possible to use the fraud laws to enable the user to proceed against the vendor, and against the individual vendor personnel responsible for the fraudulent progress report. The progress report serves as a means of informing the user, as a means of keeping the vendor honest, and as a means of determining whether or not specific progress payments are due.

8-13   Title Transfer

The software developed under contract ultimately belongs to the user, and title to such software should pass to the user upon completion. However, if progress payments are made and product deliverables produced during the product cycle, then it is desirable to stipulate that title transfer to these components takes place at the point of delivery, or at the point of payment. This means, for example, that at the completion of systems design all systems design specifications become the property of the user, whether or not they have been physically delivered. If title is transferred in the work product at that point, then the user has the legal right to obtain those materials, which allows him to continue software development in the event the vendor defaults or otherwise terminates the contract. Title transfer should include title to the documentation, title to the source code, and title to all intermediate products delivered against specific product payments. Unless the parties have a special understanding to the contrary, the contract should provide that all of the material belongs *solely* to the user. The vendor should be obliged to deliver all copies of the developed material to the user and retain nothing. (See clause 8-20).

8-14   Staged Acceptance and User Approval

It is necessary for the user to have a formalized acceptance procedure, under which specific products delivered under the contract are accepted. In addition, it is desirable for the user to approve specific products being delivered, so that the vendor can proceed without fear that product development is proceeding in the wrong direction. Thus, associated with each phase and task or with each specific product delivery should be an acceptance procedure and a separate approval procedure. The user is normally prepared to accept an intermediate product, on the basis of its quality, its conformance with the necessary standards and, of course, its ability to meet the user's requirements. Acceptance of the product is indicated by a progress payment, or by the signature of the user on a specific progress report or approval document. In addition, there may be specific approval requirements stated in the contract, where the user must positively approve a series of specifications, output documents, or other design components, where such approval is necessary to build the remainder of the software system. These stages can be defined as part of clause 8-01, or can be defined in a separate contract clause, which will also stipulate the amount of time which the user may take to perform the necessary acceptance test functions and provide his approval.

Upon completion of the software, a final acceptance test should be designed and included in the contract. This test should exercise the software in accordance with the defined requirements, and should consist at least of a running of the test data prepared by the contractor, and the test data prepared by the user. In addition, it may be desirable to include as part of the final acceptance cycle some operational activities using live test data. The system should be used on actual data as well as the fabricated test data which the user and/or the vendor have provided.

8-15   Test Data

It is desirable that the contract stipulate with precision the source of test data and the responsibility for its development and approval. It is suggested that there be at least three levels of test data, of which only one level is developed by the vendor. The initial level, which determines that the programs operate in accordance with program specifications is normally developed by the vendor. A second level, which tests each individual program to determine that each program meets the user requirements, should be developed independently by the user, and should be tested by the vendor in accordance with the acceptance procedures. Finally, it is necessary to use a third level of data which tests the linkage of the programs as a total system. Systems test data again should be fabricated by the user. In addition, as a potential fourth level of test data, or as a separate stage in the acceptance procedure, the system should be run with a sufficient amount of live data to insure that the test data has faithfully covered the normal operations which occur in live data. Live data alone is insufficient to test all components of a system, but live data is used at the final stage in testing or acceptance to insure that the system can handle the basic activity.

8-16 Rights to Cancel at Stages

It is highly desirable from the user's viewpoint to incorporate cancellation rights in a software development contract at almost any time. However, this is not necessarily a fair procedure for the vendor, if such cancellation rights can be exercised arbitrarily, or if they do not take into account the potential profits which the vendor might have made from the completion of the contract.

If cancellation is desired on the part of the user, without fault on the part of the vendor, then such cancellation rights should require the user to complete all payments for work performed to the point of cancellation, and pay the profits which the vendor could have reasonably obtained in the completion of the contract. In addition, the user should be required to compensate the vendor for the fact that the vendor will have to reassign his staff on an orderly basis, which may entail a loss of revenue for a period of time. Thus, an arbitrary cancellation right should take into account the vendor's position in as equitable a manner as possible.

On the other hand, the user should have an absolute right to cancel at each stage and at each product delivery point if for some reason the vendor fails to meet the qualitative or quantitative standards established as part of the contract. If the vendor fails to deliver a particular product on or near a scheduled date, or if the vendor delivers a product which fails to meet the defined quality standards established in the contract, or which fails to meet the specifications of that system, then the user should be able to cancel the contract and to pay only those progress payments due up to the last acceptable delivery. In addition, it is negotiable whether or not the user is required to pay any part of the potential profits of the vendor, or any part of the hold-back to the point of cancellation. Thus, a cancellation provision in the contract is desirable, and should provide for cancellation at any time, with the user obtaining rights and title in the materials developed, and the vendor obtaining those payments to which it is reasonably entitled.

E. STAFF

The most important component in the success of any data processing project is clearly the personnel assigned to that project. As a result, it is important for the using organization to obtain contractual guarantees of the caliber, level, and continuance of the staff assigned to a particular software development contract. This may be difficult to negotiate, and difficult to enforce, since vendor personnel are not wholly within the control of the user organization. However, if the letter of the contract is sufficiently specific, the spirit and the intent can be adhered to when structuring a reasonable development project.

8-17 Staff Qualifications

The first reference to staff in a software development contract will stipulate the caliber and qualifications of the staff to be used in the contract. Normally this provision would divide the staff into functional categories, such as systems analysis, programming, and operations. The classifications of personnel used can conform to those of either the vendor, if the vendor has a published personnel administration manual, or to those of the user, if the user has specific job descriptions which define staff responsibilities. The qualifications of staff in data processing professions are normally formulated in terms of years of experience and experience type. Thus a clause could indicate that "All programmers used in the development and implementation, phases N-Y, shall have not less than three years of programming experience, of which at least one year shall be with the particular machine and language being implemented." This description should be sufficient to assure a reasonable caliber of staff, without limiting the vendor to the point where it is impossible to supply the right kinds of people to complete the development process.

It is further possible to stipulate that staff shall have been in the employ of the vendor for a specific period of time, thus preventing the vendor from hiring new personnel directly for the contract. This constraint can be a troublesome one for the vendor. Normally, a contractual requirement that all staff have at least three months past service should be sufficient to insure that the vendor does not supply personnel on the project directly from the street, while also not seriously impeding the vendor.

A final constraint on staff qualification is to give the user the absolute right to approve all staff to be assigned to the contract. This is normally not a reasonable demand. Under certain conditions, however, where the contract involves sensitive areas or requires unusual security precautions, and if the user can show a need to have control over the vendor personnel, it may be possible to incorporate such a provision. Such a right of approval of personnel, particularly coupled with control over their activities, can sometimes raise legal problems for the user. An implication may arise in law that the vendor personnel are employees of the user. This may, for example, create insurance problems and, if the vendor goes bankrupt, may result in claims against the user for unpaid withholding taxes. In such situations, advice of counsel should be sought.

8-18   Full-Time Employees

All employees assigned to a software development contract should be full-time employees of the vendor, and this assurance should be given in the contract. It is the vendor's responsibility to insure that his employees are honest, bonded if necessary, and are capable of control. The use of "moonlighters" or other part-time personnel is not recommended from the user viewpoint. In addition the contract probably should stipulate that all employees assigned to the contract will be assigned on a full-time basis, except only for such minor administrative tasks as they may be asked to perform from time to time.

To insure compliance with this clause, it should be extended to say that vendor-assigned employees may be rejected by the user for cause and that any personnel substitutions shall be approved in advance by the user. This is less onerous than absolute approval rights on all personnel, but does assist the user in ridding the project of incompetents or trouble-makers, and prevents the dissolution of an acceptable team as a result of a vendor decision without user approval.

8-19   Staff Accessibility Upon Business Termination

In the event of vendor business termination, the vendor should give the user rights of access to the staff, and to offer employment to suitable members of the project team. This, of course, contravenes another recommended contract provision requiring each party not to hire the other's staff (reference clause 5-16), but that restriction should not apply in the event of business termination by the vendor. It would be unfair for the user to require the vendor's staff to agree in advance to accept employment with the user if offered upon vendor's business termination; the contingency is too remote and it unduly restricts the personnel involved. However, under certain circumstances each employee could be asked to agree that he will work for a 30-day period to effect an orderly termination of the contract in the event of vendor business termination. This approach should be taken if business termination appears possible from the financial reports submitted by the vendor prior to contract signing.

8-20   Noncompetition

The vendor should undertake not to compete with the user in offering services through use of the systems or programs developed under the contract, and the vendor should agree not to offer these programs or systems, or similar programs or systems to any other organization for some period of time. In addition, it may be desirable to request the vendor to refrain from working in *any* manner for a competing organization during and for a period of time after completion of the contract. This latter provision is most desirable in the event the vendor has developed some sensitive, competitive system which enables the user to obtain lead-time or increased efficiency over competition in a specific area; in that event it is desirable to constrain the vendor from working for competitive organizations on similar projects for a significant period of time.

8-21   Insurance

The use of vendor staff on the premises of the user will require that they be insured in accordance with the law, which calls for such policies as workmen's compensation, disability, and comprehensive liability. The user insurance department should be able to specify the types of insurance vendor personnel should have, depending on circumstances of the contract. The contract can then provide for the vendor to give the user a certification of insurance, an undertaking to keep that insurance current, and provision of similar insurance for all new personnel assigned to the contract.

8-22   Security

It is necessary for vendor personnel working at a user installation to comply with all security provisions associated with that installation, and equally necessary for vendor personnel working on user projects which are confidential to have similar security provisions enforced on the vendor's site. The security requirements will vary depending on the nature of the contract, but to the extent that security provisions are required of user personnel, they should similarly be imposed on vendor or contract personnel. Separate undertakings may be required from individual staff. Alternately, a blanket undertaking given by the vendor corporation in the contract may be sufficient, provided that the vendor corporation represents that it has in turn signed separate agreements with its employees (chapter 10). If the Industrial Security Act is applicable, then a provision should be included in the contract, and specific reference made to the appropriate sections of the act.

A. INTRODUCTION

A wide variety of processing services are available in the computer industry, many supplied by smaller companies, with potentially the same problems as software organizations. Processing services are defined to be machine-based services using equipment in some form. They can be classified in a a variety of ways, including the following:

- Keypunch or data entry services, in which media transformation is the sole product through card punching, key-to-disk, or key-to tape processing.
- Raw machine time sales, in which the service organization simply sells access to its machine time and the user provides staffing, programming, supplies and the like.
- Enhanced machine time sales, in which the service bureau provides the user with an operating center, and the user provides only the programs. Typically the service organization will also provide forms, cards, supplies and the like.
- Application processing, in which the service bureau provides the end result: the payroll checks, the inventory reports, invoices to customers, accounts payable. In this area the service bureau not only uses its own facilities, but its own programming as well.
- Time-sharing services, in which the user accesses the service bureau facility on a time-shared basis, normally through a terminal, and in which the programs may be partially supplied by the service bureau and partially supplied by the user.

In addition, in all of these cases it is possible to access a data base, which can belong to either the service bureau, the user, or to a third party. The

9 PROCESSING SERVICES

types of services offered vary widely, and contracts must take this into account.

The service bureau "industry" is to some extent in worse financial shape than the software "industry," because under-capitalization in service bureaus is often worse than in software organizations. A service organization has a larger fixed cost because it operates its own equipment. It therefore faces the prospect of making monthly payments to an equipment manufacturer in sizable amounts, regardless of revenue. Although it can discharge staff partly proportionate to the amount of business it loses, a service bureau cannot reduce the basic cost of its equipment, and therefore may find itself in a position where a significant loss of revenue can cause disaster somewhat more readily than in the typical software organization.

As a result, it is sometimes possible to find a service bureau willing to reduce its price significantly to capture enough business to load its equipment, thereby covering its basic costs. This practice, often referred to as "low-balling," is dangerous from the user's viewpoint, since the service bureau will want to find all possible means of recovering lost revenues once the crisis is over. The service bureau will then look to the user to find alternate ways of obtaining additional revenue, possibly by contract termination or other form of squeeze. An unethical service bureau may even prevent the user from changing service organizations by making data available only at exorbitant rates. A wise user should take pains to protect himself from the risks associated with dealing with a temporarily distressed service organization prepared to reduce its price on a temporary basis.

The major risks to be recognized in a service bureau or processing contract are as follows:

1. The ability to have continuous access to all data belonging to the user. The user must have the absolute right of access to its data and to remove that data from the premises of the service bureau at any time.
2. The ability to have access to the programs, if such programs were developed by the service organization for the user. Again, an unscrupulous service organization may wish to withhold programs developed for a user to protect its business base. The user's rights in these programs, when paid for by the user, should be absolute, and the user's access to these programs should be protected.
3. A breach of confidentiality. Key operating data of the user may have been supplied to the service bureau, and this data in the hands of competitors may result in significant damage to the user. The protection of data supplied to the service organization must be absolute, and confidentiality protected at all costs.
4. Loss or erasure of data. As has been suggested, the only protection to the user against loss of data comes from its duplication. The service bureau should, however, be held responsible for costs and expenses attendant to its loss or destruction of the data in its hands.

A processing service contract will include clauses obtained from other types of contracts. A service bureau contract should include clause 6-64 (No Subcontracts), clause 7-22 (Availability of Financial Statements), and clauses 8-17 through 8-22, which provide for certain qualifications and representations made with respect to employees of the organization. In addition, clause 6-35 (Tax Applicability), and clause 6-93 (Liquidated Damages) may also be appropriate for a service bureau contract.

B. PERFORMANCE

Performance of a processing service contract consists of products to be supplied, in a timely manner. In addition, product quality may be a parameter, in that errors must be limited and correction methodology provided. The following clauses are potentially applicable:

9-01   Deliverables

The products to be delivered in a processing service contract are somewhat different from the products delivered in a hardware or software contract. Normally the products include reports, or responses to inquiries, or products which allow direct access to databases and responses to inquiries. Report products are delivered on the basis of some predefined schedule normally included as a part of the contract. Daily recurring reports, weekly reports, monthly reports, year-end reports, and the like all must be defined, their frequency and delivery time stipulated, and their content included either by reference, or by example. If no examples are available, the content of the report should be described much as a system specification is defined in chapter 8.

In addition to recurring reports, certain reports may be required upon request. In that event, the response time must be indicated, and the product to be delivered against such a request must be defined explicitly.

9-02   Performance Turnaround

Not only must a report be delivered at a particular time, but that time has to be stated as relative to the time that the input was delivered to the service organization. A month-end report is required five days after the end of the month, but in no event later than three days after delivery of the materials necessary for its preparation to the service bureau. There are two parameters to be concerned with in performance turnaround; an absolute parameter, which defines the outside limitation of delivery under normal circumstances, and a relative parameter, which gears delivery to the provision of materials to the service organization. Each product defined under clause 9-01 must have its associated turnaround schedule, and must have a specific delivery commitment.

9-03   Quality Specification

The quality of materials supplied by processing services can be defined in two ways. Of minor importance is visual quality and readability. This will be the result of proper forms alignment by the service organization, ribbon quality, and adjustment of its printer. Although this is a minor point, it probably should be included in the contract so that the user organization has the opportunity to complain and obtain corrective action in the event that forms are improperly aligned, unclear, smudged or otherwise unpresentable.

A more significant qualitative concern is that the material be error free, and that it accurately represent the requirements. These factors have to be defined in greater detail, and the error percentage must be limited. In addition, an error-correcting mechanism must be established, and a means of error-detection defined if not automatically included in the system. The normal remedy for an error will be correction and necessary reprocessing of the material.

9-04   User Rights to Programs Developed

In the event the user uses programs designed and developed at its direction, and for which payment is included, either separately, or as an amortized component of the processing charges, ownership of these programs should automatically devolve upon the user, when paid for. In this event the absolute right of ownership should be stipulated in the contract. See also clauses 8-9 and 8-13.

9-05   Delivery of Owned Programs to User

To protect the user from business termination, or from potential extortive practices by the service organization, it is desirable to have copies of the programs delivered to the user at the time that they are completed. These programs were developed specifically for the user, and are owned by the user upon payment. Copies of all requisite documentation should also be delivered by the service organization to the user. In addition, any future corrections, maintenance changes, and modifications made to these progams by the service organization should be supplied as well, so that the user's copies are kept totally up-to-date. Periodically, the user should provide its version of the programs to the service organization as a test of their currency, for use by the service organization in actually performing the processing services.

9-06   Equipment Requirements

Since the user may wish to transfer his processing services from one service bureau to another, whenever programs are developed for him, or when processing services are provided using his own programs, he should insist on a statement in the contract which stipulates the minimum equipment requirements under which these programs will work. This will allow a change to another service organization with comparable equipment, because the minimum equipment configuration required to successfully run the programs is available. It will also allow the user to take over the processing on his own equipment, should he wish to do so or to obtain equipment for this purpose. Alternatively, the user will be capable of running these programs on equipment supplied to him locally, or of obtaining raw machine time and converting the contract to a machine time contract; provided again that the amount of equipment required is known and provided that he has absolute access to all the programs.

9-07   Procedures Defined

A significant part of the documentation required to process the programs for a user are the procedures necessary for complete processing. These procedures should be defined in detail, and copies should be made available to the user at the inception of the contract. They should include all steps performed by the service organization, from the point of receipt of material from the user, to the point of delivery of each and every product produced. Detailed procedures are necessary in the event the user elects to do the job himself, or elects to transfer the job to another organization. They are an integral part of the processing capability, have been paid for as part of the development of the programs, and therefore belong to the user.

9-08   User Training

The service organization may be asked for assistance in training end users of the products, in preparation of material as input, or in providing an understanding of material produced as output. It is the intent of this clause to make available the expertise of the service organization in training personnel of the user organization in input preparation or output use. Alternate ways of presenting material and alternate forms of requests and inquiries can also be explored in a user training session, which is provided by the service organization as a part of the contract.

C. CHARGES

9-09   Basis for Charging

Processing services can be billed in many different ways, and the basis for charges should be defined in the contract. The arrangements can be made for a fixed monthly fee or a price which varies based on the volume of activity or the size of the user's organization. Thus, if the service organization is asked to process a payroll, it can be charged for at a fixed price per month, or on the basis of the average number of employees, a price per employee, or on the basis of activity items, such as the number of paychecks produced. Whatever basis is used, and however it is done, the simplest methodology generally works out best, and leads to least controversy. Computations should be made in advance of signing the contract to insure that both parties understand the basis for charging, and the magnitude of the charges to be incurred, so that no surprises are possible when the service bureau's initial invoice is produced.

9-10   Term of the Contract

A processing service contract should not be for a lengthy term or it should be capable of being cancelled by the user on short notice. If the programs are the property of the user, then such cancellation should be possible on 30 to 90 days notice. The vendor will probably want the same cancellation rights. If possible the user should negotiate a provision that requires the vendor to give lengthier notice for vendor cancellation. This will give the user more turnaround time and will also prevent the vendor from using its cancellation privilege as a vehicle for frequent price renegotiation. If the programs do not belong to the user, then the user may need substantial time to replace the services and vendor cancellation should not be permitted on less than six months notice. In any event, a long-term processing service contract is probably not in the interest of either party.

9-11   Automatic Renewal with Notice

Many vendor supplied contracts provide for automatic renewal. If the contract is drawn for an initial term of one year, with automatic renewal on an annual basis, then the user should insist that a notice provision be inserted that insures that the service organization provides notice to the using organization of the existence of the automatic renewal provision not later than 90 days prior to the expiration of the term of the contract. Such notice will remind the user that unless affirmative action is taken, the user will be bound to a renewal term.

9-12   Price Protection

It is common practice in the service industry to provide price protection for the initial term of the contract, but not necessarily for renewals of the contract. It may be possible to incorporate a pricing escalator formula in the contract, which calls for adjustments in price related either to labor cost indices or a cost-of-living index, in the event of automatic renewal of the contract. If the contract is to be renewed automatically, and the price is to be adjusted using an escalator, then notice of impending renewal is definitely required to insure that the user has an opportunity to cancel, and to find alternative processing methods. Thus, it may be desirable to provide for a longer notice period if the price is to be adjusted, with a shorter notice period in the event that no price adjustments are to be made.

9-13   Options to Change the System

Business dynamics will force changes in systems on a regular basis. In the normal systems development process this is referred to as systems and program maintenance, and it is often a continuing process. Similarly, if programs have been developed for the user by the service organization, these programs will require maintenance, to cope with user changes. Since the service bureau essentially is in a "monopoly" position relative to the user with respect to these programs, the user should have the option either to make these changes directly, to subcontract them to another organization, or to obtain them from the service organization at a predefined rate. This rate can be expressed as a person-day rate, as a rate per change, or on another equitable basis. The user should see to it that the basis selected provides for reasonable nonmonopolistic attitudes on the part of the service organization.

If copies of these programs are available to the user, as defined in clause 9-05, then the user has the opportunity of making these changes on his own, or of obtaining changes from a competitive organization in the event the service bureau refuses to make these changes or wishes to charge an exorbitant price.

9-14   Options to Undertake Part of the Work Internally

It may be desirable from time to time to change the operating procedures to allow part of the processing to be done by the user organization. For example, an initial service bureau contract may call for data entry or media conversion to be done by the service organization, followed by processing, report preparation, bursting, binding, and distribution. In the future, the user may wish to undertake part of these tasks internally. Media conversion lends itself well to internal performance, if volumes are sufficient to warrant the acquisition of the necessary equipment and personnel. By doing media conversion internally the user may have better control over the quality of the product, or may be able to provide converted media as a by-product of some other form of processing. An attachment to a cash register or other device could eliminate the need for media conversion by the service organization. The contract should be sufficiently flexible so that components of the processing services can be separated without breach. This type of flexibility is important in order to enable the user to perform significant parts of the work when economical.

9-15   Protection from Levy by Creditors

A service organization may be undercapitalized, and may from time to time have its assets compromised in a creditor proceeding such as bankruptcy or an assignment for the benefit of creditors. This need not disturb the operating practices of the service bureau, but the user and his property in the possession of the service bureau must be protected from levy by the creditors. It should be noted that user files stored on magnetic media belonging to the service bureau are the property of the user. If a creditor issues a levy against and attempts to sell the tapes and disks which contain the user's files, this could create a serious problem for the user. It may be possible for the contract to be drawn so that the user maintains proprietary rights in the file, in the data and also in the media associated therewith. In addition, the programs which are the property of the user must also be protected from levy by creditors, just like any other facilities or equipment which the user may have supplied to the service bureau.

D. TERMINATION

The completion of a service bureau contract, after which the services are to be transferred to another organization, or back to the user organization, presents some particular problems. It is necessary to have free access to information belonging to the user but in the possession of an organization which is not happy about losing the business. As a result, the rights and responsibilities at termination should be defined clearly in the contract, at its inception.

9-16   Termination Rights

It is assumed that the user will negotiate certain rights to terminate the contract. These will arise upon expiration of the contract, upon notice of a vendor price increase, upon vendor's failure to perform in accordance with the quality specifications (clause 9-03), upon failure of required turnaround (clause 9-02), upon exercise of cancellation rights (clause 9-10) or for a variety of legal causes. These conditions should be specified, and the rights of the user in each type of termination should be indicated. If the termination is for cause, in that the service bureau has failed to perform, then the user should seek more stringent requirements of access to information than if the termination is orderly. In any event file and program access rights the user has on termination should be stipulated in the contract.

9-17   Assistance in Take-Over

Whether the user transfers the processing responsibility to another service organization, or assumes the responsibility directly, some assistance from the original vendor is desirable. Files must be prepared in a format readable by the replacement machine. Programs must be made available on the most current basis. Procedures should be checked to insure that they are being followed in accordance with the documentation. Assistance is needed from the service organization to make sure that the data and the programs can be properly transferred to a successor organization, regardless of the identity of that successor.

9-18   Business Termination

In the event of vendor business termination, the contract should terminate immediately, and provisions of clauses 9-16 and 9-17 should become immediately effective. In addition, all ownership rights to media, data and programs should be asserted by the user, if this is appropriate, to insure that they can be protected from levy or from being sealed by the authorities. In the event that the processing services use programs which are proprietary to the service organization, the user should negotiate a contractual provision to obtain the rights to the programs in the event of business termination. Such rights can be nonexclusive, and solely for the user's benefit. The inconvenience of transferring business in an emergency to another service organization is sufficiently great to make it necessary to compensate the user by providing him access to the programs which will simplify the conversion process and which will allow him to transfer rapidly to another service organization. Additional provisions pertaining to business termination are given in clauses 5-02 and 7-19.

E. SECURITY, ACCESS AND CONFIDENTIALITY

One of the major risks in the establishment of a processing service contract is the risk of unauthorized access to information belonging to the user organization. This requires careful consideration in a contract, as follows:

9-19   File Access

Files used by the service bureau in processing information are normally the property of the user. This applies to files maintained by the system and files used in the processing itself, such as intermediate or working files. Since these files belong to the user, access rights should be given to the user at any time for any reason whatsoever. If the user wishes to remove these files he should be entitled to do so or to make any alterations, provided that it does not interfere with the responsibilities of the service bureau to provide the turnaround established.

9-20   File Ownership

User ownership of the files should be clearly stated. Title to work files should be given to the user in exchange for specific consideration, such as a nominal payment. Ownership of the media on which these files are stored should also be provided to the user, attested to by a transfer of title arranged for at the inception of the contract for an initial payment.

9-21   File Confidentiality

The service organization must agree to protect the confidentiality of user files, and to use them solely for processing services supplied to the user, and for no other purpose. These files are the property of the user and cannot be released to anyone without the permission of the user.

9-22   Destruction of Intermediate Files

As part of the processing cycle, work files are normally destroyed, or replaced in the data file library, where they are reused from time to time and where data is wiped out by such reuse. For the protection of the user and the confidentiality of the data, it is recommended that a contractual provision be included requiring the service organization to destroy all confidential work files prior to their return to the data file library, upon completion of the necessary processing work.

9-23   Destruction of Print Media

Reports are often produced in multiple copies, with interleaved carbons, which are thrown away after the carbons have been removed from the printed report sets. Unfortunately, the data printed on the reports leaves a readable impression on the carbon. As a result the service organization should warrant that it will destroy all carbons removed from confidential reports prepared for the user. As an alternative, the service organization can deliver all materials, including work files and carbons, to the user organization, so that the user can arrange for proper disposition of this potentially sensitive material.

9-24   Constraints on Release of User Information

In addition to certification of confidentiality, the service bureau should state in the contract that all material and user information, including files, programs, operating instructions, source data supplied for data entry conversion, and the like, will be released only to designated personnel of the user organization, and will be used only by specifically designated personnel of the service organization. This will afford the necessary protection to the user, and will prevent delivery to unauthorized recipients.

9-25   Systems Controls

If the system has been developed by the service organization, whether for its own use or specifically for the user, it will normally include a number of systems and program controls. These controls should be defined in the contract, so that the user can use these controls, and determine whether control practices are being followed and are adequate to protect the integrity of the data and the system at the service organization. An integral part of the documentation supplied by the service organization to the user, regardless of program ownership, will be a list of systems and program controls incorporated in the processing system.

9-26   Rights to a Security Inspection

The user should have an unlimited right to inspect the facilities and operating practices of the service organization with a view to determining that security is adequate, and that data stored at the service organization site is protected with the same caution and protection given to data stored in the user organization itself. An absolute right to security inspections at any time is a part of a proper service organization contract.

9-27 Evidence of Proper Insurance

Another security precaution, protecting against disaster, is maintenance of the proper insurance policies for fire, theft, unauthorized entry, loss of valuable business papers, and the like. The service organization should submit a certificate of insurance to the user prior to the contract, or have it incorporated in the contract. This will provide evidence, that in the event of a disaster, unauthorized entry, or destruction of valuable papers, insurance will cover the financial responsibility associated with the problem. The service organization should be contractually obliged to keep the coverage in force during the life of the contract. It is frequently possible to have the policy amended so that it cannot be cancelled without prior notice to the user.

9-28 Guarantee of Program Ownership

If the service organization uses its own programs to perform processing for the user, it is desirable to have a guarantee that the bureau is the owner on an unrestricted basis of the programs in use, that it has the right to use such programs, that such programs do not infringe any patents, copyrights, or other proprietary rights and that the service organization will hold the user harmless from any potential infringement caused by the use of such programs. In the event that such programs are found to be infringing, or found to be the property of someone else, the service organization will replace these programs at no further cost to the user, and at no disruption in service to the user. In addition, the service organization should agree to defend the user in any actions pertaining to these warranties.

9-29 Program Protection

If the programs are developed by the service organization for the user, it is useful to accord these programs whatever protection is available under the law, such as contractual restrictions on use, copying, and disclosure as might be required to retain them as trade secrets.

9-30 No Software Infringement

As a part of the processing supplied by a service organization, software supplied by the hardware manufacturer for job control, compilation of programs, and the like, will be used. The user will not know whether the contract between the service bureau and the hardware vendor provides for indemnification in the event of infringement. Since the user can be held to be an infringing party, the user (as an adjunct to clause 9-28) should have the protection of a "hold harmless" clause which states that the service bureau will hold the user harmless against infringement claims arising out of any software utilized by the service bureau which has been purchased or licensed from an outside source.

9-31 Data Storage Facilities

As a part of the physical protection of user property at the service bureau, the contract should contain a description of the data storage facilities used to retain user data. This will allow the user to ascertain that the facilities are adequate, properly protected, and possess proper temperature and humidity control devices, smoke detectors, fire protection equipment and the like.

F. TIME-SHARING CONTRACTS

When dealing with time-sharing, the contract takes on somewhat different features. The basis for charging may be different, terminals are normally supplied for access to the system, and turnaround characteristics are different as well. Each of these need to be defined. This section explores the contractual differences and contract clauses to be added to a time-sharing contract. All preceding contract clauses not superseded by the ones which follow should be included as a part of a time-sharing contract.

9-32 Terminal Ownership

A terminal is normally a prerequisite for an effective time-sharing operation. The time-sharing vendor is often prepared to supply that terminal on a rental basis, or to arrange for terminal rental separately. It is equally possible to purchase a time-sharing terminal, and to use the telephone network for access to the time-sharing organization. The user must decide whether to purchase his own terminal, rent it from the time-sharing vendor, or rent it from someone else. In any event, a time-sharing contract should stipulate who will supply and own the terminal.

9-33 Maintenance and Installation of the Terminal

If the terminal is owned by the time-sharing organization, it would probably be maintained by them so that a maintenance contract for the terminal will be included as part of the rental. This should provide for response time to maintenance calls, and backup equipment in the event of permanent failure. The provisions of a maintenance contract under hardware (section 6-F) should be reviewed for applicability. The contract may also provide for terminal installation procedures, and charges therefor. The responsibility for installation, and the ambient environment, cabling, telephone hookups, and other connections required to make the terminal operative should be spelled out in a contract as well.

9-34 Rights to Use Terminal for Other Purposes

Regardless of who supplies the terminal, the user should have the absolute right to use it for other purposes. Such purposes should include, but not be limited to, use as a telex or TWX terminal, use as an ordinary typewriter, or use as a terminal for access to other time-sharing services. Rental of the terminal is on a 24-hour basis, and the user should be unrestricted in its use, including use of competitive time-sharing services.

9-35 Entry Turnaround

The performance characteristics of a time-sharing service relate directly to turnaround of individual entries. The user types in a program or data line and obtains a response. The response time should be defined in the contract, in terms of a maximum and an expected response time. The expected response time is the norm, computed as an average of typical responses. The maximum time is the worst case situation, after which possible penalties might apply. However, if the norm is consistently violated, and the average response time deteriorates, some cancellation provision or other alternative might have to be included in the contract.

9-36   Data Base Accessibility

Time-sharing services often provide access to central data bases which have been developed by the vendor. Such data bases may be mathematical, engineering statistics, census data obtained from the Bureau of the Census, or those compiled by the regular operation of application programs, such as insurance rate files. When these data bases are accessible to customers on a nonexclusive basis, the contract for time-sharing service should specify user access rights for all data bases offered to other customers.

9-37   Program Accessibility

Time-sharing services often provide access to programs, sometimes developed by third parties, and at other times developed by the time-sharing organization itself. Access to these programs should be available to the user upon payment of the standard charges. In this event, guarantees of ownership (clause 9-28) and guarantees of noninfringement (clause 9-30) must be included as a part of the contract.

9-38   Definition of Charges

Charging methods and their determination are somewhat more difficult to monitor, since they are almost always based on "time" usage. Thus a time-sharing organization normally will charge its users for:

- data storage charges, per thousand characters, per month,
- connect time, the time during which the terminal is hooked up to the computer requesting or providing information,
- computer resource or processing unit time, the actual computer time used for processing of the user data or programs,
- line charges, telephone costs for connecting the terminal to the time-sharing computer, which may be done on an allocated basis if the service organization provides IN-WATS or leased line capabilities,
- terminal charges, rental and maintenance on a monthly basis,
- modem charges, rentals for modulating and demodulating units to translate terminal data into telephone line data, and
- program surcharges for the use of proprietary programs, developed by the time-sharing organization or its subcontractors.

9-39   File Compatibilities

Upon termination of a time-sharing contract the user may have developed his own data base or files, accessible to him under the ownership provisions of clauses 9-20 and 9-19. In this case the time-sharing organization should identify in what form these files are stored, since systems design is not under the control of the user, and since the programs are normally not the property of the user. The formats of the files, and their compatibility with other types of equipment should be guaranteed by the time-sharing organization, so that the user can terminate the contract and transfer these files to another organization, or use them internally.

9-40   Program Compatibility

To the extent that the user has developed specific programs on the time-sharing system, modified programs belonging to the time-sharing organization with their permission, or obtained rights to the time-sharing programs as a result of negotiation or a business termination clause (see clause 9-18), the compatibility of these programs and their ability to operate on comparable systems should be warranted. Equipment requirements and the programming language should be stated in the contract so that the user has an opportunity to use these programs elsewhere in the event of contract termination.

10
OTHER FORMS OF CONTRACTS

A. INTRODUCTION

There are a number of other contracts that can be considered part of the data processing environment. Most of these are available on a fairly standardized basis, and many of these do not have significant impact on the installation. Contracts relating to hardware and software are most significant; however, a chain is as strong as its weakest link, so that computer-related contracts should be considered in the light of data processing goals and some thought given to applicable provisions to be included in each.

A number of contract types are not included in this text, because they are generally within the competence of nondata-processing staff of the user organization, or because of their remoteness to the issues raised in this text. In addition, there are certain contracts whose provisions are covered in their entirety by provisions of hardware and software contracts. For example, peripheral equipment contracts normally can be designed out of appropriate provisions selected from among the hardware contract sections. Among those contracts not covered in this text are contracts for guard services, cleaning contractors, services provided for facilities maintenance, space, letters of intent (which should be designed so as not to be binding in any event and therefore are not truly contracts), estimates, requests for quotations, and facilities management contracts, whose complexity and difficulty make them an area almost impossible to cover adequately (for a start, see checklist in Appendix B).

Areas which are covered in this chapter to the extent that there are specific contracts with data processing, are the following:

contracts with employees
contracts with vendors of various types of supplies required for computer operation

third party leases, if they are different from hardware purchase contracts
consulting and other third party contracts
used equipment agreements
advance deposit agreements
equipment relocation contracts
training contracts

In all, there are over 250 contract terms covered in this text, categorized and divided by contract types. Many of these are applicable to transactions outside the specific contract framework in which they have been listed in this text.

A user of this text, interested in constructing a specialized contract not covered in this chapter, should be able to construct a list of appropriate contract clauses from among those covered in the entire text. Common sense must prevail in establishing an agreement between two parties; the definition of the relationship of the parties and a variety of protective devices can be developed by an alert individual, assisted by counsel. This chapter attempts to highlight some aspects of data processing situations not elsewhere considered in this text.

B. CONTRACTS WITH EMPLOYEES

The contractual relationship between an employer and employee is normally fairly well defined by the employer's management policies, and requires minimal augmentation for computer-related employees. Data processing is a sensitive area, and often involves information about the entire corporation, much of which is confidential, and might be used adversely by a competitor. It is almost invariably impossible to prevent an employee from going to work for a competitive organization. In fact, the most significant career opportunities for a data processing employee are generally with a competitor of his prior employer because of his applications experience and understanding of problems associated with a given industry. As a result, some provision should be made in the relationship with employees to insure that confidential information is not disclosed and that all material developed by the employee during his employ remains the property of the employer. Nondisclosure agreements are particularly important in the data processing area because of the frequent employer use of proprietary products licensed from third parties, who will demand such protection as a condition of the transaction.

10-01   Nondisclosure

The employee should sign an agreement which insures that he will not use or disclose any proprietary or confidential information about the employer or its operations. Nondisclosure should apply to data and methodology. The information content of computer programs and systems is significant, and formulas, factors, constants, and other data used in the company's operation must be fully protected. Methodology must be equally protected, and the method under which the company's information systems operate should not be disclosed to outside parties.

10-02   Inventions—Property of the Employer

Any material developed by the employee during his tenure with the organization, and developed at the direction of the organization or as a part of the job description provided by the organization, must of necessity belong to the organization. The employee must agree, preferably prior to employment, that all material developed by him, all inventions, developments, refinements, methodology, documentation, computer programs, and systems are the property of the organization and will be protected by the employee for the benefit of the organization. In addition, the employee should give the organization blanket consent to copyrighting of any materials developed by him or in conjunction with him, or to the patenting of any inventions in whose development he may have had a part. Such patents and copyrights, if obtained, will be assigned to the organization, and the employee should waive any and all rights he may have had in such patents and copyrights. Some companies offer financial incentives for inventions and developments in addition to regular compensation.

C. CONTRACT FOR THE PURCHASE OF USED EQUIPMENT

While the recent trend has been downward, a significant market for used equipment still exists, largely as a result of the increase in the percentage of purchased equipment. Much of the used equipment business is done by third party leasing companies. It is now possible to obtain used equipment at considerably lower prices than for comparable new equipment. Caution should be exercised, since a reduction in cost is not always as significant to the end user as it might appear. A 50% reduction in hardware cost, accompanied by an increase in maintenance costs, probably represents less than a 10% reduction in the user's total budget. In addition, used equipment is not always subject to the provisions of the investment tax credit, nor to free maintenance during an initial warranty period. Computer staff does not normally like to work with obsolescent equipment, so that it may be difficult to retain or obtain qualified personnel. However, under certain circumstances, used equipment may indeed have significant value to a user. This is true, for example, when a used computer is purchased as a second machine, to double the capacity of the installation, without any necessity for conversion or redevelopment of programs. In that case, a used computer contract may be required.

In structuring a used computer contract, almost all of the provisions of the hardware contract given in chapter 6 should be included. A possible exception is clause 6-37, the applicability of the investment tax credit. This is normally not applicable when dealing with previously owned computer equipment. In addition, reference is made to clause 7-29, which provides for a guarantee of clear title when transferring a software package. Similarly, a vendor of used equipment would have to give the purchaser a warranty of ownership, so that there can be no question as to title.

Finally, the user of a used computer is cautioned to make sure that it is possible to obtain a maintenance contract for that computer, either from the original equipment manufacturer, or from a third party maintenance organization. It is desirable to include in a purchase contract some indemnification for the possibility that maintenance is not readily available for this type of equipment, or, even if available, that no reconditioning or other expense will be required to bring the equipment to a level of eligibility for standard maintenance charges.

10-03 Warranty of Condition

The equipment is used, and the previous user is selling it. It is important to know why this sale is being made. If the equipment is being sold because it is a "lemon," and it has performed poorly or it has not met reasonable reliability standards, then it is to the advantage of the second user to know this information, and to have indemnification where possible for such failures. It is important to have a warranty of condition, stating the equipment is in operating condition, has been consistently maintained in (good) working order, and performs in accordance with reasonable standards of reliability. This warranty can then be enforced by a performance bond, by placing part of the purchase price in escrow, as defined in clause 10-05, or by a period of acceptance testing during which it is possible to determine, subject to rights of rescission, the operating performance of the equipment.

10-04   Agreement to Maintain the Equipment

Computer equipment is normally maintained by the original equipment manufacturer, or in less frequent cases by a third party maintenance organization. The purchaser of a used computer should have a certificate from the original equipment manufacturer, or from a third party maintenance organization, that that organization is willing to maintain this equipment in accordance with its standard maintenance contract, for a specific period of time. Such an agreement should be the responsibility of the *seller* to obtain from a vendor of maintenance services. Normally, the vendor will be more interested in giving such certification to the seller, who may be purchasing a replacement computer from that vendor, and therefore has some leverage. In any event, the purchaser of a used machine should not find himself in a position where he is unable to get the machine maintained in accordance with proper industry standards.

Original equipment vendors often require reconditioning of a machine after title has been transferred before committing themselves to maintenance contracts. In part this is done to discourage the sale of used equipment, and in part to protect the vendor from the possibility that the equipment suffers from some unknown malfunction, which the vendor then has to assume under a blanket maintenance contract. The seller of the equipment should be held responsible for any necessary reconditioning. The seller should deliver a fully operable machine, installed on the user's site, with a maintenance contract attached, exactly as if that machine were a new machine obtained from the original equipment manufacturer. Only under these conditions is it ever worthwhile purchasing a used computer.

10-05   Performance Escrow

The seller of a used computer may be in the used computer business, a leasing company, or a user not normally in the business of transferring used equipment. The recourse which the user has to the seller is generally fairly limited, and it is desirable to establish an indemnification provision in the contract, supported by a specific performance bond. The purchase price of a used computer can be significant, and it is normally possible, in lieu of a bond, to place a percentage of the purchase price in an escrow fund to cover any damages, indemnities, performance problems, reconditioning costs, and the like. The escrow fund should be administered by an independent escrow agent capable of disbursing funds to correct defaults in the operating condition of the transferred computer.

10-06 Transfer of Rights of Original Purchaser

The purchaser of a computer from a computer manufacturer obtains therewith certain rights, options and obligations, covered in detail in chapter 6. Such rights may be capable of transfer to a second purchaser. These include the rights to documentation and education courses, the unlimited right to use the system in any activities, the right to make changes, attachments, alterations, and the like. In addition, warranties, representations, performance statistics, on-going reliability guarantees and the like might be transferable. The purchaser of a used computer should analyze the purchase contract under which the machine was originally obtained to determine which particular rights should be included in any transfer of the equipment. In addition the purchaser should evaluate clauses of chapter 6 to determine whether or not the seller of the used machine can obtain additional rights from the original vendor for transfer to the used equipment purchaser.

D. THIRD PARTY LEASES

In general, a third party lease is a financing instrument for purchasing a computer from the original equipment manufacturer using someone else's money. In a lease, a third party supplies the funds, against a contract under which the user makes payments equivalent to rental, and thus provides fund recovery on a favorable basis, often better than direct rental payments. A third party lease typically is longer than a straight rental contract, normally is cheaper, and does not involve a payment for overtime use.

In most cases, it is possible to obtain commitments from the original equipment manufacturer identical to those in a direct purchase. The leasing company purchasing from the manufacturer should then transfer all of these commitments to the user. The user, of course, should be directly involved in the purchase transaction. Often, the equipment is bought by the user from the manufacturer and resold to the leasing company at the same time, subject to a lease-back to the user from the leasing company. The rental payable by the end user is generally a function of the length of the lease and the cost of money. When third party leasing began, the only leases written with users were "full payout" (the term is self-explanatory) leases. Competition has enabled users to obtain shorter leases from third party lessors, with the consequent flexibility in potential for upgrading equipment. Two financial elements enter into the construction of a third party lease. One is a financial reporting problem; the other is a tax question.

The financial statement problem, as it affects the user, revolves around the question of whether the user is deemed the owner of the equipment, in which case it is subject to balance sheet treatment as an asset and to depreciation, or whether the user is deemed a lessee, in which case the rental payments can be treated as operating expenses, without any effect on the balance sheet. Generally speaking, if the lease provides that upon lease expiration the user becomes the owner of the equipment or has the option to buy it at a "nominal" price, the user's auditors will treat the lease as a "conditional sales contract." If so treated, the user will be deemed the owner, the equipment will be carried as an asset, the rental may be treated as a debt service and the write-offs limited to depreciation and interest. In a true lease, the rental payments will be deemed operating expenses and charged in full against income. Benefits can accrue from either approach, depending on the financial condition and goals of the user. Consultation with the accountants is urged.

The second problem relates to the availability of the investment tax credit. With new equipment, under certain conditions, the tax credit can be "passed-through" to the user-lessee. Some finance-lease deals, however, are constructed almost entirely for the purpose of giving the tax credit to the lessor. The problem should be exposed and the transaction constructed in such a manner as to properly secure the tax credit to the party entitled to it by the agreement and to meet with the requirements of the Internal Revenue Code.

The clauses identified below relate specifically to a third party lease. All of the clauses in chapter 6 apply as well. The totality of manufacturer commitments required must pass through to the end user, regardless of the format of the transaction. Since the transaction can involve a purchase by the third party lessee from the manufacturer, a simultaneous resale to the third party lessee and a lease-back, it is wise to consult with counsel to determine the appropriate methodology based on legal, tax and accounting requirements. What should not be lost in the shuffle is user protection in a proper relationship with the vendor.

10-07 Purchase Option at End of Lease

If there is no disadvantage to end user ownership for tax or financial reporting purposes, then it is possible to structure a lease under which the user has a purchase option upon making final payment. The purchase price can be negotiated, can be included as a part of the original contract, or can be made nominal to reflect the fact that the lease is a payout lease. If a purchase option exists, it should be documented in the contract. If a conditional sales agreement is not desired, then a purchase option should not be included, whether or not it is informally agreed to. If there is an *informal* agreement, it should be recognized that the Parol Evidence Rule will eliminate any possibility of its enforcement. The user should recognize that an informal option to purchase the computer at the end of the lease term is of little advantage.

10-08 Investment Tax Credit Pass-through

The investment tax credit belongs to the owner, the purchaser of the equipment when new. That credit normally can be passed through to the end user, either indirectly by the reduction of lease payments, or by an appropriate pass-through agreement, under which the end user may apply for the credit directly. In either case the machine is normally subject to the full tax credit, since the life of the lease or the life of the equipment can be assumed to be seven years or longer. Provisions should be made for this advantage.

10-09 Attorney-In-Fact with Vendor

If the lessor is the purchaser of the equipment, and if the lessor alone has established the relationship with the equipment manufacturer on a contractual basis, the lessee should have an absolute pass-through of all rights and conditions negotiated with the vendor. This can be accomplished by making the lessee the "attorney-in-fact" in representing the lessor in dealing with the vendor. Such a clause in the lease provides that the user shall have the absolute right to deal with the vendor on all matters involving this equipment. Also refer to clause 10-06 for a similar example.

10-10   Quiet Enjoyment

The financial stability of leasing organizations is not necessarily the same as that of original computer manufacturers. It is possible that the leasing organization, acting solely as a fiscal intermediary, can get into difficulty. Such difficulty should not have an impact on the lease, and as long as the user is current in maintaining his lease payments, the user should have the opportunity to continue to enjoy the use of the equipment without disruption. This clause is useful in a third party lease, to insure that creditors of the lessor will not bother the user, as long as the using organization is maintaining its obligations with respect to the lease. A similar clause is given in 7-18 for software package use.

   User's counsel should determine if the leased equipment is subject to any security interests in favor of the lessor's creditors which have priority over the lease itself. When in doubt a subordination or nondisturbance agreement should be obtained directly from the creditor.

10-11   Right to Defend in Actions

The incidents and responsibility of ownership in the equipment devolve upon the lessor, and not the end user. If ownership of the equipment generates problems which may be of interest to or disruptive to the user, then the user should have notice of and the right to defend against any actions, simultaneous with the lessor. This protects the user from the possibility of legal action which might take place without the user ever knowing it. By including in the leasing contract a clause giving the user the right to defend any actions involving the user or ownership of the equipment, then such actions must come to the attention of the user prior to their determination and may warrant user involvement.

10-12   Right to Dispute Taxes Levied

Property taxes are levied against an owner of property in many states and jurisdictions. The user of a computer is not the owner if the computer is leased from a third party. Normally the lessor protects itself from difficulty by saying it is the responsibility of the user to pay all property taxes when levied. Since taxing authorities have the right to place a lien against the equipment, and sell it at a sheriff's sale, the leasing company is not enthusiastic about disputes relating to property taxes. As a result most third party leases include wording which suggests that the user must pay all property taxes when due, and failure to do so is considered a breach of contract, resulting in termination of the lease, and further resulting in damages equal to all future lease payments due.

   Such a provision is clearly onerous, if property taxes are levied on a spurious basis, or if they can be legitimately disputed. Since the leasing company has no interest in disputing property taxes levied against its property, it must afford the right to dispute such taxes to the lessee, without onerous provisions of lease termination or default. A simple clause providing the user with the right to dispute property taxes, which can include placing the disputed amounts in escrow for the benefit of the lessor, is desirable in a lease contract.

E. SUPPLY CONTRACTS

The purchase of supplies does not normally require significant consideration, since most supplies are purchased with simple purchase orders, which typically contain appropriate standard terms. There are factors to be considered which might be critical to a successful operation. Disks, tapes, certain types of cards or optically readable documents, could be considered critical, and additional terms defined. These, of course, would have to be considered on the basis of the individual requirements of the installation, and the particular problems which experience has indicated might occur in the use of these supplies.

10-13 Supply Specifications (also see 6-13 for those supplies purchased directly from the original equipment manufacturer.)

The supply contract should include the specifications of the supplies, which match those given by the equipment manufacturer. Warranty by the supplier that the equipment or the supplies provided under the contract will meet the computer vendor's specifications, and will perform in accordance therewith should suffice to cover this point.

10-14 Workmanship

Since it is normally not possible to hold the supply manufacturer to reliability guarantees, some statement with respect to the workmanship of the supplies should be given, if feasible. A statement that the supplies are made to the highest level of workmanship and are guaranteed to be useful in operation for a period of time, or for a number of uses, as necessary, can be formulated. In the case of punch cards, for example, it is useful to insure that the cards are made to eliminate the possibilities of pin holes or other openings which might be misread by card reading equipment. Every effort should be made to excise from supplier contracts or purchase order forms any language which tends to exculpate the supplier from the warranties of merchantability and fitness for purposes afforded to users by the Uniform Commercial Code.

10-15 Functional Usability

The functions for which the supplies are to be used should be stated in a supply contract, which will hold the supply vendor responsible for successful use. A disk pack, for example, can be defined by function as capable of holding the inventory file of the organization, which consists of N records of Y characters. This will insure that the pack can contain the file so designated. Alternatively, it is possible to stipulate that the pack shall contain a total of N million characters subject to access within a given period of time, and that all such characters are accessible in the same amount of time and with the same relative ease. Punch cards, for example, should be defined in terms of function such as being capable of having information punched on them in 12 rows and eighty columns, and that the cards are sufficiently sound that punching such information will not create problems in handling them.

10-16 Continued Availability (see also 6-23 for a similar clause with respect to education.)

By definition, supplies wear out or are used up and have to be replaced. Since these supplies may be specifically tailored to a computer vendor's equipment, and since the specifications may be linked to this equipment, it may be necessary to insure that these supplies will continue to be available, even if the vendor discontinues manufacturing such equipment. If, for example, an installed machine is unique, or is the sole survivor of an unpopular series of equipment, then it may not be economical to manufacture the supplies. In this case, it would be desirable to have a clause in the contract which insures continued availability at reasonable prices for as long as the equipment is installed. A user will normally be unable to obtain such a commitment from the supplier, unless the user is willing to commit to a long-term purchase agreement for the supplies, with minimums.

   This type of agreement could be made with the original equipment manufacturer as well, in cases where such supplies were obtainable from that manufacturer. In addition, other clauses of chapter 6 which relate to payment, delivery, title passage, and the like should be considered in developing a supply contract.

F. PERSONAL SERVICE CONTRACTS

It is occasionally necessary to enter into contracts to provide for personal services, such as consulting agreements, or agreements for the provision of time and materials services to support a particular function within the data processing organization. Personal service contracts are sometimes difficult to deal with, in that it is often cumbersome to define the products to be delivered, and the time to be allotted. However, it is possible to establish a contract for personal services in which the user is more or less protected.

   Chapter 7, Software Packages, and chapter 8, Software Development Contracts, cover much of the material necessary to design a reasonable personal service contract. Where those chapters refer to fixed price contracts, some personal service contracts may be slightly different. Normally, personal service contracts are time and materials oriented, and provide for payment for the service on the basis of the time spent, and the expenses incurred. Very few contractual provisions, other than those given in chapters 5, 7, 8 and possibly 9, would have to be considered in a personal service contract.

10-17 Expenses

It is common for expenses to be included as a separate item of a personal service contract. Often these expenses are increased by a percentage, to recognize the costs of billing, paying, and servicing. Regardless of whether or not this is reasonable under particular circumstances, the contract should provide specifically how expenses are to be calculated, and what types of expenses are to be included. If air travel is included, it should be specified to be by coach, or by cheapest way, depending on the nature of the travel. Similarly, rates per mile of automobile usage, the use of public transportation as opposed to rental cars, the use of moderately priced hotels, all should be covered in a clause which defines the type of expenses to be incurred. Some service organizations have policies which allow staff members to travel with their wives or husbands, and for such travel to be reimbursed, which may mean that the service organization will attempt to pass such expenses through to the client. It is desirable to stipulate specifically which expenses the client will pay, and which expenses should be borne by the service organization as part of its own overhead.

10-18   Scope and Deliverables

In a personal service contract it is useful to define as explicitly as possible the scope of the contract and the products to be produced. In dealing with time and materials activities it is not always simple to delineate exactly what is to be accomplished. Often, the completion of one phase may alter the expectations of products in subsequent phases. In this case the scope and deliverables clause of the contract should so state, and should *by reference* incorporate into the contract the products of one phase which define the scope of subsequent phases. Staged, or unrestricted rights of cancellation are helpful (see clause 8-16).

10-19   Named Individuals

The reason that a personal service contract is often attractive to a buying organization is that the organization will obtain the services of *specific* individuals whose expertise and capabilities may be well known. Those individuals should be named in the contract, and a stipulation included that the contract can be performed only by them. Where possible, the contract should include, or incorporate by reference, a resume of each of the individuals so named, so that the experience level and caliber assumed is defined as a part of the contract in the event substitutions are proposed.

10-20   Rights to Approve Substitution or Addition of Staff

A corollary to clause 10-19 is the absolute right to approve the assignment of staff other than those individuals named. If it is necessary to substitute members of the staff, or add staff to accomplish the objectives defined, the characteristics of the individuals should be submitted for approval to the using organization and it should be afforded an opportunity to interview the candidates. An unconditional right to approve any substitutions or additions of staff is a part of a good personal service contract.

In addition to these clauses, it is strongly recommended that the clauses of section 8-E be incorporated in any personal service contract. Specifically these include clause 8-18, which presumes full-time employment; clause 8-19, staff accessibility during business termination; and clauses 8-20, 21, and 22, defining noncompetition, insurance and security. It is further desirable to include clause 8-12, progress reports, and clause 8-13, title transfer of all materials developed under the contract, or all materials defined as deliverables under clause 10-18.

G. INSTALLMENT PURCHASE

The original equipment manufacturer, when selling a computer, is often prepared to undertake the sale on an installment basis. This means that the computer manufacturer will provide a loan to the user, to be repaid in installments, and retain a security interest in the equipment as long as there is a balance outstanding on the installment purchase plan. This is very similar to the purchase of an automobile, where the automobile company or a bank acts as a fiscal intermediary to provide the necessary financing. Computer installment purchase agreements can be signed with banks as fiscal intermediaries, or the equipment manufacturer can sell the note to a fiscal organization. The benefit of installment purchase to the user is access to funds on a reasonable basis, using as security a lien on the equipment, which prevents a charge against other balance sheet assets. It is, however, a *purchase* agreement, and even if the user is dissatisfied with the equipment and decides to get rid of it, he cannot escape the obligations of the installment purchase agreement.

Failure to pay can result in repossession of the equipment. Most installment purchase agreements also provide for recourse against the general credit of the user and, consequently, to other assets, if, upon repossession, its sale results in lower proceeds than the principal balance remaining on the installment note. Often, the creditor need not even first have recourse to the security. If the original equipment manufacturer takes the lien and provides the installment purchase financing, he will be capable of arranging a fairly low resale price in the event of repossession. It is therefore desirable from a user viewpoint to recognize that this is only a financing mechanism, and does not necessarily reduce the user's investment in the equipment and the obligation of the user to project the use of the equipment for the period of the note.

If it is possible to negotiate an installment purchase contract under which the lien on the equipment is the sole recourse of the vendor (a nonrecourse note), then the user is in an excellent position. He is then capable of terminating the installment purchase contract by returning the equipment, without incurring further liability. This may be expensive, since most installment purchase plans call for a significant down payment, which means that the aggregate payments made to date of termination will far exceed those he might have made had he rented it. The "front-loading" of a nonrecourse installment sale will generally be immense.

The principal components of an installment purchase contract which differ from a purchase contract are those which protect the vendor and not the user. The lien which the vendor places on the equipment is the most significant difference between an installment purchase and a straight purchase contract. All clauses of chapter 6 are therefore applicable. This is a purchase contract, regardless of the method of financing.

10-21   Security Interest

Title to the equipment should pass to the user, upon making the down payment. However, the vendor who is providing the installment financing will have a security interest in the equipment until the final payment is made. The terms and conditions of that security interest should be defined in the installment purchase section of the purchase contract.

10-22   No Liens or Encumbrances

Since the user has an imperfect title in the equipment, and since the vendor has a lien on the equipment which predates any other encumbrance, it is in the interest of the vendor to insure that the user does not place additional liens or encumbrances on the equipment. Since the inability to place a "second mortgage" on the equipment may have a disastrous effect on subsequent user financings, particularly toward the end of the installments when user "equity" in the equipment is high, the user's financial officers may wish to battle against a clause prohibiting additional encumbrances.

Beyond that, the user should be free to do with the equipment as he sees fit, except that the user normally will not be allowed to move the equipment outside the jurisdiction where the lien can be exercised. Thus, it is probable that in an installment purchase the location of the equipment will be constrained to the country in which it is initially placed.

10-23   Rights

Most installment purchase contracts are onerous, in that they provide for acceleration of the principal balance if there is default in the payment of any installment. It is possible, however, that the user may have mechanical difficulties in making payments on a regular basis; the user's payment system may be faulty, someone may forget, an entry may not be generated. The user should accordingly provide for notice of default, and an appropriate period to cure that default before the installment note is converted into an immediate obligation to pay the total principal. It is equally desirable (but not always feasible) to request that the user be billed by the vendor for each installment payment. Such invoicing can act as a useful reminder to make the payments. However, many installment purchase contracts do not provide for invoicing since it is the obligation of the user to make the necessary payments, and since the vendor desires rapid recourse to correct the situation.

10-24   Disaster Protection

Inasmuch as the vendor has a secured interest in the equipment, it is incumbent on the user to maintain all necessary insurance protection, so that the vendor will be capable of collecting, regardless of whether the equipment is still in working condition. In the event of fire, theft, or other natural disaster which wipes out the equipment, insurance payments should be provided directly to the vendor for the principal balance. Normally, insurance is the only protection necessary to satisfy vendor obligations. However, other types of disasters which may not be insurable are normally covered by making the user responsible for payment to the vendor, regardless of what may have happened to the equipment. In the event of a sale of the equipment by the user, the obligation to the vendor should be satisfied out of the purchase price, unless the user can negotiate the right to sell the equipment subject to the debt.

10-25   Right to Prepayment

Although present law often provides that installment purchase contracts must give the consumer certain rights, an installment purchase contract entered into between two business organizations may not be covered under present consumer protection laws. Thus, it is important to have a right of prepayment without penalty, or without additional interest. This is useful in the event of a sale of the machine or in case of some disaster which results in payment of insurance. The user should have the absolute right to pay off the principal balance without further penalty at any time after entering into an installment purchase contract. Such payment should terminate the installment portion of the purchase contract, but should in no way reduce the obligations of the vendor to meet other contractual obligations entered into as a part of the purchase contract.

H. ADVANCE DEPOSIT AGREEMENT

When a user does not have a satisfactory credit rating, or when the balance sheet of the user does not reflect a sufficient net worth to support the rental of a large scale computer system, it is not uncommon for the manufacturer to request an advance deposit, which may be in the range of two to six months of rental. This deposit is then used by the manufacturer as security, in the event the user fails to pay rental or other obligations on time. It is most commonly used in a rental contract, when the manufacturer requires notice to terminate the contract. If, for example, the rental contract is a 90-day contract, it is common for the manufacturer to request a security deposit of at least 90 days, which will allow him to terminate the contract and yet assure collection of the rental which will fall due. An advance deposit agreement, which can, of course, be incorporated in the rental contract, should provide for refunding of the deposit on termination of the contract, or on the establishment of reasonable credit. Other than that, all provisions of a rental or purchase contract apply.

10-26 Advance Deposit Requirement

The requirement for the advance deposit should be stated in the contract, with an indication of the specific reasons why such a deposit is required. It may be required because of a poor credit history, because of an inadequate net worth, or because of evidence of inadequate cash flow to support continuing rental payments. Whatever the reason, the amount of the deposit and the reason for its need must be defined. This will provide the basis for eliminating the deposit when the situation has improved.

10-27 Refund Rights on Termination

Upon termination of the contract, the user should have the right to obtain an immediate refund of the amount on deposit, net of any rental payments due. It should be stated in the contract that the deposit should not be capable of being used to offset payments due to the manufacturer for reasons other than rental. If, for example, the user has purchased supplies from the manufacturer and has not yet paid invoices due for these, the advance deposit should not be usable to satisfy this obligation. The advance deposit should be requested and reserved solely for purposes of payment of rental invoices.

10-28   Refund Rights on Establishment of Good Credit

If the condition defined in clause 10-26 is cured, and the user has established reasonable credit, the requirement for continuation of the advance deposit should be waived, and an immediate refund made. In addition, the contract should provide that if the user has maintained timely payments over a period such as a year, the advance deposit should also be eliminated. If, alternately, the user can obtain other forms of security to protect the vendor, it should also generate a refund. A cosigner of the contract, a letter of credit from a bank, or an assignment of an interest in a certificate of deposit, can be provided as substitutes for the advance deposit requirement. The contract can also provide for other substitutions with vendor consent and permission for such substitution should not be unreasonably refused. When such substitution is made, a refund of the amount placed on deposit should be made immediately.

10-29   Trust Funds

Funds placed on deposit with the manufacturer should be denominated as trust funds belonging to the user. Reliance on state statutes governing use and investment of trust funds or security deposits is not encouraged, since those laws will normally be inapplicable to chattel lease security deposits. The user should insist that such funds be segregated in a separate, interest-bearing account and interest should inure to the benefit of the user, and be paid back to the user on a quarterly or annual basis. Requirements of segregation of these deposits are important to assure that the user has a better claim against them than the vendor's creditors in case of vendor bankruptcy.

I.   RELOCATION OF EQUIPMENT

It is necessary from time to time for equipment to be relocated, because the user moves his data processing center, or because the user wishes to use the equipment in another center. If the equipment is under maintenance contract, it is desirable to have the manufacturer providing the maintenance also perform the relocation. This will insure that the manufacturer will retain responsibility for keeping the equipment in good working order, and for maintaining the service functions at a uniform level of reliability.

It is usual to sign a separate relocation agreement, which stipulates the role to be performed by the manufacturer and the responsibilities assumed. Such a relocation agreement can be included as part of an original purchase contract, or as part of an original maintenance contract. Alternatively it can be negotiated at the time that relocation is contemplated.

10-30   Functions Performed During Relocation

The relocation agreement should stipulate specifically what functions are to be performed by the manufacturer during relocation. The equipment is disconnected, dismantled, crated for moving, and possibly moved by the manufacturer. In addition, the manufacturer may wish to test the equipment prior to shipment to insure that it is operating in accordance with the terms of the maintenance contract, so that any defects detected after relocation can be blamed on the mover. When the equipment has been moved, the manufacturer will be called upon to install it, to put it back into operation, and to test it to see that it works in accordance with the performance characteristics in place prior to the move. This clause serves as a statement of scope of the relocation agreement.

10-31   Applicability of All Warranties on Completion

The equipment after relocation should perform exactly as it performed before. Thus, a reaffirmation of all warranties of operability should be made as a part of the relocation agreement. The performance of the equipment is to be exactly as it was prior to the move. Even if the manufacturer does not physically move the equipment, the user is well advised to require the manufacturer to meet these requirements and to let the manufacturer seek recourse from the moving company if appropriate. Any other arrangements will permit the user to be "whip-sawed" between manufacturer and mover, each blaming the other for the damage.

10-32   Time Requirement

This clause defines the time of delivery of the relocated equipment, and stipulates the time required to perform the service of clause 10-30. Normally relocation can be performed in a matter of days, and, if that is the case, the time requirement can be strictly stipulated. If it takes significantly more time than in the contract, the user will incur damages as a result of his inability to use the equipment in the new location. Remedies could conceivably be liquidated, or other forms of recourse sought. Where time is of the essence, it should be clearly stated.

J. TRAINING

It may be desirable from time to time to contract with an outside organization to provide an in-house training program. Such programs are normally designed specifically for the user organization, or represent some modification of a standard program offered by the vending organization. The contract form need not be very complex, since the amounts involved are normally small. However, for purposes of protecting the user, some contractual obligation is desirable.

10-33   Course Content and Objectives

The product specification of a training program is the course content in outline form, and the objectives to be achieved by the course. If it is desired by the user to have people capable of designing systems using decision tables, and a decision table course is purchased, this objective should be stated in the contract. In addition, the materials to be supplied should be included. The course syllabus, agenda, instructor's notes, tests, audio-visual equipment, etc., should be defined as a part of the overall deliverables included in the contract.

10-34   Course Schedule

A course schedule must be established which delineates in time when the course is ready to be delivered, when the necessary instructors are available, and when the audience can be assembled. If the audience requires preparatory training as a prerequisite, then this should be indicated so that if there are any delays in preparation they will eliminate the obligation of the user to make an audience available. Rights to postpone the course, rights to conduct it on multiple occasions, etc., should be considered as well.

10-35 Attendee Restrictions and Characteristics

It is the user's responsibility to provide an audience, but that audience must be fairly well defined, especially if it is the responsibility of the vendor to modify the skills of that audience in some predefined way. If it is the responsibility of the training organization to enable people to use decision tables in systems analysis, then personnel entering this course must be capable of performing systems analysis. The characteristics of the audience should be defined in terms of entry level at the inception of the course. This will give teeth to the definition of end product in clause 10-33. The actual number of attendees which can be reasonably accommodated in the course must also be given. It is possible that, if the course uses workshop methods, the training organization cannot undertake to train more than 15 or 20 persons at the same time. Additional people would require additional instructor staff to assist in grading and in participation in workshop presentations. The maximum number of attendees in the training program is a part of the contract.

Other terms which should be included in a training contract are clauses 10-19 and 20, which relate to named individuals to be used in performance of the contract. The quality of the teacher often is a far greater determinant of success than the course content or the audience characteristics. The individuals conducting the course should be named and the right to substitute for them restricted. In addition all components of section 8-E, and certain components of chapters 7, 8, and 9 should be considered in drafting a training contract, depending on its size, scope and complexity.

10-36 Training Facilities

When a training course is conducted on an in-house basis, it is the user's responsibility to supply the necessary facilities. These include classrooms, blackboards, equipment, possibly computer time, and such other material as may be necessary, other than the syllabi or other material specifically identified in clause 10-33. The user's responsibilities should be clearly articulated, so that the vendor cannot blame course failure or delay on some pretended user inadequacy.

A. INTRODUCTION TO APPENDIX A

Appendix A contains some 255 clauses which could be included in a comprehensive contract. These clauses have been segregated in accordance with the chapters in which they are discussed. The appendix may be used by first referring to the chapter in which the particular type of contract has been discussed, and there locating appropriate clauses. Alternatively, clauses may be located by name in the index, or in the separate list of clauses provided. In any event, once the reader reaches appendix A, the following will be the information found with respect to each clause.

B. CONTENT OF SECTIONS OF APPENDIX A

There are 12 different components in the section related to each clause. These are briefly described below:

A. *Clause Name*. This summarizes the clause in a few words. The clause name is used in the index, in the chapter, and in the clause lists.

B. *Clause Number*. The clause number is comprised of the chapter number where the clause is referenced and a sequential number assigned randomly, in sequence by the functional grouping established in the chapter. Thus, the first clause is called 5-01, since chapter 5 is the first chapter in which specific clauses are discussed. Clause 01 is the arbitration clause, discussed in chapter 5 as fitting within the group of "substantive" clauses therein.

C. *Contract Types Used In*. This section identifies the contract types in which this clause might be found. In the case of chapter 5, clauses therein would normally

11
INTRODUCTION TO THE APPENDICES

be found in all types of contracts, since they are by definition general. A clause discussed in chapter 7, a software package clause, might also be needed in a software development contract or a service center contract. In this case the clause number used is in the first chapter in which the clause is referenced. All later chapters will refer to the original clause number.

D. *Risk Rating*. For purposes of the appendix the risk rating used is comprised of four elements:

    1 — Key
    2 — Important
    3 — Minor
    4 — Limited or no quantifiable impact.

This rating is used rather than a dollar or "point" valuation, since valuations only make sense in the context of an actual particular contract. Obviously, some clauses deemed unimportant by the authors may, in a particular case, be critically important, and *vice versa*.

E. *Intent and Scope*. The purpose of the clause is defined in this field.

F. *Protection Against*. This clause identifies the possible exposure to be covered and the problems which might occur if this clause were not to be included. Where the danger is obvious, or covered in 5, it is not repeated.

G. *Standard Clause Provided by Manufacturers*. This category shows the applicable standard clause, if any, provided by specific manufacturers, with that manufacturer referenced. Where several manufacturers supply substantially equivalent clauses, the selection has been made without regard to the manufacturer. Most clauses do not have a "standard" clause included.

H. *Ideal Coverage*. This is perhaps the most important component of the appendix, in that it identifies the authors' views on what would be an idealized clause from the *user* point of view.

I. *Fall-back Alternatives*. Where it is impossible to achieve an ideal situation, suggestions are made in this field for potential fall-back alternatives. There are cases where there are no fall-backs which are useful. The fall-backs may be obvious, in which case none are shown.

J. *Possible Remedies*. Where possible, *contractual* remedies are preferred to remedies at law. Wherever possible, therefore, contractual remedies have been identified as appropriate for reach.

K. *Comments*. Any additional comments deemed appropriate may be noted here.

L. *References to Other Clauses*. A cross-reference is given in this component where the clause does not normally stand alone, or where similar subject matter is covered by another clause. A general business termination clause might provide for an orderly termination in the event of vendor bankruptcy. A specific business termination clause in a software contract might provide for the transfer of title of the software product to the user in the event of bankruptcy. These two clauses would be cross-referenced here.

The reader should note that, in the body of this text, there is a discussion, clause by clause, of each clause appearing in the appendix. Since that textual discussion is not usually repeated in the "Comments" section in the appendix, reference to the text is strongly recommended.

C. INTRODUCTION TO APPENDIX B

Appendix B contains "checklists," or concise, preliminary guidelines for the negotiation and drafting of various, specific types of data processing contracts, corresponding to those types discussed generally in the text.

While these checklists are not exhaustive, they are more detailed, and thus more helpful, than reference to the Table of Contents as a means of identifying clauses necessary for consideration in a proposed contract. Obviously, each specific contract will include more—and less, in some cases—than the relevant checklist. The checklists are included courtesy of Brandon Consulting Group, Inc.

APPENDIX A

A. CLAUSE NAME: Arbitration **B. CLAUSE NO.:** 5-01

C. CONTRACT TYPES USED IN: All **D. RISK RATING:** 1

E. INTENT AND SCOPE

To provide a means for the resolution of a dispute under the contract without the expense, delay and formality encountered in litigation.

F. PROTECTION AGAINST

Prevents a manufacturer or user with significant resources from arbitrarily using the process of litigation to subvert or otherwise thwart the intent of the agreement between the parties.

H. IDEAL COVERAGE

Any dispute under this agreement shall be submitted to binding arbitration in the City of _____, under the rules then prevailing of the American Arbitration Association. Judgment upon any award made in such arbitration may be entered and enforced in any court of competent jurisdiction.

I. FALL-BACK ALTERNATIVES

1. Limit arbitration to claims of less than $50,000.
2. Arbitration to be non-binding. If not accepted by either party, litigation is mandated.

K. COMMENTS

Arbitration is to the advantage of the party with the lesser resources—typically the vendor in case of software contracts, and the user in case of hardware contracts. Arbitration is quick, and usually settles at a mid-point of a dispute when issues are not clear.

A. **CLAUSE NAME:** Business Termination   B. **CLAUSE NO.:** 5-02

C. **CONTRACT TYPES USED IN:** All   D. **RISK RATING:** 3

E. **INTENT AND SCOPE**

To ensure that acts of bankruptcy on the part of either party will trigger termination of the contract.

F. **PROTECTION AGAINST**

To protect either party against possible adverse developments. In the event of user business termination, to ensure that the vendor has the right to recover moneys due and possibly recover equipment owned by the vendor. To protect the user from vendor termination of business at the least possible disruption.

G. **STANDARD CLAUSE PROVIDED BY MANUFACTURERS**

Termination: Should Buyer neglect to make payment hereunder when due, or do or perform any of the Buyer's agreements hereunder, or should Buyer be or become insolvent or a party to any bankruptcy or receivership proceeding or any similar action affecting the affairs or property of Buyer, prior to payment in full of the purchase price, Seller may at its option and with or without demand or notice to Buyer (if given, notice by mail to Buyer's address, shown in this agreement being sufficient) elect to sue therefor, thereby vesting title in Buyer, or, with or without legal process, take possession of said equipment, Buyer thereby waiving all claims and damages arising from or connected with such taking and all of Buyer's rights under this agreement including rights to amounts paid and to the equipment; or Seller may pursue any alternative or additional and cumulative remedies provided by law, and may assess against Buyer all costs and attorney's fees incurred in enforcing its rights hereunder, to the extent permitted by law. (Burroughs)

H. **IDEAL COVERAGE**

In the event that either party shall cease conducting business in the normal course, become insolvent, make a general assignment for the benefit of creditors, suffer or permit the appointment of a receiver for its business or assets or shall avail itself of, or become subject to, any proceeding under the federal Bankruptcy Code of 1978, as amended, or any other statute of any state relating to insolvency or the protection of rights of creditors, then [at the option of the other party] this agreement shall terminate and be of no further force and effect and any property or rights of such other party, tangible or intangible, shall forthwith be returned to it.

L. **REFERENCES TO OTHER CLAUSES:** See also 7-19, 8-19, 10-15, 9-18, and 10-10.

A. CLAUSE NAME: Most Favored Nations   **B. CLAUSE NO.:** 5-03

C. CONTRACT TYPES USED IN: All   **D. RISK RATING:** 2

E. INTENT AND SCOPE

To ensure that there is no discrimination against the user by the vendor; to provide that no other users gain a competitive advantage over the user.

F. PROTECTION AGAINST

Protects against discrimination.

H. IDEAL COVERAGE

All of the prices, terms, warranties and benefits granted by vendor herein are comparable to or better than the equivalent terms being offered by vendor to any present customer. If the vendor shall, during the term of this contract, enter into arrangements with any other customer providing greater benefits or more favorable terms, this agreement shall thereupon be deemed amended to provide the same to purchaser.

I. FALL-BACK ALTERNATIVES

Insert the word "commercial" before "customer" in the preceding language.

K. COMMENTS

The insertion of the word "commercial" under I is particularly appropriate if the vendor has signed a GSA contract, whose terms may not be always applicable to commercial contracts.

A. **CLAUSE NAME:** Assignment of Contract by User   B. **CLAUSE NO.:** 5-04

C. **CONTRACT TYPES USED IN:** All   D. **RISK RATING:** 3

E. **INTENT AND SCOPE**

Promotes business flexibility by allowing user to assign contract without restriction.

F. **PROTECTION AGAINST**

Protects again forfeitures, price renegotiations and other actions by the vendor in the event of desired or required disposition of equipment or services supplied under the contract.

G. **STANDARD CLAUSE PROVIDED BY MANUFACTURERS**

Transfer of Equipment: The rights and license granted Customer hereunder to hold and use the Equipment are restricted solely and exclusively to Customer and may not be assigned, subleased, sublicensed, sold, offered for sale, disposed of, encumbered or mortgaged.

Notwithstanding the above, Customer shall have the right, upon written notice to ADR, to transfer this Agreement to any affiliated company to whom Customer's right to use, or its lease of, any computer equipment related to the use of the Equipment licensed hereunder has been transferred.

Assignments: This Installment Payment Agreement is not assignable by the Purchaser, nor may the Purchaser sell, transfer, substantially modify, relocate or dispose of the machines, or any of them, without prior written permission of IBM. In no event may the machines be relocated outside the United States. Any attempted assignment or transfer by the Purchaser of any of the rights, duties or obligations of this Installment Payment Agreement is void.

General: This Agreement is not assignable without written permission from IBM; any attempt to assign any rights, duties or obligations which arise under this Agreement without such permission shall be void.

General: Without the prior written consent of Honeywell, Lessee shall not assign or transfer this Agreement or permit the use of the equipment by any person other than by operators in Lessee's direct employ or by representatives of Honeywell.

H. **IDEAL COVERAGE**

This agreement may be assigned by the user without vendor's consent. Upon such assignment and an assumption of liability hereunder by the assignee, the user shall be discharged of any liability hereunder.

I. **FALL-BACK ALTERNATIVES**

(i) delete the discharge of assignor; (ii) require that assignee be of comparable net worth to user; (iii) require vendor consent, which shall not be unreasonably withheld or delayed; (iv) set standards for permitted assignment; (v) permit free assignment among user's affiliates and subsidiaries and in the event of mergers, consolidations, sales of assets, etc.

K. **COMMENTS**

It is very necessary to have at least enough assignability so that the vendor cannot interfere with business combinations and sales of businesses.

L. **REFERENCES TO OTHER CLAUSES:** See also 6-78, 6-79, 10-09, 5-05.

A. **CLAUSE NAME:** Non-Assignment of Contract by Vendor   B. **CLAUSE NO.:** 5-05

C. **CONTRACT TYPES USED IN:** All   D. **RISK RATING:** 3

E. **INTENT AND SCOPE**

To ensure that the vendor cannot assign the contract to any organization incapable of meeting the obligations hereunder.

F. **PROTECTION AGAINST**

Protects against vendor discharge of obligation by assignment.

G. **STANDARD CLAUSE PROVIDED BY MANUFACTURERS**

Assignment: ADR may assign the license fee payments reserved herein or any of its other rights hereunder. Customer, on receiving notice from ADR of any such assignment, shall abide thereby and make payments as directed.

H. **IDEAL COVERAGE**

This contract may not be assigned by the vendor.

I. **FALL-BACK ALTERNATIVES**

This contract may not be assigned by the vendor except with the written consent of the user. (This consent shall not be unreasonably withheld.)

K. **COMMENTS**

This provision is most critical where services are involved, for obvious reasons.

L. **REFERENCES TO OTHER CLAUSES:** 5-04.

A. **CLAUSE NAME:** Cross Guaranties.   B. **CLAUSE NO.:** 5-06

C. **CONTRACT TYPES USED IN:** All   D. **RISK RATING:** 3

E. **INTENT AND SCOPE**

To ensure that a contract signed by subsidiary has the support of the parent organization, and vice versa.

F. **PROTECTION AGAINST**

Prevents circumvention of obligations through use of corporate shells or subsidiaries.

H. **IDEAL COVERAGE**

(i) *Where negative covenants (restrictions or activities) are involved:* If any affiliate (as hereinafter defined) of a party shall take any action which, if done by a party, would constitute a breach of this agreement, the same shall be deemed a breach by such party with like legal effect. "Affiliate" shall mean a "parent", subsidiary or other company controlling, controlled by or in common control with a party.

(ii) *Where affirmative guaranties are sought:* By their signatures at the foot hereof, the following companies . . . hereby, jointly and severally with X, guarantee the full and timely performance hereof by X.

K. **COMMENTS**

Corporate guaranties raise tricky legal problems and special attention should be paid by counsel to ensure that they will be enforceable, including obtaining of Board resolutions and evidence of benefit to the guarantors.

L. **REFERENCES TO OTHER CLAUSES:** 5-25.

A. **CLAUSE NAME:** Indemnification Inclusion of Costs	B. **CLAUSE NO.:** 5-07
C. **CONTRACT TYPES USED IN:** All	D. **RISK RATING:** 3

E. INTENT AND SCOPE

To ensure that the expenses incurred by either party in litigation, arbitration, or costs of debt collection are included as an obligation of the party at fault.

F. PROTECTION AGAINST

Protects against the expenditure of substantial expenses to cure a default, which expense would otherwise diminish the award.

G. STANDARD CLAUSE PROVIDED BY MANUFACTURERS

Default: Purchaser agrees to pay reasonable attorney's fees (15% of the unpaid balance, unless otherwise provided by law) for enforcing UNIVAC's rights after Purchaser's default.

H. IDEAL COVERAGE

Each party hereby agrees to indemnify the other against all losses, costs and expenses (including reasonable counsel fees) which the other may incur by reason of the breach of any term, provision, covenant, warranty or representation contained herein and/or in connection with the enforcement of this Agreement or any provision hereof.

K. COMMENTS

Normally the vendor would like its costs reimbursed in the event it is required to employ collection agencies or attorneys to enforce the contract. It appears equitable, however, to make this remedy two-sided.

L. REFERENCES TO OTHER CLAUSES: 6-93.

A. CLAUSE NAME: User Limitation of Liability   B. CLAUSE NO.: 5-08

C. CONTRACT TYPES USED IN: All   D. RISK RATING: 3

E. INTENT AND SCOPE

To limit the user's liability to some maximum amount.

F. PROTECTION AGAINST

To protect against the user being held responsible for consequential or other damages in excess of some reasonable amount.

H. IDEAL COVERAGE

The user's liability shall, in the aggregate, be limited to the smaller of the following:
- The total amount payable under this contract (in the case of a software contract)
- The total amount payable by the user over a 6-month period under this contract (in the event of a rental contract)
- 10% of the purchase price of the equipment hereunder (in the event of a complete purchase contract)
- $ X. (in the event it is desired to limit the liability to a predetermined amount)

I. FALL-BACK ALTERNATIVES

Any alternative which limits the liability of the user in some fashion can be a reasonable fallback. The primary purpose is to ensure that liability is not open-ended.

L. REFERENCES TO OTHER CLAUSES: 5-09.

A. **CLAUSE NAME:** Vendor Limitation of Liability B. **CLAUSE NO.:** 5-09

C. **CONTRACT TYPES USED IN:** All D. **RISK RATING:** 3

E. **INTENT AND SCOPE**

To ensure that the vendor's liability has a finite limitation.

F. **PROTECTION AGAINST**

To protect against unreasonable damages being paid by the vendor.

G. **STANDARD CLAUSE PROVIDED BY MANUFACTURERS**

Warranty Exclusion and Limitation of Damages: Except as expressly set forth in writing in this agreement, or except as provided in the clause entitled "Contractor's Commitments, Warranties and Representations" and except for the implied warranty of merchantability, THERE ARE NO WARRANTIES EXPRESSED OR IMPLIED. IN NO EVENT WILL HONEYWELL BE LIABLE TO THE GOVERNMENT FOR CONSEQUENTIAL DAMAGES AS DEFINED IN THE UNIFORM COMMERCIAL CODE, Section 2-715, in effect in the District of Columbia as of January 1, 1973; i.e., consequential damages resulting from the seller's breach include: (a) any loss resulting from general or particular requirements and needs of which the seller at the time of contracting had reason to know and which could not reasonably be prevented by cover or otherwise; and (b) injury to persons or property proximately resulting from any breach of warranty. (Honeywell)

Limitation of Liability: **The foregoing warranties are in lieu of all other warranties express or implied, including, but not limited to, the implied warranties of merchantability and fitness for a particular purpose.**

The Purchaser further agrees that IBM will not be liable for any lost profits, or for any claim or demand against the Purchaser by any other party, except a claim for patent infringement as provided herein.

In no event will IBM be liable for consequential damages even if IBM has been advised of the possibility of such damages.

H. **IDEAL COVERAGE**

The vendor's liability shall be limited to the following:
- Amounts payable (already received by vendor) under this contract.
- $ X. (if user costs can be realistically determined, and a specific amount established)
- The aggregate of all costs incurred by the user in preparation for the use of vendor's equipment, which costs are not capable of being applied to another vendor's equipment, as determined by an independent appraiser.
- All losses incurred by the user as a result of vendor's breach, for a period not to exceed two years.

I. **FALL-BACK ALTERNATIVES**

It is not unreasonable for the vendor to have some limit to his liability. However, that limit should take into account whatever costs might be realistically incurred by the user which cannot be recovered by the user as a result of vendor failure.

Any clause limiting vendor liability should be carefully considered. Some liabilities which may flow to third parties could be excused by such a clause and leave the user exposed and unindemnified.

Another approach to vendor liability is contained in 5-04, which restricts vendor liability by *type* rather than amount. Many vendors try to get both limitations.

L. REFERENCES TO OTHER CLAUSES: 5-08, 5-10.

A. CLAUSE NAME: Consequential Damages   B. CLAUSE NO.: 5-10

C. CONTRACT TYPES USED IN: All   D. RISK RATING: 3

E. INTENT AND SCOPE

Both parties should be protected from consequential damages, if this can realistically be done.

F. PROTECTION AGAINST

To protect against the possibility of an infinite expansion of liability as a result of events which are indirect consequences of breach of the contract.

G. STANDARD CLAUSE PROVIDED BY MANUFACTURERS

Limitation of Liability: The Customer agrees that IBM will not be liable for any consequential damages, even if IBM has been advised of the possibility of such damages.

In the event any errors in processed data result from NCR's performance hereunder, NCR will correct such errors, and in the event damages result from the negligence of NCR in its performance hereunder, NCR's liability therefor shall be limited to damages arising solely, directly, and proximately therefrom. In no event shall NCR be liable for consequential or special damages arising from this Agreement or its performance.

H. IDEAL COVERAGE

Neither party shall be liable to the other for any indirect, special or consequential damages.

I. FALL-BACK ALTERNATIVES

Set a limit to consequential damages.

K. COMMENTS

It may be possible to obtain agreement from a hungry vendor to become liable for consequential damages, if it can be clearly demonstrated to the vendor that his breach will necessarily have some indirect, but important, consequences to the user. It is always difficult to get vendor agreement on consequential damages, since they are usually not prepared to risk open-ended liability or go into bankruptcy to protect themselves from being prosecuted for potentially infinite damages. A limit on amount may help conquer resistance. In the event that it is impossible to get vendor commitment for consequential damages, it is best to have a bi-lateral clause which holds both parties harmless from such damages.

L. REFERENCES TO OTHER CLAUSES: 5-08, 5-09.

A. **CLAUSE NAME:** Rights Upon Orderly Termination   B. **CLAUSE NO.:** 5-11

C. **CONTRACT TYPES USED IN:** All   D. **RISK RATING:** 3

E. **INTENT AND SCOPE**

To provide a procedure or mechanism in the event of orderly termination, that is, the expiration of the contract in accordance with its terms.

F. **PROTECTION AGAINST**

To protect each party against the other's attempts to use the termination of the contract as a means of obtaining leverage upon the other party.

H. **IDEAL COVERAGE**

Upon termination or other expiration of this contract each party shall forthwith return to the other all papers, materials and other properties of the other held by each for purposes of execution of the contract. In addition, each party will assist the other party in orderly termination of this contract and the transfer of all aspects hereof, tangible and intangible, as may be necessary for the orderly, non-disrupted business continuation of each party.

K. **COMMENTS**

Normally, when a contract expires or is terminated, a stand-by or alternate method of operation has been pre-arranged by the user. In certain types of contracts, however, it is important to ensure the goodwill of the vendor in such termination. When terminating a service bureau contract, for example, it is desirable to be able to obtain access to programs and data without additional cost, particularly where the vendor is losing out to another service bureau. Consideration should be given, in arrangements whereby the vendor has control of important materials belonging to the user, to provisions for a hold-back of final payments until the transfer has been completed, to provisions for injunctive relief or to per-diem liquidated damages. In the course of contract performance, careful records should be maintained respecting properties transferred, and receipts obtained, in order to avoid disputes as to the items returnable upon termination.

L. **REFERENCES TO OTHER CLAUSES:** 6-91, 7-28, 9-16, 9-17, 10-27.

A. **CLAUSE NAME:** Force Majeure   B. **CLAUSE NO.:** 5-12

C. **CONTRACT TYPES USED IN:** All   D. **RISK RATING:** 2

E. **INTENT AND SCOPE**

To protect against unforeseen circumstances beyond the control of either party.

G. **STANDARD CLAUSE PROVIDED BY MANUFACTURERS**

NCR shall not be responsible for delays in processing or in the delivery of the processed data caused by strikes, lockouts, riots, epidemics, war, governmental regulations, fire, communication line failure, power failure, acts of God, or other causes beyond its control.

Excused Non-Performance: Bunker Ramo shall not be liable, and Customer shall have no right, in respect of any delay in delivery or failure to deliver Equipment or any component or device used in connection therewith, or of the non-performance or delay in performance of any term or condition of this Agreement directly or indirectly resulting from any cause beyond the control of Bunker Ramo.

H. **IDEAL COVERAGE**

Neither party shall be responsible for delays or failures in performance resulting from acts beyond the control of such party. Such acts shall include but not be limited to acts of God, strikes, lockouts, riots, acts of war, epidemics, governmental regulations superimposed after the fact, fire, communication line failures, power failures, earthquakes or other disasters.

I. **FALL-BACK ALTERNATIVES**

Certain types of failures may be excluded from the force majeure clause. Power failure, communication line failure and such may be deemed to be within the control of a party, depending upon the nature of the contract.

K. **COMMENTS**

Certain types of contracts, and certain provisions of other contracts, may require some escape valves from the force majeure excuse. For example, in most purchase transactions, a purchaser should be entitled to cancel for delays in delivery, even if occasioned by force majeure, after some specific lapse of time; otherwise the user can be faced with an indefinite "over-hang" of liability, say, where the vendor's plant burns down and requires extensive reconstruction.

L. **REFERENCES TO OTHER CLAUSES:** 6-72, 6-92.

A. **CLAUSE NAME:** Confidentiality B. **CLAUSE NO.:** 5-13

C. **CONTRACT TYPES USED IN:** All D. **RISK RATING:** 2

E. **INTENT AND SCOPE**

To ensure that materials belonging to either party are kept confidential.

F. **PROTECTION AGAINST**

To protect against disclosure by either party of trade secrets or business practices of the other.

G. **STANDARD CLAUSE PROVIDED BY MANUFACTURERS**

Protection and Security: The Customer agrees not to provide or otherwise make available any licensed program or optional material, including but not limited to flow charts, logic diagrams and source code, in any form, to any person other than Customer or IBM employees without prior written consent from IBM, except during the period any such person is on the Customer's premises with the Customer's permission for purposes specifically related to the Customer's use of the licensed program or optional materials.

Customer acknowledges that the Product is proprietary to BASI and has been developed as a trade secret at BASI's expense. Customer agrees that it will hold and use the Product in the same manner as it deals with its own proprietary information and trade secrets and that the Customer will not divulge, nor permit any of its employees, agents or representatives to divulge any data or information with respect to the Product or the programs and technology embodied therein or any other documentation, models, descriptions, forms instructions or other information relating thereto. If Customer or any of its employees, agents or representatives shall attempt to use or dispose of the Product or any of its aspects or components or any duplication or modification thereof in a manner contrary to the terms of this license, BASI shall have the right, in addition to such other remedies which may be available to it, to injunctive relief enjoining such acts or attempts, it being acknowledged that legal remedies are inadequate. (Brandon Applied Systems, Inc.)

The items listed below are Customer confidential technical data to be treated in accordance with the Confidentiality paragraph of the Agreement for IBM Systems Engineering Services and terms and conditions of this Supplement. The items must be in writing and must be described specifically for identification purposes, but the description should be in non-confidential language. IBM will designate an individual to receive the items listed below and he shall give the Customer a written receipt for each item he receives. Items must be disclosed to this individual in order to be considered as Customer confidential technical data by IBM. The maximum period for treatment of Customer technical data as confidential under this Supplement is 30 months after commencement of the Schedule of Services as shown on the Service Estimate.

Description	Written Document Containing Data	Location Where Data to be Used

_____ *(hereinafter referred to as "User")* acknowledges the
receipt of _____ *the program* _____
(all of which is hereinafter referred to as the "program material"). It is agreed that said

_____ _program contains confidential information of the Sperry Rand Corporation, Univac Division (hereinafter referred to as "Univac"). In consideration of the receipt of said program material and other valuable consideration, User agrees to hold the information contained in said program material in confidence. In particular, User agrees not to disclose such information to any other party and to take such steps as are necessary to prevent the disclosure of such information to others._

H. IDEAL COVERAGE

Each party acknowledges that all material and information which has or will come into the possession or knowledge of each in connection with this contract or the performance hereof, consists of confidential and proprietary data, whose disclosure to or use by third parties will be damaging. Both parties, therefore, agree to hold such material and information in strictest confidence, not to make use thereof other than for the performance of this contract, to release it only to employees requiring such information, and not to release or disclose it to any other party. Each party agrees not to release such information or material to any employee who has not signed a written agreement expressly binding himself not to use or disclose it.

J. POSSIBLE REMEDIES

It may be possible to establish specific liquidated remedies for a breach of disclosure. It is hard to determine what these might be. As a result it is normally recommended that no specific damages be assessed with reference to a breach of confidentiality; in the event of such a breach, it is probable that significant damages can be established. Injunctive remedies should be provided for, however, to restrain further a continuing leakage of information. Normally, such a breach should also permit contract termination.

L. REFERENCES TO OTHER CLAUSES: 5-15, 5-17, 9-21, 9-24, 10-01.

A. CLAUSE NAME: Agreement with Employees	B. CLAUSE NO.: 5-14
C. CONTRACT TYPES USED IN: All	D. RISK RATING: 3

E. INTENT AND SCOPE

The protection required under clause 5-13 (Confidentiality) should require that each party have an agreement with each of its employees who may have access to such confidential information. Thus this clause supports the confidentiality clause and insures that the corporation warrants that it has an agreement with each employee with respect to confidentiality.

G. STANDARD CLAUSE PROVIDED BY MANUFACTURERS

The Customer agrees that he will take appropriate action by instruction, agreement, or otherwise with his employees or other persons permitted access to licensed programs and/or optional materials to satisfy his obligations under this Agreement with respect to use, copying, modification, and protection and security of licensed programs and optional materials. (IBM)

H. IDEAL COVERAGE

(i)   See 5-13, second and third sentences under "H".

(ii) Both parties agree to take appropriate action with respect to their employees to insure that the obligations of non-use and non-disclosure of confidential information under this agreement can be fully satisfied.

I. FALL–BACK ALTERNATIVES

A clause can be written which is less broad, but which specifically obliges each party to treat the other's information with the same confidentiality that it treats its own proprietary information. It is, however, preferable to require that specific agreements with employees be obtained, so that each party can secure rights as a third-party beneficiary with respect to the other's employees.

L. REFERENCES TO OTHER CLAUSES: 5-13, 10-01, 10-02.

A. CLAUSE NAME: Survival beyond Completion   **B. CLAUSE NO.:** 5-15

C. CONTRACT TYPES USED IN: All   **D. RISK RATING:** 3

E. INTENT AND SCOPE

To insure that all or certain clauses of the contract survive beyond completion or termination of the contract. A purchase contract, for example, completes upon delivery of the items to be purchased and payment therefor. Certain clauses, specifically those relating to confidentiality, must survive forever; others, such as warranties, must survive beyond delivery for some agreed time period.

F. PROTECTION AGAINST

Protection against expiration of promises made in the contract when the contract is completed or terminated.

G. STANDARD CLAUSE PROVIDED BY MANUFACTURERS

Survival of Provisions: The provisions of Section 7 and 8 hereof shall survive termination of employment in the manner provided in Section 6 hereof. (BASI)

H. IDEAL COVERAGE

The terms, provisions, representations and warranties contained in this contract shall survive the delivery of [the product] and the payment of the purchase price.

I. FALL-BACK ALTERNATIVES

Specify those provisions that will survive.

K. COMMENTS

Those terms which should survive forever include terms relating to 5-13, confidentiality, 5-11, rights upon orderly termination, 5-07, 08, and 09 relating to indemnification and liability, 5-28, patent indemnity, and such other terms as may be necessary to enforce those provisions. The best approach is to have a simple and complete "survival" clause and to negotiate specific time limitations on certain clauses, such as warranties, leaving all other provisions to survive forever (subject, of course, to statutes of limitation written into law, or the contract.)

L. REFERENCES TO OTHER CLAUSES: 5-29

A. CLAUSE NAME: Non-hiring of Employees   **B. CLAUSE NO.:** 5-16

C. CONTRACT TYPES USED IN: All   **D. RISK RATING:** 2

E. INTENT AND SCOPE

Neither party should raid employees of the other. This tempting but damaging activity should be contractually prohibited, particularly in personal service arrangements.

F. PROTECTION AGAINST

To protect against the loss of valuable personnel.

H. IDEAL COVERAGE

For the term of this contract, and for N months after its termination, each party agrees not to employ any employee of the other party.

I. FALL-BACK ALTERNATIVES

The clause can be softened by prohibiting solicitation only or by providing that if an employee is hired away, the guilty party will pay to the injured party liquidated damages equal to, say, one year's salary.

J. POSSIBLE REMEDIES

It is not uncommon for contracts not to prohibit employment but merely to provide for a liquidated remedy for such hiring. This is probably appropriate in the data processing industry where employee mobility is high and where unhappy employees are not only useless, but potentially dangerous.

L. REFERENCES TO OTHER CLAUSES: 8-19, 8-20

A. CLAUSE NAME: Rights to New Ideas   **B. CLAUSE NO.:** 5-17

C. CONTRACT TYPES USED IN: All   **D. RISK RATING:** 3

E. INTENT AND SCOPE

To ensure that any new ideas, methods, adaptations, processes, etc. developed as a result of the relationship contemplated in the contract remain the property of the party benefiting from such ideas and from the contract.

F. PROTECTION AGAINST

To protect against the appropriation or resale of ideas by the vendor if such ideas were developed by the user or even if developed by the vendor as a result of the contract.

H. IDEAL COVERAGE

The parties acknowledge that performance of this contract may result in the development of new proprietary and secret concepts, methods, techniques, processes, adaptations and ideas. The parties agree that the same shall belong solely and exclusively to the user, without regard to the origin thereof and that the vendor will not, other than in the performance of this contract, make use of or disclose the same to anyone.

I. FALL-BACK ALTERNATIVES

As a fall-back, ownership in methods and ideas jointly developed (or developed by either) could be deemed to belong to both parties equally. Pre-arranged participations and rights of exploitation can be provided. Confidentiality provisions should include protection from disclosure by either party, regardless of ownership.

K. COMMENTS

Normally, any new ideas developed as part of the contract which are of specific application to the user, belong to the user, and not to the vendor; more generalized ideas can sometimes be left to the vendor, provided the user gets free use. These are extremely difficult concepts, fraught with legal problems and difficult to deal with except in specific areas. Where know-how on development is being bought, as in software development contracts, the user should own everything and the vendor should have no rights.

L. REFERENCES TO OTHER CLAUSES: 5-13, 8-13

A. **CLAUSE NAME:** Headings Not Controlling   B. **CLAUSE NO.:** 5-18

C. **CONTRACT TYPES USED IN:** All   D. **RISK RATING:** 4

E. **INTENT AND SCOPE**

To allow the contract to have headings for purposes of organization, but to assure that they have no legal effect.

F. **PROTECTION AGAINST**

Protects against legal inferences being drawn from one or two-word summaries, which inferences could violate the meaning of a lengthy clause.

H. **IDEAL COVERAGE**

Headings used in this contract are for reference purposes only and shall not be deemed a part of this contract.

A. CLAUSE NAME: Entire Agreement **B. CLAUSE NO.:** 5-19

C. CONTRACT TYPES USED IN: All **D. RISK RATING:** 2

E. INTENT AND SCOPE

To ensure that the contract is the only and complete statement of the parties' under-standing and to prohibit the introduction of prior or contemporaneous verbal state-ments or earlier written material to vary or contradict the contract.

F. PROTECTION AGAINST

To protect against side issues being raised as a result of verbal commitments, discussions or other documentation not expressly contained in the contract. A good contract should speak for itself and should incorporate (by reference or otherwise) all agreed to docu-mentation, negotiations, statements, promises, etc. which are intended to be relied upon.

G. STANDARD CLAUSE PROVIDED BY MANUFACTURERS

THE PARTIES HAVE READ THIS AGREEMENT, INCLUDING THE REVERSE SIDE HEREOF, AND AGREE TO BE BOUND BY ALL ITS TERMS AND FURTHER AGREE THAT IT CONSTITUTES THE COMPLETE AND EXCLUSIVE STATEMENT OF THE AGREEMENT BETWEEN THEM WHICH SUPERSEDES ALL PROPOSALS, ORAL OR WRITTEN, AND ALL OTHER COMMUNICATIONS BETWEEN THEM RELATING TO THE LICENSE AND USE OF THE EQUIPMENT. (ADR)

This Agreement will be governed by the laws of the State of New York. It constitutes the complete and exclusive statement of the agreement between the parties which super-sedes all proposals, oral or written, and all other communications between the parties relating to the subject matter of this Agreement. (IBM)

H. IDEAL COVERAGE

This contract constitutes the entire agreement between the parties with respect to the subject matter; all prior agreements, representations, statements, negotiations and under-takings are superseded hereby.

K. COMMENTS

If several contemporaneous contracts are being entered into simultaneously covering the same subject matter, they should be cross-referenced or otherwise reflected in some master instrument.

Vendors love this clause. Far too many purchasers have been badly injured by it. It is in every standard vendor's form contract. The only protection against it is to see that the contract is, in fact, *complete and comprehensive.*

L. REFERENCES TO OTHER CLAUSES: 5-22

A. **CLAUSE NAME:** Compliance With All Laws—Partial Invalidity   B. **CLAUSE NO.:** 5-20

C. **CONTRACT TYPES USED IN:** All   D. **RISK RATING:** 3

E. **INTENT AND SCOPE**

To ensure that the contract performance is in compliance with all applicable laws; to further insure that if any part of the contract is held to be violative of law at any time, the contract shall survive with the offending clause stricken.

F. **PROTECTION AGAINST**

To protect the entire contract from being struck down by virtue of an insignificant provision which violates some law.

G. **STANDARD CLAUSE PROVIDED BY MANUFACTURERS**

If any provision or provisions of this Agreement shall be held to be invalid, illegal or unenforceable, the validity, legality and enforceability of the remaining provisions shall not in any way be affected or impaired thereby. (IBM)

Compliance With Laws: ADR agrees to comply with the provisions of the Fair Labor Standard Act of 1938 as amended and all other applicable laws and regulations in the performance of this Agreement.

Severability: If any provision, or portion thereof, of this Agreement is invalid under any applicable statute or rule of law, it is to that extent to be deemed omitted. (ADR)

Effect of Invalid or Unenforceable Provisions: If any provision of this Agreement is determined to be invalid or unenforceable, the remaining provisions of this Agreement shall not be affected thereby and shall be binding upon the parties hereto, and shall be enforceable, as though said invalid or unenforceable provision were not contained herein. (BASI)

H. **IDEAL COVERAGE**

(1) *Compliance:* Each party agrees that it will perform its obligations hereunder in accordance with all applicable laws, rules and regulations now or hereafter in effect.

(2) *Partial Invalidity:* If any term or provision of this agreement shall be found to be illegal or unenforceable then, notwithstanding, this agreement shall remain in full force and effect and such term or provision shall be deemed stricken.

K. **COMMENTS**

Some lawyers like to be very careful and to provide that if the offending provision goes to the heart of the agreement, the agreement is terminated.

A. CLAUSE NAME: Compliance with U.S. Standards   B. CLAUSE NO.:   5-21

C. CONTRACT TYPES USED IN: All   D. RISK RATING: 4

E. INTENT AND SCOPE

To ensure that the contract compiles with standards issued by the American National Standards Institute (A.N.S.I.).

F. PROTECTION AGAINST

To protect against the delivery of hardware or software elements which violate the standards established for U.S. data processing hardware or software.

H. IDEAL COVERAGE

In addition to, but not in limitation of, the representations and warranties herein contained, vendor warrants that all products or elements to be delivered hereunder shall comply with all applicable provisions of standards or draft standards issued by the American National Standards Institute.

K. COMMENTS

There is limited value to having such a provision in the contract, but to the extent it is determined during negotiation that there are useful standards and that the manufacturer's equipment or software complies with such standards, it may be of benefit. It can be further expanded to relate to standards approved by the International Standards Organization (ISO) which governs those standards which have applicability across country lines.

L. REFERENCES TO OTHER CLAUSES: 5-20

A. **CLAUSE NAME:** All Amendments in Writing   B. **CLAUSE NO.:** 5-22

C. **CONTRACT TYPES USED IN:** All   D. **RISK RATING:** 4

E. **INTENT AND SCOPE**

To ensure that the contract can be amended only by a written instrument counter-signed by both parties.

F. **PROTECTION AGAINST**

To protect against disputes surrounding claimed verbal changes in the contract.

G. **STANDARD CLAUSE PROVIDED BY MANUFACTURERS**

This Agreement may only be changed in a writing, executed on behalf of IBM and of the Purchaser. The term "this Agreement" as used herein includes any applicable Installment Payment Agreement, Supplement, or future written amendment made in accordance herewith. (IBM)

H. **IDEAL COVERAGE**

No amendment to this agreement shall be effective unless it is in writing and signed by duly authorized representatives of both parties.

I. **FALL-BACK ALTERNATIVES**

Some contracts provide that a written amendment is effective if merely signed by the party to be "charged" with that amendment. Some amendments are capable of being binding, then, on the basis of only one signature; a price reduction will stand up if signed by the vendor. Most amendments are more complex and are chargeable against both parties. This fall-back provision is, therefore, often dangerous.

K. **COMMENTS**

This, too, is a clause beloved by vendors. It can be found, in substance, in all vendor standard forms. It can, however, protect the user, too, if the user is disciplined enough to follow proper contract procedures.

L. **REFERENCES TO OTHER CLAUSES:** 5-19

A. CLAUSE NAME: Consent to Breach not Waiver   **B. CLAUSE NO.:** 5-23

C. CONTRACT TYPES USED IN: All   **D. RISK RATING:** 4

E. INTENT AND SCOPE

To ensure that, if a possible breach of the contract is excused, such tacit consent does not necessarily constitute a waiver of any other, different or subsequent breach. Thus if the vendor is late in delivery by 30 days on one occasion, and such delay is waived, this does not mean that future late delivery will in fact be tolerated or any waiver effected with respect to such subsequent delays.

F. PROTECTION AGAINST

To protect a single consent or waiver from being used as a precedent for future waivers of breach or as a future rationale for continuing such breach.

G. STANDARD CLAUSE PROVIDED BY MANUFACTURERS

Non-Waiver: No delay or failure of ADR in exercising any right hereunder and no partial or single exercise thereof, shall be deemed of itself to constitute a waiver of such right or any other rights hereunder.

ADR may accept any payments from any person tendering the same without thereby accepting such person as Customer hereunder or waiving any breach of covenant or provision against assignment or transfer by Customer.

Waiver: Waiver by the Company of any breach of any provision of this Agreement by the Employee shall not operate or be construed as a waiver of any subsequent or other breach by the Employee. (BASI)

H. IDEAL COVERAGE

No term or provision hereof shall be deemed waived and no breach excused, unless such waiver or consent shall be in writing and signed by the party claimed to have waived or consented. Any consent by any party to, or waiver of, a breach by the other, whether express or implied, shall not constitute a consent to, waiver of, or excuse for any other different or subsequent breach.

K. COMMENTS

Although such a provision should be incorporated in the contract, it should be noted that a continuing pattern of waivers, whether express or implied, may eventually be deemed, at law, to be the practice of the parties and enforceable even in the face of this clause. In other words, parties can, by their persistent, long term conduct be found to have disregarded a contract or discarded a provision.

A. **CLAUSE NAME:** Notices   B. **CLAUSE NO.:** 5-24

C. **CONTRACT TYPES USED IN:** All   D. **RISK RATING:** 4

E. **INTENT AND SCOPE**

To identify a single location where notices are to be sent. Proper dispatch or delivery of notices to the addresses indicated in the contract will be deemed effective delivery.

F. **PROTECTION AGAINST**

To protect against claims that notices were never received.

G. **STANDARD CLAUSE PROVIDED BY MANUFACTURERS**

Notices: Any notice required or permitted to be given hereunder shall be in writing and shall be given by delivering the same in the case of the Employee to him personally, and in the case of the Company to an officer of the Company on its behalf. (BASI)

H. **IDEAL COVERAGE**

All notices under this contract shall be deemed duly given: upon delivery, if delivered by hand (against receipt); or three days after posting, if sent by registered mail, receipt requested; to a party hereto at the address hereinabove set forth or to such other address as a party may designate by notice pursuant hereto.

K. **COMMENTS**

Good lawyers like to insist that notices must be addressed to the attention of a particular office (e.g., President, Vice-President-Data Processing) or of a particular individual. This helps to see to it that the notice doesn't get mis-routed. Many lawyers like to require that an extra notice be sent to their offices; it keeps them informed. Where frequent and fast communication needs are felt to be necessary contract provisions should be written to cover telegraphic and Telex notices.

L. **REFERENCES TO OTHER CLAUSES:** 5-22

A. CLAUSE NAME: Authority   **B. CLAUSE NO.:** 5-25

C. CONTRACT TYPES USED IN: All   **D. RISK RATING:** 4

E. INTENT AND SCOPE

To ensure that each party has the authority to enter into the agreement and that the agreement has in fact been properly read.

G. STANDARD CLAUSE PROVIDED BY MANUFACTURERS

The purchaser acknowledges that he has read this agreement, understands it and agrees to all terms and conditions stated herein. (IBM)

H. IDEAL COVERAGE

Each party has full power and authority to enter into and perform this contract, and the person signing this contract on behalf of each has been properly authorized and empowered to enter into this contract. Each party further acknowledges that it has read this agreement, understands it, and agrees to be bound by it.

K. COMMENTS

In most commercial transactions, this clause is mostly hocus-pocus. If the man signing has neither actual nor apparent authority, his representation that he has will not bind his employer. The statement that "the contract has been read" is generally attacked by the defense that "I didn't read any of the contract, including the section that says I did read it; I just signed on the salesman's say-so that it was only a non-binding order". The current attitude towards consumerism, however, suggests that it may help for each party to acknowledge the fact that it has in fact read the agreement and understands it. If used, the clause should probably be in solid capital letters right above the signature lines, so that the signer will have to claim either blindness or imbecility as a basis for denying he saw it.

A. CLAUSE NAME: Governing Law

B. CLAUSE NO.: 5-26

C. CONTRACT TYPES USED IN: All

D. RISK RATING: 4

E. INTENT AND SCOPE

This defines the laws of the state or other authority under which the contract will be governed.

G. STANDARD CLAUSE PROVIDED BY MANUFACTURERS

This Agreement will be governed by the laws of the State of New York. It constitutes the complete and exclusive statement of the agreement between the parties which supersedes all proposals, oral or written, and all other communications between the parties relating to the subject matter of this Agreement. (IBM)

H. IDEAL COVERAGE

This contract will be governed by and construed in accordance with the laws of [the state in which the user is resident] .

K. COMMENTS

It is desirable, from the user viewpoint, to have the governing law that of the user's residence, since user counsel will be most familiar with that law. In the United States, the governing laws of the various states are very similar, so the particular legal situs is relatively unimportant; it is helpful to choose one as a reference point.

L. REFERENCES TO OTHER CLAUSES: 5-01

A. CLAUSE NAME: UCC Applicability

C. CONTRACT TYPES USED IN: All

D. RISK RATING: 3

E. INTENT AND SCOPE

Attempts to bring the umbrella of the Uniform Commercial Code to bear on the contract. This provision is necessary if the contract relates to the delivery of services, since services are not always covered by the Uniform Commercial Code.

F. PROTECTION AGAINST

Protects against rampant unfairness on the vendor's part, since the UCC has some valuable provisions generally protective of purchasers and tending toward fairness in trade dealings.

H. IDEAL COVERAGE

Except to the extent that the provisions of this agreement are clearly inconsistent therewith, this agreement shall be governed by any applicable provisions of the Uniform Commercial Code. To the extent that this contract entails delivery or performance of services, such services shall be deemed "goods" within the meaning of the Uniform Commercial Code, except when to so deem such services as "goods" would result in an absurdity.

K. COMMENTS

This clause is in many ways helpful. It should not be deemed a substitute for a comprehensive, complete agreement.

A. **CLAUSE NAME:** Patent and Other Proprietary Rights
Indemnity

B. **CLAUSE NO.:** 5-28

C. **CONTRACT TYPES USED IN:** All

D. **RISK RATING:** 2

E. **INTENT AND SCOPE**

To ensure that the user of equipment or services produced by the vendor does not infringe upon any patents or other rights and if such use is found to be infringing to require the vendor to defend the user against any such infringement claim and to hold the user harmless.

F. **PROTECTION AGAINST**

Protects against claims against the user of infringement.

G. **STANDARD CLAUSE PROVIDED BY MANUFACTURERS**

Patent Indemnity: Bunker Ramo will indemnify, hold harmless and defend Customer against any suit claiming that Equipment shall not have been delivered free from infringement of any United States Letters Patent, but Bunker Ramo shall have no other liability in respect of any patent infringement or claimed infringement. In limitation of the foregoing, Bunker Ramo shall have no liability in respect of any patent infringement:

(a) based on specifications furnished by Customer, or

(b) resulting from use of Equipment or the inclusion or the incorporation thereof with equipment not produced by Bunker Ramo or in a manner for which the Equipment was not designed, or

(c) in connection with the leasing or resale of Equipment, or

(d) unless Customer shall notify Bunker Ramo of any claim of infringement or of commencement of any suit, action, or proceeding alleging such infringement forthwith after Customer shall have received notice thereof. Bunker Ramo shall have the right in its sole discretion and at its expense to participate in and control the defense of any such claim, suit, action or proceeding and in any and all negotiations with respect thereto, and Customer shall not settle any such claim, suit, action or proceeding without Bunker Ramo's prior written approval. Bunker Ramo shall have the right, at its option and expense, at any time to modify or replace Equipment or parts or components thereof to obviate or cure any patent infringement.

Patent Indemnity: IBM will defend at its own expense, any action brought against the Purchaser, to the extent that it is based on a claim that the machines supplied by IBM, or the operation of such machines pursuant to a current release and modification level of any Type I program or System Control Programming furnished by IBM, infringe a United States patent and, IBM will pay those costs and damages finally awarded against the Purchaser in any such claim, but such defense and payment are conditioned on the following:

(i) that IBM shall be notified promptly in writing by the Purchaser of any notice of such claim; and

(ii) that IBM shall have the sole control of the defense of any action on such claim and all negotiations for its settlement or compromise; and

(iii) should the machines, or the operation thereof, become, or in IBM's opinion be likely to become, the subject of a claim of infringement of a United States patent, that the Purchaser shall permit IBM, at its option and expense, either to procure for the Purchaser the right to continue using the machines, to replace or modify the same so that they become noninfringing, or to grant the Purchaser a credit for such machines as depreciated and accept their return. The depreciation shall be an equal amount per year over the life of the machines as established by IBM.

IBM shall have no liability to the Purchaser under any provision of this cluase with respect to any claim of patent infringement which is based upon:

(i) the combination, or utilization, of machines furnished hereunder with machines or devices not made by IBM; or

(ii) the operation of machines furnished by IBM pursuant to any program other than, or in addition to, the aforementioned Type I programs or System Control Programming; or

(iii) the modification by the Purchaser of machines furnished hereunder or of the aforementioned Type I programs or System Control Programming.

The foregoing states the entire liability of IBM with respect to infringement of patents.

H. IDEAL COVERAGE

Seller warrants that the products hereby sold do not infringe upon or violate any patent, copyright, trade secret or any other proprietary right of any third party; in the event of any claim by any third party against Purchaser, Purchaser shall promptly notify Seller and Seller shall defend such claim, in Purchaser's name, but at Seller's expense and shall indemnify Purchaser against any loss, cost, expense or liability arising out of such claim, whether or not such claim is successful.

I. FALL–BACK ALTERNATIVES

The user may be willing to surrender some of the indemnity, but only where the infringement claim is specifically based upon some act on the part of the user.

L. REFERENCES TO OTHER CLAUSES: 7-30, 9-28, 9-30.

A. CLAUSE NAME: Statute of Limitations   B. CLAUSE NO.: 5-29

C. CONTRACT TYPES USED IN: All   D. RISK RATING: 3

E. INTENT AND SCOPE

To provide for a short statute of limitations for actions to be brought under the agreement.

G. STANDARD CLAUSE PROVIDED BY MANUFACTURERS

No action, regardless of form, arising out of the services under this Agreement, may be brought by either party more than one year after the cause of action has accrued, except that an action for nonpayment may be brought within one year of the date of last payment. (IBM)

H. IDEAL COVERAGE

No party may commence an action under this agreement more than two years after the expiration of its term, or, in the event of default, more than two years after the occurrence of said default, or, in the event such default is not discoverable by the injured party when it has occurred, more than two years after such default could, in the exercise of due diligence, have been discovered by such party.

K. COMMENTS

Claims of contract defaults are normally governed by statutes of limitations established by law. In most United States jurisdictions these statutes bar claims of breach if not commenced within six years after the breach. An agreement to shorten the statute of limitations will serve to prevent hang-overs of contingent liability. These "short statute" clauses are generally felt to benefit vendors, not users. User defaults normally involve non-payment and vendors will rarely wait long to sue for collection. The user's general problem in this area will be to attempt to negotiate from a vendor a *longer* "short statute" than contained on the vendor's standard form, as for example in the four-year statute under the U.C.C.

A. **CLAUSE NAME:** Hardware Components Specification   B. **CLAUSE NO.:** 6-01

C. **CONTRACT TYPES USED IN:** Hardware contracts   D. **RISK RATING:** 2

E. **INTENT AND SCOPE**

To insure that the hardware is specified in the detail necessary to allow acceptance testing.

F. **PROTECTION AGAINST**

To protect against the delivery of hardware which does not meet the requirements of the user.

H. **IDEAL COVERAGE**

Each hardware component delivered hereunder will conform to the detailed specification respecting such component attached as Schedule A hereto in all respects including, but not limited to, physical characteristics, operating characteristics, space requirements, power requirements, maintenance characteristics, modularity, compatibility, and the like.

K. **COMMENTS**

It is desirable to have, for each hardware component, an independent set of specifications which can be attached to the contract. These specifications must of course cover the operating characteristics, but should also cover such physical and reliability characteristics as can be realistically defined by the user in advance of signing the contract. Often, the best approach is to annex the glossy component description and specification sheets that vendors use as selling tools. They generally describe the equipment in glowing terms. Vendor resistance to annexation of such sheets to a contract should give the user pause.

L. **REFERENCES TO OTHER CLAUSES:** 6-02.

A. **CLAUSE NAME:** Software Component Specification   B. **CLAUSE NO.:** 6-02

C. **CONTRACT TYPES USED IN:** Hardware and software   D. **RISK RATING:** 2
contracts

E. **INTENT AND SCOPE**

The intent of a software component specification is similar to that of a hardware component specification. It is to define the role and responsibility of the software to the user's viewpoint. Operating characteristics, core requirements, timing characteristics, all must be defined as part of the specification.

G. **STANDARD CLAUSE PROVIDED BY MANUFACTURERS**

Lessor agrees to make available to Lessee at no additional charge during the initial period of lease, on the basis hereinafter defined, all standard software which Lessor makes available as a standard price book item to equipment users, both heretofore made available and any which is subsequently developed and made available during the initial period of the lease (such software to consist of programming languages, operating systems, utility programs and application packages, but not to include software developed under separate contracts for specific customers). This provision conveys only a non-exclusive license under Lessor's proprietary rights to such program material for use on equipment leased herein, but such license does not include the right to reproduce, publish, or license such program material to others. Lessor expressly reserves and Lessee expressly consents that the entire right and title to such program material shall remain in Lessor, and Lessor has the exclusive right to protect by copyright or otherwise, to reproduce, publish, sell and distribute such material to any other customer.

In recognition of Lessor's property rights in program material delivered to Lessee, Lessee further agrees to place on each copy or reproduction of such program material for use on his equipment the identical notice contained on the program material furnished by Lessor to Lessee. (Burroughs)

H. **IDEAL COVERAGE**

Each software component supplied hereunder will conform to the software specification respecting such component attached as Schedule A in all respects, including, but not limited to, operating performance, core requirements, timing characteristics, documentation quality, compatibility, modularity and the like.

K. **COMMENTS**

See comments to 6-01.

L. **REFERENCES TO OTHER CLAUSES:** 7-01, 7-02, 8-02, 8-03, 9-01.

A. CLAUSE NAME: Hardware Configuration   **B. CLAUSE NO.:** 6-03

C. CONTRACT TYPES USED IN: Hardware contract   **D. RISK RATING:** 3

E. INTENT AND SCOPE

To identify in detail the configuration of hardware which makes up a group or a system.

F. PROTECTION AGAINST

To protect against vendor claims that the contract, or an element thereof, has been "substantially" performed, while material components are still missing or inoperative.

H. IDEAL COVERAGE

The hardware components to be supplied hereunder, for purposes of delivery and performance under this contract, shall be grouped together in one or more hardware configurations, defined in Schedule A. Any such configuration shall be deemed incomplete and undelivered if any component within that configuration has not been delivered, or if delivered, is not operational or acceptable in accordance with sections 6-05 and 6-51.

K. COMMENTS

Sufficient grouping of hardware should be accomplished so that realistic standards of usability are set. Failure to deliver one component which does not in fact interfere with the operation of the installation, should not be treated as a material breach of contract, but should be dealt with on some liquidated damage basis, per diem, until the installation is totally on-line. However, if an important component is not delivered which thereby renders the configuration useless or usable only at a serious loss of capacity or efficiency, then more serious penalties should be recognized.

L. REFERENCES TO OTHER CLAUSES: 6-01, 6-02, 6-05, 6-51.

A. **CLAUSE NAME:** Software Configuration   B. **CLAUSE NO.:** 6-04

C. **CONTRACT TYPES USED IN:** Hardware and software   D. **RISK RATING:** 3
contracts

E. **CONTENT AND SCOPE**

To identify software and hardware components together in groups or configurations, since such configurations must be delivered in total prior to beneficial use being made of them, and prior to acceptance being considered therefor.

H. **IDEAL COVERAGE**

The software components listed on Schedule A to be delivered hereunder shall, together with the hardware components listed on Schedule B, be grouped together in the configurations defined in Schedule C. Any such configuration shall be deemed incomplete and undelivered if any component, of either hardware or software, within that configuration has not been delivered, or, if delivered, is not operational or acceptable in accordance with Sections 6-05 and 6-51.

K. **COMMENTS**

See 6-03.

L. **REFERENCES TO OTHER CLAUSES:** 6-03, 6-05, 6-51.

A. CLAUSE NAME: Systems Performance	B. CLAUSE NO.: 6-05
C. CONTRACT TYPES USED IN: Hardware	D. RISK RATING: 1

E. INTENT AND SCOPE

To define from the viewpoint of the user the functional systems performance which the aggregate of all hardware and software must meet. This clause should specify the types of functions which the system must be capable of handling, within the constraints established therefor.

H. IDEAL COVERAGE

The hardware and software configurations delivered under this contract must be capable of performing the following functions, in the operating times shown: [list]

J. POSSIBLE REMEDIES

In the event that the system as delivered, cannot meet the performance characteristics outlined, the vendor should be required to correct or add such hardware and software components as he deems appropriate to make the system capable of meeting the performance characteristics described. If the vendor cannot or does not do so, the contract should be capable of rescission if the failure is a major one, or unless dealt with by liquidated damages or a reduction in price if the parties are sophisticated enough to be able to compute them in advance.

L. REFERENCES TO OTHER CLAUSES: 6-51, 8-04, 9-02.

A. **CLAUSE NAME:** Inclusion of Proposal   B. **CLAUSE NO.:** 6-06

C. **CONTRACT TYPES USED IN:** Hardware and software   D. **RISK RATING:** 2
package or software
development

E. **INTENT AND SCOPE**

To include in any agreement the proposal which originally formed the basis of the contract. Usually, the vendor's initial proposal states the offer under which the vendor is prepared to proceed in most expansive terms. Such terms should be embodied in the contract, but to the extent that they are not, the inclusion of the proposal will, of course, incorporate these into the contract.

F. **PROTECTION AGAINST**

Protects against omission in the contract of claims or promises made by the vendor in a proposal. It further protects against a sales oriented proposal containing many unrealistic statements.

H. **IDEAL COVERAGE**

The proposal, submitted by the vendor, dated _____ is incorporated herein by reference [or physically annexed as Exhibit A].

I. **FALL–BACK ALTERNATIVES**

Paragraphs A, B, C, etc. of the proposal submitted by the vendor, dated _____ are incorporated herein by reference.

K. **COMMENTS**

In developing a bid specification, prior to the submission of the proposal, it is wise to advise the vendors that their proposals will be incorporated into the contract. This will prevent the inclusion of much redundant information, will eliminate "puffing" the proposal, and will insure that the proposal is factual, to the point, and capable of being implemented.

L. **REFERENCES TO OTHER CLAUSES:** 6-07, 6-08.

A. CLAUSE NAME: Inclusion of Hardware Manuals   **B. CLAUSE NO.:** 6-07

C. CONTRACT TYPES USED IN: Hardware contracts   **D. RISK RATING:** 3

E. INTENT AND SCOPE

To incorporate by reference or directly all manuals produced by the manufacturer describing the characteristics of the hardware. This incorporation will insure that hardware performance described in any manual of the manufacturer is warranted in the contract. This will prevent unrealistic claims being made in hardware manuals, and if this clause is considered acceptable by the vendor, will insure that the hardware manuals have been in fact carefully prepared.

H. IDEAL COVERAGE

The following hardware manuals are incorporated herein by reference:

I. FALL-BACK ALTERNATIVES

Paragraphs A, B, C, D, etc. of the hardware manual No. 1234 published by the vendor are incorporated herein by reference.

L. REFERENCES TO OTHER CLAUSES: 6-06, 6-08.

A. **CLAUSE NAME:** Inclusion of Software Manuals   B. **CLAUSE NO.:** 6-08

C. **CONTRACT TYPES USED IN:** Hardware and software   D. **RISK RATING:** 3
                                                     contracts.

E. **INTENT AND SCOPE**

To ensure that all manuals describing software products are incorporated into the contract, much as hardware manuals were included in 6-07. The manuals to be included should be those which define the specifications of the software, and those which specify how the software is to be used and what functions it is capable of performing.

H. **IDEAL COVERAGE**

This contract incorporates all of the following manuals, which describe the functions and characteristics of the software supplied hereunder:

I. **FALL-BACK ALTERNATIVES**

Paragraphs A, B, C, D, etc. of software manual No. 1234 published by vendor are incorporated herein by reference.

L. **REFERENCES TO OTHER CLAUSES:** 6-07, 6-06.

A. **CLAUSE NAME:** Guarantees of Compatibility B. **CLAUSE NO.:** 6-09

C. **CONTRACT TYPES USED IN:** Hardware contracts D. **RISK RATING:** 3

E. **INTENT AND SCOPE**

To ensure that the hardware being delivered is compatible with other hardware manufactured by the vendor. Such compatibility refers to compatibility of data and programs.

H. **IDEAL COVERAGE**

The vendor acknowledges that vendor has available for sale or rental other equipment described in Schedule A similar in function to that being delivered hereunder. The vendor warrants that such other equipment is both data compatible and program compatible, so that data files created for the system being delivered pursuant hereto can be utilized without adaptation on such other equipment, and programs written for the systems contracted for herein will operate without necessity for alteration, emulation or other loss of efficiency on such other equipment.

I. **FALL–BACK ALTERNATIVES**

To the extent that compatibility may require some modification, the insertion of the word "substantially" prior to the word "compatible" in the preceding clause will ameliorate its effect somewhat.

K. **COMMENTS**

It is desirable to ensure that there is program and data compatibility in larger or newer series of equipment which the vendor is offering. Since compatibility is a sales point, it is highly desirable to incorporate this point in the contract.

L. **REFERENCES TO OTHER CLAUSES:** 9-39, 9-40.

A. **CLAUSE NAME:** Guarantees of Interface   B. **CLAUSE NO.:** 6-10

C. **CONTRACT TYPES USED IN:** Hardware contracts   D. **RISK RATING:** 3

E. **INTENT AND SCOPE**

To ensure the equipment being delivered is capable of interfacing with equipment made by others. Such interfaces may be necessary for data communications equipment, for terminals, or for other types of peripheral equipment. It is desirable to include in this clause a list of all equipment contemplated to be added to the configuration.

F. **PROTECTION AGAINST**

This clause will both assure the user's ability to interconnect with other equipment and protect against a vendor's refusal to allow connection of "foreign" equipment to its machine on some pretext, such as the fact that the interconnection may interfere with proper maintenance.

H. **IDEAL COVERAGE**

The vendor warrants that the equipment sold pursuant hereto can be connected without modification and without injury to the following equipment:

- All presently available data communications equipment supplied by common carriers in the United States,
- All terminals except those identified in Schedule A
- All peripheral equipment now available, except those identified in Schedule B

I. **FALL-BACK ALTERNATIVES**

Rather than identify on an exception basis those which cannot be connected, it may be acceptable to let the vendor identify those which can be connected, or to deal only with those intended to be connected by the user.

L. **REFERENCES TO OTHER CLAUSES:** 6-80, 6-81

A. CLAUSE NAME: Ability to Modify in Field   **B. CLAUSE NO.:** 6-11

C. CONTRACT TYPES USED IN: Hardware contracts   **D. RISK RATING:** 3

E. INTENT AND SCOPE

To require field modifications to be performed, where field modification is feasible.

F. PROTECTION AGAINST

Prohibits the vendor from requiring the purchase of a new unit, where the unit in existence is capable of being upgraded in the field. It also protects against the vendor's requiring that the unit be shipped back for upgrading, with consequent inconvenience and expense to the user.

H. IDEAL COVERAGE

The vendor represents that, in any case where expansion equipment can be installed or obtained through field modification of any component contracted for herein, the vendor will make such installation when requested by user at charges then in effect.

J. POSSIBLE REMEDIES

In the event the vendor refuses to make such changes, the remedy is at law. The user may go elsewhere for the installation and sue the vendor for the difference between the charges actually paid and the manufacturer's listed prices for the work.

L. REFERENCES TO OTHER CLAUSES: 6-80, 6-82

A. **CLAUSE NAME:** Supply Requirements   B. **CLAUSE NO.:** 6-12

C. **CONTRACT TYPES USED IN:** Hardware   D. **RISK RATING:** 3

E. **INTENT AND SCOPE**

To define the specific requirements for supplies which the system needs.

F. **PROTECTION AGAINST**

Prevents the vendor from defining unusual supply specifications after the fact, and protects against vendor established monopolies on such supplies.

H. **IDEAL COVERAGE**

Only the following supplies are required for the satisfactory operation of the system:
1. Punch cards
2. Magnetic tape
3. Magnetic disk packs
4. Printer ribbons
5. Printer paper
6. Lubricating oil
7. [Etc.]

L. **REFERENCES TO OTHER CLAUSES:** 6-13, 14, 15, 10-13, 10-15

A. **CLAUSE NAME:** Supply Specifications   B. **CLAUSE NO.:** 6-13

C. **CONTRACT TYPES USED IN:** Hardware   D. **RISK RATING:** 3

E. **INTENT AND SCOPE**

The specifications of the supplies required to operate the hardware successfully should be incorporated as part of the contract. Such specifications should be sufficient so that the manufacturer will warrant that supplies meeting the specifications will not interfere with the operation of the equipment.

F. **PROTECTION AGAINST**

Protects against vendor claims that the equipment is being injured by the use of supplies which do not meet basic requirements. This type of claim is most common where the equipment vendor is also a supply vendor but has not been getting supplies business from the user.

G. **STANDARD CLAUSE PROVIDED BY MANUFACTURERS**

Cards and Tape: Cards, tape, other supplies, accessories and disk devices used to operate the machines are to meet the necessary IBM specifications.

All supplies for use with the equipment are to be provided by Lessee and are to meet the specifications set forth by Honeywell.

H. **IDEAL COVERAGE**

The following specifications shall be met by the supplies required to operate the system:
● Punch cards: [dimensions, thickness, opacity, and the like]
● Tape: [physical and operating characteristics]
The vendor warrants that any supplies which meet these specifications will operate successfully on, and without injury to, the system.

L. **REFERENCES TO OTHER CLAUSES:** 6-12, 6-14, 10-13

A. **CLAUSE NAME:** Acceptable Supply Vendors   B. **CLAUSE NO.:** 6-14

C. **CONTRACT TYPES USED IN:** Hardware   D. **RISK RATING:** 4

E. **INTENT AND SCOPE**

To ensure that the hardware manufacturer will not object to the purchase of supplies from other vendors, it may be desirable to incorporate in the contract a listing of those sources considered acceptable by the hardware manufacturer.

H. **IDEAL COVERAGE**

The following vendors are acceptable to Seller as suppliers of supplies utilized for the system, and Seller acknowledges that such supplies as presently marketed by those suppliers meet the specifications outlined in 6-13:

for Tape: [list] etc.

L. **REFERENCES TO OTHER CLAUSES:** 6-12, 6-13.

A. CLAUSE NAME: Guarantee of Supply Availability   **B. CLAUSE NO.:** 6-15

C. CONTRACT TYPES USED IN: Hardware   **D. RISK RATING:** 3

E. INTENT AND SCOPE

If the machine vendor is the sole supplier of available supplies then the user becomes highly dependent on that vendor. To ensure that the vendor does not take advantage of this dependence, it is desirable to ensure that the supplies will be available at reasonable prices for the life of the system.

F. PROTECTION AGAINST

Protects against the vendor using the unavailability of supplies as a means of forcing the user to upgrade equipment, or as a means of forcing the user to pay outrageous prices for supplies.

H. IDEAL COVERAGE

The vendor agrees to make the supplies listed below available in sufficient quantities to meet the user's requirements for as long as the equipment contracted for hereunder is utilized by the user. Such supplies shall be made available at prices from time to time in effect, but in no event shall such prices be increased above present catalogue prices by more than ____% for each year from the date of this contract.

I. FALL–BACK ALTERNATIVES

Supply pricing can be tied to the cost of living index.

K. COMMENTS

It is possible that supply pricing can be controlled on some other basis. For example, cost-increase pass-throughs are becoming more common, but most vendors will not consent merely to pick up added costs except, perhaps, on a very short term arrangement. If a supply monopoly exists the user should seek an availability commitment and such price guarantees as can be obtained.

L. REFERENCES TO OTHER CLAUSES: 6-12, 6-56, 10-16.

A. **CLAUSE NAME:** Power Requirements   B. **CLAUSE NO.:** 6-16

C. **CONTRACT TYPES USED IN:** Hardware contracts   D. **RISK RATING:** 3

E. **INTENT AND SCOPE**

To include in the contract a statement as to the power requirements necessary for the system. This, of course, includes specification of voltage, wattage, amperage, and allowable fluctuations in such power, which will dictate whether or not rectification is required. The user should know what power requirements there are, so that the vendor cannot use power problems as an excuse for inadequate operation of the system.

F. **PROTECTION AGAINST**

Protects against a claim by the vendor that the power supply is inadequate or does not meet specifications.

G. **STANDARD CLAUSE PROVIDED BY MANUFACTURERS**

Installation and Operating Supplies: Installation facilities, including space, electrical power, cable troughs, special cable requirements, and the like, shall be furnished in accordance with installation instructions of Honeywell and at Lessee's expense, and the equipment shall not be moved from the premises where it has been installed without Honeywell's prior written consent. Honeywell shall install the equipment, at no additional charge, during its normal working hours, provided, however, that the Lessee shall furnish labor as may be necessary for placement, packing, and unpacking of equipment when in possession of Lessee. Supervision of packing, unpacking and placement of equipment shall be furnished without charge by Honeywell. If installation by Honeywell personnel is precluded by local law, union agreement or otherwise, Honeywell will supervise the installation and the Lessee shall bear any additional costs caused thereby.

H. **IDEAL COVERAGE**

Vendor represents that Schedule A sets forth the maximum electrical requirements for satisfactory operation of the system.

L. **REFERENCES TO OTHER CLAUSES:** 6-17.

A. CLAUSE NAME: Ambient Environment Requirements   **B. CLAUSE NO.:** 6-17

C. CONTRACT TYPES USED IN: Hardware contracts   **D. RISK RATING:** 3

E. INTENT AND SCOPE

The ambient environment under which the system must operate should be stipulated in the contract. This will include stipulation of satisfactory temperature ranges, acceptable changes in temperature, satisfactory humidity ranges, dust tolerance capabilities, and the like.

F. PROTECTION AGAINST

Protects against the vendor's claims that the ambient environment does not meet the specifications of the system, thereby excusing a failure of reliability.

H. IDEAL COVERAGE

Vendor represents that Schedule X is a complete statement of permitted ranges of environmental variations under which the system is capable of satisfactory operation.

K. COMMENTS

In some instances, these variables are interdependent (e.g., the maximum permissible temperature may vary with humidity), and appropriate notation of these interdependencies should be made in the Schedule.

L. REFERENCES TO OTHER CLAUSES: 6-16.

A. CLAUSE NAME: Cabling Requirements   **B. CLAUSE NO.:** 6-18

C. CONTRACT TYPES USED IN: Hardware contracts   **D. RISK RATING:** 4

E. INTENT AND SCOPE

To identify the necessary cabling needs, and the cost associated with such cabling if any. Normally computer components are cable connected by the manufacturer at no additional cost. However, the cable connections necessary sometimes exceed those which the vendor is prepared to supply at no cost. Thus it is desirable to include in the contract a configuration layout, and to have the vendor certify that all cabling will be done, at no cost to the user, if that is the case.

H. IDEAL COVERAGE

The components of the hardware will be installed substantially in accordance with the configuration diagram attached hereto as Exhibit A. The vendor warrants that it will supply and install all necessary cabling to properly connect the components in accordance with Exhibit A, at no further cost to the user.

L. REFERENCES TO OTHER CLAUSES: 6-73, 6-74.

A. CLAUSE NAME: Support Supplied by Type and Amount   **B. CLAUSE NO.:** 6-19

C. CONTRACT TYPES USED IN: Hardware contract   **D. RISK RATING:** 2

E. INTENT AND SCOPE

To identify specifically the types of support to be supplied, and the amounts of each. Normally this can be done by stipulating the number of person-years of support in each category, or the specific tasks to be accomplished by that support. Either one is acceptable provided that the definition can be made sufficiently clear so that there is no question as to the vendor's responsibility.

F. PROTECTION AGAINST

Protects against vague commitments for support which are ultimately not met, or which are met half-heartedly or by unqualified staff. Note that staff caliber to be used is specified as part of 6-20.

G. STANDARD CLAUSE PROVIDED BY MANUFACTURERS

Technical Services: Honeywell's technical personnel shall be available as specified in Honeywell's proposal to assist the Government in implementation, review and improvement of existing data processing systems and to assist in programming, development and implementation of new systems involving Honeywell equipment.

H. IDEAL COVERAGE

The vendor recognizes its responsibility to assist the user in the proper implementation of the system. Accordingly, the vendor agrees to supply the types of implementation support as set forth on Schedule A in the quantities and at the times shown. [Categories: system design assistance, programming assistance, software support assistance, software modification assistance, data base design assistance, data conversion assistance, site planning assistance, physical installation assistance, public relations assistance, direct training assistance, programming conversion assistance, etc. Show quantities in person-years or by intended result.]

I. FALL–BACK ALTERNATIVES

It is possible to stipulate ranges of support, rather than absolute numbers of person-years. As a further alternative, it is possible to stipulate that the vendor will give as much support as is reasonably necessary to achieve a result provided that the determination of what is necessary is in some way a joint effort. The timing of the support services must be described, or it must be provided that the services will be supplied on a full-time basis whenever requested by the user.

L. REFERENCES TO OTHER CLAUSES: 6-20, 8-17.

A. **CLAUSE NAME:** Staff Caliber   B. **CLAUSE NO.:** 6-20

C. **CONTRACT TYPES USED IN:** Hardware contracts   D. **RISK RATING:** 2

E. **INTENT AND SCOPE**

To identify clearly the caliber of staff necessary to provide the support. A person-year of inexperienced staff is valueless if this support is to provide direct assistance in systems implementation. Caliber normally is based upon years of experience in specific categories.

H. **IDEAL COVERAGE**

For each type of support provided described in 6-19, the vendor will supply a person with the following minimum experience; n years of experience in the computer field; m years in the employ of the vendor; y years of experience with applications similar to those being implemented by the user; and z years in the specific hardware and or software technology required for the type of assistance necessary.

K. **COMMENTS**

A perfect clause would also provide the user with some right to call upon the vendor to replace incompetent, inefficient or merely non-cooperative vendor personnel assigned. (See Clause 10-20 for an example)

L. **REFERENCES TO OTHER CLAUSES:** 6-19, 8-17, 10-19, 10-20.

A. CLAUSE NAME: Education Curriculum

B. CLAUSE NO.: 6-21

C. CONTRACT TYPES USED IN: Hardware contracts

D. RISK RATING: 3

E. INTENT AND SCOPE

Hardware vendors normally supply a significant amount of education, through a comprehensive education curriculum. It is desirable to stipulate exactly what courses are included in that curriculum.

F. PROTECTION AGAINST

This protects against a vendor claiming that it is not responsible for teaching certain types of disciplines.

H. IDEAL COVERAGE

The courses listed on Schedule A constitute the curriculum of courses provided by the vendor on a periodic basis. [With respect to each course, Schedule A should set forth the instruction.]

L. REFERENCES TO OTHER CLAUSES: 6-22, 6-60, 9-08, 10-33, 10-34.

A. **CLAUSE NAME:** Free Education Allotment and
Charges for Excess

B. **CLAUSE NO.:** 6-22

C. **CONTRACT TYPES USED IN:** Hardware contracts

D. **RISK RATING:** 2

E. **INTENT AND SCOPE**

Most vendors provide a free education allotment, or provide for all necessary training to be provided at no further charge to the user. It is desirable to stipulate specifically what such an allotment is, how long it remains available, and what the charges will be for courses used when the free allotment has been exceeded.

F. **PROTECTION AGAINST**

Protects against vendor withdrawal of support, by eliminating training courses, or uncontemplated additional charges for training necessary from the viewpoint of the user.

G. **STANDARD CLAUSE PROVIDED BY MANUFACTURERS**

Training: UNIVAC shall provide instruction in the operation of the equipment. No charge shall be made for such instruction.

Training: Upon request, ADR will make available to Customer at a location and time mutually agreed upon, up to _____ working days of training in the use and operation of STAR/ACA at no cost to Customer except for travel and living expenses connected with the training, which shall be borne by Customer.

Training and Technical Services: (a) UNIVAC shall train the Customer's operating and programming personnel at courses held on a regularly scheduled basis at a UNIVAC training center. No charge shall be made for such training. Upon mutual agreement training may be conducted at the Customer's location. (b) UNIVAC's professional personnel shall be available to advise the Customer concerning implementation, review and improvements of existing Data Processing Systems and the development and implementation of new systems involving UNIVAC's equipment.

Training and Technical Services: With respect to the equipment currently listed in the Pricelist, Honeywell shall provide training and technical services as follows:

Training. Honeywell without additional charge to the Government shall train an adequate number of operating and programming personnel including initial staff and replacements as specified in Honeywell's proposal at Honeywell's training location, or, if mutually agreed, at a Government location. Training not identified in a proposal is beyond the scope of this contract. Contact your Honeywell representative for information concerning Honeywell training courses.

H. **IDEAL COVERAGE**

For a period of _____ months after delivery of the system [for so long as the system is installed], the vendor will allow the user's personnel to attend, at any time or from time to time, all of the courses described in 6-21, without charge.

I. **FALL–BACK ALTERNATIVES**

Limit all such training to a maximum of _____ student days. Thereafter require the vendor to provide such training at a fixed cost per student-day.

J. POSSIBLE REMEDIES

A remedy for failure to provide support or assistance of this type is to obtain similar assistance from another source, and to charge the costs directly to the vendor. The contract can so provide.

K. COMMENTS

If special, non-course training is necessary, specific training arrangements should be contracted for. In the case of very large, expensive installations, it may be possible to have the vendor perform the training on the user's site.

L. REFERENCES TO OTHER CLAUSES: 6-21, 6-23 and 6-24.

A. **CLAUSE NAME:** Continued Availability of Education   B. **CLAUSE NO.:** 6-23

C. **CONTRACT TYPES USED IN:** Hardware contract   D. **RISK RATING:** 2

E. **INTENT AND SCOPE**

To ensure that the user's training requirements, which continue during the life of the equipment, will continue to be available from the vendor as long as the equipment remains installed. Training is not a one-time activity, but one which is continuous, especially since there is more than average personnel turnover in the field.

F. **PROTECTION AGAINST**

Protects against vendor discontinuance of training courses as equipment ages; also protects against excessive charges for such education.

H. **IDEAL COVERAGE**

The vendor agrees that the courses described in the curriculum under 6-21 will remain available to the user as long as the equipment to be delivered hereunder remains installed and in use by user.

Charges for such courses (to the extent not agreed by vendor to be furnished at no cost) will be made at vendor rates then prevailing, provided that such rates shall not exceed current rates by more than an increase of ＿＿% per year.

I. **FALL–BACK ALTERNATIVES**

Charges can be related to increases in the cost of living index, or to similar indexes.

J. **POSSIBLE REMEDIES**

Where the vendor fails to provide such courses, the user should have the opportunity to purchase such courses from other sources and to charge any additional cost incurred thereby to the vendor.

L. **REFERENCES TO OTHER CLAUSES:** 6-21, 6-22 and 6-24.

A. CLAUSE NAME: Availability of Instructors   **B. CLAUSE NO.:** 6-24

C. CONTRACT TYPES USED IN: Hardware contracts   **D. RISK RATING:** 3

E. INTENT AND SCOPE

The vendor may occasionally drop education courses, or may elect not to make them available on a public basis, because demand is insufficient to warrant continuance. In that event this clause will ensure that the vendor will, if all else fails, make available necessary instructors and materials for purposes of conducting such courses on the user's site.

F. PROTECTION AGAINST

Protects against total unavailability of instruction. It is an ultimate fall-back position after all other vendor commitments expire.

H. IDEAL COVERAGE

The vendor agrees, if any courses in vendor's current curriculum, related to the operation, programming or use of its system shall be discontinued, that the vendor will make available, at user request, the necessary instructors and materials to teach such courses on-site at the user's location. Charges for such instructors will not exceed then prevailing charges made for such personnel to other users.

K. COMMENTS

Charges can be based on prevailing rates plus an escalation formula.

L. REFERENCES TO OTHER CLAUSES: 6-25, 6-23, 6-22 and 6-21.

A. CLAUSE NAME: Availability of Training Materials   **B. CLAUSE NO.:** 6-25

C. CONTRACT TYPES USED IN: Hardware contracts   **D. RISK RATING:** 3

E. INTENT AND SCOPE

Concurrently with the availability of instructors it is also necessary to have available all training materials. In the event, however, that the instructors may not be available, it is still desirable to obtain training materials for use by the user to teach the course internally.

H. IDEAL COVERAGE

The vendor agrees to make available, so long as the equipment contracted for hereunder is installed, all materials used by the vendor in any and all training courses taught by the vendor connected with the use, operation or programming of such equipment. Such training materials shall include, but not be limited to, student materials such as syllabi, agendas, tests, and teaching materials such as instructors' manuals, audio-visual aids, test results, and the like.

L. REFERENCES TO OTHER CLAUSES: 6-24, 6-23, 6-21.

A. **CLAUSE NAME:** Rights to Future Courses　　　　B. **CLAUSE NO.:** 6-26

C. **CONTRACT TYPES USED IN:** Hardware contracts　　　D. **RISK RATING:** 3

E. **INTENT AND SCOPE**

To provide the user with access to all future courses developed by the vendor which may be useful to the user with respect to the system.

F. **PROTECTION AGAINST**

Protects against excessive charges for newly developed courses, or for new courses which represent minor adaptations of courses contracted for.

H. **IDEAL COVERAGE**

The user will have the right to attend all courses developed by the vendor after the signing of this contract, and all revisions of courses included in the curriculum described in 6-21. The provisions of 6-21, 6-22, 6-23, 6-24 and 6-25 shall apply to such new and revised courses.

L. **REFERENCES TO OTHER CLAUSES:** 6-25, 6-24, 6-23, 6-22, 6-21.

A. **CLAUSE NAME:** Rights to Teach Internally B. **CLAUSE NO.:** 6-27

C. **CONTRACT TYPES USED IN:** Hardware contract D. **RISK RATING:** 3

E. **INTENT AND SCOPE**

To provide the user the right to teach any and all courses on an internal basis, after having obtained the necessary instruction material under the purview of clause 6-25. Such right should, of course, be limited to the in-house needs of the user and should continue only so long as equipment supplied under the contract is still in use.

H. **IDEAL COVERAGE**

The user shall have the right, so long as the equipment contracted for hereunder is in use by user, to give instruction to user personnel in all courses described in the curriculum in 6-21 (and all future and revised courses defined under 6-26) without charge, using materials supplied by the vendor. Such use by user of vendor materials shall include the right to reproduce the same solely for the permitted use, which use and reproduction shall not be deemed to violate or infringe upon any patent, copyright or other proprietary right of vendor.

L. **REFERENCES TO OTHER CLAUSES:** 6-21, 6-22, 6-23, 6-24, 6-25, 6-26.

A. **CLAUSE NAME:** Test Time Supplied	B. **CLAUSE NO.:** 6-28
C. **CONTRACT TYPES USED IN:** Hardware contract	D. **RISK RATING:** 2

E. INTENT AND SCOPE

To identify specifically the amount of machine time to be supplied at no charge prior to installation of the equipment. Such machine time is normally used to test programs being prepared for use on the machine, to run benchmarks, or to run initial compilations. The general term "test time" is used to describe this machine time.

The test time to be supplied should be supplied at a convenient location, and upon a reasonably convenient schedule. If for example the vendor supplies 24 hours of free time, it is useless if provided in unreasonably small segments, or if provided in Southwest Africa. Thus, test time provisions should disclose (or geographically define) the site at which it is to be supplied and the schedule and time of day under which it is to be supplied.

F. PROTECTION AGAINST

Protects against inadequacy or practical unavailability.

G. STANDARD CLAUSE PROVIDED BY MANUFACTURERS

Program Testing and Compiling Time: a. Honeywell's proposals solicited for planned installations shall include upon request a statement of the total program testing and compiling time which is estimated to be required for each program application area specified by the Government to permit the Government to use the equipment productively immediately following the installation date.

b. The amount of the program testing and compiling time specified above which shall be provided without additional charge, shall be specified in the proposal; and shall be provided on equipment identical in configuration with that on order or mutually agreed as adequate, at Honeywell's facilities, or at a Government site, or by mutual agreement at another installation or a combination of the above prior to installation of the ordered system.

At the Government's option, any or all of the no-charge pre-installation testing and compiling time may be exchanged for program testing time to be used during the ninety (90) day period following the start of the acceptance test provided in Paragraph 4 on the basis of two (2) hours of post-installation testing and compiling time for one hour of pre-installation testing and compiling time. The Basic Monthly Rental (Special Item 132-1) will not be reduced as a result of the post-installation testing time, nor will any credit be given for unused time.

c. Honeywell shall, as specified in its proposal, provide without charge the necessary translation compilers and machine time to permit the conversion from source programs written in COBOL, FORTRAN, etc., to programs of the particular data processing systems covered by this Contract.

d. In those instances where programs are to be developed at a single installation for use of multiple installations, the time which accrues to the multiple installations may be utilized at the option of the Government at a single installation.

H. IDEAL COVERAGE

The vendor agrees to furnish to user, at no charge, _____ hours of test time on a configuration substantially equivalent to that being delivered hereunder. Test time will be provided at the dates and times described in Schedule A, and at a location within a 50-mile radius from the user's site. Test time will normally be provided during normal working hours of the user's staff, unless permission has been given by the user for use of test time at other times. During test time, user may make such use of the test facilities as user shall determine.

J. POSSIBLE REMEDIES

Like other services provided by the vendor, failure to provide this one should permit the user the opportunity to purchase such additional time from other sources and to charge the cost thereof to the vendor's account.

L. REFERENCES TO OTHER CLAUSES: 6-51.

A. CLAUSE NAME: Documentation Availability   **B. CLAUSE NO.:** 6-29

C. CONTRACT TYPES USED IN: Hardware and some   **D. RISK RATING:** 3
software contracts

E. INTENT AND SCOPE

To identify specifically which documentation is required to operate the system, and which will be made available. This can take the place of a list of all available documentation, or be done as a general statement of types of documentation necessary to run the system effectively.

G. STANDARD CLAUSE PROVIDED BY MANUFACTURERS

Manuals and Documentation: ADR will provide Customer one copy of each of the following: (A) STAR/ACA User's Guide (B) STAR/ACA Maintenance Documentation.

H. IDEAL COVERAGE

The vendor will provide the user with copies of each of the following manuals which vendor represents are the only manuals necessary for the effective operation of the system: [list]

I. FALL-BACK ALTERNATIVES

Limit the number of manuals provided free and obtain the right to reproduce them at user expense (free from copyright violation); or obtain the right to purchase additional manuals at published prices.

L. REFERENCES TO OTHER CLAUSES: 6-30, 6-31, 7-03, 7-04, 8-03, 9-07.

A. CLAUSE NAME: Future Rights to Documentation   **B. CLAUSE NO.:** 6-30

C. CONTRACT TYPES USED IN: Hardware and some software contracts   **D. RISK RATING:** 3

E. INTENT AND SCOPE

To ensure for the user the ability to obtain all documentation developed in future for the system or any related systems.

F. PROTECTION AGAINST

Protects against the vendor's refusal to provide, except possibly at exorbitant cost, the documentation necessary for later-devised methods of operation of the system, or future modifications and improvements on existing documentation.

H. IDEAL COVERAGE

The vendor agrees that all future documentation and revisions of existing documentation developed for the system or similar systems, which may be useful to the user, shall be furnished to the user. Where such future or revised documentation is furnished without charge to any customer of vendor, it shall be furnished without charge to user; where not so available without charge, it shall be furnished to user, upon request, at then published prices.

L. REFERENCES TO OTHER CLAUSES: 6-29, 7-03.

A. CLAUSE NAME: Rights to Reproduce Material   **B. CLAUSE NO.:** 6-31

C. CONTRACT TYPES USED IN: Hardware and software contracts   **D. RISK RATING:** 3

E. INTENT AND SCOPE

If additional copies of documentation are required, and the vendor's charges for additional copies are significant, then it may be desirable to reproduce existing documentation. It is generally more convenient to reproduce such documentation, but this represents a violation of copyright (incidentally, a widespread one) unless permission is granted by the vendor. This clause provides such permission on a blanket basis, provided that such rights are exercised solely for internal use by the user.

H. IDEAL COVERAGE

All documentation and printed materials provided by the vendor to the user may be reproduced by user, provided that such reproduction is made solely for the internal use of employees of the user and further provided that no charge is made to anyone for such reproductions.

I. FALL-BACK ALTERNATIVES

The user may reproduce documentation, provided that reproduction is made only after requesting permission from the vendor, which permission will not unreasonably be withheld.

L. REFERENCES TO OTHER CLAUSES: 7-04.

A. CLAUSE NAME: Term of Agreement **B. CLAUSE NO.:** 6-32

C. CONTRACT TYPES USED IN: Hardware and software contracts **D. RISK RATING:** 2

E. INTENT AND SCOPE

To define the term under which the basic agreement will run. For a purchase contract the term expires when the hardware has been delivered, accepted, paid for, and title has transferred; thereafter, however, the maintenance contract will run, and most terms of the purchase contract should survive transfer of title. In a rental contract, the term of the agreement should run from the installation and acceptance of the equipment until expiration of the lease. Rights to cancel by the user can be negotiated. A 30- or 90-day user cancellation clause can often be contracted for.

H. IDEAL COVERAGE

Purchase Agreements: This agreement and all of its provisions shall survive the transfer of Title. *Rental Agreements:* The term of this agreement shall commence upon acceptance of the equipment by user, as elsewhere herein defined, and shall continue for a term of ＿＿ months, unless sooner terminated by user, at its option, on at least 30 days prior written notice to vendor. Upon termination, this agreement shall thereafter be of no force and effect, but the terms and provisions hereof shall otherwise survive such termination.

K. COMMENTS

If it is the vendor's obligation to remove the equipment upon termination, this should be specifically dealt with.

L. REFERENCES TO OTHER CLAUSES: 5-11, 7-16, 9-10, 9-11.

A. **CLAUSE NAME:** Method of Payment   B. **CLAUSE NO.:** 6-33

C. **CONTRACT TYPES USED IN:** Hardware contract   D. **RISK RATING:** 3

E. **INTENT AND SCOPE**

Payments should be made in accordance with normal and reasonable business practices. This would normally mean that payment is to be made against an approved invoice, possibly within 30 days from receipt of that invoice.

F. **PROTECTION AGAINST**

Protects against the calling of defaults prior to the expiration of sufficient time for the user to make payment under normal business practices.

G. **STANDARD CLAUSE PROVIDED BY MANUFACTURERS**

Price and Payment: Customer shall pay to Bunker Ramo the purchase price specified in *Schedule A* for each item of Equipment within 30 days after delivery thereof. The price of Equipment is f.o.b. Bunker Ramo's point of shipment.

H. **IDEAL COVERAGE**

All payments otherwise due under this contract shall not be payable until ____ days after receipt of invoice from vendor.

L. **REFERENCES TO OTHER CLAUSES:** 6-38, 7-15, 8-11, 9-09, 10-26.

A. **CLAUSE NAME:** Hold-backs for Contract Compliance   B. **CLAUSE NO.:** 6-34

C. **CONTRACT TYPES USED IN:** Hardware and other contracts   D. **RISK RATING:** 3

E. **INTENT AND SCOPE**

If elements of the contract are to be completed after delivery and installation, it is desirable to withhold sums from the vendor in order to ensure complete contract compliance. If, for example, some software modifications are to be made after hardware installation, a portion of the price should be withheld from the payment due upon acceptance of the hardware. It is best for the hold-back to be under user control. If the vendor resists, escrow can be created to hold the funds.

H. **IDEAL COVERAGE**

The parties acknowledge that certain performance will be required by vendor subsequent to acceptance of the equipment by user. Accordingly, $_____ (or ____%) of the purchase price otherwise payable upon such acceptance shall be retained by user and shall be payable upon performance and acceptance of tasks described on Schedule A.

I. **FALL-BACK ALTERNATIVES**

Provide for a deposit of the hold-back into escrow.

K. **COMMENTS**

The Schedule may provide for releases of parts of the hold-back as each element is performed and accepted. Consideration should be given to per diem liquidated damages to be retained out of the hold-back for delays in performance.

L. **REFERENCES TO OTHER CLAUSES:** 7-15, 8-11, 10-05, 10-26.

A. **CLAUSE NAME:** Tax Applicability   B. **CLAUSE NO.:** 6-35

C. **CONTRACT TYPES USED IN:** Hardware and some   D. **RISK RATING:** 3
software contracts

E. **INTENT AND SCOPE**

To explicitly define the tax obligation of the user with respect to the services and equipment provided. All taxes applicable to the contract should be defined in this clause.

F. **PROTECTION AGAINST**

Protects against unforeseen tax expenses. Normally, a user should only expect to be responsible for sales and use taxes and personal property taxes.

G. **STANDARD CLAUSE PROVIDED BY MANUFACTURERS**

In addition to payment of the purchase price Customer shall pay, or reimburse Bunker Ramo for any and all sales, use taxes and any other governmental charges upon or measured by Equipment sold or services rendered pursuant to this Agreement, or otherwise exacted in connection with the performance hereof except Bunker Ramo's net corporate income taxes or corporate franchise taxes.

Taxes: Notwithstanding the provisions of Clause 27 of GSA Form 1424, GSA Supplemental Provisions, the contract price excludes all state and local taxes levied on or measured by the contract or sales price of the services or completed supplies furnished under this Contract. Taxes so excluded from the contract price pursuant to the preceding sentence shall be separately stated on the Contractor's invoices, and the Government agrees either to pay to the Contractor amounts covering such taxes or to provide evidence necessary to sustain an exemption therefrom. (Honeywell)

Buyer agrees to pay Seller any tax on this Agreement or on or measured by the prices and/or other charges herein or the equipment hereunder or its use, however designated, levied or based, whether or not specifically included in the pricing breakdown on the face page hereof, whenever Seller must itself pay and/or must collect such tax from Buyer according to the applicable statutes or ordinances, as interpreted by the departmental authorities of the taxing unit. It shall be Buyer's sole obligation after payment to Seller to challenge the applicability or propriety of any such tax by contact with or action against said taxing unit. Seller agrees to refund any tax collected which it is subsequently determined need not have been paid and/or collected and for which a credit or refund may be obtained from the taxing unit. Personal property taxes levied after delivery shall be paid by Buyer. (Burroughs)

H. **IDEAL COVERAGE**

The user shall pay any sales, use and personal property taxes arising out of this contract and the transaction contemplated hereby. Any other taxes levied upon this contract, the transaction or the equipment or services delivered pursuant hereto shall be borne by the vendor.

J. **POSSIBLE REMEDIES**

In a rental contract, it can be provided that any claims made against user for taxes payable by vendor can be paid by user, after notice, and deducted from the rent.

L. **REFERENCES TO OTHER CLAUSES:** 7-17, 10-08, 10-12.

A. CLAUSE NAME: Warranty of New Equipment   B. CLAUSE NO.: 6-36

C. CONTRACT TYPES USED IN: Hardware contracts   D. RISK RATING: 3

E. INTENT AND SCOPE

To ensure that under a purchase contract all equipment delivered is new and of original manufacture. This is necessary to ensure that the provisions of the investment tax credit will apply to the equipment, and to ensure that the user obtains new equipment.

F. PROTECTION AGAINST

Protects against vendor delivery of reconditioned or rebuilt equipment under a purchase contract, and protects the tax credit.

G. STANDARD CLAUSE PROVIDED BY MANUFACTURERS

Warranty: Machines purchased under this Agreement may be either newly manufactured by IBM from new and serviceable used parts which are equivalent to new in performance in these machines, or assembled by IBM from serviceable used parts, or machines which have been previously installed. Machines assembled from serviceable used parts and machines previously installed will at the time of shipment meet product functional specifications currently applicable to new machines.

H. IDEAL COVERAGE

The vendor warrants that all equipment supplied hereunder will be new and of original manufacture in the United States and, as such, eligible for the investment tax credit.

L. REFERENCES TO OTHER CLAUSES: 6-37, 10-08.

A. CLAUSE NAME: Pass Through of Investment Tax Credit   **B. CLAUSE NO.:** 6-37

C. CONTRACT TYPES USED IN: Hardware *rental* contracts   **D. RISK RATING:** 2
only

E. INTENT AND SCOPE

To ensure, in a rental contract, that the Investment Tax Credit is passed through to the user.

H. IDEAL COVERAGE

The vendor warrants that the leased equipment is eligible for Investment Tax Credit and vendor assigns to the user the full benefit thereof, and vendor will not claim the same.

K. COMMENTS

The best approach to the tax credit is often to have the amount computed and to reduce the rent by that amount. The user, then, need not worry about availability of the credit or about the implications on the user's financial statements and tax returns. A tax credit is of little use to a user who is operating at a loss for tax purposes. The entire area deserves careful consideration by tax counsel and by qualified accountants.

L. REFERENCES TO OTHER CLAUSES: 6-36, 10-08.

A. **CLAUSE NAME:**   Method of Charging by Type of Charges   B. **CLAUSE NO.:** 6-38

C. **CONTRACT TYPES USED IN:**   Hardware contracts   D. **RISK RATING:** 2

E. **INTENT AND SCOPE**

To clearly define the charges to be incurred by the user, and the method under which these charges will be computed. This clause should cover charges for all types of supporting services, for supplies, for the equipment, for overtime usage, for maintenance services and the like.

F. **PROTECTION AGAINST**

Protects against surprises.

G. **STANDARD CLAUSE PROVIDED BY MANUFACTURERS**

Invoices and Payments:

a. Rental (Special Item 132-1)

(1) Subject to the provisions of Paragraph 4 of Special Item 132-1, rental charges shall begin on the installation date.

(2) Honeywell shall render invoices (five copies) for Basic Monthly Rental Charges at the end of the month for which the charges accrue. Such charges are due when billed and are payable to Honeywell at the address shown on the invoice. Invoices shall provide as a minimum:

    (a) Type and description of equipment

    (b) Serial number

    (c) Basic Monthly Charge for each machine

    (d) Total charges

(3) In case of unscheduled or emergency maintenance charges, the Government shall furnish Honeywell monthly with an authorization to bill which shall list the following information:

    (a) Number of hours of extra maintenance

    (b) Extra maintenance rate applied

    (c) Total extra maintenance charges for the month

(4) Any credits due the Government may be applied against Honeywell's invoices with appropriate information attached.

(5) Invoices for Honeywell prepaid transportation charges must be accompanied by a bill of lading.

(6) The Basic Monthly Rental for a machine, initially installed for a fraction of a calendar month, shall be computed at the rate of one thirtieth (1/30th) of the Basic Monthly Rental for each day the machine was installed beginning on and including the installation date through the last calendar day of the month.

(7) A machine discontinued at other than the last day of a calendar month shall be billed for its Basic Monthly Rental less one thirtieth (1/30th) of the Basic Monthly Rental for each calendar day in that month following the date of discontinuance.

(8) In the event that the Government is of the opinion that a charge or credit on an invoice is not billed properly, every effort should be made to promptly pay the portion of the invoice not in question and give detailed written notice to Honeywell concerning the item in question.

(9) The Government shall be entitled to a rental renewal order incentive equal to 0.9 percent of the Basic Monthly Rental Charge for July 1974, multiplied by the number of months for which rental is ordered, for all funded renewal orders issued for the Fiscal Year 1975 provided that such renewal orders are received by Honeywell no later than August 15,

1974. Such orders should cover the full period contemplated for rental within the fiscal year.

b. Purchase (Special Item 132-6)

On equipment to be shipped from a Honeywell factory, Honeywell shall render an invoice at the time of shipment. Payment of such invoice shall be made in full upon acceptance of the equipment by the Government in accordance with Paragraph 3, Special Item 132-6. Title to the equipment shall remain with Honeywell until the purchase price is paid. On equipment already installed, Honeywell shall render an invoice upon receipt of the Government's order to purchase and payment is due when billed and shall be made in full before title passes. Honeywell shall issue invoices for such additional charges, including transportation, rigging, and drayage as may be applicable to each sale and such charges are due and upon full acceptance of the equipment by the Government in accordance with Paragraph 3 of Special Item 132-6 are payable to Honeywell at the address shown on the invoice. Upon mutual written agreement between Honeywell and the Government, title to identical rented and purchased equipment may be exchanged. Refusal to agree to exchange title is at the sole discretion of either party.

c. Maintenance (Special Item 132-11)

(1) All charges for maintenance service shall be invoiced at the end of the month for which such charges accrued and are payable when billed.

(2) Payment for maintenance services of less than one (1) month's duration shall be prorated at one thirtieth (1/30th) of the Monthly Maintenance Charges for each calendar day except that the thirty-first (31st) day of any month shall not be included in the computation.

(3) In case of extra maintenance charges, the Government shall furnish Honeywell with an authorization to bill which shall list the following information:

(a) Number of hours of extra maintenance.

(b) Extra maintenance rate applied and total extra maintenance charges for the month.

(4) Extra maintenance charges shall be rounded to the nearest fifteen (15) minutes.

(5) Invoices for extra maintenance charges are payable when billed.

(6) In case maintenance credits apply, the Government shall request in writing the applicable credits for the month to be applied against other charges. The request shall list the following information:

(a) Type and model number(s) of machine(s)

(b) Date of occurrence

(7) The Government shall be entitled to a maintenance renewal order incentive equal to ten percent (10%) of the Basic Monthly Maintenance Charges for the month of July 1974 for all funded renewal orders issued provided that such renewal orders are received by Honeywell no later than August 15, 1974. Such orders should cover the full period contemplated for maintenance within the fiscal year.

d. Repair Service (Special Item 132-15) and Repair Parts (Special Item 132-16)

Invoices for repair services and parts shall be submitted by Honeywell as soon as possible after completion of the work and are payable by the Government when billed.

H. IDEAL COVERAGE

The charges described in this contract are the only charges now or hereafter to be levied by vendor for the equipment, support and services to be performed by it. There are no other charges to be made by the vendor to the user except as follows:

[Equipment usage—possible overtime charges, installed meter; Sunday and holiday use charges; off-hour maintenance charges; transportation charges; insurance charges; removal charges; late charges; charges for service and supplies; etc.]

K. COMMENTS

If the contract is comprehensively drawn, there should be *no* exceptions in the above written clause.

L. REFERENCES TO OTHER CLAUSES: 6-33, 7-14, 8-10, 9-09.

A. **CLAUSE NAME:** Credits for Malfunction   B. **CLAUSE NO.:** 6-39

C. **CONTRACT TYPES USED IN:** Hardware contracts   D. **RISK RATING:** 3

E. **INTENT AND SCOPE**

If the equipment malfunctions for some significant period of time, the user should be given credit against charges. In a purchase transaction, at least a maintenance charge credit should be supplied; in a rental machine, rental credits should be made available. It should be recognized that an equipment malfunction will cost the user more than just the lost time. As a result, credits for malfunction probably should be computed on a reasonably generous basis, and might be the equivalent of twice the number of hours lost due to malfunction. Since a rental contract and a purchase transaction including maintenance are very similar in practical terms, in both instances it might be feasible to establish credits on the basis of prevailing rental rates.

G. **STANDARD CLAUSE PROVIDED BY MANUFACTURERS**

Customer Credit for Equipment Malfunction Rider: If customer is unable to use the Equipment covered by this Agreement for a continuous period of ninety-six (96) hours due to malfunction of such Equipment (not including software), ITEL shall provide for Customer a Credit equal to the pro rata portion of the monthly rent payable under the Lease with respect to such Equipment for each successive continuous 24-hour period thereafter during which the such Equipment continues to malfunction, up to an aggregate of ten (10) such periods. Any request by Customer for a Credit hereunder must be substantiated by IBM Maintenance Logs.

Temporary inoperability of the Equipment during maintenance or installation of engineering changes by IBM shall not be considered to be equipment malfunction hereunder.

H. **IDEAL COVERAGE**

The vendor will provide credits [*in a purchase contract:* against maintenance charges; *in a rental contract:* against rent] for equipment malfunction equal to twice the amount of time lost due to the malfunction at rates equal to the rental rate for such equipment prevailing at the time of this delivery.

I. **FALL–BACK ALTERNATIVES**

As an alternative, a specific amount can be set aside as a credit for malfunction. A fee of $_____ per hour of time lost to be credited against invoices due to the vendor could be used as an index of approach.

L. **REFERENCES TO OTHER CLAUSES:** 6-62.

A. CLAUSE NAME: Price Protection Prior to Delivery   **B. CLAUSE NO.:** 6-40

C. CONTRACT TYPES USED IN: Hardware contracts   **D. RISK RATING:** 2

E. INTENT AND SCOPE

The price protection clauses, 6-40, 41, 42, 43 and 44 ensure that the vendor does not unreasonably increase prices for products or services as a result of the lapse of time. Prior to delivery of equipment, the price at which the equipment is to be delivered should be protected. If one enters into a contract to purchase an item for delivery N months from now, the contract price should hold at the time of delivery.

F. PROTECTION AGAINST

Protects against increases in price after the contract, but before delivery.

G. STANDARD CLAUSE PROVIDED BY MANUFACTURERS

(b) If UNIVAC's established purchase price for any equipment shall be lower upon the date of shipment than the purchase price for such equipment as specified in the Schedule of Equipment of this Agreement, the Purchaser shall have the benefit of such lower price.

(c) The purchase price for any such equipment scheduled for delivery within the eighteen (18) month period commencing on the date the Agreement is accepted by UNIVAC, shall not be increased unless the delivery is delayed beyond this period and such delay is caused or requested by the Purchaser.

(d) If UNIVAC's established purchase price for any equipment shall be higher on a date not within the protection period as defined in Paragraph (c), the price stated in the Agreement shall be increased accordingly.

(e) UNIVAC shall furnish the Purchaser with personal, direct notice in writing of any price increase affecting the equipment hereunder; the Purchaser may thereafter terminate his order for such equipment provided the Purchaser mails or otherwise furnishes UNIVAC with written notice of termination within thirty (30) days after the date of UNIVAC's notice of such price increase.

H. IDEAL COVERAGE

If the vendors established purchase [or rental] price for any item of equipment or software delivered hereunder shall be less on the date of installation thereof than the price for such equipment as specified herein, this contract shall be deemed to provide such lower price; if such price shall be higher, the prices set forth herein shall prevail.

K. COMMENTS

Some vendors will want a time limit. That can be acceptable if the delivery is delayed by the purchaser, but is not acceptable if delivery delays are occasioned by vendor.

L. REFERENCES TO OTHER CLAUSES: 6-41, 42, 43, 44, 6-88, 7-20, 7-21, 9-12.

A. **CLAUSE NAME:** Price Protection During Term of Contract   B.   **CLAUSE NO.:** 6-41

C. **CONTRACT TYPES USED IN:** Hardware rental contracts   D.   **RISK RATING:** 2
                                           only

E. **INTENT AND SCOPE**

In a rental contract, the rental price should be protected for some period of time. In addition, a notice requirement should exist in the event vendor desires to increase rental rates after expiration of the protected period. The notice period will give the user the opportunity to cancel the contract if the price increase is not acceptable. The best rental contracts are obviously those with fixed rents over a long term, and with rights of early termination by the user only.

F. **PROTECTION AGAINST**

Protects against unreasonable increases in rental prices during the term of the contract.

H. **IDEAL COVERAGE**

The rentals for the equipment and software shown herein shall not be increased for a period of 24 months after installation and acceptance of the system. Thereafter, if this contract shall still be in effect and if the vendor decides to increase such prices, at least 90 days notice of intended increase, setting forth the amount thereof, shall be given to the user. Notwithstanding anything herein to the contrary, upon receipt of such notice the user may terminate this contract, effective any time within nine months after the date of such notice from vendor on 30 days notice to vendor.

J. **POSSIBLE REMEDIES**

Limit, by formula or otherwise, the amounts of increases.

K. **COMMENTS**

A user should also try to get automatic benefit of any price reductions which take effect during the term. See 5-03.

L. **REFERENCES TO OTHER CLAUSES:** 6-40, 42, 43, 44, 6-88, 7-20, 7-21, 9-12.

A. CLAUSE NAME: Price Protection for Expansion Equipment   **B. CLAUSE NO.:** 6-42

C. CONTRACT TYPES USED IN: Hardware   **D. RISK RATING:** 3

E. INTENT AND SCOPE

To provide some mechanism for assuring that additional equipment for expansion is capable of being obtained at realistic prices. This clause is important if the equipment being purchased is relatively unique, if it is a test model for a contemplated larger system, or if expansion equipment is routinely required as the business grows. For example, a bank contemplating the addition of branches each year would have to purchase additional teller terminals for such new branches. If these teller terminals were relatively unique, and it were possible for the vendor to increase the prices for these unrealistically, a clause such as this would be highly desirable to ensure the continued viability of the total system approach.

F. PROTECTION AGAINST

Protects against the possibility of vendor price escalation to compensate for the necessity to continue to manufacture certain special types of equipment.

H. IDEAL COVERAGE

The vendor agrees for the next N years, to manufacture, on request, additional equipment similar to those items listed on Schedule A, for sale [or rental] to user at prices then in effect, but in no event shall such prices be increased by more than 10% per annum for each year from the date of this contract to the date of such order.

I. FALL–BACK ALTERNATIVES

Increases can be limited by any other formula, such as cost of living index.

K. COMMENTS

If substantial additions are contemplated in the near future the user should attempt to get fixed price commitments for some agreed to time period.

L. REFERENCES TO OTHER CLAUSES: 6-40, 41, 43, 44, 6-88, 6-89, 7-20, 7-21, 9-12.

A. CLAUSE NAME: Price Protection for Supplies and Services

B. CLAUSE NO.: 6-43

C. CONTRACT TYPES USED IN: Hardware

D. RISK RATING: 3

E. INTENT AND SCOPE

To ensure that supplies and services which may be required to augment the contract, from time to time, can be obtained at prices not increased on an unreasonable basis.

F. PROTECTION AGAINST

Protects against vendor use of supply or services pricing as a means of increasing profits from a dependent customer.

H. IDEAL COVERAGE

The charges shown in 6-38 for supplies and services shall not be increased for a period of 24 months after delivery of the equipment herein contracted for. Thereafter, such supplies and services shall be available at published prices then in effect, which prices shall, however, not represent an increase of more than ____% per annum over current prices for each year after the date of delivery of the equipment.

I. FALL-BACK ALTERNATIVES

The cost of living index or another formula may be used as an alternative to a fixed percentage increase.

K. COMMENTS

Initial price protection is probably desirable for some minimum period, during which the majority of the services, if not the majority of the supplies as well, will be purchased. For example, initial supplies of tapes, disks, ribbons, etc. will be purchased most heavily during the first few months surrounding delivery. Similarly, support services, installation systems and other services will all peak around the delivery period and for a few months thereafter. Thus, it is highly desirable to establish firm prices for those supplies and services to be bought prior to and soon after delivery. Thereafter, should it be necessary to obtain additional supplies and services they can be adjusted on the basis of price increase limitations which are considered reasonable.

L. REFERENCES TO OTHER CLAUSES: 6-15, 6-19, 6-23, 6-38, 6-44, 9-12.

A. CLAUSE NAME: Price Protection for Maintenance   **B. CLAUSE NO.:** 6-44

C. CONTRACT TYPES USED IN: Hardware or maintenance   **D. RISK RATING:** 2

E. INTENT AND SCOPE

To provide realistic pricing methods for maintenance services which, perhaps more than any other types of services, are principally obtained from the original equipment manufacturer.

F. PROTECTION AGAINST

Protects against arbitrary or excessive manufacturer maintenance price increases to recover costs incurred in other parts of the contract or to unreasonably profit from a dependent customer.

G. STANDARD CLAUSE PROVIDED BY MANUFACTURERS

Burroughs may, effective after the expiration of the original term of this Agreement, and at the end of any billing period thereafter, increase or decrease the rates set forth hereunder to those then currently in effect.

H. IDEAL COVERAGE

Prices given in 6-38 for maintenance services shall not be increased for a period of two years after delivery of the equipment. Thereafter such prices may be increased to prevailing prices, which prices, however, shall not represent an increase of more than ____% per year over current prices for each year after the date of delivery of the equipment.

I. FALL-BACK ALTERNATIVES

The period of price protection should be established either from the point of delivery, or the point at which the warranty expired. The cost of living index may be used as an indicator of maintenance cost increases, since maintenance is primarily a labor intensive cost.

J. POSSIBLE REMEDIES

If maintenance prices are increased beyond a defined reasonable amount, it may be possible to obtain such maintenance services from another organization, and to charge the difference in cost so incurred to the vendor.

L. REFERENCES TO OTHER CLAUSES: 6-56, 6-58.

A. **CLAUSE NAME:** Reliability Parameters	B. **CLAUSE NO.:** 6-45
C. **CONTRACT TYPES USED IN:** Hardware	D. **RISK RATING:** 2

E. **INTENT AND SCOPE**

To define the parameters to be used in computing reliability characteristics, for establishment of reliability guarantees in clause 6-46.

F. **PROTECTION AGAINST**

Protects against disputes as to the definition of what exactly reliability is.

H. **IDEAL COVERAGE**

For purposes of this contract, reliability of equipment shall be defined as follows:

"Downtime percentage" shall mean unavailable time minus time for scheduled maintenance divided by total time available, computed on a monthly [bi-weekly] basis.

"Unavailable time" is the time involved while any of the following shall take place and continues:

- the system fails to operate;
- the system fails to operate in accordance with specifications attached hereto as Exhibit A;
- the system operates inconsistently or erratically;
- the system is in the process of being maintained or repaired;
- a hardware or software component of the system is inoperative which renders the entire system useless for user purposes;
- the system is not operated because there is potential danger from operation of the system to operators or employees;
- there is a defect in software supplied by the manufacturer.

J. **POSSIBLE REMEDIES**

See 6-48, 6-39 and 6-62.

K. **COMMENTS**

Reliability definitions should be made as simple as possible, since their ultimate interpretation may be in a court of law. It is, accordingly, desirable to try to reduce reliability characteristics to as simple a standard as possible.

L. **REFERENCES TO OTHER CLAUSES:** 6-05, 6-46, 6-48, 6-51.

A. CLAUSE NAME: Guarantees of Performance	B. CLAUSE NO.: 6-46
C. CONTRACT TYPES USED IN: Hardware	D. RISK RATING: 1

E. INTENT AND SCOPE

To provide a mechanism for measurement of reliability, which will ensure that the equipment being supplied will meet the necessary standards, without excessive interruption for maintenance and repair.

F. PROTECTION AGAINST

To protect against vendor attempts to continually maintain equipment when its performance is sub-standard, rather than replace it.

G. STANDARD CLAUSE PROVIDED BY MANUFACTURERS

When, in the opinion of Burroughs, overhaul is necessary, it will be provided at no additional cost up to the 5th anniversary of the equipment. Overhaul after the 5th anniversary will be provided at the customer's expense.

H. IDEAL COVERAGE

The "downtime" percentages attached in Schedule A represent agreed reliability standards and vendor agrees that all equipment installed will meet such standards. The vendor agrees that if the downtime percentages are exceeded, the System [component] will be considered unreliable and the System will, at user's request, be promptly replaced with new substitute equipment, which for the purposes of this contract shall be deemed delivered on the date of installation and acceptance.

I. FALL-BACK ALTERNATIVES

(1) The vendor will use its best efforts to meet the reliability standards shown in the attached schedule, including the replacement of unreliable equipment as it may reasonably determine to be appropriate.

(2) The vendor agrees that the reliability standards shown in the attached schedule are reasonable. The vendor will therefore attempt to maintain the equipment in such a way that these standards can normally be achieved.

J. POSSIBLE REMEDIES

In the event reliability standards are not met, various remedies are possible. For example, it is possible to require the vendor to make rebates of rental, maintenance payments or purchase payments. It is wise to require the vendor to replace unreliable components, as set forth above and as is recommended in 6-48. It is further possible to insist that the user has the right to have maintenance provided by an external organization, with the vendor paying any cost differentials. Finally, it is possible to insist that the vendor provide necessary backup equipment so that if the System is unavailable because of unreliable operations the user will have an alternative system on which production can be achieved. See 6-39, 6-48, 6-49, and 6-62 for other remedies.

K. COMMENTS

The issue of reliability boils down principally to duration of unavailable time, and to frequency. Both of these must be covered in a reliability clause. Unfortunately, with current systems and types of functions currently being performed, a reliability clause which calls for a percentage reliability acceptable to the vendor, such as the 90% level required in the GSA contract, is not normally satisfactory to a user. If a main computer were to operate at only 90% reliability, it would be a disaster for any company using it in a real time mode. In such cases, reliability below 98% would be deemed to be disastrous, even though no vendor realistically could guarantee its equipment to operate at 98% or above. As a result, it is extremely difficult to establish realistic reliability parameters and guarantees of performance. Even if no guarantees can be obtained, it is desirable to have a reasonable schedule of reliability parameters set forth in the contract, even as a non-binding expression of intent. If claims are made against the vendor it is possible to demonstrate the intent of the parties, and to determine what was deemed to be reasonable reliability. This normally will allow claims to be pursued if the operational results fall far below reliability targets although it still raises significant questions if the operational results are close to but still below the defined targets.

It should be noted that in arbitration or litigation, the person standing in judgment will be a person who is not familiar with the high levels of reliability expected in today's computer environment. Such a person is more likely to be familiar with the reliability problems involving automobiles or television sets, and is therefore likely to consider 90% reliability realistic as a target. Although expert testimony will help to educate a judge, it is highly desirable to stipulate some level of operating effectiveness which is expected from the viewpoint of reliability.

L. REFERENCES TO OTHER CLAUSES: 6-05, 6-39, 6-45, 6-48, 6-49, 6-51, 6-62.

A. **CLAUSE NAME:** Warranty and Free Maintenance   B. **CLAUSE NO.:** 6-47

C. **CONTRACT TYPES USED IN:** Hardware   D. **RISK RATING:** 2

E. **INTENT AND SCOPE**

To ensure that, for an initial period, the equipment is warranted against defects in material, workmanship and failure of operation in ordinary use. Maintenance during such period should be at no cost to the user.

F. **PROTECTION AGAINST**

To protect against levies of charges during an initial period; to establish a free "shaking-out" period.

G. **STANDARD CLAUSE PROVIDED BY MANUFACTURERS**

Warranty: Seller warrants that: (1) no applicable statute, regulation or ordinance of the United States or of any State has been violated in the manufacture and/or sale of the equipment; (2) Seller has title to said equipment and the right to sell same; (3) For a period of one (1) year from installation, the equipment delivered under this Agreement shall be free from defects in material or workmanship. Written notice and an explanation of circumstances concerning any claim that the equipment has proven defective in material or workmanship shall be given promptly to Seller. Seller agrees thereupon as its only liability for such defects to take reasonable and prompt action to correct such defect either by repair or by replacement, at its election, except that there shall be no obligation to replace or repair items which by their nature are expendable, such as but not limited to, transistors, tubes, lamps, resistors, capacitors, belts, and diodes. Seller shall not in any event be liable for loss or damage arising from any cause beyond Seller's reasonable control, nor for incidental, indirect or consequential damages. Seller's liability under this Agreement shall in no case exceed refund of the purchase price less reasonable rental for past use, upon return of the equipment delivered hereunder by mutual agreement. This warranty is in lieu of any and all other warranties, express or implied, regarding the equipment and service supplied hereunder, including any regarding merchantability or fitness for a particular purpose. In the event of employment by Buyer of any non-Burroughs attachment, feature or device on the Burroughs equipment, or any part thereof, furnished by Seller hereunder Seller shall not be liable under this warranty.

Warranties: There shall be no representation or warranty of Bunker Ramo, of any kind, express or implied, in respect of any of the Equipment, or the use or results of the use thereof or otherwise, except that Bunker Ramo hereby represents and warrants that:

(a) Each item of Equipment delivered hereunder shall be free of defects in material and workmanship at the date of delivery thereof. In limitation of the foregoing, Bunker Ramo shall in no event have any liability or obligation in connection with any Equipment failure occurring more than 12 months after the date of delivery thereof or any defect causing such failure nor any liability or obligation at any time in respect of expendable components such as, but not limited to, cathode ray tubes, light bulbs, transistors, diodes or tubes.

(b) Bunker Ramo will transfer and convey to Customer good and marketable title to Equipment purchased by Customer hereunder.

You warrant the above described equipment for a period of _____ months after delivery against defects in material, workmanship and operational failure from ordinary use. Your obligation if the equipment does not meet these warranties is limited solely to correcting the defect or failure, without charge. The foregoing warranties are exclusive of all other warranties whether written, oral or implied, and whether of merchantability, fitness or otherwise. In no event shall you be liable for special or consequential damages from any cause whatsoever. Any repairs not covered by the foregoing warranties shall be paid by the undersigned. Subsequent to above mentioned warranty period you will make maintenance service available to the undersigned in accordance with the terms of your standard maintenance agreement. (NCR)

For a ninety (90) day period following delivery, the Equipment sold hereunder is warranted against defects and workmanship and material under normal use. Any defects reported to ADR within this period shall be remedied by ADR at its factory provided the Equipment is returned, prepaid and in accordance with the shipping instructions supplied by ADR.

Guarantee:

a. Honeywell will furnish all maintenance service and parts for a period of ninety (90) days beginning on the first day of the acceptance unless such maintenance service and parts are required because of fault or negligence of the Government. If rental equipment is purchased during this ninety (90) day period, the guarantee shall apply for the remainder of the period. If Series 60 equipment initially on rental is purchased, a 90-day guarantee period will begin on the effective date of the purchase. All replaced parts shall become the property of Honeywell. Prior to the expiration of this ninety (90) day guarantee period, whenever equipment is shipped for mechanical replacement purposes, Honeywell shall bear all costs of such shipment including, but not limited to, cost of packing, transportation, rigging, drayage, and insurance. The unexpired portion of the ninety (90) day guarantee period shall apply to the mechanical replacement provided, however, that the ninety (90) day guarantee period is suspended for any period of time between the date of removal of the units to be replaced and the installation and ready-for-use date of the mechanical replacement. However, if the replacement was necessitated due to the fault or negligence of the Government, the Government shall bear those costs.

b. These machines may contain some used parts which are warranted equivalent to new in performance when used in these machines.

c. Service pursuant to this guarantee will be furnished on an on-call basis and by Honeywell's local Field Engineering District Office. Honeywell shall not be responsible for failure to render service due to causes beyond its control and without the fault or negligence of Honeywell.

I. *Service and Parts Warranty:* Commencing on the Date of Installation, IBM will maintain in good working order each Warranty Category A machine for one year and each Warranty Category B or C machine for three months, at no additional charge to the Purchaser. At the Purchaser's request, IBM will make all necessary adjustments, repairs and parts replacements. All replacement parts will be new or equivalent to new in performance when used in these machines. All replaced parts will become the property of IBM on an exchange basis. IBM may, at its option, store maintenance equipment or parts on the Purchaser's premises that IBM deems necessary to fulfill this Warranty.

Service pursuant to this Warranty as required at any time will normally be furnished by IBM's nearest Branch Office or resident location. IBM shall have full and free access to the machines to perform this service. There will be no charge for travel expense associated with warranty services except that actual travel expense shall be charged in those unusual instances where the site at which the machine is located is not normally accessible by private automobile or scheduled public transportation. The Purchaser shall promptly inform IBM of any change in the machine location during the warranty period. Service outside the scope of this Warranty will be furnished at IBM's applicable hourly rates and terms then in effect.

II. *Parts Warranty:* For one year commencing on the Date of Installation, IBM warrants each Warranty Category B or C machine (excluding vacuum tubes and solid state and other electronic devices which are warranted for three months) to be free from defects in material and workmanship. IBM's obligation is limited to furnishing on an exchange basis replacements for parts which have been promptly reported by the Purchaser as having been, in his opinion, defective and are so found by IBM upon inspection. All replacement parts will be new or equivalent to new in performance when used in these machines. All replaced parts will become the property of IBM on an exchange basis. No service will be furnished pursuant to this parts warranty.

III. *Limitations:* The foregoing warranties will not apply to repair of damage or increase in service time caused by: accident, transportation, neglect or misuse; alterations (which shall include, but not be limited to, any deviation from circuit or structural machine design as provided by IBM, installation or removal of IBM features, or any other modification or maintenance related activities, whenever any of the foregoing are performed by other than IBM representatives); any machine other than those owned by IBM, under warranty provision of an IBM Purchase Agreement or under an IBM Maintenance Agreement; failure to provide a suitable installation environment with all facilities prescribed by the appropriate IBM Installation Manual—Physical Planning (including but not limited to, failure of, or failure to provide adequate electrical power, air conditioning or humidity control); the use of supplies or materials not meeting IBM specifications for such installation; or the use of the machine for other than data processing purposes for which designed.

IBM shall not be responsible for failure to provide service or parts due to causes beyond its control or required to adjust or repair any machine or part if it would be impractical to do so because of alterations in the machine or its connection by mechanical or electrical means to another machine or device or if the machine is located outside the United States, Puerto Rico or the Canal Zone.

H. IDEAL COVERAGE

The equipment purchased hereunder is warranted for a period of N months after delivery against defects in material and workmanship and from failure of operation from ordinary use, and vendor during such period will furnish all maintenance, service and parts and replacements necessary to maintain the equipment in operation and in working order, at no cost to the user.

I.   FALL–BACK ALTERNATIVES

The warranty period can be staged over two periods, one of which involves availability of free labor and material and a second which involves the supply of free parts, although labor may be charged. Since most standard maintenance contracts combine these, this may be difficult to obtain.

L.   REFERENCES TO OTHER CLAUSES: 6-36, 6-51, 7-32, 10-03.

A. **CLAUSE NAME:** Right to Replace Components   B. **CLAUSE NO.:** 6-48

C. **CONTRACT TYPES USED IN:** Hardware   D. **RISK RATING:** 1

E. **INTENT AND SCOPE**

This is the so called "lemon" clause. It protects against serious frustrations surrounding the retention of an item that through maintenance or repair is brought to operational level, but promptly goes "down" again, requiring more repair. It provides the user the right to request replacement of a component which does not make the reliability standards on a consistent basis.

F. **PROTECTION AGAINST**

There is sometimes subtle discrimination between renters and buyers. In many rental contracts, particularly short term leases favored by some vendors, it is possible to request replacement of an ineffective component, either by simply making the request, or cancelling the component and requesting a replacement under a new lease. In a purchase contract, this is not possible; if a component consistently fails it is often not possible to have it replaced, despite the fact that it is supposed to be maintained in good working order under a maintenance contract. As a result it is highly desirable to have a clause in the purchase (or long term rental) contract which allows the user upon persistent failure of the vendor to meet reliability standards to request replacement of a component.

H. **IDEAL COVERAGE**

The vendor shall, upon request, immediately replace any component whose operating characteristics exceed the "Downtime Percentages" in Schedule A by 5% in any 90 days, 10% in any 60 days and 20% in any 30 days.

I. **FALL-BACK ALTERNATIVES**

The parameters involved, duration and frequency, can be adjusted to reflect reasonable compromises from the viewpoint of the user and vendor.

K. **COMMENTS**

The principal objective of the clause is to force replacement of a component which is consistently troublesome and therefore interferes with the reasonable operation of the entire system.

L. **REFERENCES TO OTHER CLAUSES:** 6-45, 6-46.

A. **CLAUSE NAME:** Backup Availability B. **CLAUSE NO.:** 6-49

C. **CONTRACT TYPES USED IN:** Hardware or maintenance D. **RISK RATING:** 2

E. **INTENT AND SCOPE**

To provide a mechanism for obtaining backup equipment in the event of a temporary failure of the system which threatens to be sufficiently long in duration to upset the user's operational schedule.

F. **PROTECTION AGAINST**

To protect against vendor delays in making repairs to equipment and to protect against calamities.

G. **STANDARD CLAUSE PROVIDED BY MANUFACTURERS**

Emergency Equipment: UNIVAC shall use its best efforts to assist the Customer in obtaining use of equipment compatible with that used by the Customer to meet emergency needs.

H. **IDEAL COVERAGE**

In the event the equipment is unavailable for use due to maintenance or repair for a period of more than N hours, or in the event that it is reasonably anticipated that maintenance will exceed N hours, the vendor will make available within a M-mile radius from the user installation, a comparable installation for use without charge within P hours after request. This substitute installation will be equipped with a compatible configuration of hardware and software, to enable the user to operate the emergency system necessary to maintain effective operation. Such substitute installation may be utilized for as many hours as equals the length of time that user's equipment is inoperative.

I. **FALL-BACK ALTERNATIVES**

Fall-back considerations relate to length of downtime periods, or length of notice.

K. **COMMENTS**

It is possible to make separate arrangements with another customer of the same vendor located nearby, to provide similar backup services sometimes on a reciprocal basis.

L. **REFERENCES TO OTHER CLAUSES:** 6-46, 6-50.

A. CLAUSE NAME: Disaster Availability   **B. CLAUSE NO.:** 6-50

C. CONTRACT TYPES USED IN: Hardware   **D. RISK RATING:** 3

E. INTENT AND SCOPE

To provide a means for obtaining replacement equipment in the event a disaster permanently disables the computer system. Disasters include fire, flood, earthquake, bomb damage, or anything else which permanently makes the system inoperative.

F. PROTECTION AGAINST

To protect against long delivery delays for replacement equipment.

H. IDEAL COVERAGE

In the event the computer system or any component thereof is rendered permanently inoperative as a result of a natural or other disaster, the vendor will deliver a replacement system, within N days from the date of user request. In such event, the vendor agrees to waive any delivery schedule priorities, and to make the replacement system available from the manufacturing facility currently producing such equipment, or from inventory. The price for replacement equipment will be the then current published price or the price payable under this contract plus _____ % per year for each full year between the delivery date of the equipment hereunder and the request for replacement, whichever is lower. If the inoperability is due to the negligence or fault of the vendor, replacement equipment will be delivered at no cost to the user.

I. FALL-BACK ALTERNATIVES

The variable factors in terms of time and price can be negotiated.

L. REFERENCES TO OTHER CLAUSES: 6-46, 6-49.

A. **CLAUSE NAME:** Acceptance Tests	B. **CLAUSE NO.:** 6-51
C. **CONTRACT TYPES USED IN:** Hardware and software contracts	D. **RISK RATING:** 1

E. INTENT AND SCOPE

To ensure that the equipment delivered in fact operates in accordance with *all* specifications.

F. PROTECTION AGAINST

To protect against delivery of a machine which is not warranted to the user.

G. STANDARD CLAUSE PROVIDED BY MANUFACTURERS

Acceptance, Price and Payment: Customer agrees to pay the purchase price of $_____ for STAR/ACA to ADR at the address set forth above within thirty (30) days of delivery. Customer is deemed to have accepted STAR/ACA if Customer does not serve upon ADR written notice to the contrary within ten (10) days following delivery.

Standard of Performance and Acceptance of Equipment:

a. This Paragraph 4 establishes a standard of performance which must be met before any equipment listed on a purchase order is accepted by the Government.

   This also includes replacement, substitute machines, and machines which are added, or field modified at the Government's request (when the modification substantially affects the capability), after a system has completed a successful performance period.

b. The performance period shall begin on the installation date and shall end when the equipment has met the standard of performance for a period of thirty (30) consecutive days by operating in conformance with Honeywell's published equipment specifications or as published in the Honeywell proposal at an effectiveness level of ninety percent (90%) or more.

c. In the event the equipment does not meet the standard of performance during the initial thirty (30) consecutive days the standard of performance test shall continue on a day-by-day basis until the standard of performance is met for a total of thirty (30) consecutive days.

d. If the equipment fails to meet the standard of performance after one hundred and twenty (120) calendar days, from the installation date, or the first day from the start of the performance period if such is delayed by the Government, the Government may at its option request a replacement or terminate the order in accordance with the provisions of Paragraph 11 entitled "Default", Standard Form 32, November 1969 Edition, incorporated by reference.

H. IDEAL COVERAGE

After delivery and upon completion of installation, the vendor shall certify to the user that the equipment has been properly installed and is ready for use. Thereafter, a three step acceptance test shall be performed by the user, assisted by the vendor.

1. During the first business day following such certification the user will operate the equipment to determine whether the equipment meets the specifications attached hereto as Schedule A. Such tests will determine that the operating characteristics of each of the components delivered shall in fact match those given in the attached specifications.

2. During the seven business days following such certification the user shall run the "bench mark" tests described in Schedule B to determine that the performance of the system matches that in the "bench marks" performed prior to installation of the equipment.

3. During the 30 day period following such certification, the user shall operate the system in accordance with its normal operating practices. It shall determine during this period if the systems operating characteristics meet the reliability standards defined in Schedule C and incorporated as part of 6-46.

In the event that the operating performance of the system in any of these tests fails to meet the established specifications, the vendor shall either a) modify or adjust the equipment to meet the necessary specifications; b) replace or add such components as may be necessary to make the system meet the specifications; c) at the option of the user, reduce the price by an amount to be mutually agreed; if no reduction can be agreed to within two days after purchaser shall request renegotiation, vendor shall perform under a) or b). After *any* adjustment, modification, repair or replacement, the three tests described above shall be run again and, if the system still fails to meet the established acceptance characteristics, the user shall have the right to cancel this contract, and obtain the damages identified in 6-93 and 6-94. In no event shall payment be due for any part of the system, and in no event shall the system be deemed to be fully installed and accepted until the established standards described for all three acceptance tests have been met.

L. REFERENCES TO OTHER CLAUSES: 6-05, 6-45, 6-46, 6-93, 6-94.

E. **INTENT AND SCOPE**

To define maintenance types and maintenance availability.

F. **PROTECTION AGAINST**

Protects against incomplete maintenance coverage and against inadequate maintenance.

G. **STANDARD CLAUSE PROVIDED BY MANUFACTURERS**

1. Equipment maintenance service hereunder covers periodic preventive maintenance (including testing, cleaning, lubricating and adjusting), and the replacement of parts (the replaced parts becoming the property of Burroughs).

2. Preventive maintenance needs will be determined by Burroughs and will be provided between the hours of 5:30 a.m. and 8:30 p.m. during those days specified on the Addendum, excluding national holidays, at a time mutually agreeable to both parties.

3. In addition to regular preventive maintenance, equipment maintenance service covers emergency call service during a daily "basic period" of any eight (8) consecutive hours on those days (except national holidays) selected by the Customer and agreeable to Burroughs as stated on the Maintenance Agreement Addendum, as it may be amended from time to time hereafter.

Maintenance Service: IBM agrees to provide maintenance service availability during periods selected by the Customer to keep the machines in good working order while they are located within the United States and Puerto Rico. This maintenance service includes scheduled preventive maintenance based upon the specific needs of the individual machines as determined by IBM, and unscheduled, on-call remedial maintenance. Maintenance will include lubrication, adjustments and replacement of maintenance parts deemed necessary by IBM.

Maintenance parts will be furnished on an exchange basis regardless of when installed by IBM and will be new or equivalent to new in performance when used in these machines. Replaced maintenance parts become the property of IBM.

Exclusions: Maintenance service does not include:

(a) electrical work external to the machines or maintenance of accessories, alterations, attachments or other devices not furnished by IBM;

(b) repair of damage or increase in service time caused by: accident, transportation, neglect or misuse; alterations, which shall include, but not be limited to, any deviation from circuit or structural machine design as provided by IBM, installation or removal of IBM features, or any other modification, whenever any of the foregoing is performed by other than IBM; any machine other than those owned by IBM, under warranty provision of an IBM purchase agreement or under an IBM Maintenance Agreement;

(c) repair of damage or increase in service time resulting from failure to provide a suitable installation environment with all facilities prescribed by the appropriate IBM Installation Manual—Physical Planning (including but not limited to, failure of, or failure to provide adequate electrical power, air conditioning or humidity control) or from use of supplies or materials not meeting IBM specifications for such installation;

(d) repair of damage or increase in service time attributable to the use of the machines for other than data processing purposes for which designed;

(e) furnishing platens, supplies or accessories; painting or refinishing the machines or furnishing material therefor; making specification changes or performing services connected with relocation of machines; or adding or removing accessories, attachments or other devices; and,

(f) such service which is impractical for IBM to render because of alterations in the machines or their connection by mechanical or electrical means to another machine or device.

Maintenance: IBM will keep the machines in good working order and will make all necessary adjustments and repairs. For this purpose IBM shall have full and free access to the machines. The required suitable electric current to operate the machines and a suitable place of installation with all facilities as specified in IBM's Installation Manual will be furnished by the Customer. IBM will not furnish maintenance service if the machines are located outside the United States, Puerto Rico or the Canal Zone.

H. IDEAL COVERAGE

Hardware maintenance shall be available at any time that the equipment is in use by the user and shall be available on a full-time on-site basis during the hours of _____ to_____ Monday through _____, except for the following holidays:

At all other times, hardware maintenance shall be provided not less than _____ hours after telephone request. All maintenance shall be performed by qualified maintenance engineers, totally familiar with all of the equipment installed at the user's site. Software maintenance shall be provided on an on-call basis only not more than _____ hours after telephone request. Software maintenance shall be provided by qualified software specialists familiar with the software installed at the user's site.

J. POSSIBLE REMEDIES

The contract may provide as a remedy that if maintenance is not delivered when demanded, the user may obtain it from outside sources and charge the vendor. Additional per hour liquidated damages should also be sought.

K. COMMENTS

Particular users will want to define with greater specificity the skills, experience and qualifications to be required of all maintenance personnel supplied, and the possible right to reject unqualified personnel.

L. REFERENCES TO OTHER CLAUSES: 6-53, 6-54, 6-66, 7-08, 10-04.

A. **CLAUSE NAME:** On Site Maintenance Provided   B. **CLAUSE NO.:** 6-53

C. **CONTRACT TYPES USED IN:** Maintenance, hardware   D. **RISK RATING:** 2

E. **INTENT AND SCOPE**

To define when on-site maintenance will be made available. On-site maintenance should be available during the early stages of installation, or if a significant amount of equipment is installed at the user site (see 6-52). On-site maintenance should also be required if, for some reason, equipment performance deteriorates.

G. **STANDARD CLAUSE PROVIDED BY MANUFACTURERS**

On-Site Maintenance: On-site maintenance service will be provided under this Contract in accordance with the terms, conditions, and prices set forth in Appendix II (Appendixes appear at the end of the Terms and Conditions). (Honeywell)

H. **IDEAL COVERAGE**

The vendor shall provide full-time on-site maintenance from _____ to _____, Mondays to _____, during the first sixty days after acceptance by user of the equipment. If during such sixty day period the systems operation exceeds the Downtime Percentages listed in Schedule A, full-time on-site maintenance shall continue until sixty days have elapsed in which the Downtime Percentages have not been exceeded. Nothing herein contained shall be deemed a waiver of any other rights or remedies of the user with respect to excessive Downtime Percentages or other failure of the equipment. If after discontinuance of on-site maintenance, Downtime Percentages shall be exceeded for two successive weeks, the user may request resumption of full-time on-site maintenance, which shall continue until sixty days have elapsed in which Downtime Percentages have not been exceeded.

K. **COMMENTS**

For permanent full-time on-site maintenance on larger systems see 6-52.

L. **REFERENCES TO OTHER CLAUSES:** 6-45, 6-52.

A. CLAUSE NAME: Response Time for Off-Site Maintenance   **B. CLAUSE NO.:** 6-54

C. CONTRACT TYPES USED IN: Hardware, maintenance   **D. RISK RATING:** 2

E. INTENT AND SCOPE

To define the period of time within which the vendor will respond by providing qualified maintenance personnel on site after having been notified of an unscheduled failure.

F. PROTECTION AGAINST

To protect against unwarranted delays in providing maintenance services.

G. STANDARD CLAUSE PROVIDED BY MANUFACTURERS

Service Calls: Except for equipment that is installed at a location which is more than thirty (30) miles from a Honeywell Service Center, Honeywell's maintenance personnel, barring circumstances that are beyond the control of Honeywell, shall arrive at the Government's location during the scheduled use period(s) or Principal Periods of Maintenance within two (2) hours after notification that on-call service is required. With respect to that equipment excluded above, Honeywell's Maintenance personnel shall normally arrive within one (1) hour plus travel time. For service requested outside the scheduled use period(s) or the Principal Period of Maintenance, Honeywell's maintenance personnel shall arrive at the Government's location as soon as possible.

Government personnel shall not attempt any repairs or maintenance while such equipment is under the purview of this Contract unless mutually agreed.

H. IDEAL COVERAGE

The vendor shall provide a qualified maintenance engineer in response to telephone notice by the user within two hours after notification, in all instances; on a monthly basis, 80% of maintenance responses shall be within one hour after notification.

K. COMMENTS

Response time obviously is a function of the distance between the engineering facility of the vendor and the user's site, and the available public or private transportation between the two locations. The vendor will want exculpatory language based upon transportation delays and other factors beyond its control. Some leeway should be given to the vendor, although the vendor should be encouraged to meet more stringent criteria than those in the contract. Parking facilities and any other assistance or comforts which can be provided to maintenance personnel (even including free coffee and cookies) is helpful in reducing the response time and making maintenance more efficient.

L. REFERENCES TO OTHER CLAUSES: 6-52, 6-66.

A. CLAUSE NAME: Access Needs   **B. CLAUSE NO.:** 6-55

C. CONTRACT TYPES USED IN: Hardware maintenance   **D. RISK RATING:** 3

E. INTENT AND SCOPE

To define access requirements to the equipment for purposes of preventive maintenance. Access must be provided to the equipment on an unrestricted basis in the event of a failure which disrupts operations.

G. STANDARD CLAUSE PROVIDED BY MANUFACTURERS

Access to Equipment: Employees of UNIVAC shall have access to the equipment at all reasonable times.

H. IDEAL COVERAGE

Vendor maintenance personnel shall be given access to the equipment when necessary for purposes of performing the maintenance services hereunder. Preventive maintenance shall be performed at the times listed on Schedule A, it being understood that such Schedule reflects periods when the equipment is not normally in operation. If user, because of operational or other needs, shall desire to reschedule preventive maintenance, either in single instances or in patterns, the vendor shall use its best efforts to accommodate to such changes. In any event, user shall have the right to require vendor to adjourn scheduled preventive maintenance from any scheduled time, to a date and time not later than _____ days thereafter, by offering to vendor at least_____ adjourned times within the adjournment period, out of which vendor may select any one most convenient to him.

I. FALL-BACK ALTERNATIVES

There is much room for negotiation on scheduling and rescheduling arrangements.

L. REFERENCES TO OTHER CLAUSES: 6-66.

A. CLAUSE NAME: Spare Parts Availability **B. CLAUSE NO.:** 6-56

C. CONTRACT TYPES USED IN: Hardware, maintenance **D. RISK RATING:** 3

E. INTENT AND SCOPE

To ensure that an adequate supply of spare parts is readily available to allow proper maintenance of the equipment.

F. PROTECTION AGAINST

To protect against extended downtime of equipment by reason of parts unavailability.

H. IDEAL COVERAGE

The vendor shall maintain a supply of spare parts on the user's site to make emergency repairs. Such parts shall include the items and quantities listed on Schedule A plus such others as the vendor may deem appropriate to maintain the equipment in working order. The vendor shall maintain all other spare parts necessary for the repair of the equipment within a 50 mile radius from user's site. The user shall make available a secure, locked room of at least _____ cubic feet for vendor part storage; the keys to such room shall be maintained and kept only by the vendor and the Treasurer of the user.

I. FALL-BACK ALTERNATIVES

As an alternative, have the vendor list all parts which will not be available in less than two hours, so that downtime for parts unavailability can be restricted to those listed parts.

L. REFERENCES TO OTHER CLAUSES: 6-61.

A. **CLAUSE NAME:** Space and Facilities   B. **CLAUSE NO.:** 6-57

C. **CONTRACT TYPES USED IN:** Hardware, maintenance   D. **RISK RATING:** 4

E. **INTENT AND SCOPE**

To ensure that the vendor is given the necessary space and operating facilities within the user organization to allow him to make the necessary repairs.

G. **STANDARD CLAUSE PROVIDED BY MANUFACTURERS**

Maintenance Facilities: The Government shall provide adequate storage space for spare parts and adequate working space and maintenance of the same, including heat, light, ventilation, electric current and outlets for the use of Honeywell's maintenance personnel. These facilities shall be within a reasonable distance of the equipment to be serviced and shall be provided at no charge to Honeywell.

If required, Customer shall provide, at its own expense and convenient to the Equipment, adequate storage space for Bunker Ramo tools and spare parts and adequate working space including heat, light, ventilation, electric current and outlets for the use of Bunker Ramo's maintenance personnel.

The Lessee shall provide adequate storage space for spare parts and adequate working space including heat, light, ventilation, electric current and outlets for use by Honeywell's maintenance personnel. These facilities shall be within a reasonable distance of the equipment to be serviced and shall be provided at no charge to Honeywell.

H. **IDEAL COVERAGE**

The user shall provide space and facilities described in Schedule A for vendor's maintenance staff and for the storage of spare parts, tools and other equipment necessary to maintain the system in good working order. Such space and facilities shall be located in reasonable proximity to the equipment and shall be secured by locks, the keys to which shall be kept only by authorized vendor personnel and user's Treasurer.

L. **REFERENCES TO OTHER CLAUSES:** 6-55, 6-56.

A. **CLAUSE NAME:** Continuity and Renewal Rights	B. **CLAUSE NO.:** 6-58
C. **CONTRACT TYPES USED IN:** Hardware, maintenance	D. **RISK RATING:** 2

E. INTENT AND SCOPE

To ensure that maintenance will be available as long as the equipment is installed on the user's site.

F. PROTECTION AGAINST

To protect against discontinuance of maintenance because the equipment's age or operating characteristics make it too expensive for the vendor to maintain.

G. STANDARD CLAUSE PROVIDED BY MANUFACTURERS

Option 1: NCR may require, subject to the approval of the CUSTOMER, the performance of any necessary overhaul of such equipment, at a charge in addition to the Annual Maintenance charge for such equipment. Should the CUSTOMER elect to have the applicable equipment overhauled, NCR agrees to continue this Agreement at 100% of NCR's then applicable Maintenance charge from year to year, for a period of three (3) years, or the equivalent of three (3) years of one shift usage. No overhaul will be required during this period provided said equipment continues on an NCR Maintenance Agreement during this period. At the end of such three (3) year period, NCR may elect to continue the applicable equipment under the terms of this option from year to year, unless cancelled as provided below.

Option 2: The CUSTOMER may elect to pay an additional charge of ____% of the basic undiscounted Maintenance rate during each year after the time specified herein, and NCR agrees to continue this Agreement in effect for not more than five (5) years, or the equivalent of five (5) years of one shift usage. After the end of such five (5) year period, this Agreement shall continue in effect from year to year at the increased rate unless cancelled as provided below. No overhaul shall be required as a condition to continuation of this Agreement at the increased rate as provided for in this paragraph.

It may be terminated by either party at the expiration of one year or at the end of any calendar month thereafter, provided written notice of termination is given to the other party at least ninety (90) days prior to the date of termination. (Burroughs)

Maintenance, Service and Parts: IBM will, if requested, provide the Purchaser with maintenance service for the machines, and repair or replacement parts, as long as they are generally available, on the basis of IBM's established prices and terms prevailing at the time.

Term: This Agreement is effective from the date on which it is accepted by IBM and shall remain in force until terminated by the Customer upon one month's prior written notice or by IBM upon twelve months' prior written notice. Individual machines may be withdrawn from this Agreement by the Customer one month following written notice. Except as otherwise provided herein, IBM may withdraw individual machine(s) from this Agreement at the end of the first year after maintenance service for such machines has commenced or thereafter three months following written notice.

H. IDEAL COVERAGE

The vendor agrees to provide the maintenance services as defined in this contract for as long as the equipment is installed. Such services shall be provided at prices in effect from time to time, but shall not exceed current prices plus ____% per year for each year after acceptance. User may at its option, elect to terminate maintenance services hereunder at any time on 30 days prior written notice.

I. FALL–BACK ALTERNATIVES

Use a formula more directly related to vendor labor cost.

K. COMMENTS

The best arrangement is one which binds the vendor perpetually but leaves the user free to cancel at any time. Note that by not stipulating site of installation, resale and assignment of the maintenance contract is facilitated (see 6-59).

L. REFERENCES TO OTHER CLAUSES: 6-44, 6-59, 10-04.

A. CLAUSE NAME: Reconditioning on Resale   **B. CLAUSE NO.:** 6-59

C. CONTRACT TYPES USED IN: Hardware, maintenance   **D. RISK RATING:** 3

E. INTENT AND SCOPE

To provide a mechanism at the time of the original purchase under which the vendor will agree to recondition the equipment should the user decide to resell the equipment. Such reconditioning is potentially necessary as a prerequisite to continuing the maintenance arrangements with the second user.

H. IDEAL COVERAGE

The user may assign its rights under this contract, subject to the obligations hereunder, without vendor consent.

I. FALL-BACK ALTERNATIVES

The vendor agrees to make maintenance available to any purchaser (second user) of this system, if the system is sold within the next _____ years. If such sale takes such place after _____ years the user agrees that such transfer of maintenance availability may be effected only after reconditioning of the equipment. In such event, vendor agrees to provide such reconditioning, upon request, at a charge not to exceed _____ dollars, and upon such reconditioning the vendor will continue to be bound to furnish maintenance to such second user upon the terms and provisions of 6-58.

K. COMMENTS

The principal objective is to make sure that maintenance can be provided to a second user. Variations can be made in the number of years during which the vendor is prepared to continue such maintenance, and the number of years after which reconditioning may be necessary. However, as long as the vendor has a maintenance contract and agrees to keep the equipment in good working order, significant charges for reconditioning would be unfair. The best possible deal would be a contract provision under which the user can freely assign its rights under a long-term maintenance contract, provided it has continuity rights (6-58) which do not stipulate the specific location or installation.

L. REFERENCES TO OTHER CLAUSES: 6-58, 10-03.

A. CLAUSE NAME: Rights to Training of User Staff   **B. CLAUSE NO.:** 6-60

C. CONTRACT TYPES USED IN: Hardware, maintenance   **D. RISK RATING:** 3

E. INTENT AND SCOPE

To provide a mechanism under which the user can train its own staff in maintenance functions, using the technology, materials, blueprints and other knowhow of the vendor.

F. PROTECTION AGAINST

To protect against unreasonable maintenance charges and against a discontinuity of maintenance under certain conditions.

H. IDEAL COVERAGE

The vendor agrees to make available, upon 60 days notice by the user, a training program (either in-house or on the vendor's site) for a sufficient number of trainee maintenance personnel supplied by the user to provide the user with sufficient capability to perform all necessary equipment maintenance. Such training program shall be similar to that given by the vendor to its own maintenance staff, it being intended hereby that the completion of such training program will enable user personnel to maintain the equipment at levels comparable to those established by vendor personnel.

L. REFERENCES TO OTHER CLAUSES: 6-46, 6-56, 6-61.

A. **CLAUSE NAME:** Rights to Purchase Spares   B. **CLAUSE NO.:** 6-61

C. **CONTRACT TYPES USED IN:** Hardware, maintenance   D. **RISK RATING:** 3

E. **INTENT AND SCOPE**

To ensure that the user has the right to purchase all necessary spare parts, at reasonable prices. Such capability is necessary if the vendor declines to continue to supply maintenance, or if the user decides to provide its own maintenance.

H. **IDEAL COVERAGE**

The vendor agrees, for so long as the equipment shall remain in use by the user, to sell to the user, at prevailing delivery and payment times, all necessary spare parts required for the maintenance of the equipment. Such sales shall be made at prices then in effect, but prices shall not be increased by more than _____ % per year for each year between any order for such parts and the date of acceptance of the equipment herein contracted for.

I. **FALL-BACK ALTERNATIVES**

A formula for increase tied to the cost of living is equally acceptable for such spares. However, it should be noted that such spares are often manufactured for inventory long before their sale, and may be rebuilt from used equipment. Accordingly, price increases for spares should not be quickly or heavily escalated.

K. **COMMENTS**

It may also be desirable to require a vendor warranty that spares, when purchased, will be new and of original manufacture. In certain cases, when spares are replacements for entire sections or components, such purchases may be eligible for investment tax credit.

L. **REFERENCES TO OTHER CLAUSES:** 6-36, 6-56, 6-60.

A. **CLAUSE NAME:** Rebates for Failures not Corrected Promptly   B. **CLAUSE NO.:** 6-62

C. **CONTRACT TYPES USED IN:** Hardware, maintenance   D. **RISK RATING:** 3

E. **INTENT AND SCOPE**

If the vendor fails to correct a malfunctioning component promptly, some rebate should be due to the user. This rebate need not be limited to a credit for maintenance charges paid, but can include recognition of the equipment rental value of the lost time, or a percentage of the purchase price based on the ratio of elapsed downtime to total useful life.

G. **STANDARD CLAUSE PROVIDED BY MANUFACTURERS**

Maintenance Credit for Equipment Malfunction:

(a) If Honeywell is unable to restore a machine to good operating condition and equipment failure causes the machine to remain inoperative for a continuous period of twelve (12) hours or more from the time the Government notifies Honeywell that the machine is inoperative, or if a machine remains inoperative for a total of fourteen (14) hours in any 24-hour period, and it is determined that (1) the equipment failure was not caused by conditions external to the machine, and (2) the machine became inoperative through no fault or negligence of the Government, Honeywell shall grant a credit to the Government for each hour the machine was inoperative. Such credit shall be in the amount of one two hundredth (1/200th) of the Basic Monthly Rental Charges for inoperative machines plus one two hundredth (1/200th) of the Basic Monthly Rental Charges for any Honeywell machine interconnected entirely by Honeywell power and/or signal cables which is not usable as a result of the equipment failure. However, the amount of credit granted for each machine shall not exceed one thirtieth (1/30th) of the Basic Monthly Rental Charge for the machine for any calendar day and for any month shall never exceed the Basic Monthly Rental Charge. The number of inoperative hours shall be adjusted to the nearest half hour.

(b) When maintenance credit is due under the provisions of Paragraph 6.a.(7)(a) and Government-owned equipment is being maintained by Honeywell under the provisions of Special Item 132-11 and such equipment is not usable as a result of the equipment failure of Honeywell's rented equipment, the credit provisions of Paragraph 3.n., Special Item 132-11, to the extent they are applicable shall apply to such Government-owned equipment.

(c) In the event that a machine is inoperative, due to machine failure, and the total number of hours of downtime exceeds fifteen percent (15%) of the total operational use time for three consecutive calendar months, the Government reserves the right to require Honeywell to replace the machine. In the event the machine is out of production or is not available, Honeywell will at its option either refurbish the machine or provide substitute equipment at no additional charge. Should Honeywell choose to refurbish the machine, then it will provide substitute equipment until the work is completed.

H. **IDEAL COVERAGE**

If a malfunction shall continue for more than four hours, or if the aggregate malfunction time in any consecutive 30 day period exceeds _____ hours, the vendor shall pay, or credit to the user against future payments, the sum of _____ dollars per hour for each hour that the system is unavailable for use, in excess of four hours.

I. **FALL-BACK ALTERNATIVES**

Time and dollar variables can be negotiated. Dollars can be negotiated down to merely maintenance credit.

J. POSSIBLE REMEDIES

This clause is a liquidated damages remedy.

K. COMMENTS

This clause should be drafted so that it does not derogate from any other remedies that the user may have for excessive downtime.

L. REFERENCES TO OTHER CLAUSES: 6-39, 6-45, 6-46.

A. **CLAUSE NAME:** Malfunction and Correction Reporting   B. **CLAUSE NO.:** 6-63

C. **CONTRACT TYPES USED IN:** Hardware, maintenance   D. **RISK RATING:** 4

E. **INTENT AND SCOPE**

To ensure that a proper log is kept on all malfunctions and all corrective steps taken. This will allow the user to inspect malfunction and correction reports to determine whether or not maintenance is being performed properly. If, for example, a part continues to fail and replacements do not function effectively, the log may assist the user in pinpointing where vendor maintenance has been deficient.

G. **STANDARD CLAUSE PROVIDED BY MANUFACTURERS**

Malfunction Reports: Honeywell shall furnish a malfunction incident report to the installation upon completion of each maintenance call. The report shall include, as a minimum, the following:

(a) Date and time notified
(b) Date and time of arrival
(c) Type and model number(s) of machine(s)
(d) Time spent for repair
(e) Description of malfunction
(f) List of parts replaced
(g) Additional charges, if applicable

H. **IDEAL COVERAGE**

The vendor shall maintain, at the user's site, a written maintenance and repair log and shall record therein each incident of equipment malfunction, date, time and duration of all maintenance and repair work performed on the equipment, together with a description of the cause for the work, either by description of the malfunction or as regularly scheduled maintenance and a diagnostic report of corrections or adjustments and parts repaired or replaced. The information in the log shall be aggregated into a management report, which shall be provided on a monthly basis by the vendor to the user.

K. **COMMENTS**

It is often possible to use data from these reports for trend analysis of reliability, which can point to qualitative differences among maintenance personnel.

L. **REFERENCES TO OTHER CLAUSES:** 6-39, 6-62.

A. **CLAUSE NAME:** No Subcontract   B. **CLAUSE NO.:** 6-64

C. **CONTRACT TYPES USED IN:** Hardware, maintenance   D. **RISK RATING:** 4

E. **INTENT AND SCOPE**

To prevent the vendor from subcontracting any work associated with the maintenance function.

H. **IDEAL COVERAGE**

The vendor will not subcontract or permit anyone other than vendor personnel to perform any of the work, services or other performance required of vendor under this contract without the prior written consent of the user.

I. **FALL–BACK ALTERNATIVES**

The user consent can be defined as not to be unreasonably withheld.

K. **COMMENT**

As worded, this clause applies to all services under the contract and will thus include software maintenance and development. If desired, this can be reduced to cover only those portions of the contract where sub-contracting is felt to be undesirable, such as maintenance. However, software development and maintenance and other functions might also be preferable if performed only by vendor personnel rather than sub-contractor personnel. This can be individually decided.

L. **REFERENCES TO OTHER CLAUSES:** 8-18.

A. CLAUSE NAME: Engineering changes   **B. CLAUSE NO.:** 6-65

C. CONTRACT TYPES USED IN: Hardware, maintenance   **D. RISK RATING:** 3

E. INTENT AND SCOPE

To ensure that all engineering changes generally adopted by the manufacturer are incorporated into the equipment, even after purchase and installation. Such engineering changes should be made at no cost to the user.

G. STANDARD CLAUSE PROVIDED BY MANUFACTURERS

Engineering Changes—Installation and Control: Engineering changes, determined applicable by IBM, will be controlled and installed by IBM on equipment covered by this Agreement. The Customer may, by providing notice subject to written confirmation by IBM, elect to have only mandatory changes, as determined by IBM, installed on machines so designated.

H. IDEAL COVERAGE

All engineering changes generally adopted hereafter by vendor on similar equipment, shall be made to the equipment installed hereunder at no cost to the user.

I. FALL–BACK ALTERNATIVES

Where engineering changes represent enhancements which are generally only sold for extra cost and effect an increase in price of later-marketed equipment, the user could agree to pay such increase in order to obtain the engineering change. There could also be an agreed-to time limitation on the user's right to obtain free changes.

K. COMMENTS

If an engineering change is charged for, the user should have the option to purchase it. However, in certain cases engineering changes may be generally required and adopted to simplify maintenance or to increase reliability of the equipment. In those cases, they should be made available at no cost.

L. REFERENCES TO OTHER CLAUSES: 6-11, 6-82.

A. **CLAUSE NAME:** Right to Schedule Preventive   B. **CLAUSE NO.:** 6-66
                 Maintenance

C. **CONTRACT TYPES USED IN:** Hardware, maintenance   D. **RISK RATING:** 4

E. **INTENT AND SCOPE**

To ensure that the user has the capability of scheduling and re-scheduling preventive maintenance, and has some say in determining how much preventive maintenance is required.

H. **IDEAL COVERAGE**

The vendor shall perform preventive maintenance under this contract of approximately _____ hours per week. Such time shall be scheduled during non-operational hours, from a list of available hours submitted to the vendor by the user. In the event the user decides that equipment performance warrants an increase or reduction in the preventive maintenance hours, the vendor shall so increase or decrease such maintenance, provided such requested increase or decrease is reasonable.

I. **FALL–BACK ALTERNATIVES**

A maximum limitation on increases or decreases in scheduled maintenance can be negotiated. Vendor decision to increase or decrease shall be with written user permission.

K. **COMMENTS**

It is often difficult to determine how much preventive maintenance is realistic, so that an initial amount in the contract often serves only as a guideline for what will later be deemed reasonable. In some cases preventive maintenance is of little value, in which case it can be reduced or eliminated. In other cases it is highly desirable to perform preventive maintenance, especially on mechanical equipment such as tape drives and printers. Notwithstanding this, the user should have a voice in the type and extent of preventive maintenance necessary, if the user feels that the amounts provided are incorrect. In addition, since preventive maintenance essentially renders the equipment useless while being performed, the user should provide the schedule under which it should be performed.

L. **REFERENCES TO OTHER CLAUSES:** 6-55 describes other aspects of maintenance access.

A. CLAUSE NAME: User Right to Perform Maintenance in Rental Contract

B. CLAUSE NO.: 6-67

C. CONTRACT TYPES USED IN: Hardware rental

D. RISK RATING: 3

E. INTENT AND SCOPE

To separate the maintenance cost component from the total rental payment amount, and to allow the user to withhold the maintenance portion and to undertake its own maintenance or subcontract it to others. This right should exist in a rental contract, since it is often available in a purchase contract.

H. IDEAL COVERAGE

In the event the user elects not to require vendor to maintain and repair the equipment the vendor will, immediately upon receipt of notice thereof, reduce his rental by $_____ per month. In such event, the vendor shall be relieved from any obligation to repair or maintain the equipment in good working order, but the provisions of 6-60 and 6-61 shall continue in full force.

I. FALL-BACK ALTERNATIVES

The vendor will normally insist upon an undertaking from the user that if the election is made, the *user* will obligate itself to maintain the equipment in working order and make necessary repairs and replacements, or agree to reconditioning upon termination, if necessary.

J. POSSIBLE REMEDIES

This is a difficult issue. Some vendors have agreed to separate maintenance cost from rental charges. Others have not, on the theory that if the user provides his own maintenance on a rental item, the quality of maintenance is no longer under vendor control, leaving the risk that when the lease is over and the equipment is returned, the vendor will have to recondition or upgrade to compensate for deficient maintenance. As a result, some vendors argue that if the user is to be permitted to perform its own maintenance the vendor should have the right, at the end of the lease, to repair and recondition the machines to levels determined by vendor. These issues lead to complex negotiations. In long-term "full-payout" leases or conditional sale leases (leases which give the user the right to buy the equipment for a nominal sum on expiration) there may be less resistance by the vendor but not much less, since the vendor deems the equipment's condition important if the equipment is repossessed on default of the user.

L. REFERENCES TO OTHER CLAUSES: 6-59, 6-60, 6-61.

A. CLAUSE NAME: Delivery Dates by Component or Group   **B. CLAUSE NO.:** 6-68

C. CONTRACT TYPES USED IN: Hardware   **D. RISK RATING:** 2

E. INTENT AND SCOPE

To define specifically the dates of delivery of each component and/or each group of components, including not only hardware but software as well.

F. PROTECTION AGAINST

To protect against delayed delivery of one or more components or groups, and against delivery of items out of logical sequence.

G. STANDARD CLAUSE PROVIDED BY MANUFACTURERS

Delivery: Delivery will be made as soon as practicable by Lessor. In the event Lessee should desire delivery and installation of any component prior to installation of the total system and Lessor has same available such partial delivery and installation will be performed by Lessor. (Burroughs)

H. IDEAL COVERAGE

The components and groups shall be delivered in accordance with Schedule A, and in the order stated therein, it being understood that if a component or group has been delivered while a prior-listed component or group remains undelivered, the later-listed component shall be deemed undelivered until the prior-listed one is actually delivered.

I. FALL–BACK ALTERNATIVES

It is possible to define delivery simply by month rather than month and date. Delivery within a 30 day tolerance may often be satisfactory to the user, and will help the vendor deal with installation problems. Delivery normally means transporting the equipment to the receiving dock of the user; however, it can be defined as including unpacking, uncrating and installation. It is recommended that only one definition of delivery be used and that it be deemed to mean on-line installation; there is no benefit to a user from possession of a crated, non-usable item of equipment. This is often referred to as RFU (Ready for use).

L. REFERENCES TO OTHER CLAUSES: 6-40, 7-23, 8-02, 9-01.

A. **CLAUSE NAME:** Option for Early Delivery	B. **CLAUSE NO.:** 6-69
C. **CONTRACT TYPES USED IN:** Hardware	D. **RISK RATING:** 4

E. INTENT AND SCOPE

To provide the user with the ability to accelerate delivery, if feasible from the viewpoint of the manufacturing cycle.

G. STANDARD CLAUSE PROVIDED BY MANUFACTURERS

In the event that Buyer should desire delivery of any component(s) prior to installation of the total system, and Seller has same available, Seller will deliver and install such component(s). Such component(s) will be invoiced at the list price in effect as of the date of this Agreement, plus applicable taxes, transportation, and handling. Payment received as a result thereof will be applied against the total amount payable under this Agreement upon completion of installation of the entire system. (Burroughs)

H. IDEAL COVERAGE

The user shall have the option to advance delivery dates, provided that such advanced delivery shall not unreasonably interfere with vendor's manufacturing and delivery schedule. The user shall notify the vendor of its election to advance a delivery date, which the vendor shall promptly acknowledge.

K. COMMENTS

As drafted, this is essentially a statement of intent, and not really a contractual obligation. It is difficult to hold a vendor to an early delivery date, especially if the vendor does not know when that date is, or when the option will be exercised. If there exists a need for a *real* user option to advance delivery, this must be specifically negotiated and should include the outer limits of advancement, the amount of notice to be given and the bonus to vendor if the option is exercised. With proper planning, delivery should be capable of realistic scheduling and there should be no need for advancement rights except under peculiar circumstances.

L. REFERENCES TO OTHER CLAUSES: 6-70, 6-71.

A. CLAUSE NAME: Rights to Delay Delivery   **B. CLAUSE NO.:** 6-70

C. CONTRACT TYPES USED IN: Hardware   **D. RISK RATING:** 3

E. INTENT AND SCOPE

To afford the right to delay delivery of the equipment or components or groups thereof if the user is not ready to accept such equipment. Such delay right should not be permitted to delay delivery beyond some outside date, and should not be exercisable as the scheduled delivery date approaches.

G. STANDARD CLAUSE PROVIDED BY MANUFACTURERS

Customer may delay shipment one time for a period not in excess of ninety (90) days provided written notice is given to Bunker Ramo at least thirty (30) days prior to the scheduled shipping date specified in *Schedule A.*

H. IDEAL COVERAGE

The user shall have the right to postpone delivery of the equipment or any component or group hereunder for periods of not less than _____ days nor more than _____ months, upon notice to the vendor given not later than _____ days prior to the scheduled delivery date of such equipment, component or group. No more than _____ postponements will be permitted to user with respect to any item, component or group.

I. FALL–BACK ALTERNATIVES

A number of parameters hereunder can be varied, but after exercise of a certain number of delaying options, the vendor should have the right to treat the user as in default, or to cancel the contract under 6-91.

L. REFERENCES TO OTHER CLAUSES: 6-76, 6-91.

A. **CLAUSE NAME:** Notices of Delivery and Shipment   B. **CLAUSE NO.:** 6-71

C. **CONTRACT TYPES USED IN:** Hardware, software   D. **RISK RATING:** 4

E. **INTENT AND SCOPE**

To provide the user with reasonable notice of impending delivery and notice of actual shipment.

H. **IDEAL COVERAGE**

The vendor shall notify the user of impending shipment _____ days prior to actual shipment. The vendor shall further notify the user by telegram of the actual shipment on the date of such shipment, including in such telegram the waybill number, transportation method and carrier.

L. **REFERENCES TO OTHER CLAUSES:** 6-68.

A. **CLAUSE NAME:** Delays Considered Irreparable   B. **CLAUSE NO.:** 6-72

C. **CONTRACT TYPES USED IN:** Hardware, software   D. **RISK RATING:** 2

E. **INTENT AND SCOPE**

To define delays deemed to be irreparable which, accordingly, trigger damages and cancellation rights.

F. **PROTECTION AGAINST**

To protect against significant delays.

G. **STANDARD CLAUSE PROVIDED BY MANUFACTURERS**

Seller shall not be liable for any damages caused by delay in delivery. (Burroughs)

H. **IDEAL COVERAGE**

Any delay in delivery of the equipment or any component or group in excess of 60 days beyond the scheduled delivery date shall be considered an irreparable delay and the user shall thereupon have the right to cancel this contract. If user shall, at its option, elect to excuse such irreparable delay, the user may do so by an instrument which shall include an adjourned date for the delayed delivery, as to which time shall be of the essence.

L. **REFERENCES TO OTHER CLAUSES:** 6-68, 6-92.

A. **CLAUSE NAME:** Site Preparation Responsibility   B. **CLAUSE NO.:** 6-73

C. **CONTRACT TYPES USED IN:** Hardware   D. **RISK RATING:** 4

E. **INTENT AND SCOPE**

To define responsibilities for preparation of the site in which the computer equipment shall be housed.

G. **STANDARD CLAUSE PROVIDED BY MANUFACTURERS**

Site Preparation: Customer will provide, at its own expense, temperature controlled space adequate in size and design for installation and operation of the Equipment and necessary electric current outlets, circuits and wiring and will furnish, at its own expense, during the term of this Agreement electric current of sufficient quality and quantity to operate the Equipment. (Bunker Ramo)

Site Preparation:

a. Equipment specifications for site preparation shall be furnished in writing by Honeywell as part of the equipment proposals. These specifications shall be in such detail as to ensure the equipment to be installed shall operate efficiently from the point of view of environment.

b. The Government shall prepare the site at its own expense including nonstandard cabling, connectors, and other special Government requirements, including associated labor costs, and in accordance with the specifications furnished by Honeywell. It is the Government's responsibility to adhere to these specifications and not operate the system when the environmental conditions do not meet these specifications. The Government at its expense will also have the responsibility to see that all local electrical and building codes are met.

c. Any alterations or modifications in site preparation that are directly attributable to incomplete or erroneous environmental specifications provided by Honeywell that involve additional expense to the Government shall be made at the expense of Honeywell.

d. Any such site alterations or modifications as specified in Subparagraph c. above that cause a delay in the installation date will also result in liquidated damages for equipment as specified under Paragraph 2.a. if the delay was attributable to incomplete or erroneous environment specifications provided by Honeywell.

e. Unless specified otherwise in Honeywell's proposal, all arrangements for procurement, installation, maintenance of, and payment for communications media (telephone, teletype, etc.) not supplied by Honeywelll necessary to the remote transmission of data are the responsibility of the Government. Any charges for such media in connection with installation, operation or maintenance of machines shall be borne by the Government.

H. **IDEAL COVERAGE**

The user shall, at its own expense, prepare the site in accordance with the installation specifications set forth on Schedule A, not later than _____ days prior to the scheduled delivery date of the equipment, and the site shall thereafter be available for inspection and approval. If vendor shall fail to inspect the site prior to delivery, vendor shall be deemed to have approved it and all further site responsibility shall be that of vendor. If vendor shall inspect, notice in writing shall be given promptly to user of approval or disapproval; if disapproved, vendor shall set forth in detail each deficiency discovered and user shall correct such deficiency within _____ days after receipt of vendor's notice; and if user shall fail to correct such deficiencies within the permitted time, vendor shall have the right to do so, at user's expense.

K. COMMENTS

This clause, as shown above, is in very skeletal form. Where two parties are involved in performance of interdependent activities, and timing is important, the description of the inter-relationships and respective rights can become very complex. For guidance, a reader might examine any real estate development lease, such as a new shopping center lease, where there can be found some very complex clauses defining the relationship between landlord and tenant work.

L. REFERENCES TO OTHER CLAUSES: 6-16, 6-17, 6-18, 6-74.

A. **CLAUSE NAME:** Installation Responsibility   B. **CLAUSE NO.:** 6-74

C. **CONTRACT TYPES USED IN:** Hardware   D. **RISK RATING:** 3

E. **INTENT AND SCOPE**

To define the responsibility of the vendor in installing the equipment and making it ready for use.

G. **STANDARD CLAUSE PROVIDED BY MANUFACTURERS**

Transportation and Installation of Equipment:

a. Transportation

(1) Machines shall be preserved, packed and marked in accordance with Honeywell's standard practice. Shipments to the installation site shall be made at Government expense by padded van or air freight either on a Government bill of lading or a commercial bill of lading for conversion to a Government bill of lading at destination, or Honeywell shall prepay the transportation charges and thereafter invoice such charges for payment by the Government.

(2) Authorization for the method of transportation shall be furnished to Honeywell prior to shipment.

(3) Transportation charges for the shipment of empty packing cases shall be paid by Honeywell except when equipment is moved from one Government location to another.

(4) Transportation charges, regardless of point of origin or destination of the equipment, shall not exceed the cost of shipment between the Government's location and the location of Honeywell's nearest plant of manufacture or refurbishment for the equipment involved.

(5) The Government shall pay only those rigging and drayage costs incurred at the Government's location, except that Honeywell shall pay all rigging and drayage costs when the equipment is moved for mechanical replacement purposes during the ninety (90) day guarantee period as provided in Paragraph 4.

b. Installation

(1) The Government shall furnish such labor as may be necessary for placement and unpacking equipment at the Government's site.

(2) Supervision of unpacking and placement of equipment shall be furnished by Honeywell without additional charge to the Government.

Installation: Customer shall be solely responsible for installing the Equipment, except that if Customer requests Bunker Ramo will unpack and install the Equipment at its standard per diem rates for such service. Customer will provide, at its own expense, space adequate in size and design for the installation of the Equipment and all electric current outlets, circuits and wiring required by the Equipment.

H. **IDEAL COVERAGE**

The vendor shall be responsible for unpacking, uncrating, and installing the equipment, including the installation of all necessary cabling, connection with power, utility and communications services, and in all other respects making the equipment ready for operational use. Upon completion, the vendor shall notify the user that the equipment is ready for use.

L. **REFERENCES TO OTHER CLAUSES:** 6-51, 6-68.

A. **CLAUSE NAME:** Risk of Loss Prior to Installation   B. **CLAUSE NO.:** 6-75

C. **CONTRACT TYPES USED IN:** Hardware   D. **RISK RATING:** 3

E. **INTENT AND SCOPE**

To define the party responsible for any damage or loss to the equipment prior to the installation of the equipment.

G. **STANDARD CLAUSE PROVIDED BY MANUFACTURERS**

Insurance:

5.1 During the period the equipment ordered hereunder is in transit or in the possession of the Lessee, Honeywell and its insurers relieve the Lessee of all risk of loss or damage to the equipment except for the Lessee's responsibility for loss or damage caused by nuclear reaction, nuclear radiation or radioactive contamination.

5.2 Lessee shall indemnify and hold Honeywell harmless from any loss, claim or damage to persons or property arising out of Lessee's use or possession of the equipment, which indemnity shall survive the termination of this Agreement, provided that such loss, claim or damage was not caused by the fault or negligence of Honeywell or the fault or negligence of its employees or representatives.

Risk of Loss: If any licensed program or optional material is lost or damaged during shipment, IBM will replace the licensed program or optional material and program storage media at no additional charge to the Customer.

If any licensed program or optional material is lost or damaged while in the possession of the Customer, IBM will replace the licensed program or optional material at a charge for program storage media unless it is provided by the Customer.

Risk of Loss: During the period the machines are in transit or in the possession of the Customer, IBM and its insurers, if any, relieve the Customer of responsibility for all risks of loss or damage to the machines except for his responsibility for loss or damage caused by nuclear reaction, nuclear radiation or radioactive contamination.

H. **IDEAL COVERAGE**

Any risk of loss prior to installation and certification of the equipment's readiness for use shall be borne by the vendor, and until such time, the vendor shall maintain insurance covering all conventional risks in an amount equal to the replacement cost of the equipment, which insurance shall waive rights of subrogation against the user.

K. **COMMENTS**

The user will normally not pay for the equipment until completion of the acceptance test. As a result, the vendor should be responsible for any risk of loss until title is transferred or rentals commence. However, to the extent that the particular installation or site may involve special risks, the risk of loss should be negotiated, and proper insurance provided.

L. **REFERENCES TO OTHER CLAUSES:** 8-21, 10-24.

A. **CLAUSE NAME:** Cancellation of Components Prior to Installation   B. **CLAUSE NO.:** 6-76

C. **CONTRACT TYPES USED IN:** Hardware   D. **RISK RATING:** 3

E. **INTENT AND SCOPE**

To provide the user with the ability to cancel components or reduce or alter the configuration prior to installation.

H. **IDEAL COVERAGE**

The user has the right to cancel any components deliverable hereunder by notice given not less than _____ days prior to scheduled installation.

K. **COMMENTS**

If agreed to at all, vendor will seek to limit cancellation to some fraction of the dollar value of the deal. If open-ended this provides a means for total contract cancellation by the user prior to delivery.

L. **REFERENCES TO OTHER CLAUSES:** 6-70, 6-77, 6-91.

A.	**CLAUSE NAME:** Substitution of Components Prior to Installation	B.	**CLAUSE NO.:** 6-77
C.	**CONTRACT TYPES USED IN:** Hardware	D.	**RISK RATING:** 3

E. **INTENT AND SCOPE**

To provide the right to upgrade or substitute components or alter configurations prior to installation.

G. **STANDARD CLAUSE PROVIDED BY MANUFACTURERS**

Substitutions and Additions:

a. Substitutions

(1) Subject to the provisions of Subparagraph c., the Government or its authorized agent(s) may replace any equipment components of a system or subsystem with substitute equipment which is similar or identical to the equipment being replaced, whether or not the substitute equipment is obtained from or manufactured by Honeywell. Equipment being replaced by substitutions shall be discontinued in accordance with the provisions of this Contract.

(2) When equipment substitutions are made by the Government or its agent(s):

(a) The Government shall be responsible to Honeywell for damage caused to Honeywell equipment which would not have occurred had the substitute equipment obtained from another supplier not been installed, used, maintained or removed.

(b) Honeywell shall be relieved of the obligation(s), if any, specified elsewhere in this Special Item 132-1 to provide credits to the Government for equipment malfunctions provided the malfunction would not have occurred had the substitute equipment obtained from another supplier not been installed, used, maintained or removed.

(c) Honeywell shall not be held responsible for software failure provided the failure would not have occurred had the substitute equipment obtained from another supplier not been installed, used, or maintained.

b. Additions

(1) Subject to the provisions of Subparagraph c., the Government or its authorized agent(s) may add equipment (such as additional memory, tape drives, etc.) to systems (or subsystems) whether or not the additions are obtained from or manufactured by Honeywell.

(2) When additions are made by the Government or its agent(s):

(a) The Government shall be responsible to Honeywell for damage caused to Honeywell equipment which would not have occurred had the additional equipment obtained from another supplier not been installed, used, maintained or removed.

(b) Honeywell shall be relieved of the obligation(s), if any, specified elsewhere in this Special Item 132-1 to provide credits to the Government for equipment malfunctions provided the malfunction would not have occurred had the additional equipment obtained from another supplier not been installed, used, maintained or removed.

(c) Honeywell shall not be held responsible for software failure provided the failure would not have occurred if the equipment obtained from another supplier had not been installed, used, or maintained.

c. Procedure and Conditions

(1) The Government shall provide Honeywell with a written notice of its intention to make a substitution or addition which will include the description and specification of the item(s). When possible, such notice should be ninety (90) days before a substitution or addition is made. Honeywell shall have no obligation or liability with regard to any additions or substitutions planned or made by the Government, its agents, or contractors.

(2) Any additional maintenance service regardless of when performed, required because

of an addition or substitution, will be at Honeywell's hourly rates set forth in Paragraph 6.c.(4), with a minimum service charge of two (2) hours.

(3) Honeywell may, at its option, have a field service engineer in attendance to observe the installation of any additions or substitutions to its systems or subsystems.

d. Honeywell provides peripheral (excluding communications equipment) interface modules for Series 200 and 2000 systems for which interface specifications on the peripheral side are provided. For Honeywell equipment other than Series 200 and 2000, upon request of the Government, for a specific requirement, Honeywell will, within a reasonable time, submit a reasonable price proposal for an interface module and/or specifications as described above.

Customer may change and modify the configuration of the Equipment, without penalty, no later than sixty (60) days prior to the scheduled shipping date. Customer will reimburse Bunker Ramo for actual expenses required to make such changes and modifications when made later than sixty (60) days prior to the scheduled shipping date.

H. IDEAL COVERAGE

The user has the right to substitute other components offered by vendor for any components deliverable hereunder by notice given not less than _____ days prior to scheduled installation.

I. FALL–BACK ALTERNATIVES

If such substitution results in a reduction of dollar value, the dollar value thereof can be limited to some fraction of the total dollar value of the deal.

K. COMMENTS

If 6-76 is in effect, 6-77 may not be necessary, since the objective can be achieved by cancellation and a new order.

L. REFERENCES TO OTHER CLAUSES: 6-76.

A. **CLAUSE NAME:** Unrestricted Use and Function   B. **CLAUSE NO.:** 6-78

C. **CONTRACT TYPES USED IN:** Hardware, software   D. **RISK RATING:** 3

E. **INTENT AND SCOPE**

To afford the user the absolute and unrestricted right to use the acquired equipment for any purpose.

F. **PROTECTION AGAINST**

Protects against vendor claims that equipment is being over-used or misused solely because time is sold or because the user's data processing activities compete in some way with vendor.

H. **IDEAL COVERAGE**

The user may use the equipment [components] purchased [leased] hereunder for any purpose whatsoever without restriction, including without limitation, the right to "sell time" or provide processing services to others, with or without charge and whether or not such use may now or hereafter compete with the business of vendor.

L. **REFERENCES TO OTHER CLAUSES:** 6-79

A. **CLAUSE NAME:** Unrestricted Location   B. **CLAUSE NO.:** 6-79

C. **CONTRACT TYPES USED IN:** Hardware, rental or   D. **RISK RATING:** 4
installment purchase
contracts

E. **INTENT AND SCOPE**

To permit the user to re-locate equipment.

H. **IDEAL COVERAGE**

The user may re-locate the equipment anywhere in the world without restriction, at any time and from time to time, provided such re-location is carried out with due care under the supervision of qualified maintenance personnel. Any damage to the equipment as a result of such re-location shall be promptly repaired by user, at user's expense, unless a relocation agreement is in effect.

I. **FALL–BACK ALTERNATIVES**

There will be vendor resistance, in a rental contract, to re-location outside the United States, since the equipment is the vendor's property. The other resistance will be to the user's control over a move. A satisfactory fall-back is to require the user to have the move performed by vendor, obligating the vendor to do so on request and fixing cost by amount or formula; this should be coupled with total vendor responsibility for damage, and, as so conceived, probably makes great sense to the user since there will be no gap in vendor maintenance and repair responsibility.

K. **COMMENTS**

Properly drawn hardware purchase contracts probably do not need this clause, since, unless otherwise restricted (say, if money is owed on the equipment) the user–owner can re-locate the equipment at will. Continuity of maintenance is always the problem, especially if maintenance facilities of the vendor at an alternate site are less than those at the original site. Also note that spare parts availability may be tied to a specific site, and that several other clauses specify an N-mile radius for test time, back-up, etc.

L. **REFERENCES TO OTHER CLAUSES:** 6-56, 6-78, 10-30, 10-31, 10-32.

A. **CLAUSE NAME:** Changes and Attachments   B. **CLAUSE NO.:** 6-80

C. **CONTRACT TYPES USED IN:** Hardware, maintenance or   D. **RISK RATING:** 3
rental contracts

E. **INTENT AND SCOPE**

To permit the user to make changes to the equipment, or to attach components or parts to it, unless such changes or attachments interfere with proper maintenance or lessen the value of the equipment. In a purchase agreement (other than an installment purchase) the user should have the unrestricted right to use or change the equipment.

G. **STANDARD CLAUSE PROVIDED BY MANUFACTURERS**

The Customer is not to employ additional attachments, features, or devices on the equipment, make alterations in the equipment nor participate in the maintenance of the equipment without the written consent of Burroughs.

Alterations and Additions: Alterations and/or additions to the equipment may be made solely with the prior written consent of Honeywell. This written consent may be withdrawn by Honeywell if the equipment operation or maintenance is impaired.

Modification, Alterations, and Attachments: With the prior written consent of UNIVAC, the Customer may make alterations or modifications or install attachments to the equipment at its expense. Upon termination of this Agreement the equipment shall be restored to its original configuration at the Customer's expense.

Alterations and Attachments:

a. Subject to the provisions of this Paragraph 10, the Government or its authorized agent(s) may make alterations or install attachments to equipment supplied by Honeywell.

b. The Government shall provide Honeywell with written notice of its intention to make an alteration or attachment which will include the description and specification of the item(s). When possible such notice should be ninety (90) days before an alteration or attachment is made. Honeywell shall have no obligation or liability with regard to any alteration or attachment planned or made by the Government or its agent(s).

c. The Government shall be responsible to Honeywell for damage caused to Honeywell equipment provided the damage would not have occurred had the alteration or attachment (not supplied by Honeywell) not been installed, used, maintained or removed.

d. Honeywell may, at its option, have a field service engineer in attendance to observe the installation of any alterations or attachments to its system or subsystems.

e. If such changes increase the cost of maintenance, mutually agreeable arrangements for additional maintenance charges shall be made on an individual installation basis. Prior to establishing a mutually agreeable arrangement, any additional maintenance service regardless of when performed required because of an alteration or attachment will be at Honeywell's hourly rates set forth in Paragraph 6.c.(5).

f. Such alterations or attachments shall be removed and the equipment restored to the prior conditions, reasonable wear and tear excepted, at Government expense prior to discontinuance of rental of the equipment.

g. The maintenance credit provisions specified elsewhere under Special Item 132-1 will not apply if equipment failure is caused by such alterations or attachments not furnished by Honeywell.

h. Any programming changes necessitated by such alterations and attachments will be the responsibility of the Government.

H. IDEAL COVERAGE

The user shall have the right to make changes and attachments to the equipment, provided such changes or attachments do not lessen the value of the equipment, or prevent proper maintenance from being performed, or unreasonably increase vendor's cost of performing maintenance.

J. POSSIBLE REMEDIES

This clause should be the subject of arbitration, if the entire contract isn't.

K. COMMENTS

A general arbitration clause or a specific one relating to disputes as to permitted attachment or change is helpful, since it is probably difficult to determine in advance what types of changes or attachments may be undesirable. When the user owns the equipment, the problem still arises in terms of the maintenance contract, but the question of "lessening the value" of the equipment should no longer be vendor's concern.

L. REFERENCES TO OTHER CLAUSES: 6-46, 6-81.

A. **CLAUSE NAME:** Interface with Other Manufacturers Equipment

B. **CLAUSE NO.:** 6-81

C. **CONTRACT TYPES USED IN:** Hardware

D. **RISK RATING:** 2

E. **INTENT AND SCOPE**

To give the user the absolute right to connect the equipment to any other equipment including peripheral equipment, terminal devices, communications equipment or other computers or devices which may interface in some way with the equipment. The right of the user to do this should be absolute, except only to the extent that such connection interferes with the ability to perform proper maintenance.

H. **IDEAL COVERAGE**

The user shall have the right to connect the equipment herein contracted for to any equipment manufactured or supplied by others including, but not limited to, peripheral equipment, other computers, communications equipment, terminal devices, and the like. The user shall notify vendor at least 5 days prior to any such connection and if vendor shall deem it necessary or desirable for proper maintenance of the equipment, the vendor shall make or supervise the interconnection, at vendor's expense, and supply any interface devices required as described in published vendor manuals at published prices.

K. **COMMENTS**

It should normally be possible to provide interface protection to prevent damage to the original equipment. Current flows and information flows can be monitored and governed to ensure that no damaging surges reach the equipment in question.

L. **REFERENCES TO OTHER CLAUSES:** 6-80.

A. CLAUSE NAME: Hardware Upgrades   B. CLAUSE NO.: 6-82

C. CONTRACT TYPES USED IN: Hardware   D. RISK RATING: 3

E. INTENT AND SCOPE

To give the user the ability to upgrade hardware, where additional or substitute hardware is available that is capable of performing better or faster. The user should be required to pay for the new hardware, less a trade-in allowance. The predetermination of this trade-in allowance is desirable.

H. IDEAL COVERAGE

The user may, at any time upon demand, require the vendor to substitute upgraded equipment for any component purchased (leased) hereunder, and the user will pay the difference between the purchase price (rental) of the equipment installed hereunder, and the purchase price (rental) in effect for the upgraded equipment.

I. FALL–BACK ALTERNATIVES

The clause, as drafted, provides only for the payment of the purchase (rental) price differential, when upgrading. It is probably not acceptable to most vendors, at least on a purchase situation, and to a lesser extent in a rental environment since it presumes that the old equipment will be traded in at a value equal to 100% of its purchase cost. Thus a discount based on the age of the surrendered equipment can be negotiated as a fall-back.

L. REFERENCES TO OTHER CLAUSES: 6-77, 6-83, 7-09.

A. **CLAUSE NAME:** Software Upgrades   B. **CLAUSE NO.:** 6-83

C. **CONTRACT TYPES USED IN:** Hardware, software   D. **RISK RATING:** 3

E. **INTENT AND SCOPE**

To ensure that the user obtains access to all software upgrades, at no additional cost. To the extent that upgraded versions of software are made available to customers at higher prices, the user should *perhaps* pay the differential cost. This again can be negotiated at the time of contract signing.

H. **IDEAL COVERAGE**

The user shall receive all necessary elements of any upgraded version of the software to be delivered hereunder at any time that the vendor shall make the same available to other customers. To the extent that such software as upgraded is sold or licensed at prices in excess of prices herein provided, the user will pay the increased cost differential only.

K. **COMMENTS**

Software does not deteriorate or depreciate with age, and, therefore, the payment of the cost differential only appears reasonable.

L. **REFERENCES TO OTHER CLAUSES:** 6-82, 7-09.

A. CLAUSE NAME: Trade-in   **B. CLAUSE NO.:** 6-84

C. CONTRACT TYPES USED IN: Hardware   **D. RISK RATING:** 3

E. INTENT AND SCOPE

If the user decides to replace an entire configuration, rather than upgrade a component (as defined in 6-82) the user should have the opportunity to trade-in the equipment previously installed. A trade-in value should be negotiated and established in the contract at the time of purchase. It does not benefit the user to negotiate trade-in values at the time of trade-in, since the user will have little negotiating strength unless there then exists a viable used equipment market for the unwanted configuration.

G. STANDARD CLAUSE PROVIDED BY MANUFACTURERS

Price Adjustment: The Trade-in Allowance may be adjusted downward if upon reinspection by IBM within one month prior to the trade-in, the Trade-in Machines are determined to have been damaged or their condition to have deteriorated from the condition which existed, as determined by IBM's inspection, immediately prior to the signing of this Agreement.

Cancellation of Agreement: In the event that title to the Trade-in Machines has not passed to IBM on or before the stated scheduled trade-in date, IBM's obligation to credit the Trade-in Allowance to the Customer and the Customer's obligation to trade-in the machines shall be terminated. The execution of this Agreement supersedes all prior trade-in agreements covering the above designated Trade-in Machines.

Application of Trade-in: The Trade-in Allowance credit will be issued promptly after passage of title of the Trade-in Machines to IBM and applied only as part payment of the purchase price of the On-Order machines or against sums due or to become due to IBM.

H. IDEAL COVERAGE

The user may at any time require the vendor to substitute any upgraded or later-developed configuration for the configuration purchased herein. In such event the manufacturer will allow a trade-in credit for the old equipment toward the purchase price of the new configuration equal to the following percentages of the purchase price of the old equipment based upon the number of months elapsed between the date of acceptance of the old equipment and user's election to substitute: less than _____ months— _____%; between _____ and _____ months— _____% [etc.]

K. COMMENTS

There is also required, in any properly drawn contract, a clause to assure that the upgraded equipment, when ordered, will be treated as if it were originally-ordered equipment *under the contract*, so as to attach to the new equipment all of the warranties, representations and vendor obligations that would exist if the upgraded equipment was included in the original contract.

L. REFERENCES TO OTHER CLAUSES: 6-82.

A. **CLAUSE NAME:** Title Transfer   B. **CLAUSE NO.:** 6-85

C. **CONTRACT TYPES USED IN:** Hardware purchase   D. **RISK RATING:** 4

E. **INTENT AND SCOPE**

To define the point at which title and risks are transferred to the user.

F. **PROTECTION AGAINST**

To protect against possible user risk of loss or damage during the period that the equipment has not yet been unequivocally accepted by the user.

G. **STANDARD CLAUSE PROVIDED BY MANUFACTURERS**

Title: Title to each machine passes to the Purchaser on the date of shipment from IBM, or on the date of acceptance of this Agreement by IBM, whichever is later.

Deliveries: All deliveries of Equipment by Bunker Ramo pursuant to this Agreement shall be made f.o.b. Bunker Ramo's point of shipment on the dates and otherwise as specified in *Schedule A*. Title to Equipment shall pass to Customer, and all risk of loss, damage or destruction of all Equipment delivered hereunder shall be assumed by Customer upon delivery. Neither purchase orders, acknowledgements thereof, nor invoices issued pursuant hereto shall add to, change or in any way affect the terms and conditions of this Agreement.

H. **IDEAL COVERAGE**

Title to the equipment shall pass to the user only after satisfactory completion of all acceptance tests described in 6-51.

L. **REFERENCES TO OTHER CLAUSES:** 6-33, 6-51, 6-75, 8-13, 10-21.

A. **CLAUSE NAME:** Purchase Option   B. **CLAUSE NO.:** 6-86

C. **CONTRACT TYPES USED IN:** Hardware rental contracts   D. **RISK RATING:** 3
only

E. **INTENT AND SCOPE**

In a rental contract, to provide the user with an option to purchase the equipment after the elapsing of a period of rental.

G. **STANDARD CLAUSE PROVIDED BY MANUFACTURERS**

At any time within the first 18 months after commencement of rental thereon Lessee may purchase any or all of the equipment leased as herein provided, so long as such equipment is in Lessee's possession under the terms of this lease and Lessee is not in default. Lessee shall give Lessor written notice of its election of purchase and the effective date thereof. After payment of all rentals and other charges due under the lease through the effective date of purchase, Lessee shall pay Lessor a sum equal to Lessor's established price for that classification of equipment leased hereunder, in effect on the date of purchase, plus any taxes applicable to purchase at such time, less seventy percent (70%) of all rental charges (excluding taxes) paid during the first six months of rental payments and forty percent (40%) of all rental paid during the second six months of such payments on the equipment. As an alternative, such earned rental credit may be applied on one occasion only to a purchase of any other Burroughs more advanced system, and/or components thereof, of equal or greater total price, during such 18 month period. Thereafter said options and credits shall lapse, become void and be of no further force and effect. Upon completion of payment for purchased equipment as herein provided title to all such equipment purchased shall automatically pass to the Lessee.

Purchase Option:

(a) The Customer, if he is not then in default hereunder, may at any time following commencement of monthly charges purchase any item or all items of equipment then covered by this Agreement at the purchase prices specified in the Schedule of Equipment less applicable credits. UNIVAC will credit against the purchase price of each item of equipment so purchased, an amount equal to the lesser of:

(1) 75% of the total of all monthly equipment charges for such item (excluding all maintenance charges) paid under this Agreement by the Customer up to the time of exercise of this option; or

(2) nine months of the monthly equipment charges for such item. This option shall be exercised by the Customer mailing or otherwise delivering to a Univac Sales Representative the then standard form of agreement of sale duly executed by the Customer.

(b) This option shall not survive the termination of this Agreement.

Right to Purchase:

(a) Customer may purchase any item of Equipment during the term of this Agreement upon thirty (30) days written notice to Bunker Ramo.

(b) The purchase price shall be the purchase price listed in Schedule A less the following credits (i) if purchased within ninety (90) days from the Commencement Date of each item of equipment, a credit of 100% for all monthly rental payments made, (ii) if purchased later than ninety (90) days from the Commencement Date for each item of equipment a credit of 60% for all monthly rental payments made up to a maximum of forty-eight (48) months. Such credits shall be based on the actual monthly rental charges paid on each item of equipment.

(c) The terms and conditions of such purchase shall be Bunker Ramo's standard terms and conditions for purchase of Equipment effective on the date of exercise of the option to purchase. Upon purchase of Equipment this Agreement shall terminate as to such Equipment.

H. IDEAL COVERAGE

The user may, at any time, purchase any or all items of equipment rented hereunder, upon 30 days written notice to the vendor, at the published prices for such equipment now in effect, as listed on Schedule A, less the credits described in 6-87. Title shall transfer upon full payment.

K. COMMENTS

Any contract containing a purchase option should contain all of the provisions applicable to a purchase contract, which should become operative upon exercise of the option. An equipment lease with a purchase option will in effect be two complete contracts, one for rental and one for purchase, with the latter coming into effect only upon option exercise.

L. REFERENCES TO OTHER CLAUSES: 6-85, 6-87, 6-88, 10-07.

A. **CLAUSE NAME:** Rental Credit on Exercise of Option   B. **CLAUSE NO.:** 6-87

C. **CONTRACT TYPES USED IN:** Hardware rental contract only   D. **RISK RATING:** 3

E. **INTENT AND SCOPE**

If a purchase option is exercised, a credit should be given for all or part of the rental payment to the point of purchase. The point of purchase normally occurs when the rental payments are stopped and the purchase price is paid.

G. **STANDARD CLAUSE PROVIDED BY MANUFACTURERS**

Option to Purchase: Honeywell, following the date the equipment is installed and made ready for use, shall make the items of equipment available to the Lessee for purchase during the rental period at the purchase prices specified in Section I. Credits against the purchase price from all rentals previously paid on the equipment being purchased will be accrued on the basis of the following schedule in effect at the time this option is exercised.

(1) 80% of total rentals paid to date if the option is exercised during the first twelve (12) months following the date the equipment is installed and made ready for use.
(2) 60% of total rentals paid to date if option is exercised during the next twelve (12) months following the date the equipment is installed and made ready for use.
(3) 50% of total rentals paid to date if option is exercised during the next twelve (12) months following the date the equipment is installed and made ready for use on all Model 110, 115, 120, 125, 200, 1200, 1250, 2200 systems and related peripherals. Specifically excluded from this option are all Model 3200, 4200, 8200 Central Processors, related options and peripheral units used exclusively with these Central Processors.

H. **IDEAL COVERAGE**

If the user shall exercise its purchase option described in 6-86, the purchase price listed on Schedule A shall be reduced by an amount equal to _____ % of aggregate rentals paid to the date of payment of the purchase price.

I. **FALL–BACK ALTERNATIVES**

Another approach, not necessarily a fall-back, is to reduce the price by a depreciation-age factor rather than by a rental credit factor. Most vendors, in fact, work out their trade-in and purchase options based upon their standard depreciation guidelines.

L. **REFERENCES TO OTHER CLAUSES:** 6-86, 10-07.

A. CLAUSE NAME: Protection of Purchase Price   **B. CLAUSE NO.:** 6-88

C. CONTRACT TYPES USED IN: Hardware rental contract   **D. RISK RATING:** 3

E. INTENT AND SCOPE

To ensure that the purchase price under a purchase option is fixed and unalterable. Since the machine is installed in user's site, was manufactured and delivered at a time when a particular price was in effect, that price, less depreciation or rental credit (6-87) should be fixed and not subject to escalation because of price increases occurring after installation.

G. STANDARD CLAUSE PROVIDED BY MANUFACTURERS

In the event the Lessee elects to exercise this option at any time during the rental period and subsequent to the above twenty-four (24) or thirty-six (36) (whichever is applicable) months' period following the date the equipment is installed and made ready for use, the price for such item of equipment shall not exceed the price at the end of the twenty-four (24) or thirty-six (36) (whichever is applicable) months' period had the purchase option been exercised at that time. (Honeywell)

H. IDEAL COVERAGE

The purchase price in the event of user exercise of its purchase option shall be the price in effect on the date of this contract as set forth in Schedule A, less the credits pursuant to 6-87. Increases in vendor prices hereafter occurring shall have no effect upon the exercise price herein provided.

L. REFERENCES TO OTHER CLAUSES: 6-86, 6-87.

A. CLAUSE NAME: Availability of Expansion Units

B. CLAUSE NO.: 6-89

C. CONTRACT TYPES USED IN: Hardware contract

D. RISK RATING: 2

E. INTENT AND SCOPE

To the extent that the user needs additional components from time to time, especially in a case where components are necessary to meet expanding business opportunities, the user should have the right to obtain such expansion equipment from the manufacturer. This right probably should be limited in time to take into account that the manufacturer may not wish to continue to stay ready to manufacture expansion components, especially in small quantity lots, for a single user.

H. IDEAL COVERAGE

For a period of _____ years from the installation date of the equipment delivered hereunder vendor agrees to produce, at user's request, additional units of each component listed on Schedule A or components functionally equivalent thereto. Each such additional component shall be sold [leased] at a price equal to the lower of (a) vendor's then prevailing price or (b) the price for such component set forth in this contract plus _____ % per year for each year between the installation date of the equipment delivered hereunder and the date of user request for additional components. Except for the price variation the purchase [lease] of each additional component shall be governed by all of the terms of this contract.

K. COMMENTS

See 6-42 for a discussion of price protection clauses.

L. REFERENCES TO OTHER CLAUSES: 6-42, 6-56, 7-05.

A. **CLAUSE NAME:** Alternate Sources for Components   B. **CLAUSE NO.:** 6-90

C. **CONTRACT TYPES USED IN:** Hardware   D. **RISK RATING:** 3

E. **INTENT AND SCOPE**

To cover the time after the expiration of the period designated in 6-89, when the vendor no longer manufactures expansion components, it may be possible to have the vendor now designate another source of such components and to represent that those other components are functionally equivalent.

H. **IDEAL COVERAGE**

Vendor represents and warrants that the components manufactured by others listed on Column 2 of Schedule A are functionally equivalent to and compatible and interchangeable with, the components delivered hereunder listed in Column I of Schedule A.

I. **FALL-BACK COVERAGE**

As a fall-back it is possible to provide that when the vendor stops manufacturing the needed units, the vendor will make available to the user the necessary blueprints, tools and dies so that the user can have the component made on a custom basis by another manufacturer. This is not necessarily a viable solution, since the cost of manufacturing components on a low quantity basis or on a custom basis is often prohibitive.

K. **COMMENTS**

It is a difficult problem to have the vendor designate where outside expansion components can be obtained. However, if expansion components are necessary to the survival of the user, such as teller terminals in banks, airline reservation terminals or other specialized equipment, then it is desirable to have the vendor stipulate the outside sources available for supply of these components in the event the original vendor decides to stop making them. The vendor's representation, of course, can speak only of the present, and provide no assurance that outside makers will not discontinue manufacture of the units or radically modify them so as to make them unacceptable.

It may also be possible to obtain functionally equivalent components which require alteration to the software or hardware—in which case negotiation for this may be feasible.

L. **REFERENCES TO OTHER CLAUSES:** 6-14, 6-89.

A. **CLAUSE NAME:**   Termination Prior to Delivery   B. **CLAUSE NO.:**   6-91

C. **CONTRACT TYPES USED IN:**   Hardware and software   D. **RISK RATING:**   2

E. **INTENT AND SCOPE**

To define remedies for vendor or user default under the contract prior to actual delivery of the components of the contract.

H. **IDEAL COVERAGE**

The parties acknowledge that actual damages for the breach of this contract may be difficult to determine with exactitude and, accordingly, have agreed to the following provisions for liquidated damages which the parties acknowledge are reasonable estimates of their potential losses. In the event the contract is terminated by reason of the default of either party *prior to complete delivery* the defaulting party shall pay to the other party liquidated damages computed as follows:

K. **COMMENTS**

The damages to be defined on the user's side against the vendor could include the losses incurred by user in its performance of the contract up to its cancellation, plus some compensation for the increased cost of obtaining substituted equipment. Thus, all site preparation, software, systems and other developmental costs which are incurred and not otherwise usable should be covered, as well as damages for the delay. Liquidated amounts in a contract must be reasonable or they will not be enforced in court. See Chapter IV. Vendors want to receive, from defaulting customers, their lost profits on the aborted transaction plus any out-of-pocket losses sustained. A user can attempt to negotiate a lesser liquidated amount by arguing that the equipment or software package can be sold to someone else. Since vendors would get their lost profits in court, they will not be very receptive and will question the user's good faith in entering into the contract. If an agreement is reached it will have to involve substantial damages to the vendor.

Industry practice historically has been to allow user cancellation for any reason up to some "confirmation" date without penalty—which reduces the ability to negotiate a vendor penalty in case of vendor cancellation.

L. **REFERENCES TO OTHER CLAUSES:**   5-09, 5-11, 6-72, 6-76, 6-92, 6-93, 6-94, 7-24 8-16, 9-16.

A. CLAUSE NAME: Failure to Deliver   **B. CLAUSE NO.:** 6-92

C. CONTRACT TYPES USED IN: Hardware contracts   **D. RISK RATING:** 2

E. INTENT AND SCOPE

If the vendor ultimately fails to deliver, the contract should be terminable by the user as a result of vendor breach. Presumably, the user was prepared to accept delivery, and had completed all of the efforts associated with preparation for delivery, including site preparation, systems design, programming, and purchase of the necessary supplies and facilities. As a result, damages based on default at the time delivery is scheduled will be most significant, and will be heaviest.

G. STANDARD CLAUSE PROVIDED BY MANUFACTURERS

Damages:

a. Lessor shall not be liable for any loss or damage caused by delay in delivery. Lessor shall not in any event be liable for any loss or damage arising from any cause beyond Lessor's reasonable control, nor for incidental indirect or consequential damages. In no event shall Lessor's liability for loss or damage exceed a refund of rental theretofore paid under this agreement.

b. Lessee shall not be responsible for any loss or damage to such equipment unless such loss or damage is due to nuclear reaction, nuclear radiation or radioactive contamination arising out of the use by Lessee of radioactive materials. (Burroughs)

H. IDEAL COVERAGE

In the event that all the equipment is not delivered and accepted by user on _____ , the vendor shall pay to the user damages equal to (a) all costs incurred by the user in preparation for this equipment, including but not limited to training, systems, programming, site preparation, costs of supplies and facilities, excepting only such costs which can be applied to equipment obtained from any other manufacturer, plus (b) the difference in price between the equipment to be delivered hereunder and equivalent substitute equipment, plus (c) the sum of $_____ , representing compensation for the lost time and use between the vendor's default and the delivery to user of substituted equipment.

K. COMMENTS

It is difficult to establish exact damages; the philosophy of remedies should be to make the user whole. Note that this is unilateral whereas 6-91 is bilateral.

L. REFERENCES TO OTHER CLAUSES: 5-11, 6-72, 6-91, 6-93, 8-16.

A. **CLAUSE NAME:** Liquidated Damages	B. **CLAUSE NO.:** 6-93
C. **CONTRACT TYPES USED IN:** Hardware and software	D. **RISK RATING:** 1

E. **INTENT AND SCOPE**

In the event of delays, or of failure to meet specifications, it is possible to structure a liquidated damage provision in the contract, which provides a formula for compensating the user based on the extent of delays, or based on percentage failure to meet the specifications.

G. **STANDARD CLAUSE PROVIDED BY MANUFACTURERS**

Liquidated Damages:

a. Equipment

(1) If Honeywell does not install the system and/or machines and features in the price list included on the same order (designated by Honeywell's type and model numbers) ready for use as defined in Paragraph 2.a.(4) above on or before the installation date, Honeywell shall pay to the Government, as fixed and agreed, liquidated damages for each machine whether or not installed, for each calendar day's delay beginning with the installation date, but not for more than one hundred and eighty (180) calendar days, 1/1250th of the purchase price of such machines or one-thirtieth (1/30th) of the Basic Monthly Rental Charges, whichever is greater; but the charges for any month shall not exceed the Basic Monthly Rental Charges.

(2) If some, but not all, of the machines on an order are installed, ready for use, during a time when liquidated damages would otherwise be applicable, and the Government uses any such installed machines, liquidated damages shall not accrue against the machines used for any calendar day the machines are used.

(3) If the delay is more than thirty (30) calendar days, then by written notice to Honeywell, the Government may terminate the right to Honeywell to install, and may obtain substitute equipment. In this event Honeywell shall be liable for liquidated damages until substitute equipment is installed ready for use or for one hundred and eighty (180) days from the installation date, whichever occurs first.

(4) If the Government is unable to use the equipment on the installation date because Honeywell failed to furnish the programming aids or their equivalent on or before the delivery date or furnished programming aids which do not perform in accordance with Paragraph 2.b.(1), liquidated damages as specified in Paragraph 3.a.(1) shall apply in addition to the liquidated damages as specified in Paragraph 3.b.(1) provided, however, that the total charges for any month shall not exceed one hundred and thirty percent (130%) of the damages provided in 3.a.(1) above but not for more than one hundred and eighty (180) days.

b. Programming Aids (Software)

(1) If Honeywell does not deliver the programming aids identified on the order for the equipment or their equivalent ready to perform as prescribed in Paragraph 2.b.(1) on or before the delivery date specified on the order, Honeywell shall pay to the Government as fixed and agreed liquidated damages in the amount of $100 for each calendar day's delay for each programming aid not delivered as prescribed in Paragraph 2.b.(1) and for any other programming aids not usable as a result thereof, or for each calendar day an amount equal to one thirtieth (1/30th) of the Basic Monthly Rental for the equipment, whichever is greater, but not for more than one hundred and eighty (180) calendar days. The charges for any month shall not exceed the Basic Monthly Rental Charges.

(2) In the event the provisions of Paragraph 3.a.(3) are applicable and substitute equipment is installed, Honeywell shall be liable for liquidated damages for the period of time between the date of delivery until the programming aids are delivered, ready for use, or for one hundred and eighty (180) days from the delivery date, whichever occurs first.

c. Exception

Except with respect to defaults of subcontractors, Honeywell shall not be liable for liquidated damages when delays raise out of causes beyond the control and without the fault or negligence of Honeywell. Such causes may include, but are not restricted to acts of God or of the public enemy, acts of the Government in either of its sovereign or contractual capacities, fires, floods, earthquakes, epidemics, quarantine restrictions, strikes, freight embargoes, and unusually severe weather; but in every case the delays must be beyond the control and without the fault or negligence of Honeywell. If the delays are caused by the default of the subcontractor, or if such default arises out of causes beyond the control of both Honeywell and the subcontractor, and without the fault or negligence of either of them, Honeywell shall not be liable for liquidated damages for delays unless the supplies or services to be furnished by the subcontractor were obtainable from other sources in sufficient time to permit Honeywell to meet the required performance schedule.

H. IDEAL COVERAGE

In the event of a delay in delivery, and in addition to and not in limitation of any other rights or remedies of user, the vendor shall pay to the user the sum of $_____ for each day of such delay in delivery as agreed liquidated damages.

I. FALL-BACK ALTERNATIVES

In a complex contract, some delays can be excused for a time or can be subject to very modest damages; others must be compensible.

K. COMMENTS

Liquidated damages are difficult to reach agreement on, since amounts that would be meaningful to the user would probably be much too large, and amounts that are not meaningful tend to be rather awkward. In the past, governmental institutions have insisted on liquidated damages of $100 or $200 a day on contracts of any substance and when one recognizes that although these add up to $36,000 or $72,000 a year, such amounts may be minuscule relative to the potential losses involved. However, defaults or delays will never be permitted to last that long without contract cancellation. One effective approach to the problem is to choose a per diem figure that is large enough to motivate the vendor to use its best efforts, and to limit the total amount payable under this provision. Thereafter provisions of 6-92 could take over if failure continued.

L. REFERENCES TO OTHER CLAUSES: 5-09, 6-72, 6-92.

A. CLAUSE NAME: User Costs　　　　　　　　**B. CLAUSE NO.:** 6-94

C. CONTRACT TYPES USED IN: Hardware and software　　　**D. RISK RATING:** 4

E. INTENT AND SCOPE

The costs to be incurred by the user can be described in the contract, specifically to assist in arbitration or litigation, in the event damages are to be assessed. This clause is a recitation of the estimates of costs to be incurred by the user in the operation and planning for use of the system purchased. This recitation has no purpose, except as an identification by the user and recognition by the vendor of the user's cost elements, their method of computation, and the applicability of these elements to the equipment being purchased.

H. IDEAL COVERAGE

The vendor acknowledges that the user will incur costs in preparation for and installation of the equipment purchased hereunder in the following areas and that the estimated costs set forth are reasonable estimates:

Site preparation, $_____ ;

planning, $_____ ;

systems design, $_____ ;

programming, $_____ ;

testing, $_____ ;

initial purchase of supplies, $_____ ;

data file conversion, $_____ ;

program conversion, $_____ ;

parallel operation, $_____ ;

installation, $_____ ;

user training, $_____ ;

cost of money, $_____ , etc.

L. REFERENCES TO OTHER CLAUSES: 6-91, 6-92.

A. CLAUSE NAME: Software Package Specifications   **B. CLAUSE NO.:** 7-01

C. CONTRACT TYPES USED IN: Software package contracts   **D. RISK RATING:** 2

E. INTENT AND SCOPE

To describe the specifications which the package will meet in terms of function and performance.

G. STANDARD CLAUSE PROVIDED BY MANUFACTURERS

Responsibilities of the Parties: IBM will publish design objectives and estimated avail-ability dates for licensed programs which it announces. However, IBM does not represent or warrant that such design objectives or estimated availability dates will be met.

IBM will publish Program Product Specifications for each licensed program with Pro-gramming Service Classification A or B as the licensed program is included in the IBM Program Information Department Library (Library).

IBM will provide a functional description of each licensed program with Programming Service Classification C as it is included in the Library.

The Customer shall be exclusively responsible for the supervision, management and control of his use of the licensed programs, and/or optional materials, including but not limited to: (1) assuring proper machine configuration, program installation, audit controls and operating methods, (2) establishing adequate backup plans, based on alter-nate procedures and/or based on access to qualified programming personnel to diag-nose, patch, and repair licensed program defects, in the event of a licensed program malfunction and, (3) implementing sufficient procedures and checkpoints to satisfy his requirements for security and accuracy of input and output as well as restart and recovery in the event of a malfunction.

H. IDEAL COVERAGE

The vendor warrants that the package is designed to and will meet the functional and performance specifications and standards described in Schedule A.

K. COMMENTS

The best way to begin an approach to the description of the specifications is to use (and attach) vendor's selling materials, since these will most glowingly describe the package. Of course, if specific functions are important to the user, these should also be incorporated. A goal-oriented approach to performance specifications is always recommended; it is more important to the user that the package does a particular job and does it quickly and well than specifically *how* the package does it.

L. REFERENCES TO OTHER CLAUSES: 6-02, 6-46, 8-01, 8-04, 9-01.

A. **CLAUSE NAME:**   Definition of Documentation   B. **CLAUSE NO.:**   7-02

C. **CONTRACT TYPES USED IN:**   Software and software   D. **RISK RATING:**   2
                                   package contracts

E. **INTENT AND SCOPE**

To describe the extent of documentation to be included as part of the software package when delivered.

H. **IDEAL COVERAGE**

The vendor will furnish the user with the following documentation as part of the package to be delivered hereunder, which will be in form and substance at least equal to comparable materials generally in use in the industry, in the following quantities:

Manual type   *No. of Pages*   *Quantity*

User's manual
Systems manual
Operating manual
Programming manual
Modification manual

K. **COMMENTS**

See also 6-08 for possible inclusion of manuals as a part of the contract.

L. **REFERENCES TO OTHER CLAUSES:**   8-03, 9-07.

A. CLAUSE NAME: Availability of Documentation and Future Rights   **B. CLAUSE NO.:** 7-03

C. CONTRACT TYPES USED IN: Software and hardware   **D. RISK RATING:** 3

E. INTENT AND SCOPE

To assure that the user has the right to obtain revised and later-developed documentation.

H. IDEAL COVERAGE

If the documentation described in 7-02 is revised at any time or if additional documentation is developed by the vendor with respect to the package, the vendor shall, forthwith upon publication, deliver to user N copies of such revised or additional documentation, at no cost to the user.

L. REFERENCES TO OTHER CLAUSES: 6-29, 6-30.

A. **CLAUSE NAME:** Rights to Reproduce Documentation   B. **CLAUSE NO.:** 7-04

C. **CONTRACT TYPES USED IN:** Software contracts   D. **RISK RATING:** 4

E. **INTENT AND SCOPE**

If insufficient number of documentation copies are made available or if the user requires more copies than are normally available from the vendor, the user should attempt to obtain the right to reproduce the documentation.

G. **STANDARD CLAUSE PROVIDED BY MANUFACTURERS**

Customer may make copies of any computer tapes, disks, or other material provided by BASI to the extent required for Customer's internal use of the Product at the Customer-site specified herein, or at any authorized Customer-site to which Customer may move the Product.

Customer agrees not to make any copies or partial copies, for the purpose of supplying them to others, of any computer tapes, disks, or other material provided by BASI, and agrees to supply to BASI any and all such copies in the event of termination for any reason.

Permission to Copy or Modify Licensed Programs: The Customer shall not copy, in whole or in part, any licensed programs or optional materials which are provided by IBM in printed form under this Agreement. Additional copies of printed materials may be licensed from IBM at the charges then in effect.

Any licensed programs or optional materials which are provided by IBM in machine readable form may be copied, in whole or in part, in printed or machine readable form in sufficient number for use by the Customer with the designated CPU, to understand the contents of such machine readable material, to modify the licensed provided below, for backup purposes as provided in the section of this Agreement entitled "License", or for archive purposes, provided however, that no more than five printed copies will be in existence under any license at any one time without prior written consent from IBM. The Customer agrees to maintain appropriate records of the number and location of all copies that he may make of licensed programs or optional materials which are provided by IBM in machine readable form. The original, and any copies of the licensed programs and/or optional materials, in whole or in part, which are made by the Customer shall be the property of IBM.

If the original or any copy of the licensed program or optional materials will be kept at other than the location of the designated CPU, the Customer will notify IBM in writing of a designated location for the original or copy. However, the Customer may transport or transmit a copy or the original of any licensed program to another location when the license is temporarily transferred as provided in the section of this Agreement entitled "License", provided the copy or the original is destroyed or returned to its designated location when the period of temporary transfer is concluded and the license reverts back to the designated CPU.

The Customer may modify any licensed programs and/or optional material, in machine readable form, for his own use and merge it into other program material to form an updated work, provided that, upon discontinuance of the license for such licensed program, the licensed program and optional material supplied by IBM will be completely removed from the updated work and dealt with under this Agreement as if permission to modify had never been granted. Any portion of the licensed program or optional material included in an updated work shall be used only on the designated CPU except during a period of temporary transfer as provided in the section of this Agreement entitled "License", and shall remain subject to all other terms of this Agreement.

The Customer agrees to reproduce and include IBM's copyright notice on any copies, in whole or in part, in any form, including partial copies, in modifications, of licensed programs or optional materials made hereunder in accord with the copyright instructions to be provided by IBM.

H. IDEAL COVERAGE

The user shall have the right to reproduce all documentation supplied hereunder, provided that such reproduction shall be solely for the use of the user, and that such reproductions shall be subject to the same restrictions on use and disclosure as are contained in this contract with respect to the original documentation.

I. FALL-BACK ALTERNATIVES

See 6-31 for another approach.

L. REFERENCES TO OTHER CLAUSES: 6-31.

A. CLAUSE NAME: Rights to Future Package Options   **B. CLAUSE NO.:** 7-05

C. CONTRACT TYPES USED IN: Software   **D. RISK RATING:** 2

E. INTENT AND SCOPE

To provide the user with the right to acquire enhancements to the package or to obtain additional options which the vendor may thereafter make available for the package.

H. IDEAL COVERAGE

In the event the vendor shall produce any enhancements or functional changes in the package after delivery of the package hereunder, the user shall have the right to obtain such enhancements, at the lesser of (a) prices then in effect or (b) the difference between the then current price of the package including such enhancements and the purchase price paid hereunder.

K. COMMENTS

If a user purchases a software package, additional enhancements should be made available, at reasonable prices. If such enhancements are made available to new purchasers of the package and the purchase price of the package has not been significantly increased, then the price of the enhancements is presumably reflected in the price of the new package and the price to the old user for the enhancement should not exceed the increase in the package price.

L. REFERENCES TO OTHER CLAUSES: 6-83, 7-09.

A. **CLAUSE NAME:** Run Time (Performance)   B. **CLAUSE NO.:** 7-06

C. **CONTRACT TYPES USED IN:** Software   D. **RISK RATING:** 1

E. **INTENT AND SCOPE**

To describe the operating performance of the software package. If the package requires 15 minutes per day of machine time on the particular configuration in which it is to be used, then that time should be warranted as a performance characteristic which must be met prior to acceptance of the package. Significant changes in such run time which are not cured should be cause for cancellation of the contract or adjustment of the purchase price. (See 6-93)

G. **STANDARD CLAUSE PROVIDED BY MANUFACTURERS**

Warranties: ADR represents and warrants that: (a) the Equipment, when delivered and installed, will operate on the computer specified on front of this Agreement; and (b) any service rendered by ADR will be performed in a professional manner by qualified personnel.

H. **IDEAL COVERAGE**

The running time performance characteristics of the software package sold hereunder are warranted by the vendor as follows:

On a daily basis per _____ of volume the package will require 10 minutes to run; on a monthly basis per _____ of volume the package will require 10 minutes to run.

I. **FALL-BACK ALTERNATIVES**

Fall-backs generally involve negotiated margins for error.

J. **POSSIBLE REMEDIES**

Remedies for performance failure should be provided in the contract. The vendor should be given an opportunity to bring the package up to standard. If this is not possible, the user should be given the right of cancellation or, as a fall-back regarding insubstantial variations in running time, the purchase price should be reduced by some agreed-to formula. For running time which is substantially in excess of warranted time the user should insist upon the right to cancellation and refund.

L. **REFERENCES TO OTHER CLAUSES:** 6-05.

A. **CLAUSE NAME:** Facility Requirements   B. **CLAUSE NO.:** 7-07

C. **CONTRACT TYPES USED IN:** Software   D. **RISK RATING:** 2

E. **INTENT AND SCOPE**

To ensure that the user's facilities will be adequate for proper use of the package. If the package requires certain storage capacity and certain peripheral equipment, the vendor should warrant the adequacy of the user's configuration.

H. **IDEAL COVERAGE**

The software package purchased hereunder will operate in accordance with the specifications attached as Schedule A on an equipment configuration comprised of the following: [here insert the user's equipment configuration]

J. **POSSIBLE REMEDIES**

The remedy for any breach of warranty which results in non-usability must always be cancellation and full refund, plus such damages as can be negotiated.

K. **COMMENTS**

If the user projects any changes in equipment or data processing operations and expects the package to continue to operate in the changed environment, the adequacy of the new environment should also be warranted.

L. **REFERENCES TO OTHER CLAUSES:** 8-06.

A. CLAUSE NAME: Fixes	B. CLAUSE NO.: 7-08
C. CONTRACT TYPES USED IN: Software	D. RISK RATING: 2

E. INTENT AND SCOPE

To ensure vendor responsibility for any corrections or fixes required to be made to the package. This responsibility is absolute although it can be limited in time.

G. STANDARD CLAUSE PROVIDED BY MANUFACTURERS

Maintenance: During the term of this Restricted License Agreement, BASI will maintain the Product to operate with all updated or revised versions of the operating system for which it is herein licensed, supply technical bulletins and updated user guides from time to time and supply Customer with any improvements or modifications to the Product which are not charged for as Options. BASI will correct any errors that are found to exist in the original Product.

If BASI is called upon by Customer to correct an error, and such error is found to be caused by Customer negligence, modification by Customer, Customer supplied data, machine or operator failure, or any other cause not inherent in the original Product, BASI reserves the right to charge Customer for such service on a time and materials basis, at BASI's standard rates then in effect.

Programming Services: For specified licensed programs, IBM will provide programming services after delivery, without additional charge, to correct licensed program errors and issue corrected releases. However, IBM does not guarantee service results or represent or warrant that all errors will be corrected.

The Programming Service Classification of each licensed program will be specified by IBM in the Program Product List for each license. The Programming Service Classification of any licensed program may be changed by IBM upon six months' notice except as provided in the section of this Agreement entitled "Patent and Copyright Indemnification". Some reclassifications may constitute a discontinuance of services.

The Programming Service Classifications are:

Class A

When the Customer encounters a problem which IBM Field Engineering diagnosis indicates is caused by a defect in a current unaltered release of the licensed program, IBM Field Engineering will (1) if the licensed program is inoperable, apply a Program Temporary Fix (PTF) or make a reasonable attempt to develop an emergency by-pass, and (2) prepare an Authorized Program Analysis Report (APAR) and submit it to an IBM Central Programming Service location.

IBM Central Programming Service will respond to any problem caused by a defect in a current unaltered release of the licensed program by issuing a PTF to the originator of the APAR and/or issuing corrected code or notice of availability of corrected code. Corrections will be incorporated into new releases of the licensed program which will be made available to the Customer by IBM. Any other programming services or assistance will be provided at a charge.

Class B

When the Customer encounters a problem which his diagnosis indicates is caused by a licensed program defect, the Customer may submit an APAR to an IBM Central Programming Service location.

IBM Central Programming Service will respond to any problem caused by a defect in a current unaltered release of the licensed program by issuing a PTF to the originator of the APAR and/or issuing corrected code or notice of availability of corrected code. Corrections will be incorporated into new releases of the licensed program which will be made available to the Customer by IBM.

On request, and subject to availability, IBM Systems Engineering personnel will assist the Customer in (1) diagnosing defects and preparing APARs for submission to an IBM Central Programming Service location, and (2) if the licensed program in inoperable, applying a PTF, or making a reasonable attempt to develop an emergency by-pass pending the IBM Central Programming Service response to the APAR submitted. Any other programming services or assistance will be provided at a charge.

Class C

Programming services or assistance will be provided at a charge. Central Programming Service will not be provided, except for corrections applicable to APARs received prior to the date Class C becomes effective for a licensed program previously assigned Class A or Class B.

For program documentation shipped prior to shipment of the complete program, programming services or assistance will be provided at a charge; central programming services will not be provided.

IBM shall have the right to make additional charges for any additional effort required to provide programming services resulting from Customer use of other than a current unaltered release of the licensed program.

During the time that the Equipment is under ADR maintenance, ADR will correct or replace it and/or provide services necessary to remedy any programming error which is attributable to ADR. Such correction, replacement or services will usually be accomplished within 30 days from the date that Customer has identified and notified ADR of any such error in accordance with ADR's prescribed reporting procedures.

H. IDEAL COVERAGE

During the term of this license [for a period of N years after installation] the vendor will correct all errors found by the user, any other user or the vendor. Such corrections shall be made within 24 hours after their discovery, and shall be at no cost to the user.

L. REFERENCES TO OTHER CLAUSES: 7-27, 7-32.

A. **CLAUSE NAME:** Upgrades

B. **CLAUSE NO.:** 7-09

C. **CONTRACT TYPES USED IN:** Software

D. **RISK RATING:** 3

E. **INTENT AND SCOPE**

To the extent the package vendor makes an improvement designed to enhance the operating performance which represents no change in the basic function, such "upgrades" should be made available to the user, at no cost.

G. **STANDARD CLAUSE PROVIDED BY MANUFACTURERS**

Maintenance:

(a) ADR will supply updated Equipment to operate with all updated or revised versions of the operating system for which the Equipment is licensed.

(b) ADR will supply technical bulletins and updated user guides as required to insure their continued usefulness.

(c) ADR will provide such telephone assistance as ADR, in its discretion, considers reasonable to aid Customer in its use of the Equipment.

(d) ADR will make such changes in the Equipment as ADR considers to be logical improvements.

(e) ADR will supply any improvements or modifications to the Equipment which are not charged for as options.

H. **IDEAL COVERAGE**

All "upgrades" made by vendor to the package will be furnished to the user at no cost. For the purposes of this paragraph, the term "upgrades" shall mean improvements in the package which relate to operating performance but do not change the basic function of the package.

K. **COMMENTS**

Additional package options, which alter or improve functions are covered under 7-05.

L. **REFERENCES TO OTHER CLAUSES:** 6-83, 7-05.

A. **CLAUSE NAME:** Source Availability and Access   B. **CLAUSE NO.:** 7-10

C. **CONTRACT TYPES USED IN:** Software   D. **RISK RATING:** 3

E. **INTENT AND SCOPE**

Vendors of software do not always like to make source code available to the user. Upon expiration of vendor maintenance obligations or expiration of warranties, vendors will sometimes release source code. The vendor may treat source code as an extra cost option depending on the extent of the vendor's negotiating strength or may require an escrow as discussed in 7-11.

H. **IDEAL COVERAGE**

The vendor agrees to furnish to the user, upon request and without charge, a single copy of the source code used in the preparation of the package, brought up to date to the date of delivery, after the occurrence of any of the following events, provided that, at the time of request, the user is not in default hereunder: (a) expiration of maintenance provisions of this contract; (b) expiration of _____ years from the date of installation of the package; or (c) when such source code is made available to other users of the package. Upon taking possession thereof, the user agrees that the source code shall be subject to the restrictions on the package itself.

I. **FALL-BACK ALTERNATIVES**

Fall-backs include paying for the source or escrowing it.

K. **COMMENTS**

Remedies can include specific performance (See Chapter IV) or damages equal to the cost to user of producing a source code from its object code, or a listing, which could be substantial.

L. **REFERENCES TO OTHER CLAUSES:** 7-11.

A. CLAUSE NAME: Escrow of Source   **B. CLAUSE NO.:** 7-11

C. CONTRACT TYPES USED IN: Software package   **D. RISK RATING:** 3

E. INTENT AND SCOPE

So long as source code is not available to the user, copies of source programs should be escrowed with an independent third party, to protect against source unavailability in case of business failure of the vendor, upon lapse of its obligation to maintain the package or if some dispute takes place between the vendor and the user which causes the vendor to refuse to make available the necessary source code.

F. PROTECTION AGAINST

Protects against the possibility of total unavailability of source.

H. IDEAL COVERAGE

The vendor agrees to keep, and maintain current, a copy of the source code in escrow with _____, as escrow agent. The escrow agent shall be paid by vendor and shall be authorized to release the source code in accordance with 7-10 or vendor's cessation, for any reason, to do business, or in accordance with the escrow agreement annexed hereto as Exhibit A.

I. FALL–BACK ALTERNATIVES

See 7-10. A user can agree to pay the escrow agent's fees.

J. POSSIBLE REMEDIES

Various remedies can be sought against the escrow agent for failure to perform.

K. COMMENTS

The key to an arrangement like this is the escrow agreement itself. The user should be a party to the escrow agreement, and should see to it that the agreement directs the escrow agent to act on the appropriate occasions. A good escrow agreement can give some access to the source when necessary, even if the vendor objects, provided that the user gives appropriate indemnities or cash deposits to protect vendor and if proper restrictions are imposed on use and disclosure.

L. REFERENCES TO OTHER CLAUSES: 7-10.

A. **CLAUSE NAME:** Rights to Modify Source   B. **CLAUSE NO.:** 7-12

C. **CONTRACT TYPES USED IN:** Software package   D. **RISK RATING:** 3

E. **INTENT AND SCOPE**

Once the source code has been given to the user, the user should have the right to make whatever changes the user deems desirable, provided that the source is used solely for the user's internal purposes. Any maintenance responsibility of the vendor would have to lapse if the user makes changes to the source code.

G. **STANDARD CLAUSE PROVIDED BY MANUFACTURERS**

User agrees that Univac is relieved of all responsibility in the event that modifications made to said program by User affect the performance of the program adversely; Univac will, however, provide User information as to any modifications made by Univac to said program, and User further agrees that any such information will be considered as if part of the original program material.

_____

The Customer may modify any Licensed Program and/or Optional Material, in machine readable form, for his own USE and merge all or part of it into other program material to form an updated work, provided that, upon discontinuance of the license for such Licensed Program, the Licensed Program and Optional Material supplied by IBM will be completely removed from the updated work and destroyed. Any portion of the Licensed Program or Optional Material included in an updated work shall be USED only on the Designated CPU except during a period of temporary transfer as provided in the section of this Agreement entitled "License", and shall remain subject to all other terms of this Agreement.

H. **IDEAL COVERAGE**

When the user shall come into possession of the source code in accordance with this contract, the user shall thereafter have the absolute right to modify it to perform any functions which the user deems desirable, limited, however, to the user's internal use only, and the source code as so modified shall, nonetheless, remain subject to the same restrictions on use, reproduction and disclosure as are contained in this contract with respect to the package itself. Upon any such modification, the vendor shall thereafter be released and discharged from any responsibility to maintain the package, except that vendor shall continue to disclose to user any errors discovered by vendor.

L. **REFERENCES TO OTHER CLAUSES:** 7-10.

A. **CLAUSE NAME:** Compliance with Standards   B. **CLAUSE NO.:** 7-13

C. **CONTRACT TYPES USED IN:** Software   D. **RISK RATING:** 2

E. **INTENT AND SCOPE**

To cause the vendor to represent that the software package, the source code and the documentation comply with basic reasonable standards. These should either be negotiated standards, or external standards such as the standards issued by ANSI. The contract should be specific, and if the vendor or user standards are used, a copy of such standards shall be referred to in, or attached to, the contract.

H. **IDEAL COVERAGE**

Vendor represents that the package and all its elements, including, but not limited to, documentation, and source code, shall meet and be maintained by vendor to conform to the standards set forth on Schedule A and to those issued by the American National Standards Institute with respect to software.

L. **REFERENCES TO OTHER CLAUSES:** 7-01, 8-08.

A. **CLAUSE NAME:** Charges by Type   B. **CLAUSE NO.:** 7-14

C. **CONTRACT TYPES USED IN:** Software   D. **RISK RATING:** 3

E. **INTENT AND SCOPE**

To avoid hidden, unspecified or other surprise charges. Any charges for travel, installation, personnel, documentation copies, modifications, or the source code itself should be explicitly defined in the contract.

H. **IDEAL COVERAGE**

The charges contained in Paragraph _____ hereof are the total of all charges to be made under this contract and, unless specifically to the contrary provided elsewhere herein, no additional charges shall be claimed by vendor for the package, any element thereof, including source and documentation, training, copies of materials, assistance in installation, error correction, upgrades, maintenance, or expenses for any other material or service to be performed hereunder.

K. **COMMENT**

A general contract which covers all charges in one price is best.

L. **REFERENCES TO OTHER CLAUSES:** 6-38, 8-10, 9-09, 10-17.

A. **CLAUSE NAME:** Payment Terms   B. **CLAUSE NO.:** 7-15

C. **CONTRACT TYPES USED IN:** Software   D. **RISK RATING:** 3

E. **INTENT AND SCOPE**

Payment for the package is usually either made upon installation and acceptance or, if the transaction is on a lease basis, on a periodic basis. Payments for incidental charges, if charged as extras, such as installation assistance, documentation copies, travel expenses and the like should be made upon invoice after the services are performed.

H. **IDEAL COVERAGE**

(1) *For purchases:* Payment hereunder shall be made within 30 days after invoice, which invoice shall be sent only in accordance with 7-27. Payment for incidental services separately payable under this contract shall be within 30 days after invoice upon completion of any such services.

(2) *For leases:* For the license herein granted, the user shall pay the vendor a [monthly; quarterly; annual] fee, within _____ days after invoice, during the term of this license.

I. **FALL-BACK ALTERNATIVES**

Most vendors will want some down payment prior to delivery. The down payment can be small, since packages are normally in inventory and require little expense to produce. No matter what payment terms are arrived at, the purchase of a package should involve a hold-back, or series of holdbacks, until the program is fully accepted after a period of normal use. Also see 7-33 for rights of rescission and payment refund after acceptance and payment, during warranty.

L. **REFERENCES TO OTHER CLAUSES:** 6-33, 7-27, 7-33, 8-11.

A. **CLAUSE NAME:** Term of License and Renewal   B. **CLAUSE NO.:** 7-16

C. **CONTRACT TYPES USED IN:** Software package   D. **RISK RATING:** 3

E. **INTENT AND SCOPE**

To define the duration of the license and the right to renew, if any. If the contract is an outright purchase, the term of the license should be perpetual. If the package is leased, at stated periodic payments, the license should be renewable indefinitely.

G. **STANDARD CLAUSE PROVIDED BY MANUFACTURERS**

Term, License Fee, and Maintenance: This License shall be effective on the date it is accepted by ADR at Princeton, New Jersey, and shall remain in force permanently. License fee is $_____, payable as follows:

☐ Single payment of $_____ due 30 days after the date the Equipment is placed in operation at Customer's location.

☐ One payment of $_____ due 30 days after the date the Equipment is placed in operation at Customer's location, and two equal payments of $_____ due one and two years respectively thereafter.

☐ One payment of $_____ due 30 days after the date the Equipment is placed in operation at Customer's location and $_____ per month for _____ consecutive months thereafter.

Term: This Agreement is effective from the date on which it is accepted by IBM and shall remain in force until terminated by the Customer upon one month's prior written notice, or by IBM as provided below.

Certain programs licensed hereunder shall be made available for a pre-installation testing period (testing period) as specified by IBM in the Program Product list on the last page of this Agreement or in a Supplement to License Agreement for IBM Program Products. The testing period will begin 10 days after shipment of the program by IBM and will end upon expiration of the specified period, or upon the Customer achieving productive use of the program, whichever is earlier. After this testing period the minimum use period for each license under this Agreement is one month from the commencement of monthly charges. For programs for which IBM does not specify a testing period, the minimum use period will begin 10 days after shipment of the program by IBM. Any license under this Agreement may be discontinued by the Customer upon written notice at any time during the testing period, or at the conclusion of the minimum use period, or at any time thereafter upon one month's prior written notice. IBM may discontinue any license or terminate this Agreement if the Customer fails to comply with any of the terms and conditions of this Agreement, or as provided in the section of this Agreement entitled "Patent and Copyright Indemnification". Notice of discontinuance of any program license will be notice of discontinuance of any license for optional material obtained in connection with such program license. Notice of discontinuance of any or all licenses shall not be considered notice of termination of this Agreement unless that is specifically stated.

H. **IDEAL COVERAGE**

User's right to use the package shall continue for the term of this agreement [in perpetuity]. The term hereof may be extended by user for additional one-year periods in perpetuity upon the same terms and conditions as are provided herein with respect to the original term. Failure by user to give notice of termination prior to the expiration of the term hereof or any extension shall be deemed renewal for such one-year period.

K. COMMENTS

The clause, as drafted, is a type of automatic renewal provision. It has been so drafted to avoid a forfeiture by user of a license for failure to give notice of renewal. The clause can also be drawn so as to require vendor to give written notice of expiration sometime prior thereto, to be followed by user notice of termination or renewal. This puts the onus on the vendor.

A user can often negotiate a reduced rental for renewals after some stated number of years or even, possibly, a free license, when the aggregate payments total the purchase price.

L. REFERENCES TO OTHER CLAUSES: 9-10, 9-11.

A. **CLAUSE NAME:** Non-taxability as Property   B. **CLAUSE NO.:** 7-17

C. **CONTRACT TYPES USED IN:** Software   D. **RISK RATING:** 3

E. **INTENT AND SCOPE**

A stipulation that the software package is not taxable under personal property tax laws is desirable, though self-serving.

G. **STANDARD CLAUSE PROVIDED BY MANUFACTURERS**

Taxes and Duties: There shall be added to any charges under this Agreement, amounts equal to any tariff, duties and/or sales or use tax or any tax in lieu thereof imposed by any government or governmental agency with respect to the services rendered by ADR, the Equipment or its use, the license of the Equipment, or this Agreement itself.

H. **IDEAL COVERAGE**

The software package licensed hereunder is non-tangible property, inasmuch as it is merely a license to use a proprietary method and its tangible attributes are only incidental. If personal property taxes are levied upon the package, they shall be borne by _____ .

K. **COMMENTS**

This clause, however hypnotic, does not bind any taxing authority and will be readily disregarded by it. It may have some value in the ultimate tax litigation, but the reality will be infinitely more important than the parties' description or agreement.

Normally personal property taxes are levied upon the *owner* of the property. This suggests that no title transfer should take place for a package and that the transaction should be called a license, perpetual or otherwise.

L. **REFERENCES TO OTHER CLAUSES:** 6-35.

A. **CLAUSE NAME:** Quiet Enjoyment   B. **CLAUSE NO.:** 7-18

C. **CONTRACT TYPES USED IN:** Software   D. **RISK RATING:** 3

E. **INTENT AND SCOPE**

To ensure that the license for the package will be undisturbed, provided only that payments for use of the package have been properly made.

H. **IDEAL COVERAGE**

The user shall be entitled during the term of this license and all renewals to use the package without disturbance, subject only to its obligation to make the required payments hereunder. Vendor represents that this agreement is not subject or subordinate to any right of vendor's creditors, or if such subordination exists, that the agreement or instrument creating the same provides for non-disturbance of the user so long as it shall not be in default hereunder.

L. **REFERENCES TO OTHER CLAUSES:** 5-02, 7-19, 9-15, 10-10.

A. **CLAUSE NAME:** Business Termination Rights   B. **CLAUSE NO.:** 7-19

C. **CONTRACT TYPES USED IN:** Software package   D. **RISK RATING:** 3

E. **INTENT AND SCOPE**

To give the user a perpetual license in the event of business termination regardless of the term of license heretofore stated.

H. **IDEAL COVERAGE**

In the event that vendor shall, for any reason, cease to conduct business the within license shall automatically and without notice be converted into a perpetual license and shall thereafter be free of any cost.

I. **FALL–BACK ALTERNATIVES**

The fall-back is to negotiate a right to perpetual renewal, with rights of quiet enjoyment (see 7-16 and 7-18), but subject to payment obligations. If maintenance is an element in the transaction, the license after business termination should be at a reduced fee.

K. **COMMENTS**

The vendor's creditors, if they are sophisticated, will normally prohibit the vendor to contract for free licenses upon business termination, since the package licenses are probably part of the basis for loans and constitute a potential for recoupment. A reduced license fee, based on loss of maintenance and error corrections, will probably not violate the vendor's loan agreements.

L. **REFERENCES TO OTHER CLAUSES:** 5-02, 7-18, 8-19, 9-18.

A. **CLAUSE NAME:** Price Protection on License   B. **CLAUSE NO.:** 7-20

C. **CONTRACT TYPES USED IN:** Software contracts   D. **RISK RATING:** 2

E. **INTENT AND SCOPE**

Since the software package is normally already developed prior to its initial delivery, and since no additional costs are incurred by reason of its continued use by user, it is desirable to ensure that the license fee remains constant.

H. **IDEAL COVERAGE**

The License fee stipulated hereunder shall not be increased during the term of this license and all renewals hereof.

I. **FALL-BACK ALTERNATIVES**

If maintenance is included, a limited increase in that portion of the license may be allowable to compensate for increased costs.

K. **COMMENTS**

A user may be able to negotiate a reduced license fee for use after some specified period of time. Vendors who offer outright purchases, as well as leases, often offer reduced rentals after they have recouped the equivalent of a full purchase price, after giving effect to time differentials.

L. **REFERENCES TO OTHER CLAUSES:** 6-41, 7-16, 7-21, 9-12.

A. CLAUSE NAME: Price Protection on Maintenance and Enhancements   **B. CLAUSE NO.:** 7-21

C. CONTRACT TYPES USED IN: Software package   **D. RISK RATING:** 3

E. INTENT AND SCOPE

To ensure, to the extent that maintenance and enhancements are separately paid for, that such charges will be protected from significant increases. It is desirable to attach a rate table of maintenance and enhancement charges, and to stipulate the limits of increased charge time.

H. IDEAL COVERAGE

Schedule A attached hereto represents vendor's current charges for maintenance and enhancement services. Said charges shall not be increased by vendor for _____ months after installation. Thereafter, said charges to user shall be lower of (a) then prevailing charges of vendor or (b) current charges increased by _____% for each year after installation.

I. FALL-BACK ALTERNATIVES

Escalation formulas or criteria can be negotiated.

L. REFERENCES TO OTHER CLAUSES: 6-43, 6-44, 7-20.

A. CLAUSE NAME: Financials Available   B. CLAUSE NO.: 7-22

C. CONTRACT TYPES USED IN: Software package, services   D. RISK RATING: 2

E. INTENT AND SCOPE

To require the vendor to furnish financial statements on a periodic basis.

F. PROTECTION AGAINST

Protects against vendor's financial decline without early warning to the user, so that user can make appropriate plans, if any.

H. IDEAL COVERAGE

The vendor agrees to furnish to user copies of all of its financial statements quarterly, not later than 45 days after the close of each of vendor's fiscal quarters, except its year-end statements which shall be furnished not later than 90 days after fiscal year-end and shall be audited.

L. REFERENCES TO OTHER CLAUSES: 5-02, 8-21, 9-27.

A. **CLAUSE NAME:** Delivery B. **CLAUSE NO.:** 7-23

C. **CONTRACT TYPES USED IN:** Software D. **RISK RATING:** 1

E. **INTENT AND SCOPE**

To describe the delivery schedule for the software package. To the extent a package has already been delivered to other users, delivery normally poses very few problems, unless the package needs adaptation for the particular user.

G. **STANDARD CLAUSE PROVIDED BY MANUFACTURERS**

Delivery: When available from the Library, licensed programs will be shipped to customers generally within one month after confirmation of order, subject to conditions beyond IBM's control, unless the Customer requests a later delivery date. Announced licensed programs will be included in the Library in accordance with IBM's estimated availability date for each licensed program. However, IBM does not represent or warrant the shipment or availability dates will be met.

Program storage media (Magnetic tapes and disks) will be provided at a charge by IBM if not supplied by the Customer. Licensed programs will be shipped to the Customer without charge.

H. **IDEAL COVERAGE**

The entire package, all documentation, and the necessary installation assistance shall be delivered at the times and in the order described on Schedule A. No item or element shall, for any purpose, be deemed delivered if a prior-listed item is undelivered.

L. **REFERENCES TO OTHER CLAUSES:** 6-68, 7-24, 7-27.

A. **CLAUSE NAME:** Delivery Failure　　　　　　B. **CLAUSE NO.:** 7-24

C. **CONTRACT TYPES USED IN:** Software package　　D. **RISK RATING:** 2

E. **INTENT AND SCOPE**

If the vendor fails to deliver all or any essential part of the package, the usefulness of the package will undoubtedly be significantly impaired. Failure to deliver the necessary documentation is almost as bad as failing to deliver the object code itself. As a result delivery failure of any component should be deemed to be a total failure of delivery. At a point, continued failure to deliver should be deemed grounds for cancellation.

H. **IDEAL COVERAGE**

A failure to deliver any component of the package, whether documentation, object code, source code or installation support, shall be deemed to be a total failure to deliver and the package shall not be deemed delivered until all of its elements are delivered. If such delivery failure persists for more than _____ days after the scheduled delivery date, the user shall have the right to cancel the contract.

J. **POSSIBLE REMEDIES**

There should be damages on a per diem basis for late delivery and damages upon contract cancellation similar to those discussed for hardware transactions.

L. **REFERENCES TO OTHER CLAUSES:** 6-72, 6-92, 6-93.

A. **CLAUSE NAME:** Installation and Modification Assistance   B. **CLAUSE NO.:** 7-25

C. **CONTRACT TYPES USED IN:** Software, software packages   D. **RISK RATING:** 2

E. **INTENT AND SCOPE**

To the extent that installation and modification assistance is included as a part of the package, such services should be defined explicitly.

H. **IDEAL COVERAGE**

Included in the within transaction, without additional cost to the user are the following vendor supplied services:

For installation assistance and supervision, the full-time services of a qualified installation engineer, for a period of not less than _____ days or until the package has successfully completed the acceptance tests described in 7-27; for modification to meet the required specifications, all manpower necessary to make such modification within the prescribed time periods.

L. **REFERENCES TO OTHER CLAUSES:** 6-19, 7-26.

A. **CLAUSE NAME:** Support Requirements   B. **CLAUSE NO.:** 7-26

C. **CONTRACT TYPES USED IN:** Software package   D. **RISK RATING:** 3

E. **INTENT AND SCOPE**

To ensure, if necessary, that during the life of the contract, certain types of necessary support is furnished by vendor in order to make periodic changes or to update the package to reflect changing requirements.

H. **IDEAL COVERAGE**

During the last 30 days immediately preceding the anniversary date of the installation of the package and annually thereafter, vendor will furnish to user, at user's site, without charge, the services of a qualified technician or technicians for _____ man hours to make such modifications or adjustments to the package and its components or to user systems related to the package as user may request.

L. **REFERENCES TO OTHER CLAUSES:** 6-19, 7-25.

A. **CLAUSE NAME:** Acceptance Method   B. **CLAUSE NO.:** 7-27

C. **CONTRACT TYPES USED IN:** Software package   D. **RISK RATING:** 1

E. **INTENT AND SCOPE**

To define a methodology for acceptance of a software package. The method under which the package is tested is largely a function of the manner in which the specifications have been formulated. Basic operation of the package should be attempted, on the equipment configuration on which it will run, and should involve operation of software systems, operating systems and hardware components which would be operated under normal operating conditions.

F. **PROTECTION AGAINST**

Protects against the purchase of packages which do not successfully or efficiently perform.

H. **IDEAL COVERAGE**

Upon notification that the package is installed and ready for use, the user shall perform the following acceptance test, which shall be completed within _____ days from the date of such notification. The acceptance test shall be conducted on the user's site and upon the configuration described in 7-07 to determine whether:

a) the package meets the specifications, performs the functions and does not exceed the facilities usage limits all as required by 7-01 and the standards described in 7-13

b) the run time meets the requirements of 7-06

c) the package is capable of running on a repetitive basis on a variety of data, without failure.

d) the documentation and support meets the requirements of 7-02 and 7-25.

If the package successfully meets these acceptance tests, the user will notify the vendor that the package is being accepted and the term of the license shall commence. If the user shall fail to give notice of acceptance or of non-acceptance within _____ days after notification by vendor of installation and readiness for use, the package shall be deemed accepted by the user.

If the package fails to meet any of the foregoing specifications, the user shall forthwith notify the vendor and vendor shall have _____ days thereafter within which to correct, modify or improve the package to meet such level of specifications and user shall thereafter have an additional _____ days to re-conduct the acceptance tests. Failure of the package to meet the acceptance specifications upon the second user test, shall, at user's option, be deemed a failure by vendor to deliver the package and user shall have all of the rights afforded to it as are applicable on non-delivery hereunder.

L. **REFERENCES TO OTHER CLAUSES:** 6-51, 7-24, 8-14.

A. **CLAUSE NAME**: Destruction on Termination B. **CLAUSE NO.**: 7-28

C. **CONTRACT TYPES USED IN**: Software package D. **RISK RATING**: 4

E. **INTENT AND SCOPE**

When a contract for a software package expires it is usually the responsibility of the user to return or destroy all copies of materials, since they are proprietary to the vendor.

F. **PROTECTION AGAINST**

Protects against vendor claims of possible trade secret infringement.

G. **STANDARD CLAUSE PROVIDED BY MANUFACTURERS**

Discontinuance: Within one month after the date of discontinuance of any license under this Agreement, the Customer will furnish IBM a completed IBM Program Product Certificate of Discontinuance certifying that through his best effort, and to the best of his knowledge, the original and all copies, in whole or in part, in any form, including partial copies in modifications, of the licensed program and any optional material received from IBM or made in connection with such license have been destroyed, except that, upon prior written authorization from IBM, the Customer may retain a copy for archive purposes. However, where the Customer has licensed a successive version of the program, which carries a different program number, the Customer may retain the prior version of the program for backup purposes for a period not to exceed three months following the date of discontinuance. The Customer agrees that any such backup copy will be used only in the event of a problem in the successive version of the program which prevents its use. In no case will both the prior and the successive versions of the program be used simultaneously for productive purposes. Within one month following this three month period, the Customer will furnish IBM a completed IBM Program Product Certificate of Discontinuance as indicated above.

H. **IDEAL COVERAGE**

Upon expiration of this contract the user will either return all copies of the package and all of its elements, or will represent in writing to the vendor that all such copies have been destroyed.

K. **COMMENTS**

The clause is primarily for vendor protection. It can be useful, however, to the user, by setting forth a procedure which, if followed, can avoid claims that the user was responsible for disclosure of vendor's proprietary material.

L. **REFERENCES TO OTHER CLAUSES**: 5-13, 9-22, 9-23.

A. **CLAUSE NAME:** Guarantee of Ownership   B. **CLAUSE NO.:** 7-29

C. **CONTRACT TYPES USED IN:** Software package   D. **RISK RATING:** 3

E. **INTENT AND SCOPE**

To assure the user that the vendor is the owner of the package and has the unrestricted right to license it to the user.

F. **PROTECTION AGAINST**

Protects against infringement claims.

H. **IDEAL COVERAGE**

The vendor warrants that it is the sole owner of the package and has full power and authority to grant the rights herein granted without the consent of any other person and will indemnify and hold the user harmless from and against any loss, cost, liability and expense (including reasonable counsel fees) arising out of any breach or claimed breach of this warranty. During the pendency of any claim against vendor or user with respect to vendor's ownership and/or authority, user may withhold payment of any sums otherwise required to be paid hereunder.

I. **FALL-BACK ALTERNATIVES**

During the pendency of claims, payments can be escrowed, if the vendor refuses to agree to withholding.

K. **COMMENTS**

The withholding or escrow of payments is recommended in order to provide user with a fund to pay the adverse claimant, if successful. Since many software package vendors are not financially strong, their indemnities may be of little practical value. If there is a possibility that the user will owe damages to an adverse claimant, it is helpful to assemble a fund out of payments otherwise due vendor.

L. **REFERENCES TO OTHER CLAUSES:** 5-07, 7-30, 8-09, 9-28, 9-30.

A. **CLAUSE NAME:** Infringement   B. **CLAUSE NO.:** 7-30

C. **CONTRACT TYPES USED IN:** Software package   D. **RISK RATING:** 3

E. **INTENT AND SCOPE**

To assure the user that the package does not infringe upon the rights of others.

G. **STANDARD CLAUSE PROVIDED BY MANUFACTURERS**

Patents: ADR agrees at its own cost to defend, or at its option to settle, any claim, suit or proceeding brought against Customer on the issue of infringement of any United States patent by the Equipment, providing Customer notifies ADR promptly in writing of any such claim, suit or proceeding and gives ADR full information and assistance to settle and/or to defend. ADR shall not be liable for any costs or expenses incurred without ADR's written authorization.

THE FOREGOING STATES THE ENTIRE WARRANTY BY ADR AND THE EX-CLUSIVE REMEDY OF CUSTOMER WITH RESPECT TO ANY ALLEGED PATENT INFRINGEMENT.

Patent and Copyright Indemnification: IBM will defend at its expense any action brought against the Customer to the extent that it is based on a claim that licensed programs or optional materials, used within the scope of the license hereunder, infringe a copyright in the United States or a United States patent, and subject to the limitation of liability stated herein, IBM will pay any costs, damages, and attorney fees finally awarded against the Customer in such action which are attributable to such claim, provided that, the Customer notifies IBM promptly in writing of the claim and IBM may fully participate in the defense and/or agrees to any settlement of such claim. Should the licensed programs or optional materials become, or in IBM's opinion be likely to become, the subject of a claim of infringement of a copyright or a patent, IBM may procure for the Customer the right to continue using the licensed programs or optional materials, or replace or modify them to make them noninfringing. If neither of the foregoing alternatives is reasonably available to IBM, then IBM may discontinue the licensed program and/or optional materials upon one month's written notice to the Customer. If, however, the licensed program and/or optional materials is not the subject of a claim of copyright infringement, the Customer may notify IBM in writing during the one month after IBM's notice of discontinuance that the Customer elects to continue to be licensed with respect to the licensed program or optional materials until there has been an injunction or the claim has been withdrawn, and agrees to undertake at the Customer's expense the defense of any action against the Customer and to indemnify IBM with respect to all costs, damages, and attorney fees attributable to such continued use after such notice is given to IBM; it being understood that IBM may participate at its expense in the defense of any such action if such claim is against IBM. Upon IBM's written notice of discontinuance to the Customer, a licensed program with Programming Service Classification A or B will be changed to Programming Service Classification C. IBM shall have no liability for any claim of copyright or patent infringement based on (1) use of other than a current unaltered release of the licensed program or optional materials available from IBM if such infringement would have been avoided by the use of a current unaltered release of the licensed program or optional materials available from IBM or (2) use or combination of the licensed program or optional material with non-IBM programs or data if such infringement would have been avoided by the use or combination of the licensed program or optional material with other programs or data. The foregoing states the entire liability of IBM with respect to infringement of any copyrights or patents by the licensed programs or optional materials or any parts thereof.

H. IDEAL COVERAGE

Vendor warrants that the package is original to vendor and that neither the package nor any of its elements nor the use thereof does or will violate or infringe upon any patent, copyright, trade secret or other property right of any other person, and vendor will indemnify and hold the user harmless from and against any loss, cost, liability and expenses (including reasonable counsel fees) arising out of any breach or claimed breach of this warranty. During the pendency of any claim against vendor or user with respect to infringement, user may withhold payment of any sums otherwise required to be paid hereunder.

I. FALL-BACK ALTERNATIVES

See fall-backs discussed in 7-29.

K. COMMENTS

In any areas where the user has reason for concern (such as a transaction with an ex-employee of a package vendor, who is offering a "competitive" package) it may be wise to require the vendor to furnish an indemnity bond. Users making use of packages which infringe upon proprietary rights of third parties can be sued. See chapter 4.

L. REFERENCES TO OTHER CLAUSES: 5-28, 7-29, 8-09, 9-29, 9-30.

A. CLAUSE NAME: Guarantee of Operation   **B. CLAUSE NO.:** 7-31

C. CONTRACT TYPES USED IN: Software package   **D. RISK RATING:** 2

E. INTENT AND SCOPE

To warrant continued performance over an extended time period. The acceptance test determines that the package will operate in accordance with the specifications. The continuation of such operation cannot be determined by an acceptance test, unless the test is extended for a long period of time. As a result, a warranty of continued operation, similar to the warranty provided by a vendor of equipment, should be included in a software contract.

H. IDEAL COVERAGE

The vendor warrants that the software package delivered hereunder is free from defects in manufacture or materials and will continue to meet the specifications described in this contract for _____ months after installation and vendor will, without charge to user, correct any such defects and make such additions, modifications or adjustments to the package as may be necessary to keep the package in operating order, in accordance with such specifications, during such time period.

J. POSSIBLE REMEDIES

Provide for user rights to get support elsewhere and charge to vendor.

K. COMMENTS

A procedure should be established in the contract for the giving of notices of defects or failures, the time in which responses and corrections must be commenced and completed and the remedies for non-compliance. The reader may refer back to the clauses on hardware for guidance in these areas.

L. REFERENCES TO OTHER CLAUSES: 6-47, 6-62, 6-63, 7-33.

A. **CLAUSE NAME:** Period of Free Maintenance   B. **CLAUSE NO.:** 7-32

C. **CONTRACT TYPES USED IN:** Software package   D. **RISK RATING:** 2

E. **INTENT AND SCOPE**

To ensure that warranties made by vendor are kept. In the same way that a warranty of freedom from defects and workmanship in hardware contracts provides for free maintenance and repairs, a warranty of continued operation, such as provided in 7-31, should require free maintenance, repair and adjustment of a software package.

G. **STANDARD CLAUSE PROVIDED BY MANUFACTURERS**

During the first _____ year(s) of this Permanent License Agreement, ADR will maintain the Equipment to operate with all updated or revised versions of the operating system for which it is herein licensed, supply technical bulletins and updated user guides from time to time and supply Customer with any improvements or modifications to the Equipment which are not charged for as options. Thereafter customer may continue to receive this maintenance upon Customer's execution of ADR's standard Maintenance Agreement, and payment of ADR's then-current charge for such maintenance.

H. **IDEAL COVERAGE**

During N months subsequent to installation of the package vendor will, without charge to user, furnish such materials and services as shall be necessary to correct any defects in the operation of the package and to maintain it in good working order in accordance with the specifications contained in this contract.

J. **POSSIBLE REMEDIES**

See comments to 7-31.

K. **COMMENTS**

See comments to 7-31 for a discussion of response times.

L. **REFERENCES TO OTHER CLAUSES:** 6-47, 7-31, 7-33.

A. CLAUSE NAME: Rescission During Warranty Period   **B. CLAUSE NO.:** 7-33

C. CONTRACT TYPES USED IN: Software package   **D. RISK RATING:** 1

E. INTENT AND SCOPE

To provide a means for terminating the contract if the package does not properly perform. If, for any reason, the package fails to meet functional specifications during the warranty period and is not, or cannot be, repaired, the user should have the right to return the package and receive a refund.

G. STANDARD CLAUSE PROVIDED BY MANUFACTURERS

If for any reason Customer is not satisfied with the Equipment, Customer may return it within thirty (30) days from the date it was first placed in operation at Customer's location and this License will be cancelled without any financial obligation on the part of the Customer. (ADR)

H. IDEAL COVERAGE

During a period of six months from date of acceptance, the contract can be terminated by the user without penalty. At such termination, the user's sole responsibility shall be to destroy or return all materials hereunder (See 7-28) and to pay the appropriate license fee for the period of use.

I. FALL-BACK ALTERNATIVES

In the event of any breach of vendor's warranties and/or covenants contained in 7-31 or 7-32 of this contract, or if, for any other reason, except only the fault of the user, the package does not operate in accordance with the specifications provided in this contract and vendor has not adjusted, or cannot adjust the same within _____ days after notice to vendor, user shall have the right at its option to cancel this contract and to receive the return of all sums theretofore paid by user to vendor in addition to such other damages to which user may be legally entitled.

K. COMMENTS

ADR's clause, shown above, is excellent from the user point of view, except for the thirty day time limit. Unfortunately, no serious appraisal can be made that quickly; more unfortunately, few vendors will extend the "no obligation" trial period for much longer. Resourceful users will attempt to incorporate both "G" and "H" above into their contracts.

L. REFERENCES TO OTHER CLAUSES: 7-28, 7-31, 7-32, 8-16.

A. **CLAUSE NAME:** Freedom of Use   B. **CLAUSE NO.:** 7-34

C. **CONTRACT TYPES USED IN:** Software package   D. **RISK RATING:** 3

E. **INTENT AND SCOPE**

To afford user the rights to unrestricted use of the package, provided such use is for the user alone.

G. **STANDARD CLAUSE PROVIDED BY MANUFACTURERS**

License: Each program license granted under this Agreement authorizes the Customer to use the licensed program in any machine readable form on a single central processing unit designated by type/serial number and its associated units (together referred to as CPU) or on the CPU designated under another then current license for the identical Program Product. Each optional material license granted under this Agreement authorizes the Customer to use the optional material in any machine readable form on the designated CPU or on the CPU designated under another then current license for the identical Program Product. A separate license is required for each CPU on which the licensed program and/or optional materials in any machine readable form will be used, provided, however, that the license granted under this Agreement for the designated CPU shall be temporarily transferred to (1) one back-up CPU if the designated CPU is inoperative due to malfunction, or during the performance of preventive maintenance, engineering changes or changes in features or model, until the designated CPU is restored to operative status and processing of the data already entered into the back-up CPU is completed, and (2) to one other CPU for assembly or compilation of the licensed program if the specifications of the designated CPU are such that the licensed program cannot be assembled or compiled on the designated CPU. For each program for which IBM specifies "Installation License Applies" in the Program Product List on the last page of this Agreement or in a Supplement to the License Agreement for IBM Program Products, the reference to "a single Central Processing Unit designated by type/serial number and its associated units" in this section and all references to "the designated CPU" shall mean "the designated CPU and any other CPU located in the same installation as the designated CPU". For the purposes of this Agreement "same installation" shall mean a single room or contiguous rooms unless otherwise agreed to in writing by IBM and "use" is defined as copying any portion of the licensed program's and/or optional material's instructions or data from storage units or media into the CPU for processing. Licenses granted under this Agreement authorize the Customer to utilize licensed programs and/or optional materials, in printed form, in support of the use of such licensed programs and/or optional materials in machine readable form.

Licensed programs and related optional materials which are provided by IBM in printed form under the terms of this Agreement (referred to as program documentation) can be shipped to the Customer by IBM up to six months prior to shipment of the complete program (which includes machine readable materials). Each program license authorizes the Customer to utilize program documentation which is shipped prior to shipment of the complete program, provided that the Customer agrees not to use any such program documentation in machine readable form for any purpose. Within the six month period following the date of shipment of the program documentation by IBM, the Customer agrees that he will request that the complete program be shipped prior to, or at the conclusion of, the six month period or will discontinue his license for that particular program. The provisions for discontinuing a program license hereunder are in addition to those set forth in the section entitled "Term". The provisions of the section entitled "Discontinuance" apply to all program licenses even though only program documentation is shipped.

This Agreement and any of the licenses, programs or materials to which it applies may not be assigned, sublicensed or otherwise transferred by the Customer without prior written consent from IBM. No right to print or copy, in whole or in part, the licensed programs or optional materials is granted hereby except as hereinafter expressly provided.

Said program material is to be used by User for his own use and for no other purpose unless the written consent of Univac is first obtained.

H. IDEAL COVERAGE

The user may use the package for any purpose (and at any location) whatsoever, without restriction, subject only to the restrictions herein elsewhere contained with respect to user disclosure, reproduction or permitting others to use the package.

L. REFERENCES TO OTHER CLAUSES: 6-78, 6-79.

A. CLAUSE NAME: Definition of Stages and Tasks   **B. CLAUSE NO.:** 8-01

C. CONTRACT TYPES USED IN: Software development   **D. RISK RATING:** 2

E. INTENT AND SCOPE

To define stages and tasks in a software development contract. Figure 8-1 is a comprehensive list of tasks in a software development project which should be consulted.

H. IDEAL COVERAGE

Schedule A attached hereto describes specifically the nature and goals of each task to be performed by vendor hereunder, when each shall be performed and the order of performance.

I. FALL-BACK ALTERNATIVES

Schedule A may also list estimated completion percentages of each phase, used to determine payment amounts. See 8-11.

L. REFERENCES TO OTHER CLAUSES: 8-02, 8-04, 9-01.

A. CLAUSE NAME: Deliverables by Stage   **B. CLAUSE NO.:** 8-02

C. CONTRACT TYPES USED IN: Software development   **D. RISK RATING:** 1

E. INTENT AND SCOPE

To define explicitly the products of each task or stage, for purposes of acceptance and quality specification. Figure 8-1 also identifies specific deliverables.

H. IDEAL COVERAGE

Schedule A to 8-01 also contains a detailed description of the required products to be delivered by vendor upon completion of each task, and the form each product shall take.

I. FALL-BACK ALTERNATIVES

Standards established under 8-03 could be used to define deliverables of each stage.

L. REFERENCES TO OTHER CLAUSES: 9-01.

A. CLAUSE NAME: Documentation and Documentation Standards **B. CLAUSE NO.:** 8-03

C. CONTRACT TYPES USED IN: Software development **D. RISK RATING:** 2

E. INTENT AND SCOPE

To require the vendor to provide the necessary documentation, meeting the documentation standards established by the user. Documentation is an integral part of the product, without which the user will be unable to make effective use of the software.

H. IDEAL COVERAGE

The vendor shall deliver the following documentation:

Manual Type	Approximate Number of Pages	To Comply With Following Standards Listed on Schedule A
User manual		
Systems manual		
Operating manual		
Program manual		
Manufacturer manual		

All documentation delivered hereunder shall conform to the documentation standards attached as Schedule A.

J. POSSIBLE REMEDIES

In the event quality standards are not met it may be possible for the user to subcontract the development of documentation to the proper quality standards, and to charge that cost to the vendor. It is almost always preferable to have the vendor who develops the programs develop the documentation as well, however.

L. REFERENCES TO OTHER CLAUSES: 7-02, 8-02, 9-03, 9-07.

A. CLAUSE NAME: Project Scope　　　　　　　　**B. CLAUSE NO.:** 8-04

C. CONTRACT TYPES USED IN: Software development　　**D. RISK RATING:** 2

E. INTENT AND SCOPE

To define the scope of the contract, by function and performance characteristics. This identifies the range of the system, its scope and boundaries, and the basic function to be performed by the end product.

G. STANDARD CLAUSE PROVIDED BY MANUFACTURERS

The Scope of Effort, Original Materials to be delivered to the Customer, Customer Responsibilities and Completion Criteria are as follows:

Statement of Work: IBM will provide services to the Customer in an effort to accomplish the Statement of Work referenced on the last page of this Agreement. These services will be provided up to a maximum of the estimated number of hours at the stated hourly rate also shown on the last page of this Agreement.

In providing these services, IBM will exert its best efforts to accomplish the Statement of Work within this estimated number of hours. The Customer and IBM recognize, however, that due to the nature of work being performed, the Statement of Work may not be accomplished before the estimated number of hours of services have been provided.

Services: This Agreement shall cover all assistance in the installation and use of data processing products by IBM systems engineering personnel at the Customer's request, including, but not limited to, special studies, programming and application design and development, systems analysis and design, conversion and implementation planning, and installation evaluation. These services may be performed at either the Customer's or IBM's premises.

H. IDEAL COVERAGE

The project scope is defined in the scope statement attached hereto as Schedule A:

K. COMMENTS

Since development contracts often cannot be defined with exactitude and sometimes shift in direction and emphasis during the course of development, it is wise to include, as part of, or in addition to, the specific listing of tasks, as in 8-01, a more generalized and broad description of the functional and operational goals of the project and its scope. This will assist both parties in maintaining direction and may protect the user against being required to pay the vendor for excursions into unrelated areas.

L. REFERENCES TO OTHER CLAUSES: 8-01, 10-18

A. CLAUSE NAME: Specifications and Scope by Stage   **B. CLAUSE NO.:** 8-05

C. CONTRACT TYPES USED IN: Software development   **D. RISK RATING:** 2

E. INTENT AND SCOPE

To define explicitly the specifications of each component by stage. It may not be feasible at the outset to define the specifications and scope of later stages of the project, in which case the contract should define the point at which such additional specifications will be developed, and the points at it which it may be necessary to provide for cancellation rights. Certainly, at some point, if prior specifications have not been or cannot be met, or the cost of further implementation is too expensive or substantially exceeds previous estimates, then cancellation should be available to the user. It is best for the user to provide for its right to cancel the contract at any stage, without any cause required.

H. IDEAL COVERAGE

The parties acknowledge that the detailed specifications of each phase attached hereto as Schedule A to 8-01 contain only outlines and no detailed specifications with respect to phases [X] through [Z]. Such specifications will be developed by the parties at the conclusion of phase [D], whereupon they shall become a part of this contract. If the parties cannot agree within _____ days after the completion of Phase [D] to detailed specifications for such phases, the contract may be terminated at any time after the completion of said phase [D] by user or by vendor after completion of phase [W].

L. REFERENCES TO OTHER CLAUSES: 8-01, 8-04, 8-14, 8-16, 9-03.

A. **CLAUSE NAME:**   Facility Requirements   B. **CLAUSE NO.:**   8-06

C. **CONTRACT TYPES USED IN:**   Software development   D. **RISK RATING:**   3

E. **INTENT AND SCOPE**

To ensure that the developed software will be functional and efficient on user's equipment. The expected limits of configuration utilization in terms of memory usage, facility
usage, peripheral equipment usage, etc., must all be clearly defined, or else a system will
be developed which might use far more facilities than are readily or economically available.

H. **IDEAL COVERAGE**

The software system being developed hereunder will be designed by vendor to operate on a
facility comprising the following components, and subject to the following limits on times
of operation and equipment utilization: [List]

K. **COMMENTS**

It should be noted that facility usage limitations can also include the use of data entry
facilities, bursting and binding facilities, and such other facilities as are involved, in addition to those associated with direct operation of the computer system itself.

Obviously, the user must define for the vendor the permissible burden on equipment
and operations that the software being developed must not exceed. Otherwise, a set of
programs can be developed by vendor which may be less efficient than those now being
used, or, if the system is a new one, the new program can be too expensive to operate
even if it produces the desired output.

L. **REFERENCES TO OTHER CLAUSES:**   7-07, 8-01, 9-06.

A. CLAUSE NAME: Constraints on Resource Usage by Vendor   **B. CLAUSE NO.:** 8-07

C. CONTRACT TYPES USED IN: Software development   **D. RISK RATING:** 3

E. INTENT AND SCOPE

Under certain conditions the software vendor is requested to use resources of the user, to reduce total cost. For example, it is less costly to the user if the vendor uses the user's equipment for testing than it is to purchase equipment time elsewhere. Vendor use of equipment should be constrained, however, so that the vendor does not take advantage of this "free" equipment availability, and so that user operations are not interfered with.

H. IDEAL COVERAGE

The user will make available to the vendor, for vendor's use in fulfillment of this contract, the following resource types and amounts:

(a) Data entry personnel and equipment for _____ data entry lines.

(b) _____ hours of computer time, as selected by vendor from the availability list set forth in Schedule A.

(c) Desks and conventional office facilities for location of _____ employees of the vendor.

In the event the amounts above are exceeded vendor will reduce the contract amount by the following:

$_____ per line of data entry
$_____ per machine hour, etc.

K. COMMENTS

The nature of the contract will determine the types and quantities of facilities which the vendor will need. Facilities supplied by user such as communications equipment, supplies, desks, and, of course, machine time, all cost money and should be given effect in computing the cost of the installation.

L. REFERENCES TO OTHER CLAUSES: 6-57.

A. CLAUSE NAME: Compliance with Installation Standards   **B. CLAUSE NO.:** 8-08

C. CONTRACT TYPES USED IN: Software development   **D. RISK RATING:** 3

E. INTENT AND SCOPE

In addition to documentation standards identified in 8-03, the user will normally have established standards for operating practices, programming, systems design and user relationships. These standards normally are defined in a user standards manual, which should be incorporated as a part of the contract.

H. IDEAL COVERAGE

The vendor warrants that all software and other products delivered hereunder will comply with user standards as set forth in the user data processing standards manual attached hereto as Exhibit "A".

I. FALL-BACK ALTERNATIVES

If the vendor reviews the standards manual and takes objection to certain aspects thereof, exceptions can be carved out of the generalized vendor obligation to comply. If vendor standards exist and are acceptable to user, they may be substituted.

K. COMMENTS

If the user has not codified its standards for data processing operations, it would be wise to have the staff compile a brief outline of basic procedures and operational guide-lines for attachment to the contract. This will avoid the production by vendor of soft-ware that is "foreign" in thrust, tone or approach from the general approach of the user.

L. REFERENCES TO OTHER CLAUSES: 7-13, 8-03, 9-25.

A. **CLAUSE NAME:**   Guarantee of Original Development   B. **CLAUSE NO.:**   8-09

C. **CONTRACT TYPES USED IN:**   Software development   D. **RISK RATING:**   3

E. **INTENT AND SCOPE**

Much as the vendor must warrant ownership of a software package (see 7-29) the vendor in the development project should warrant that the material to be developed will be original and will not infringe.

H. **IDEAL COVERAGE**

The vendor warrants that all materials produced hereunder will be of original development by vendor, and will be specifically developed for the fulfillment of this contract and will not infringe upon or violate any patent, copyright, trade secret or other property right of any third party, and vendor will indemnify and hold user harmless from and against any loss, cost, liability or expense (including reasonable counsel fees) arising out of any breach or claimed breach of this warranty.

In the event the vendor shall elect to use or incorporate in the materials to be produced any components of a system already existing, vendor shall first notify the user, who, after whatever investigation user may elect to make, may direct the vendor not to so use or incorporate any such components. If the user shall not object, vendor may use or incorporate such component at vendor's expense after obtaining the written consent of the party owning the same, and furnishing a copy thereof to user; in all events, such components shall be similarly warranted (except for originality) by the vendor and the vendor will arrange to transfer title or the perpetual license to use such components to the user for purposes of this contract, and shall indemnify user, in the manner aforesaid, with respect thereto.

J. **POSSIBLE REMEDIES**

A performance bond may be the sole remedy if the vendor's financial statement (7-22) does not support the indemnity given.

L. **REFERENCES TO OTHER CLAUSES:**   5-28, 7-29, 7-30.

A. CLAUSE NAME: Expenses and Other Charges   **B. CLAUSE NO.:** 8-10

C. CONTRACT TYPES USED IN: Software development   **D. RISK RATING:** 3

E. INTENT AND SCOPE

To fix responsibility for expenses and other charges. A software development contract may sometimes be a fixed price contract, and, in such event the charges could be covered as in 7-14. However, these contracts, by their nature, are often open-ended with respect to certain types of expenses, such as machine time, travel costs, overtime payments, supplies, photocopies, copies of documentation and the like. As a result, the user would be wise to set limits to other extra charges.

G. STANDARD CLAUSE PROVIDED BY MANUFACTURERS

Charges: The Customer agrees to pay charges for these services, including billable travel time, in accordance with IBM's established rates and minimums in effect when the services are rendered.

All charges, rate classifications and minimum hours are subject to change by IBM upon three months' notice.

Charges will be invoiced monthly for services rendered and will be payable on receipt of invoice.

There shall be added to any charges under this Agreement amounts equal to any applicable taxes however designated, levied or based on such charges or on this Agreement or the services rendered hereunder, including state and local privilege or excise taxes based on gross revenue, and any taxes or amounts in lieu thereof paid or payable by IBM in respect of the foregoing, exclusive of taxes based on net income.

The Customer will reimburse IBM for special or unusual expenses incurred at the Customer's specific request.

H. IDEAL COVERAGE

In addition to the software development charges provided in this contract, the user agrees to reimburse the vendor, after justification, for the following out-of-pocket expenses actually incurred in connection with this contract in the following categories and limited in the aggregate to the amounts shown adjacent to each category:

> Travel $
> Reproduction
> Overtime (clerical)
> Overtime (technical)
> Extra computer time
> Data entry

No more than _____ % of the amount set forth as the maximum for any category will be reimbursable from user if incurred within a single one-month period.

K. COMMENTS

The user should take steps in the contract to restrain "bunching" or "front-loading" of expenses. Furthermore, in any transaction involving expense reimbursement, the user's contract should require expenses to be: (a) actually incurred; (b) reasonable in amount; (c) related to the contract and (d) necessary for contract performance. All expenses should be justified by receipts, vouchers and explanations.

L. REFERENCES TO OTHER CLAUSES: 6-38, 7-14, 10-17

A. **CLAUSE NAME:** Progress Payments and Holdbacks   B. **CLAUSE NO.:** 8-11

C. **CONTRACT TYPES USED IN:** Software development   D. **RISK RATING:** 2

E. INTENT AND SCOPE

To ensure that payment is related to performance. Payments for a software development contract should be made on the basis of delivery of certain products, and a percentage of the contract payment should be held back for performance of the entire
contract. It is recommended, therefore, that a percentage of completion be established for each task and deliverable. A progress payment schedule would then show
the percentage of the contract price applicable to particular products or deliverables.
A portion of the amount due on each deliverable should further be held back against
completion of the entire contract.

G. STANDARD CLAUSE PROVIDED BY MANUFACTURERS

IBM agrees to perform the services under the Scope of Effort for the "Fixed Price"
shown below in accordance with the terms of the referenced Agreement for IBM
Systems Engineering Services as modified in the third paragraph below. IBM will invoice the Customer in equal monthly amounts over the period covered by the Estimated Schedule of Services. If the Scope of Effort is completed prior to the "To"
date, the invoice in the month of completion will include the balance of the charges
due. Invoices will be payable upon receipt. Any changes to the Scope of Effort or
failure of the Customer to meet his responsibilities as described below may result
in an adjustment to the Fixed Price and the Estimated Schedule of Services and shall
release IBM from its obligations hereunder to the extent that IBM is affected by such
changes or Customer failure.

H. IDEAL COVERAGE

Schedule A attached hereto sets forth the amount [percentage] of the contract price
applicable to each phase of the required performance. 80% of the amount applicable to
each phase shall be paid to the vendor upon its completion and acceptance. The balance
shall be retained by the user until delivery and acceptance of the entire performance
required by this contract. In the event this contract is terminated by vendor, or by
user on account of vendor default, prior to completion of the entire contract, user
shall be entitled to retain said balances as liquidated damages for vendor's breach.

I. FALL–BACK ALTERNATIVES

If vendor is badly financed, as is often the case in the software area, either the deliverables
will have to be broken down into minuscule elements or progress payments will have to be
made at regular intervals, so that vendor can meet his payroll and overhead expenses.

K. COMMENTS

See 8-01 and Figure 8-1 for the method of project staging.

L. **REFERENCES TO OTHER CLAUSES:** 8-01, 10-05.

A. CLAUSE NAME: Progress Reports   **B. CLAUSE NO.:** 8-12

C. CONTRACT TYPES USED IN: Software development   **D. RISK RATING:** 2

E. INTENT AND SCOPE

To permit proper evaluation of performance through receipt and appraisal of regular progress reports.

H. IDEAL COVERAGE

The vendor shall submit a monthly progress report to the user, not less than 10 days after the close of each calendar month signed by an authorized officer of the vendor. Each progress report shall describe the status of the vendor's performance since the preceding report, including the products delivered, and the progress expected to be made in the next succeeding period. Each report shall describe vendor activities by reference to the schedule of stages and tasks attached to 8-01 as Schedule A.

K. COMMENTS

It may be possible to obtain the *personal* signature of an officer, thereby protecting the Company from possible fraud, or at least giving recourse to one or more individuals, as well as the corporation.

L. REFERENCES TO OTHER CLAUSES: 8-01, 8-11.

A. CLAUSE NAME: Title Transfer   **B. CLAUSE NO.:** 8-13

C. CONTRACT TYPES USED IN: Software development   **D. RISK RATING:** 2

E. INTENT AND SCOPE

To assure that sole title to the products of the development project passes to the user.

G. STANDARD CLAUSE PROVIDED BY MANUFACTURERS

Rights in Data: All original written material including programs, card decks, tapes, listings and other programming documentation originated and prepared for the Customer pursuant to this Agreement shall belong exclusively to the Customer.

The ideas, concepts, know-how, or techniques relating to data processing, developed during the course of this Agreement by IBM personnel or jointly by IBM and Customer personnel can be used by either party in any way it may deem appropriate. Each invention, discovery or improvement which includes ideas, concepts, know-how, or techniques relating to data processing developed pursuant to this Agreement shall be treated as follows: (a) if made by Customer personnel, it shall be the property of the Customer; (b) if made by IBM personnel, it shall be the property of IBM and IBM grants to the Customer a non-exclusive, irrevocable, and royalty-free license throughout the world; (c) if made jointly by personnel of IBM and the Customer, it shall be jointly owned without accounting.

H. IDEAL COVERAGE

The products of this contract shall be the sole and exclusive property of the user, free from any claim or retention of rights thereto on the part of the vendor except as herein specifically provided. Upon completion or other termination of this contract the vendor shall deliver to user all copies of any and all materials related or pertaining to this contract. Vendor shall have no right to disclose or use any of such products or materials for any purpose whatsoever, and vendor acknowledges that such products and materials are proprietary to user having been secretly developed for user for its own and sole use.

J. POSSIBLE REMEDIES

Injunction is the proper remedy for vendor breach, in addition to damages. A restrictive covenant will help (see 8-20).

L. REFERENCES TO OTHER CLAUSES: 6-85, 8-20.

A. CLAUSE NAME: Acceptance by Stage   **B. CLAUSE NO.:** 8-14

C. CONTRACT TYPES USED IN: Software development   **D. RISK RATING:** 2

E. INTENT AND SCOPE

To provide a methodology of acceptance of software. During the course of development, for each stage of the project, specific product deliverables should be described (8-01). For each stage, a specific acceptance test or method must be devised, designed to determine that the product is acceptable, meets the standards of quality, conforms with the installation, and performs in accordance with specifications. Final acceptance must verify that the entire package works as planned, performs the defined functions as an entirety and with internal consistency, and meets all specifications and standards.

H. IDEAL COVERAGE

Upon notification to user of the completion of each stage described in Schedule A to 8-01 and of delivery of the products attendant to such stage, the user shall within _____ days perform the following acceptance tests, at the user site upon the configuration described in 8-06, to determine whether: (a) the products meet the specifications and standards described in this contract and (b) that they perform repetitively on a variety of data without failure. Upon completion of the last stage described, the aforesaid tests shall be performed as to the entirety of the products, and also to determine whether the totality of the products meets the generalized specifications for the totality and operates with internal consistency. If any test shall disclose deficiencies the vendor shall within _____ days correct such deficiencies and user shall thereafter have an additional _____ days to re-conduct the acceptance tests. Failure to meet specifications after the second test shall entitle the user at its option, to cancel this contract on the same basis as if vendor had failed to deliver the products required.

K. COMMENTS

Note that failure of the acceptance tests at any stage gives the user the benefit of the products delivered up to the previous stage. The vendor will have received 80% of the revenue due, and the contract can be cancelled with equity for both parties.

L. REFERENCES TO OTHER CLAUSES: 7-27, 8-01, 8-15, 8-16.

A. **CLAUSE NAME:** Test Data to be Used   B. **CLAUSE NO.:** 8-15

C. **CONTRACT TYPES USED IN:** Software development   D. **RISK RATING:** 3

E. **INTENT AND SCOPE**

One way of insuring that the final acceptance test is performed in a realistic manner is to insure that test data can be chosen by the user. As a result, a preliminary specification of test data should be included in the contract.

F. **PROTECTION AGAINST**

Protects against the claims of satisfactory contract completion on the basis of vendor produced test data only.

H. **IDEAL COVERAGE**

The test data to be used in the acceptance test under 8-14 shall be furnished and prepared by the user.

L. **REFERENCES TO OTHER CLAUSES:** 8-14.

A. **CLAUSE NAME:** Right to Cancel at Each Stage   B. **CLAUSE NO.:** 8-16

C. **CONTRACT TYPES USED IN:** Software development   D. **RISK RATING:** 1

E. **INTENT AND SCOPE**

By giving the user the unilateral right to cancel at each stage, regardless of whether the product is acceptable or not, the software development contract is simplified considerably. This approach can also benefit the user by eliminating the necessity for significant disputes and substantial losses or litigation.

H. **IDEAL COVERAGE**

The user may, at its option, elect to cancel the contract at any time, by notice to vendor, upon completion of any stage described in Schedule A to 8-01. In such event the user will pay to the vendor the amount due by virtue of completion of the products therefore delivered, and if such cancellation is not based upon any claim of vendor default such payment shall include any sums withheld pursuant to 8-11.

K. **COMMENTS**

Note acceptance test discussion under 8-14.

L. **REFERENCES TO OTHER CLAUSES:** 8-01, 8-11, 8-14.

A. CLAUSE NAME: Staff Qualifications   **B. CLAUSE NO.:** 8-17

C. CONTRACT TYPES USED IN: Software development   **D. RISK RATING:** 2

E. INTENT AND SCOPE

To set standards for qualification of staff to be supplied by vendor in the development project.

F. PROTECTION AGAINST

To protect against use of unqualified staff, thereby decreasing prospects for delay, error and unsatisfactory performance.

H. IDEAL COVERAGE

Personnel assigned by the vendor to the performance of the work required by this contract shall meet the following minimum standards:

　　Education— _____ years after secondary school
　　Data processing training— _____ months
　　Data processing employment experience— _____ months
　　Tenure with vendor— _____ months
　　Software applications experience— _____ months

I. FALL-BACK ALTERNATIVES

Another approach is to have each person assigned subject to approval by prior interview with the user's staff. Still another is to limit personnel standards to supervisory personnel of vendor.

K. COMMENTS

The user should note, particularly in the "art" of data processing, that standard tests of qualification such as education and experience are not to be overly relied upon. Many creative software people are quite young, relatively uneducated and inexperienced. Tenure on a particular job is often not particularly relevant, especially in light of the extreme mobility of data processing people. However, a minimum of two years of experience is probably necessary for technically proficient personnel.

L. REFERENCES TO OTHER CLAUSES: 6-20, 10-19, 10-20.

A. CLAUSE NAME: All Employees Full-time   **B. CLAUSE NO.:** 8-18

C. CONTRACT TYPES USED IN: Development contracts   **D. RISK RATING:** 2

E. INTENT AND SCOPE

To ensure that employees assigned to the project are full-time employees of the vendor, and are assigned to the contract on a full-time basis.

F. PROTECTION AGAINST

Protects against use of moon-lighting or part-time staff, thereby decreasing prospects of inefficiency, discontinuity and other deleterious effects upon performance, timing and quality.

H. IDEAL COVERAGE

The vendor warrants and represents that all employees to be assigned to the performance of this contract shall be full time employees of the vendor, and shall be assigned to the project on a full time basis.

L. REFERENCES TO OTHER CLAUSES: 5-14, 10-19.

A. **CLAUSE NAME:** Right to Staff Access Upon Vendor
Business Termination

B. **CLAUSE NO.:** 8-19

C. **CONTRACT TYPES USED IN:** Software development

D. **RISK RATING:** 3

E. **INTENT AND SCOPE**

Clause 5-16 provides reciprocally for non-"raiding" of personnel. This clause should be inoperative in the event the vendor ceases to do business. The user can then have the opportunity to enroll vendor staff, so that the project can be completed without serious delays or discontinuity.

H. **IDEAL COVERAGE**

In the event the vendor shall cease conducting business, the user shall have the right to offer employment, on a permanent or part time basis, to all employees of the vendor assigned to the performance of this contract, notwithstanding anything to the contrary provided elsewhere herein. To this end, vendor shall, each week, furnish to user a list of all employees so assigned, and their addresses and telephone numbers, and shall advise all employees of the existence of this clause.

L. **REFERENCES TO OTHER CLAUSES:** 5-02, 5-16, 7-19, 9-18.

A. CLAUSE NAME: Non-Competition   **B. CLAUSE NO.:** 8-20

C. CONTRACT TYPES USED IN: Software development   **D. RISK RATING:** 3

E. INTENT AND SCOPE

In developing a software product for the user the vendor will become knowledgeable about the user's business activities, and in the processing associated with the software product being developed. This skill is potentially usable by the vendor in competing with the user. This competition should be constrained.

F. PROTECTION AGAINST

Protects against competition by the vendor and against use of vendor knowledge gained on the project for the purpose of assisting user's competitors.

G. STANDARD CLAUSE PROVIDED BY MANUFACTURERS

This Agreement shall not preclude IBM from developing materials which are competitive, irrespective to their similarity, to materials which might be delivered to the Customer pursuant to this Agreement.

H. IDEAL COVERAGE

During the performance of this contract and for _____ months after its completion or other termination, the vendor agrees not to enter into any business competitive with the user in the United States, and not to transact business of any kind with any third party engaged in any line of business competitive with that of user. In addition, vendor will not make use of or disclose, at any time during or after the termination of this contract any information concerning the user not already known to the general public or any information, methods, systems or other elements created, learned or developed in connection with vendor's performance under this contract.

I. FALL–BACK ALTERNATIVES

There may be vendor resistance to a restriction upon any business activities with competitors of user. A fall-back restriction can be limited to the performance of similar types of work for competitors. In that case, the types of work restricted should be broadly defined.

L. REFERENCES TO OTHER CLAUSES: 8-13, 10-02.

A. CLAUSE NAME: Staff Insurance   **B. CLAUSE NO.:** 8-21

C. CONTRACT TYPES USED IN: Software development   **D. RISK RATING:** 4

E. INTENT AND SCOPE

To require vendor to obtain necessary insurance for its staff, whether or not they work on the premises of the user.

F. PROTECTION AGAINST

Protects against claims made by employees of the vendor against the user.

H. IDEAL COVERAGE

The vendor agrees, during the term of this contract, to maintain at vendor's expense all necessary insurance for its employees, including but not limited to, workmen's compensation, disability, and unemployment insurance, and to provide user with certification upon request.

L. REFERENCES TO OTHER CLAUSES: 6-75, 9-27, 10-24.

A. **CLAUSE NAME:** Security

C. **CONTRACT TYPES USED IN:** Software Development

D. **RISK RATING:** 3

E. **INTENT AND SCOPE**

To require vendor personnel assigned to the project to comply with security regulations of the user.

H. **IDEAL COVERAGE**

The vendor agrees that it and its personnel will at all times comply with all security regulations in effect from time to time at the user's premises, and externally for materials belonging to user or to the project.

L. **REFERENCES TO OTHER CLAUSES:** 9-26.

A. CLAUSE NAME: Deliverables and Products　　**B. CLAUSE NO.:** 9-01

C. CONTRACT TYPES USED IN: Service Bureau　　**D. RISK RATING:** 2

E. INTENT AND SCOPE

To define the products to be produced on a recurring basis under a service contract. Such products typically are reports, file maintenance, and mailing material, such as bills and invoices.

H. IDEAL COVERAGE

The vendor agrees to deliver to the user, at user's premises, the following materials on the schedule shown:

Exhibit A Reference No.	Product or Report	Frequency	Day (or date) and Time of Delivery
1	Invoices for prior month's sales	Monthly	_____ day of every month, at _____ p.m.
2	Statement for outstanding receivables	Monthly	_____ day of every month, at _____ p.m.
3	Receivables aging Statement [Etc.]	Monthly	_____ day of every month, at _____ p.m.

Each of the foregoing materials shall be furnished in the form and shall contain the information set forth on Exhibits A1 through A_ hereof.

L. REFERENCES TO OTHER CLAUSES: 8-02, 10-18.

A. CLAUSE NAME: Performance Turnaround   **B. CLAUSE NO.:** 9-02

C. CONTRACT TYPES USED IN: Services   **D. RISK RATING:** 1

E. INTENT AND SCOPE

The responsiveness of a service organization is a function of its ability to rapidly turn around the necessary material. Turnaround time is the lapse of time between receipt of the material from the user, and the delivery of the processed products required by the contract. The turnaround requirements of the user are an important part of the service contract.

G. STANDARD CLAUSE PROVIDED BY MANUFACTURERS

Report Processing: The NCR DPC shall make available to the Customer, at the office of the NCR DPC, the daily reports described in the attached Schedules on the morning of the working day following the day on which the reported transactions occurred, such time to be no later, under normal conditions, than 7:30 A.M. local time. Regularly scheduled reports (weekly, monthly) shall be made available within 48 hours following the close of the period. Other reports will be available on a mutually agreed upon schedule. In the event that the Customer should desire that the reports be delivered to it at some place other than at the NCR DPC, the Customer shall be responsible for arranging and paying the costs of any required transportation.

H. IDEAL COVERAGE

The vendor agrees to deliver the following within the elapsed time periods set forth below, after receipt of the input material from the user.

Product	Elapsed time in hours after receipt (turnaround time) for delivery
Statement of Cash Receipts and Cash Position [Etc.]	_____ hours

For the purposes of this paragraph the hours between midnight Friday and 7 A.M. the following Monday shall be excluded from the computation of elapsed time.

I. FALL-BACK ALTERNATIVES

The vendor may require some leeway based upon machine down-time and other occurrences beyond its control.

K. COMMENTS

Holidays and other exceptions to turnaround requirements should be set forth. Note that 9-01 contains date and time of delivery, *assuming* on-time delivery of input. 9-02 provides for turnaround independent of input delivery.

L. REFERENCES TO OTHER CLAUSES: 7-23, 9-01.

A. **CLAUSE NAME:** Quality Specifications

B. **CLAUSE NO.:** 9-03

C. **CONTRACT TYPES USED IN:** Services

D. **RISK RATING:** 3

E. **INTENT AND SCOPE**

To define the quality level of products to be produced. A rapidly produced product may otherwise be totally inadequate. Quality can be specified in two ways: accuracy (in terms of error percentages); and appearance quality. The former is obviously more important than the latter.

H. **IDEAL COVERAGE**

Vendor warrants that the reports produced shall be consistently error free. All errors discovered shall be corrected by the vendor without cost to the user. In furtherance but not in limitation of the foregoing, vendor shall be deemed in default if errors occur in excess of the Error Percentages for the period shown. Error Percentages shall be determined by dividing the total number of output lines produced from the applicable period which are correct into the total number of output lines which are incorrect:

Type of Report	Maximum Error Percentages	Period
Invoices		
addresses	_____%	Monthly
amounts	_____%	Monthly
[Etc.]		

Vendor further warrants that the products shall be uniform in appearance, clean and presentable, in accordance with generally accepted standards in the industry.

J. **POSSIBLE REMEDIES**

Remedies may include non-payment for any period in which quality standards are not met.

L. **REFERENCES TO OTHER CLAUSES:** 7-01, 10-14.

A. CLAUSE NAME: Rights to Programs   B. CLAUSE NO.: 9-04

C. CONTRACT TYPES USED IN: Services   D. RISK RATING: 2

E. INTENT AND SCOPE

If the payments made to the service bureau include amortization or direct payment for programs developed or modified for the user, the user should be granted the right to obtain them and to use them either internally or with another service organization on termination of this contract. In the event that the service organization goes out of business, similar rights should be included. These are identified in 9-18.

F. PROTECTION AGAINST

Protects against vendor unwillingness to turn over programs developed for the user at its expense; protects against user necessity to repurchase systems or program development whenever it changes service bureaus.

H. IDEAL COVERAGE

Ownership of all programs used to process the products under this contract shall vest in the user organization upon completion of the payments described under the category "Systems and Programs Development Costs" in Schedule A. Any programs not specifically developed for the user, shall be deemed licensed to user on a non-exclusive basis, in perpetuity, without restriction as to use.

K. COMMENTS

The key to all service bureau arrangements lies in an understanding of the fact that *excessive dependency promotes the risk of extortion.* The protections to be sought by the user should be designed to minimize user dependence on the service organization, since the relationship by its nature, is one of high user dependence.

L. REFERENCES TO OTHER CLAUSES: 8-13, 9-18, 9-37.

A. **CLAUSE NAME:** Delivery of Program Copies and Changes B. **CLAUSE NO.:** 9-05

C. **CONTRACT TYPES USED IN:** Services D. **RISK RATING:** 2

E. **INTENT AND SCOPE**

To ensure that, with respect to programs belonging to the user, such programs will be delivered to user at the time of their completion, at the commencement of the processing contract *and* simultaneously with the making of upgrades and modifications.

F. **PROTECTION AGAINST**

Protects against difficulties associated with ownership claims not coupled with possession.

H. **IDEAL COVERAGE**

Copies of all programs used in the processing services to be performed hereunder will be delivered to the user as soon as developed and accepted by the user. Any program changes made to correct errors, to enhance the program, or to change the output as a result of changed requirements, shall be furnished to the user upon their completion. Simultaneously with delivery of the programs the vendor shall deliver copies of all documentation and amended documentation produced by the vendor.

K. **COMMENTS**

This clause has at least three valuable aspects. It provides security against loss; possession of the material acts as a hedge against extortion in the event of contract disputes or termination; and it eliminates some of the problems that might arise if the service bureau goes out of business or has its assets levied upon by a creditor.

Note that is it probably desirable to include *all* programs used by the bureau, including those in the public domain, or supplied by the hardware vendor. It is possible these are modified by the bureau, or that specific versions or generations are needed. By having a complete set, the user becomes vendor-independent.

L. **REFERENCES TO OTHER CLAUSES:** 7-05, 9-04, 9-13.

A. CLAUSE NAME: Equipment Requirements

B. CLAUSE NO.: 9-06

C. CONTRACT TYPES USED IN: Services

D. RISK RATING: 3

E. INTENT AND SCOPE

The facilities and equipment required by the service bureau are of some consequence to the user, since the user may be required to utilize the data and programs, after termination of the service bureau contract, on an internal basis, or through another service organization. As a result it is necessary to stipulate the equipment configuration in the contract which will allow the user to find alternatives when necessary.

F. PROTECTION AGAINST

Protects against user receipt from the service bureau of programs and systems which will have to be adapted for utilization internally or by another service bureau.

H. IDEAL COVERAGE

The vendor warrants that the user's data will be processed on the following equipment configuration and systems and that all programs and data files will be compatible therewith:

L. REFERENCES TO OTHER CLAUSES: 7-07, 8-01, 8-06, 9-39, 9-40.

A. CLAUSE NAME: Procedures Defined   B. CLAUSE NO.: 9-07

C. CONTRACT TYPES USED IN: Services   D. RISK RATING: 3

E. INTENT AND SCOPE

To ensure that the user knows the procedures followed and standards applied by vendor in using the programs, copies of the service bureau's procedures and manuals should be provided to the user, and updated on a periodic basis.

G. STANDARD CLAUSE PROVIDED BY MANUFACTURERS

The Customer shall include error detection routines in his programs to detect machine errors. The Customer is solely responsible for the accuracy and adequacy of the programs, the operation of the machines and resultant output thereof. IBM assumes no responsibility for loss or security of records or damages, caused by IBM's negligence or otherwise, arising in connection with the Hourly IBM Machine Service furnished hereunder. In no event shall IBM be liable for consequential damages. IBM personnel are not permitted to operate the machines.

H. IDEAL COVERAGE

The vendor shall supply the user with copies of the operating, systems, programming and standards manuals and procedures in use by vendor for the user's programs, after the initial processing cycle has been completed. Whenever such manuals and procedures are changed, the vendor shall immediately supply copies of the changes to the user.

L. REFERENCES TO OTHER CLAUSES: 9-04, 9-05.

A. CLAUSE NAME: User Training Supplied   **B. CLAUSE NO.:** 9-08

C. CONTRACT TYPES USED IN: Services   **D. RISK RATING:** 2

E. INTENT AND SCOPE

To define the user training to be supplied. User training is important, since it is likely that user familiarity with data processing procedures will be relatively limited at the time when a services contract is entered into.

H. IDEAL COVERAGE

The vendor will supply all necessary instruction to enable the user to supply input and to utilize output of the services contracted for hereunder, including, but not limited to, a training program of _____ days duration for user personnel to be conducted at least twice on the user's site at times determined by user, which instruction shall be given by qualified vendor personnel.

L. REFERENCES TO OTHER CLAUSES: 6-23, 6-60.

A. CLAUSE NAME: Basis for Charging	B. CLAUSE NO.: 9-09
C. CONTRACT TYPES USED IN: Services	D. RISK RATING: 2

E. INTENT AND SCOPE

To define the basis for payment to the service bureau. The charges made by a service organization will vary, depending on volume and on types of products produced.

G. STANDARD CLAUSE PROVIDED BY MANUFACTURERS

Charges: The charges for Hourly IBM Machine Service shall be the regular hour and off hour rates currently in effect at the IBM Datacenter for the availability of the machines to be used by the Customer. All charges are subject to change upon three months' prior notice. However, no notice shall be required for such changes occurring within three months after the effective date of this Agreement and announced by IBM prior to such date. If a charge is changed, the Customer may terminate this Agreement on the effective date of such change; otherwise, the new charge shall become effective.

The charges accrue when the machines are available for Customer's use. The hourly charge includes the cost of the building services necessary for the Customer's use of the machines at the IBM Datacenter.

The regular hourly rate shall apply between the hours of 9 a.m. and 6 p.m. Mondays through Fridays, exclusive of IBM holidays. IBM Machine Service furnished outside of these hours shall be at the off hour rate. Charges will be invoiced at the end of each month, and payment shall be made in full within thirty days after the date of the invoice.

H. IDEAL COVERAGE

The following basis will be used for charges computed under this contract.

$_____ per line of output
$_____ per report page
$_____ per hour of processing input.

If, in any week, the volume of output shall exceed _____ lines, the cost thereof set forth above shall be reduced by _____%. [Etc.]

L. REFERENCES TO OTHER CLAUSES: 6-38, 7-14.

A. **CLAUSE NAME:** Term of Contract   B. **CLAUSE NO.:** 9-10

C. **CONTRACT TYPES USED IN:** Services   D. **RISK RATING:** 3

E. **INTENT AND SCOPE**

To define the duration of the term of contract.

H. **IDEAL COVERAGE**

The contract shall be for a term of _____ months, and shall be extended automatically for additional like terms unless the vendor shall terminate this contract by notice to user not less than 6 months prior to the expiration of the term or any renewal term or the user shall terminate this contract by notice to vendor not less than 30 days prior to the expiration of the term or any renewal.

K. **COMMENTS**

A contract with a service organization normally should be cancellable only by the user, or, if cancellable by the vendor, only after substantial prior notice. In order to ensure that the user's operations are not disrupted in the event of termination and during the process of finding a substitute avenue for processing user data, the user should demand lengthy prior notice of vendor termination. Also see 9-17 for assistance to be supplied by vendor in the event of termination.

L. **REFERENCES TO OTHER CLAUSES:** 9-11, 9-17.

A. **CLAUSE NAME:** Notice of Automatic Renewal   B. **CLAUSE NO.:** 9-11

C. **CONTRACT TYPES USED IN:** Services   D. **RISK RATING:** 4

E. **INTENT AND SCOPE**

To ensure notice to the user that, unless action is taken, the contract will be automatically renewed.

F. **PROTECTION AGAINST**

Protects against automatic extensions of a contract on a surprise basis.

H. **IDEAL COVERAGE**

Not more than _____ nor less than _____ [here insert a number of days greater than the number of days' notice required to be given by user to cancel the contract] days prior to the expiration of the term or any renewal term, vendor shall give notice to the user of such expiration, which notice shall state the date of expiration and that if not cancelled by the user not less than _____ days prior thereto the contract will be automatically renewed. If vendor shall fail to give such notice during the permitted period then (a) user shall thereafter have the right to cancel the contract at any time (whether or not the cancellation date shall be the expiration of the term or any renewal) upon 30 days notice to vendor, which right shall lapse only upon vendor's giving timely and proper notice hereunder to user of the next scheduled expiration date, assuming this contract shall not have been theretofore cancelled by user and (b) vendor shall thereafter have no right to cancel this contract except upon 6 months notice prior to the expiration date next succeeding the expiration date as to which vendor has so failed to give notice, pursuant hereto.

K. **COMMENTS**

Many users understandably do not favor automatic renewal clauses, since they can result in unexpected, but binding commitments. Such clauses are, however, useful in articulating an understanding between parties that they will define a short term relationship and, so long as matters progress satisfactorily and circumstances do not change, they will continue to extend it, over and over, on the same basis.

To protect against the element of surprise, the above clause requires the vendor to give the user advance notice that a contract time segment is coming to a close and that if the user wants to end the relationship it had better take action or else the contract will renew.

Another approach to the problem is to write a contract for an extended term, say five years, and cover all the elements which would be required in a long-term-relationship. Then give each party the right at any time to advance contract expiration on specified notice.

L. **REFERENCES TO OTHER CLAUSES:** 6-58, 9-10.

A. CLAUSE NAME: Price Protection   **B. CLAUSE NO.:** 9-12

C. CONTRACT TYPES USED IN: Services   **D. RISK RATING:** 2

E. INTENT AND SCOPE

To ensure that price increases cannot be arbitrary or extortive.

F. PROTECTION AGAINST

To protect against unreasonable price increases levied by a supplier whose contract is difficult to terminate.

H. IDEAL COVERAGE

During any renewal term vendor may increase prices hereunder upon at least _____ [here insert at least the same notice period that vendor must give to cancel, since a price increase may have the same effect] days notice to user, setting forth the increased prices and the effective date thereof. Upon receipt of such notice user may cancel this contract effective at any time prior to the effective date of such increased prices or within 6 months thereafter, upon _____ days notice to vendor. Notwithstanding anything herein to the contrary contained, vendor shall not increase prices more often than once in any 12 months period and no price increase shall exceed the lower of (a) vendor's then prevailing prices to other customers (b) _____% in excess of the previous prices changed by vendor to user; or (c) the proportionate increase in the Consumer Price Index between the effective date of the prior prevailing prices hereunder and the date of vendor's notice of increase.

I. FALL–BACK ALTERNATIVES

Some service bureaus like to base their escalations on actual increases in labor and computer costs. That, as a fall-back can be acceptable only if coupled with maximums and with cancellation rights, since those costs are capable of being manipulated by the vendor. Escalations can be tied to any number of standards including escalations in computer rental rates, prevailing wages for some industry that publishes such rates, etc.

K. COMMENTS

If the contract is, by term or renewal rights, capable of long duration some right must be given to the service bureau to increase its charges, but the user should protect against excessive increases.

L. REFERENCES TO OTHER CLAUSES: 6-43, 6-44, 7-20, 7-21.

A. **CLAUSE NAME:** Options to Change System at Defined Rates   B. **CLAUSE NO.:** 9-13

C. **CONTRACT TYPES USED IN:** Services   D. **RISK RATING:** 3

E. **INTENT AND SCOPE**

Price protection should be applied to programming changes as well, otherwise exorbitant charges may be levied by the vendor against a dependent user.

F. **PROTECTION AGAINST**

To protect the prices at which program modifications will be made.

H. **IDEAL COVERAGE**

The user shall have the right to request the vendor to make modifications to the system. Such modifications shall be made by qualified vendor personnel, at charges then in effect, which charges, however, shall not be higher than those charges in effect at the date hereof, [or, those annexed as Schedule A] multiplied by _____% for each elapsed year from the date hereof. Within 5 days after receipt of user's request for such a change the vendor shall give a quotation of price for such change and in the event the vendor's quotation is deemed to be too costly, the user shall have the option to have the change performed by any other service organization. The making of such changes shall not affect the prices set forth in 9-09.

K. **COMMENTS**

This is a difficult clause, principally because it may complicate matters if another agency is used to modify programs. There can be an adverse impact on the efficiency of the operation of the entire system. If the efficiency of the rest of the programs is impacted by outside changes the vendor will want to increase its prices to reflect its increase in processing costs.

L. **REFERENCES TO OTHER CLAUSES:** 7-05.

A. CLAUSE NAME: Options to Undertake Part of Work   **B. CLAUSE NO.:** 9-14
In-House

C. CONTRACT TYPES USED IN: Services   **D. RISK RATING:** 2

E. INTENT AND SCOPE

To permit the user to recover some processing work for in-house operation. The user may wish to do so because its internal capabilities have expanded, because costs are too high, or because error standards are not being met.

H. IDEAL COVERAGE

The user shall have the right, on 30 days notice to vendor, to undertake any part of the processing services covered hereby to be performed by it. To the extent that such services are being performed by the user, the vendor shall be free from further liability for the quality or performance thereof.

I. FALL-BACK ALTERNATIVES

Some dollar restrictions or percentage of contract restrictions may be negotiated.

K. COMMENTS

If it may become desirable to perform part of the processing services on an internal basis the user should seek vendor agreement thereto in the initial contract. This can become important in connection with processing components such as data entry, report bursting, binding and distribution. These are readily separable from the main service bureau activities and in-house performance can save money, or improve quality.

L. REFERENCES TO OTHER CLAUSES: 6-76.

A. CLAUSE NAME: Protection from Levy by Creditors   **B. CLAUSE NO.:** 9-15

C. CONTRACT TYPES USED IN: Services   **D. RISK RATING:** 3

E. INTENT AND SCOPE

To segregate user property in order to minimize it from claims of vendor's creditors. This can probably be done by recitation of the fact that ownership of certain materials belongs to the using organization and not to the vendor.

H. IDEAL COVERAGE

The vendor agrees that the files, programs, input materials and output materials, and the media upon which they are located including cards, tapes, disks and other storage facilities, utilized in performing the processing services covered by this contract, all are the property of the user, and the vendor agrees to use its best efforts to protect the same from levy by or upon the authority of creditors of the vendor, or committees, representatives or trustees thereof.

L. REFERENCES TO OTHER CLAUSES: 7-18, 10-10.

A. CLAUSE NAME: Termination Rights   **B. CLAUSE NO.:** 9-16

C. CONTRACT TYPES USED IN: Services   **D. RISK RATING:** 3

E. INTENT AND SCOPE

To ensure that contract termination will not unduly disrupt user's operations or give rise to a vendor vendetta.

F. PROTECTION AGAINST

To protect against hasty terminations, which can disrupt or impair the user's ability to process its data.

H. IDEAL COVERAGE

Upon termination of this contract for any reason (including default by user) the user shall have the right immediately upon demand to obtain access to and possession of all its properties, including, but not limited to, current copies of all programs and necessary documentation, all files, intermediate materials and supplies held by vendor. Vendor acknowledges that any failure or delay on its part in the delivery of such access and possession to user is and will be deemed willful and malicious and will cause irreparable injury to user, not adequately compensable in damages and for which user may have no adequate remedy at law, and vendor accordingly agrees that user may, in such event, seek and obtain injunctive relief in any court of competent jurisdiction as well as punitive damages in the sum of $_____ per day for each day of such failure or delay.

I. FALL-BACK ALTERNATIVES

Removal of liquidated damages.

L. REFERENCES TO OTHER CLAUSES: 5-11, 9-17, 9-19, 9-20.

A. CLAUSE NAME: Assistance in Take-Over Upon Termination

C. CONTRACT TYPES USED IN: Services

D. RISK RATING: 2

E. INTENT AND SCOPE

It is desirable to require the assistance of the service organization in the takeover necessary to shift the processing services to the user or to another service organization upon contract termination.

F. PROTECTION AGAINST

To protect against drastic contract terminations.

H. IDEAL COVERAGE

The vendor agrees to make available to the user all services necessary for an orderly take-over at the time of termination of the contract regardless of the reason for such termination, including but not limited to, providing all files in the format defined by the user, providing all intermediate materials in the format defined by the user, and providing all supplies and other properties of the user. Charges for such assistance shall be the lower of those in effect for the services of the personnel listed on Schedule A at the time the assistance is rendered, or those in effect on the date hereof for such personnel plus _____ % per year for each year between the date hereof and the date of termination.

L. REFERENCES TO OTHER CLAUSES: 5-11, 9-16.

A. CLAUSE NAME: Business Termination **B. CLAUSE NO.:** 9-18

C. CONTRACT TYPES USED IN: Services **D. RISK RATING:** 3

E. INTENT AND SCOPE

In the event of vendor business termination the user should be given access to all materials, and be given these materials in any format desired. Rights to own and operate programs should all devolve upon the user.

H. IDEAL COVERAGE

In the event vendor shall cease conducting business, the user shall thereupon own all programs and other vendor materials used in the processing services contracted for herein. Access thereto shall be unrestricted, and vendor shall assist the user in obtaining access thereto and possession thereof in such manner so as to prevent disruption of user's operations. To the extent feasible, the vendor shall assist the user in every possible manner in arranging for the orderly transfer of all processing activities to the user or another vendor.

K. COMMENTS

Both the legal and practical value of this clause can be marginal, if any, dependent upon the nature of and reasons for vendor's cessation of business.

L. REFERENCES TO OTHER CLAUSES: 5-02, 7-19, 8-19.

A. **CLAUSE NAME:** File Access

C. **CONTRACT TYPES USED IN:** Services

D. **RISK RATING:** 2

E. **INTENT AND SCOPE**

The user should have access to all files at any time. No one else should ever have access to the files.

H. **IDEAL COVERAGE**

The user shall be permitted access to all files used in the processing of his information, at any time, which access shall not be denied by vendor for any reason whatsoever.

K. **COMMENTS**

Injunction and punitive damage language such as found in 9-16 may be useful here. The denial of access to others is covered in 9-21.

L. **REFERENCES TO OTHER CLAUSES:** 9-16, 9-19, 9-21.

A. CLAUSE NAME: File and Media Ownership   **B. CLAUSE NO.:** 9-20

C. CONTRACT TYPES USED IN: Services   **D. RISK RATING:** 3

E. INTENT AND SCOPE

User files and the media on which those files are inscribed should be the user's property. The necessary payments to establish and evidence such ownership should be made as an integral part of the contract.

H. IDEAL COVERAGE

All files used in the processing of user information and the media upon which such files are inscribed are the sole and exclusive property of the user, and vendor shall evidence such ownership by plaque, emblem and/or decal theron.

L. REFERENCES TO OTHER CLAUSES: 9-16, 9-19.

A. **CLAUSE NAME:** File Confidentiality   B. **CLAUSE NO.:** 9-21

C. **CONTRACT TYPES USED IN:** Services   D. **RISK RATING:** 2

E. **INTENT AND SCOPE**

The confidentiality of files is of extreme importance, and must be provided for in any service contract.

H. **IDEAL COVERAGE**

The vendor warrants that it will retain all information belonging to the user in strictest confidence, and will neither use it nor disclose it to anyone without the explicit written permission of the user, and that each and every employee of vendor has executed a binding agreement to the same effect. The vendor recognizes that irreparable harm can be occasioned to the user by disclosure of information relating to its business and, accordingly, that user may enjoin such disclosure. The user shall from time to time furnish to vendor lists of authorized user personnel who may be permitted access to information in the files held by the vendor organization, and vendor agrees not to permit any access thereto to any user personnel except those so listed.

L. **REFERENCES TO OTHER CLAUSES:** 5-13, 9-24, 10-01.

A. CLAUSE NAME: Destruction of Intermediate Files   **B. CLAUSE NO.:** 9-22

C. CONTRACT TYPES USED IN: Services   **D. RISK RATING:** 3

E. INTENT AND SCOPE

To reduce the possibility of information leakage through the retention of excess materials.

F. PROTECTION AGAINST

The vendor agrees to destroy all intermediate and work files used in the processing, immediately upon completion of their processing. Such destruction shall take the form of degaussing of magnetic media, or shredding of paper media.

K. COMMENTS

In processing it is often necessary to create intermediate or work files, which reflect information in certain relevant formats. Such intermediate files have limited utility, except in the processing itself, but is it possible that these files could be used in an unscrupulous manner to obtain information relative to the user. It is therefore desirable to have these files destroyed immediately upon their completion.

L. REFERENCES TO OTHER CLAUSES: 9-21, 9-23.

A. **CLAUSE NAME:** Destruction of Carbons   B. **CLAUSE NO.:** 9-23

C. **CONTRACT TYPES USED IN:** Services   D. **RISK RATING:** 3

E. **INTENT AND SCOPE**

If reports are run in multiple copies, the carbon in-between is normally deleafed and discarded. Such carbon, however, contains in readable form the information reflected on the reports. The service organization therefore should destroy carbons or deliver them to the user with the reports.

H. **IDEAL COVERAGE**

The vendor agrees to immediately destroy, by shredding, all carbons removed from reports produced for the user, or to deliver them separately to the using organization, simultaneously with the production of such reports.

L. **REFERENCES TO OTHER CLAUSES:** 9-22.

A. CLAUSE NAME: Release of User Information to Designated Personnel   **B. CLAUSE NO.:** 9-24

C. CONTRACT TYPES USED IN: Services   **D. RISK RATING:** 3

E. INTENT AND SCOPE

The user shall supply a list of designated personnel authorized to obtain information. Such personnel are the sole persons to whom reports can be delivered or to whom information about file contents can be supplied.

H. IDEAL COVERAGE

The user shall from time to time supply the vendor with lists of personnel authorized to receive information in the possession of vendor. The vendor agrees not to deliver any reports or information to any other personnel of user.

L. REFERENCES TO OTHER CLAUSES: 9-19, 9-21.

A. **CLAUSE NAME:** System Controls   B. **CLAUSE NO.:** 9-25

C. **CONTRACT TYPES USED IN:** Services   D. **RISK RATING:** 3

E. **INTENT AND SCOPE**

To ensure accuracy of information.

F. **PROTECTION AGAINST**

Protects against excessive audit costs and questions concerning the veracity of user's financial statements, and provides positive information with respect to controls in effect.

H. **IDEAL COVERAGE**

Schedule A contains a list and description of the system controls incorporated into the user programs and systems by vendor. Such controls will be furnished to the user monthly, together with a separate control report.

K. **COMMENTS**

Controls incorporated in systems are quite important to insure that information flow is accurate, that audit trails are protected, and that financial information is correct. To the extent that system controls are built-in to the processing function by the service organization they should be described as a part of the information control for understanding and evaluating these controls and for determining that the system is carefully protected from outside interference. This is of course especially important in systems run outside of the organization.

L. **REFERENCES TO OTHER CLAUSES:** 9-03.

A. CLAUSE NAME: Rights to Security Inspection   **B. CLAUSE NO.:** 9-26

C. CONTRACT TYPES USED IN: Services   **D. RISK RATING:** 3

E. INTENT AND SCOPE

To ensure that user information is properly secured by the service bureau.

H. IDEAL COVERAGE

The vendor agrees that, at all times during the term of this agreement, vendor will maintain the procedures, provisions, conditions and equipment for the security of its processing site described on Schedule A. The user shall have the unconditional right to make security inspections of the vendor's organization at any time, without notice to vendor. If user shall request additional security provisions, vendor shall not unreasonably delay or refuse to adopt the same.

K. COMMENTS

The security of the vendor is as important as the security of the user, since a breach of vendor security, in a service bureau context, will expose property of the user. As a result the user should have the right to control and inspect the security conditions at the vendor's site.

L. REFERENCES TO OTHER CLAUSES: 8-22, 9-21, 9-24.

A. **CLAUSE NAME:** Evidence of Proper Insurance   B. **CLAUSE NO.:** 9-27

C. **CONTRACT TYPES USED IN:** Services   D. **RISK RATING:** 3

E. **INTENT AND SCOPE**

To ensure that the service organization has appropriate insurance to cover liability, loss or destruction of valuable business papers, and misconduct of employees.

H. **IDEAL COVERAGE**

The vendor will at its own expense maintain insurance during the term of this agreement, and furnish the user with evidence thereof, including but not limited to, comprehensive liability, fire and theft with extended coverage, valuable papers insurance, and fidelity bonds covering each vendor employee, at least in the amounts set forth on Schedule A.

L. **REFERENCES TO OTHER CLAUSES:** 8-21.

A. **CLAUSE NAME:** Guarantee of Ownership of Programs   B. **CLAUSE NO.:** 9-28

C. **CONTRACT TYPES USED IN:** Services   D. **RISK RATING:** 3

E. **INTENT AND SCOPE**

To ensure that the user, by utilizing products produced by the service bureau, does not become involved in claims of infringement.

F. **PROTECTION AGAINST**

Protects against possible infringement claims.

G. **STANDARD CLAUSE PROVIDED BY MANUFACTURERS**

Ownership of Programs: All programs developed by NCR in connection with this Agreement are and shall remain the sole property of NCR.

H. **IDEAL COVERAGE**

The vendor warrants that it is the sole owner of the programs being used for user processing purposes, and that it has the absolute right to transfer ownership to the user of those programs herein provided to be transferred to user, or to provide the user with a non-exclusive license for the use of any other programs so utilized by vendor.

K. **COMMENTS**

The ownership of programs presumably is vested initially in the service organization who develops them. To the extent these programs are used to process information for the user, the ownership must be warranted by the vendor organization, since the user of the products thereof may involve the user in claims of infringement of such ownership provisions. If the programs were developed for the user, ownership thereof should be transferred to user; if they are of generalized utilization by vendor, the user should possess a non-exclusive license to their use and products.

This clause should be expressed with conventional indemnities by the vendor.

L. **REFERENCES TO OTHER CLAUSES:** 5-28, 7-29, 8-09.

A. **CLAUSE NAME:** Program Protection   B. **CLAUSE NO.:** 9-29

C. **CONTRACT TYPES USED IN:** Services   D. **RISK RATING:** 3

E. **INTENT AND SCOPE**

To protect proprietary rights.

H. **IDEAL COVERAGE**

The vendor agrees to apply for United States copyrights on any programs and associated documentation produced hereunder for the user promptly upon and only upon user request, and/or to assign all rights of copyright thereto to user. In all events, whether or not copyright registration is sought, the vendor agrees to treat the programs as proprietary and secret.

K. **COMMENTS**

It is the initial responsibility of the developer of the programs to protect them. If it is considered desirable or necessary by the user to obtain copyright protection for such programs then such action should be taken by the vendor if the user requests. If it is desirable to provide trade secret protection, then the vendor must warrant that it has not done and will not do anything to disturb the proprietary aspects of the material.

L. **REFERENCES TO OTHER CLAUSES:** 7-30, 9-28.

A. **CLAUSE NAME:** No Infringement of Software   B. **CLAUSE NO.:** 9-30

C. **CONTRACT TYPES USED IN:** Services   D. **RISK RATING:** 4

E. **INTENT AND SCOPE**

To ensure that software utilized by vendor in processing data is properly licensed to vendor.

H. **IDEAL COVERAGE**

The vendor warrants and represents that all manufacturer supplied and other non-vendor-owned software in use at vendor's installation has been procured by vendor under valid licenses from the equipment manufacturer or other owners thereof, and that vendor is not now, nor will vendor be, during the term of this agreement, in default under any such license. Vendor will not utilize any software during the term of this agreement which might cause the user to be charged with infringement upon or violation of the rights of any owner thereof. Vendor will indemnify and hold user harmless from and against any loss, cost, liability, or expense (including reasonable counsel fees) which user may incur by reason of any breach or claimed breach of the foregoing representations and warranties.

K. **COMMENTS**

A service bureau undoubtedly uses software developed by the manufacturer of the computer used by it. Such software will obviously be used in processing user data. To insure against the remote possibility that the user might be charged with infringement, the vendor should represent that it has paid the original equipment manufacturer for a license to use the software, and vendor should hold the user harmless from any possible infringement claim.

L. **REFERENCES TO OTHER CLAUSES:** 5-07, 5-28, 7-30, 9-29.

A. **CLAUSE NAME:** Data Storage Facilities   B. **CLAUSE NO.:** 9-31

C. **CONTRACT TYPES USED IN:** Services   D. **RISK RATING:** 3

E. **INTENT AND SCOPE**

To arrange that vendor facilities for storage of data are protected from natural and other disaster as well as from potential man-made disaster.

H. **IDEAL COVERAGE**

The vendor agrees that it will during the term of this agreement, maintain data storage facilities which meet the specifications set forth on Schedule A. The vendor agrees not to store any user files or other user material except at such data storage facilities.

K. **COMMENTS**

There is no known solution to file security other than duplication.

The service bureau's insurance, described in 9-27 also should cover the storage facilities.

L. **REFERENCES TO OTHER CLAUSES:** 9-26.

A. **CLAUSE NAME:** Ownership of Time Sharing Terminal   B. **CLAUSE NO.:** 9-32

C. **CONTRACT TYPES USED IN:** Services - Time Sharing   D. **RISK RATING:** 3

E. **INTENT AND SCOPE**

To define ownership of terminal equipment.

H. **IDEAL COVERAGE**

The terminal supplied hereunder for use by the user in time sharing services is, and shall remain, the property of vendor.

K. **COMMENTS**

The terminal provided by the vendor for time-sharing use belongs either to the user, the vendor, or a third party, and such ownership should be made clear in the contract. It should be noted that, absent specific provisions to the contrary, ownership implies that certain risks of loss or destruction of the equipment normally attach to the owner, who should, accordingly, procure insurance upon it.

Note that *hardware* is being supplied to the user as a part of a time-sharing contract. In this case, certain provisions of a hardware contract might be appropriate. (See Chapter 6)

L. **REFERENCES TO OTHER CLAUSES:** 6-75, 6-85.

A. **CLAUSE NAME:** Maintenance and Installation of Time   B. **CLAUSE NO.:** 9-33
Sharing Terminal

C. **CONTRACT TYPES USED IN:** Services - Time Sharing   D. **RISK RATING:** 3

E. **INTENT AND SCOPE**

To require the vendor to install and maintain the terminal.

H. **IDEAL COVERAGE**

The vendor shall install the time sharing terminal at the user's site, and shall certify its readiness for use. The vendor shall also maintain and repair it, so as to keep it in good working order and agrees to respond to requests for repairs within two hours from the time that the vendor is notified by telephone that the terminal is not operating properly.

K. **COMMENTS**

Regardless of who owns the time sharing terminal, its installation and maintenance should be the responsibility of the vendor, who has the technical competence to install it, and to provide for its proper operation in the time-sharing environment.

Note maintenance provisions of hardware contract.

L. **REFERENCES TO OTHER CLAUSES:** 6-47, 6-52 thru 6-67, 6-74.

A. CLAUSE NAME: Right to Use Terminal for Other Purposes   **B. CLAUSE NO.:** 9-34

C. CONTRACT TYPES USED IN: Services - Time Sharing   **D. RISK RATING:** 3

E. INTENT AND SCOPE

To afford the user the right to unrestricted use of the terminal.

H. IDEAL COVERAGE

The user is hereby granted the absolute right to use the time sharing terminal supplied under this contract for any purpose whatsoever, including, but not limited to, its use with other time sharing services, as a free standing typewriter, or as a Telex or TWX terminal.

K. COMMENTS

Since the time sharing terminal is paid for by the user on a full time basis, it should be available for user utilization for any purpose. Such purposes might include its use with another time sharing service, or as an independent free standing typewriter, or as a Telex-terminal. In any event, the methodology of use of the terminal should be explicitly defined.

Location may also be specified as unrestricted, but this may depend on communications links. See 6-79 for this.

L. REFERENCES TO OTHER CLAUSES: 6-78, 6-79.

A. CLAUSE NAME: Entry Turnaround **B. CLAUSE NO.:** 9-35

C. CONTRACT TYPES USED IN: Services - Time Sharing **D. RISK RATING:** 2

E. INTENT AND SCOPE

To define the performance characteristics of the time sharing service.

H. IDEAL COVERAGE

The service organization warrants and agrees that the system will supply a response (turnaround) to an entry made by the user within 10 seconds from the time the entry is received at the vendor's installation; except between the times of _____ and _____ when such turnaround time shall not exceed 15 seconds. Vendor shall not be responsible for delays in turnaround occasioned by transmission difficulties or other circumstances beyond vendor's control.

I. FALL-BACK ALTERNATIVES

If the vendor will not agree to absolute turnaround time guarantees, fall-backs include an agreement to average response time over a monthly period, to some other statistical formulation, or to a best efforts commitment.

K. COMMENTS

The turnaround time required to respond to an entry must be fixed on some basis, since that time is the basis for measuring the performance characteristics of the time sharing service. This clause becomes the basis for judging the effectiveness with which the time sharing service operates.

L. REFERENCES TO OTHER CLAUSES: 6-46, 9-02.

A. CLAUSE NAME: Date Base Accessibility   **B. CLAUSE NO.:** 9-36

C. CONTRACT TYPES USED IN: Services - Time Sharing   **D. RISK RATING:** 3

E. INTENT AND SCOPE

To insure user access to a generalized data base which is unique to vendor.

F. PROTECTION AGAINST

To protect against a cessation by the time sharing organization in providing a specific data base.

H. IDEAL COVERAGE

The vendor agrees during the entire time of this agreement to make available its _____ data base for use by the user organization for such purposes as user may determine.

K. COMMENTS

A time sharing service often provides access to a data base, which is either in the public domain or, at least, is being furnished to all users of the service. A warranty of its continued accessibility should be included in the contract, to insure that the vendor organization does not arbitrarily cease providing this information.

L. REFERENCES TO OTHER CLAUSES: 6-15, 7-03.

A. **CLAUSE NAME:**   Program Accessibility   B. **CLAUSE NO.:**   9-37

C. **CONTRACT TYPES USED IN:**   Services - Time Sharing   D. **RISK RATING:**   3

E. **INTENT AND SCOPE**

To obtain user access to programs provided by the time sharing service.

H. **IDEAL COVERAGE**

The vendor, upon user request, agrees to furnish copies to user of any and all programs used by the user at the charges set forth in 9-09 or 9-38. When requested, programs shall be furnished in object and source code, and shall include all documentation.

K. **COMMENTS**

To the extent that a time sharing service has provided significant programming, access thereto may be potentially desirable, if the user desires to convert to internal processing, or to shift to a different time sharing organization. Program accessibility may be a negotiated part of a time sharing contract, which will permit the user to obtain the programs on some agreed basis.

L. **REFERENCES TO OTHER CLAUSES:**   9-04, 9-09, 9-38.

A. CLAUSE NAME: Definition of Charges

B. CLAUSE NO.: 9-38

C. CONTRACT TYPES USED IN: Services - Time Sharing

D. RISK RATING: 2

E. INTENT AND SCOPE

To describe the entire cost to the user for time-sharing.

H. IDEAL COVERAGE

The user shall pay to vendor monthly the sum of $_____ as a minimum fee against the following use charges:

Program access	– $	per
Data base access	$	per
Computer resource unit	$	per
Terminal connect time	$	per
File storage	$	per
Terminal rental	$	per month
Terminal maintenance	$	per month
Communications	$	per month

K. COMMENTS

The charges incurred in time sharing are somewhat different from those incurred in other services. They should be explicitly defined, and parameters used in their computation should be established. Such charges include charges for program access, data base access, terminal rental and maintenance, computer resource units,* terminal connect time, storage of data files, and minimum charges which may be levied against the user as well.

*This is an especially insidious charge, if its derivation or calculation method is not defined.

L. REFERENCES TO OTHER CLAUSES: 9-09.

A. CLAUSE NAME: File Compatibility   **B. CLAUSE NO.:** 9-39

C. CONTRACT TYPES USED IN: Services - Time Sharing   **D. RISK RATING:** 3

E. INTENT AND SCOPE

To require the vendor to maintain file compatibility with user, or with another service.

F. PROTECTION AGAINST

Protects against disruption upon termination of time sharing contract.

H. IDEAL COVERAGE

The vendor warrants that all files maintained in the provision of these services will be on a user-compatible basis, and that they will match in every respect the files of the user organization. [or those of other commonly used files].

K. COMMENTS

If the user desires to change time sharing organizations or to undertake the processing internally, it will be necessary to obtain copies of the files. In that event, it is desirable to have the vendor agree that the files will be and remain compatible with files of another organization, and that they are compatible with files of the internal organization. File compatibility, therefore, should be defined in the contract, since at the time of termination the vendor is less likely to be willing to be cooperative.

In this clause it is desirable to indentify the equipment manufacturer with whose equipment the files are compatible. Since the various equipment manufacturers have different file structures, some of which are not compatible with one another, it is desirable to stipulate explicitly what the file structures are.

L. REFERENCES TO OTHER CLAUSES: 5-21, 6-09, 9-40.

A. **CLAUSE NAME:** Program Compatibility   B. **CLAUSE NO.:** 9-40

C. **CONTRACT TYPES USED IN:** Services - Time Sharing   D. **RISK RATING:** 3

E. **INTENT AND SCOPE**

To establish standards for program compatibility.

H. **IDEAL COVERAGE**

The vendor warrants that the programs used in processing the time sharing services supplied hereunder are and will remain compatible with the equipment installed at the user organization, and will perform on all of the types of equipment listed on Schedule A without modification. Programs are written in COBOL, [FORTRAN, PL/1, or any other language], and can be recompiled to perform on the types of equipment listed on Schedule A.

K. **COMMENTS**

If the user decides to change time sharing services, or to process in-house, it is desirable for the programs under which the processing is being performed to be compatible with the machine used by the user or by another time sharing vendor. A description of the programming in the contract at the outset enables the user to know what conversion costs, if any, may be incurred in the event of a change-over.

Absolute compatibility cannot be guaranteed, except for identical machines. However, the vendor can make representations of this kind without significant peril, although some may desire to qualify a representation of absolute "compatibility."

L. **REFERENCES TO OTHER CLAUSES:** 5-21, 6-09, 9-39.

A. CLAUSE NAME: Non-Disclosure by Employees   **B. CLAUSE NO.:** 10-01

C. CONTRACT TYPES USED IN: Employee contracts   **D. RISK RATING:** 2

E. INTENT AND SCOPE

When a party signs a contract which includes a non-disclosure or confidentiality clause (see 5-13), it in turn should have an underlying agreement with its employees binding them in like manner.

F. PROTECTION AGAINST

Protects against the breach of confidentiality by the employee both for the protection of the employer's confidences and for the protection of the employer's customers with whom it has entered into a confidential relationship.

G. STANDARD CLAUSE PROVIDED BY MANUFACTURERS

Disclosure of Information: The Employee recognizes and acknowledges: that the services the Company performs for its clients are confidential and that to enable the Company to perform those services its clients furnish to the Company confidential information concerning their affairs; that the good will of the Company depends, among other things, upon its keeping such services and information confidential and that unauthorized disclosure of the same would irreparably damage the Company; and that by reason of his duties hereunder, the Employee may come into possession of information concerning the services performed by the Company for its clients, and concerning information furnished to the Company by its clients, even though the Employee does not himself take any direct part in or furnish the services performed for those clients. The Employee accordingly agrees that, except as directed by the Company, he will not at any time during or after his employment hereunder, disclose any of such services or information to any person whatsoever, or permit any person whatsoever to examine or make copies of any reports or other documents prepared by him or coming into his possession by reason of his employment hereunder, and that upon the termination of his employment hereunder, he will turn over to the Company all documents, papers, memoranda, and other matter, in his possession or under his control, that have in any way to do with the clients of the Company and that came into his possession or under his control by reason of his employment hereunder. (BASI)

H. IDEAL COVERAGE

The employee agrees, during the term of his employment and forever thereafter to keep confidential all information and material provided to him by employer, excepting only such information as is already known to the public, and including any such information and material relating to any customer, vendor or other party transacting business with the employer, and not to release, use or disclose the same except with the prior written permission of the employer. The within understandings shall survive the termination or cancellation of this agreement or of the employee's employment, even if occasioned by the employer's breach or wrongful termination. Employee recognizes that the disclosure of information by the employee may give rise to irreparable injury to the employer or to the owner of such information, inadequately compensible in damages and that, accordingly, the employer or such other party may seek and obtain injunctive relief against the breach or threatened breach of the within undertakings, in addition to any other legal remedies which may be available.

L. REFERENCES TO OTHER CLAUSES: 5-13, 5-14, 8-20, 8-22, 9-21, 10-02.

A. CLAUSE NAME: Inventions by Employees—Property of Employer   **B. CLAUSE NO.:** 10-02

C. CONTRACT TYPES USED IN: Employee contracts   **D. RISK RATING:** 3

E. INTENT AND SCOPE

To afford to the employer and its licensees or customers the benefit of all discoveries and innovations made by the employee.

G. STANDARD CLAUSE PROVIDED BY MANUFACTURERS

Assignment of Patents: The Employee shall notify the Company of any discovery, invention, innovation, or improvement conceived or developed by the Employee during the term of his employment and related to the business of the Company or to the business of any client of the Company; and all such discoveries, inventions, innovations, and improvements shall be the exclusive property of the Company. The Employee shall, when appropriate, file for patents and thereafter assign his rights in such patents to the Company. (BASI)

H. IDEAL COVERAGE

The employee agrees that any inventions, discoveries, developments, modifications, procedures, ideas, innovations, systems, programs, know-how or designs developed by the employee during his employment shall be the property of the employer and agrees further to execute applications for patents or copyrights thereon to the extent so requested by the employer and/or to assign the same to the employer. The employee agrees that all of the foregoing shall be the subject of the confidentiality, non-use and non-disclosure requirements of 10-01.

J. POSSIBLE REMEDIES

A remedy for breach is injunctive relief.

K. COMMENTS

To the extent that an employee may make discoveries, design or develop new systems, invent new solutions or increase employer know-how, the employee should relinquish any rights he or she may have therein to the employer. This is very necessary where the employer has given a "rights-in-data" representation to another organization. Thus, a service organization, having agreed to develop a system and to transfer title to that system, can do so comfortably only if the employees who actually develop that system and who may, therefore, have some rights to the discoveries or innovations contained therein, have agreed to relinquish any such rights.

L. REFERENCES TO OTHER CLAUSES: 5-17, 10-01.

A. **CLAUSE NAME:** Warranty of Used Equipment Condition   B. **CLAUSE NO.:** 10-03

C. **CONTRACT TYPES USED IN:** Used equipment purchase   D. **RISK RATING:** 1
contract

E. **INTENT AND SCOPE**

To describe and guaranty the condition of used equipment to a purchaser thereof.

H. **IDEAL COVERAGE**

The seller warrants that the equipment hereby sold is in good working order, and has been maintained under a standard maintenance contract by _____ , the manufacturer of the equipment. Seller further warrants that the equipment will be accepted by _____, its manufacturer, under its standard maintenance contract at prevailing standard rates, without upgrading or reconditioning costs.

I. **FALL-BACK ALTERNATIVES**

As an alternative it may be possible to obtain certification of maintenance eligibility directly from the original equipment manufacturer.

J. **POSSIBLE REMEDIES**

A possible remedy is to provide for the escrow of a part of the purchase price, sufficient to provide for major overhaul or reconditioning of the equipment, until manufacturer's inspection can be made. (10-05)

K. **COMMENTS**

The seller of a used computer should provide the purchaser with a warranty of the condition of the used equipment. This warranty can take the form of a statement that the equipment is in good working order, and that the equipment will not require reconditioning prior to acceptance by the manufacturer of a new maintenance contract at standard rates. Alternatively, the warranty can describe the specific condition of the equipment, and its historical record of performance. From the purchaser's viewpoint the principal objective is that the equipment will be eligible for maintenance at rates then in effect for comparable equipment.

L. **REFERENCES TO OTHER CLAUSES:** 6-59, 10-04, 10-05.

A. **CLAUSE NAME:** Agreement to Maintain Used Equipment   B. **CLAUSE NO.:** 10-04

C. **CONTRACT TYPES USED IN:** Used equipment purchase   D. **RISK RATING:** 2
contract

E. **INTENT AND SCOPE**

To ensure that the equipment being purchased will immediately be subject to maintenance.

G. **STANDARD CLAUSE PROVIDED BY MANUFACTURERS**

If Burroughs has not had immediately prior equipment maintenance responsibility for the system, the equipment is to be placed in acceptable working order before equipment maintenance is provided.

H. **IDEAL COVERAGE**

Attached hereto as Exhibit A is a certificate signed by the manufacturer that the equipment will be accepted under its standard maintenance contract at standard rates.

I. **FALL-BACK ALTERNATIVES**

Attached hereto as Exhibit A is a signed maintenance contract from the original equipment manufacturer, with rights of renewal.

As a second fallback, the seller can agree that in the event costs are incurred in obtaining a maintenance contract from the original equipment manufacturer, such costs will be borne by the seller, and funds may be placed in escrow for such performance. (See 10-03.)

K. **COMMENTS**

The used equipment contract should require the seller to deliver a separate agreement for maintenance, signed by a reputable maintenance organization or the original equipment manufacturer. This maintenance agreement normally would be a separate maintenance contract between maintainer and purchaser. Alternately, a warranty should be given by the seller that such a maintenance contract can be obtained. (See 10-03.)

L. **REFERENCES TO OTHER CLAUSES:** 10-03, 10-05.

A. CLAUSE NAME: Escrow of Funds Against Performance   **B. CLAUSE NO.:** 10-05

C. CONTRACT TYPES USED IN: Used equipment purchase contract   **D. RISK RATING:** 2

E. INTENT AND SCOPE

To provide a fund to secure the purchaser of used equipment that it will operate as warranted.

F. PROTECTION AGAINST

Protects against misrepresentations by leaving a portion of the price outside seller's hands until the veracity of the representation is tested.

H. IDEAL COVERAGE

The seller agrees that _____ percent of the purchase price hereunder shall be placed in escrow in accordance with the escrow agreement annexed as Exhibit A, to secure the warranties made in 10-03. [10-04] In the event that the equipment requires reconditioning, or other repair, the escrow agent will be authorized to release the cost thereof to the purchaser upon presentation of the manufacturer's invoice therefore, all in accordance with the notice requirements and all of the other provisions of said escrow agreement.

K. COMMENTS

It may be desirable to place in escrow a portion of the purchase price for a reasonable period of time to secure the performance of the used equipment and the warranties made by the seller. In many instances, the seller is not as financially responsible as an original equipment manufacturer might be. As a result, an escrow is probably a good idea, if the seller has made warranties of equipment condition or performance.

L. REFERENCES TO OTHER CLAUSES: 6-39, 8-11.

A. **CLAUSE NAME:** All Rights of Original Purchaser   B. **CLAUSE NO.:** 10-06
Transferred

C. **CONTRACT TYPES USED IN:** Used equipment purchase   D. **RISK RATING:** 2
contract

E. **INTENT AND SCOPE**

To pass through to a purchaser of used equipment all rights which the seller has against the manufacturer.

H. **IDEAL COVERAGE**

Seller hereby transfers and assigns to purchaser all of seller's right, title and interest in and to the purchase agreement with _____ , dated _____ , a copy of which is annexed hereto as Exhibit A and hereby irrevocably appoints the purchaser as seller's attorney-in-fact to exercise in seller's name or in purchaser's name any and all of the rights granted to seller in said purchase agreement.

K. **COMMENTS**

An original equipment purchaser has certain rights against the manufacturer of the equipment, or against the maintenance organization, if different. To the extent that these rights are transferrable, they should be passed on to the second user. Such rights may include continued availability of documentation (6-29, 6-30) continued availability of education (6-23), reconditioning on future resale (6-59), rights to maintenance training (6-60), upgrades and other significant continuing rights granted under the original purchase contract. The user would be wise to examine the original purchase contract to insure that such transfer is possible, and to determine which rights remain capable of being transferred. (See 5-04)

L. **REFERENCES TO OTHER CLAUSES:** 5-04, 10-09.

A. **CLAUSE NAME:** Purchase Options at End of Lease   B. **CLAUSE NO.:** 10-07

C. **CONTRACT TYPES USED IN:** Third party lease   D. **RISK RATING:** 3

E. **INTENT AND SCOPE**

To afford the user-lessee the right to purchase the leased equipment at the time of lease expiration.

H. **IDEAL COVERAGE**

Option to Terminate at any Time By Payment of Termination Value: This lease may be terminated by the lessee at any time, by payment to the lessor of the applicable termination value amount shown in Schedule A. Upon such payment, lessor will transfer title in the equipment to lessee.

Option to Purchase at End of Term: Upon the expiration of the lease, the lessee shall have the option, to be exercised upon _____ days notice prior to such expiration, to purchase the equipment.

K. **COMMENT**

It may be desirable at the termination of the lease for the user to have a purchase option at some predefined amount. The inclusion of such an option in the lease should not be done cavalierly, and should be inserted in the lease only after consultation with tax and audit counsel, since the mere existence of the option may, under certain circumstances, have both balance sheet, income statement and federal income tax effects. Some third-party lessors will agree to user termination at any time based upon scheduled termination value payments. Thus, if the lease is terminated early, the user is required to make a significant termination value payment which compensates the leasing company for the use of its money and for the equipment value at the time of termination.

Note that the exercise of such an option is comparable to the purchase of a used computer from the view of the manufacturer. Thus review 10-03 thru 10-06 for applicability.

L. **REFERENCES TO OTHER CLAUSES:** 6-86, 10-03 thru 10-06.

A. **CLAUSE NAME:** Pass-through of Investment Tax Credit   B. **CLAUSE NO.:** 10-08

C. **CONTRACT TYPES USED IN:** Third party lease   D. **RISK RATING:** 3

E. **INTENT AND SCOPE**

To pass investment tax credits on to the user in a long-term lease.

H. **IDEAL COVERAGE**

The lessor warrants to lessee that the equipment has a useful life in excess of seven (7) years, is new and of original manufacture, and is, therefore, eligible for the full investment tax credit, as that credit is defined under existing federal tax law. The lessor agrees not to claim such credit and further agrees that the credit may be claimed by user. Lessor will execute such returns, forms and other instruments as may be required to effectuate the intent hereof.

K. **COMMENTS**

To the extent that the lessee needs or can make use of the tax credit, and to the extent the lessor is prepared to pass it on, the credit may be directly given to the lessee. Alternatively, the amount of the credit can be computed and passed through by reduction in rents payable. The best approach depends upon the earnings pictures of the parties and the structure of the deal. Tax counsel should be consulted.

L. **REFERENCES TO OTHER CLAUSES:** 6-37.

A. CLAUSE NAME: Attorney-in-fact with Vendor   **B. CLAUSE NO.:** 10-09

C. CONTRACT TYPES USED IN: Third party lease   **D. RISK RATING:** 2

E. INTENT AND SCOPE

To give the user-lessee the ability to deal directly with the manufacturer of the equipment, where the purchase from the manufacturer was made by the lessor.

F. PROTECTION AGAINST

Protects against dependency by the user upon the lessor for relief against the manufacturer.

G. STANDARD CLAUSE PROVIDED BY MANUFACTURERS

No Warranties: Lessor makes no warranty or representation, either expressed or implied, as to the design and condition of, or as to quality of the material, equipment or workmanship in the equipment, and lessor makes no warranty of merchantability or fitness of the equipment for any particular purpose, it being agreed that all such risks as between lessor and lessee are to be borne by lessee. Lessor shall not be responsible for incidental or consequential damages. Lessor hereby irrevocably appoints and constitutes Lessee its agent and attorney-in-fact during the term of this Lease, so long as Lessee shall not be in default hereunder, to assert and enforce from time to time, in the name of and for account of Lessor; but for the benefit of Lessee, whatever claims and rights including warranties of the Equipment which Lessor may have against IBM. (ITEL).

H. IDEAL COVERAGE

Lessor represents that it has purchased the leased equipment from the manufacturer thereof _____ , under a purchase agreement between lessor and _____ , dated _____ , a copy of which is annexed hereto as Exhibit A. Lessor hereby assigns to lessee all of lessor's right, title and interest in and to said purchase agreement and hereby appoints lessee its attorney-in-fact, irrevocably during the term of this lease, and coupled with an interest, to exercise and enforce all of the rights granted to lessor under said purchase agreement, in lessor's name (or in lessee's name) and stead.

L. REFERENCES TO OTHER CLAUSES: 10-06.

A. **CLAUSE NAME:** Quiet Enjoyment   B. **CLAUSE NO.:** 10-10

C. **CONTRACT TYPES USED IN:** Third party lease   D. **RISK RATING:** 2

E. **INTENT AND SCOPE**

The leasing company may have financial problems, which should not affect the lessee. A quiet enjoyment clause is therefore mandatory in a third party lease.

G. **STANDARD CLAUSE PROVIDED BY MANUFACTURERS**

Quiet Enjoyment: Lessor hereby covenants that Lessee, upon paying the Rents herein provided for, and performing the covenants, agreements and conditions to be performed by Lessee hereunder, shall and may presently and quietly have; hold, and enjoy the Equipment and every part thereof leased hereunder, for the term aforesaid, free from repossession or disturbance by Lessor or the Lender or their respective officers, agents, employees or servants or by any one (whether the holder of a lien or otherwise) claiming through or under them or either of them. (ITEL).

Quiet Enjoyment: Provided the Lessee duly performs its obligations under this lease the Lessee shall be entitled to possess and use the Equipment during this lease without interruption by the Lessor or any person claiming under or through the Lessor. (Leasco).

H. **IDEAL COVERAGE**

The lessee shall be entitled to possess and use the equipment during this lease, without interruption by the lessor or any person claiming under or through the lessor, provided only that the lessee has duly performed its obligation under this lease. The lessor warrants and represents that the leased equipment is not subject to any lien, claim or encumbrance inconsistent herewith.

L. **REFERENCES TO OTHER CLAUSES:** 7-18, 9-15.

A. **CLAUSE NAME:** Right to Defend in Actions   B. **CLAUSE NO.:** 10-11

C. **CONTRACT TYPES USED IN:** Third party lease   D. **RISK RATING:** 3

E. **INTENT AND SCOPE**

To give the lessee the right to defend any actions brought which may affect the user's rights to or use of the equipment.

H. **IDEAL COVERAGE**

Lessor agrees to notify lessee immediately upon the commencement of any actions brought against lessor whose outcome may affect the rights of the user herein granted or its use of the leased equipment and user shall have the right to appear in and defend such actions and user's expenses (including reasonable counsel fees) shall be borne by lessor.

I. **FALL-BACK ALTERNATIVES**

Lessee may be charged with the costs of such defense.

L. **REFERENCES TO OTHER CLAUSES:** 5-28, 10-12.

A. **CLAUSE NAME:** Right to Dispute Taxes   B. **CLAUSE NO.:** 10-12

C. **CONTRACT TYPES USED IN:** Third party lease   D. **RISK RATING:** 3

E. **INTENT AND SCOPE**

To afford the user the right to contest taxes levied upon leased equipment without subjecting itself to claims of default.

G. **STANDARD CLAUSE PROVIDED BY MANUFACTURERS**

Taxes: Lessee agrees that, during the term of this Lease, in addition to the Rent and all other amounts provided herein to be paid, it will promptly pay all taxes, assessments and other governmental charges (including penalties and interest, if any, other than those resulting from the failure of Lessor on request to supply information to, or otherwise cooperate with, Lessee, and fees for titling or registration if required) levied or assessed:

(a) upon the interest of Lessee in the Equipment or upon the use or operation thereof or on the earnings of Lessee arising therefrom; and

(b) against Lessor on account of its acquisition or ownership of the Equipment or any part thereof, or the use or operation thereof or the leasing thereof to Lessee, or the Rent herein provided for, or the earnings of Lessor arising therefrom, provided, however, that Lessee shall not be responsible for any taxes based on net income of Lessor or for any taxes based on gross income of Lessor (other than gross receipts taxes) which may hereafter be imposed in a particular jurisdiction as a substitute for and not in addition to taxes based on net income. Lessee agrees to file, on behalf of Lessor, all required tax returns and reports concerning the Equipment (other than where Lessee as a result of a requirement of a particular law notifies Lessor that such returns or reports must be filed by Lessor) with all appropriate governmental agencies, and within not more than 45 days after the due date of such filing to send Lessor and the Lender confirmation, in form satisfactory to Lessor, of such filing; provided, however, that if Lessee shall in good faith and by appropriate legal or administrative proceedings contest the validity, applicability, or amount of any such taxes assessed or proposed to be assessed, the obligation to make prompt payment thereof shall be deferred until such proceedings are concluded unless thereby in the judgment of Lessor the rights or interests of Lessor may be materially or adversely affected. Lessor will cooperate with Lessee in any such contest and will permit Lessee to conduct the same in the name of Lessor or in the name of Lessee, as Lessee may determine, all at Lessee's own cost and expense. (ITEL).

H. **IDEAL COVERAGE**

The lessee may in good faith and by appropriate legal proceedings contest the validity, applicability or amount of any personal property or other taxes assessed or levied upon the leased equipment or its use and lessor agrees to cooperate with lessee in any such contest, and will permit lessee to contest the same in the name of lessor or in the name of lessee as lessee may determine, all at lessee's cost and expense. Notwithstanding anything to the contrary contained in this lease, the non-payment of any such taxes by lessee in connection with such contest, shall not be deemed a default hereunder, until final determination in such contest and expiration of any due date established therein.

I. **FALL-BACK ALTERNATIVES**

The lessor may insist that the taxes be escrowed during the pendency of such contest, to establish a fund for payment of the amount finally determined.

K. COMMENTS

Inasmuch as property taxes are normally levied upon the owner of equipment, such property taxes can usually only be disputed by lessor. Since the lessor normally passes the obligations to pay such taxes through to the lessee, the lessor may not be motivated to contest any such taxes. Accordingly, the user, as the ultimate obligor, should be given the right to dispute any taxes levied.

L. REFERENCES TO OTHER CLAUSES: 6-35, 10-11.

A. **CLAUSE NAME:** Supply Specifications | B. **CLAUSE NO.:** 10-13

C. **CONTRACT TYPES USED IN:** Supply contracts | D. **RISK RATING:** 4

E. **INTENT AND SCOPE**

In a supply contract, it is desirable to restate the fact that the specifications to be met must be those identified by the original equipment manufacturer. These specifications therefore should mirror those contained in clause 6-13.

H. **IDEAL COVERAGE**

The specifications for the supplies to be purchased hereunder are attached as Exhibit A. The supplier warrants that all supplies to be provided hereunder shall meet the specifications issued, from time to time, and in force at the time of delivery of such supplies, by the original equipment manufacturer, as well as the specifications attached as Exhibit A.

L. **REFERENCES TO OTHER CLAUSES:** 6-12, 6-13.

A. **CLAUSE NAME:** Workmanship B. **CLAUSE NO.:** 10-14

C. **CONTRACT TYPES USED IN:** Supply contracts D. **RISK RATING:** 4

E. **INTENT AND SCOPE**

To establish that the supplies will be of good quality and workmanship.

H. **IDEAL COVERAGE**

The supplier warrants that the quality standards used in the manufacturing of the supplies are equal to or higher than those in general use in the industry, and that all supplies will be of good workmanship, free from defects, of merchantable quality and fit for their intended general use by the purchaser.

K. **COMMENTS**

If specific or unusual uses are intended to be made of the supplies, these should be made known to the supplier who should warrant their fitness for such use.

L. **REFERENCES TO OTHER CLAUSES:** 6-13, 10-13.

A. CLAUSE NAME: Functional Usability of Supplies   **B. CLAUSE NO.:** 10-15

C. CONTRACT TYPES USED IN: Supply contracts   **D. RISK RATING:** 3

E. INTENT AND SCOPE

Supplies, such as tapes and disks, purchased independently should probably be warranted as functionally usable in the applications for which they are being considered.

H. IDEAL COVERAGE

The supplier warrants that the supplies being delivered pursuant hereto will meet the user's functional requirements described in Schedule A.

L. REFERENCES TO OTHER CLAUSES: 6-13, 10-14.

A. **CLAUSE NAME:** Continued Availability of Supplies   B. **CLAUSE NO.:** 10-16

C. **CONTRACT TYPES USED IN:** Supply contracts   D. **RISK RATING:** 2

E. **INTENT AND SCOPE**

To insure the uninterrupted flow of supplies.

H. **IDEAL COVERAGE**

The supplier warrants that for a period of _____ years from the date of this contract it will continue to manufacture and sell to user supplies of equivalent specifications to those being delivered hereunder, at prices then in effect, which shall not exceed the within prices by more than _____ percent.

I. **FALL–BACK ALTERNATIVES**

Fallbacks involve different methods of price adjustment, such as the cost of living index.

K. **COMMENTS**

In many supply contracts the supplier is required to make available such supplies on a repetitive basis. Supplies are consumable, and, therefore, must be reordered at periodic intervals. Since data processing supplies generally are quite specialized, it is desirable to obtain the supplier's agreement that subsequent orders will continue to be honored, that the supplier will in fact continue to manufacture such supplies to the specifications outlined, all for some defined period of time.

L. **REFERENCES TO OTHER CLAUSES:** 6-15, 6-43.

A. CLAUSE NAME: Expenses—Personal Services   **B. CLAUSE NO.:** 10-17

C. CONTRACT TYPES USED IN: Personal service or   **D. RISK RATING:** 3
consulting contract

E. INTENT AND SCOPE

To control expenses attendant to service arrangements.

H. IDEAL COVERAGE

Vendor's aggregate expenses under this contract shall not exceed $_____, and shall consist only of the following, which shall be justified as actually and necessarily expended in connection with the performance of this contract, and evidenced by receipts: air travel, at coach fare rates between the supplier's base and the user's site; actual hotels, meals, and local transportation, not to exceed _____ dollars per day.

K. COMMENTS

In a personal service contract, expenses are normally reimbursed at cost. Since this can be fairly open-ended, the buyer would be wise to limit the amount of expense, either in an absolute sense, or in terms of which expenses may be deemed to be reasonable.

L. REFERENCES TO OTHER CLAUSES: 8-10.

A. **CLAUSE NAME:** Scope and Deliverables   B. **CLAUSE NO.:** 10-18

C. **CONTRACT TYPES USED IN:** Personal service contract   D. **RISK RATING:** 2

E. **INTENT AND SCOPE**

To articulate the scope of and performance expected in a personal service contract.

H. **IDEAL COVERAGE**

The vendor will perform the project with the following stated objectives: [List]

At the conclusion of the project, the extent and manner to which the objectives have been met will be described in a final report. An outline (or table of contents) of the final report to be furnished is set forth on Schedule A.

K. **COMMENTS**

The deliverables under a personal services or consulting contract should be defined in detail. The simplest way to do this, in the event the deliverable is a project report of some type, is to annex a table of contents of the report to be produced as part of the contract.

L. **REFERENCES TO OTHER CLAUSES:** 8-02, 8-04, 9-01.

A. **CLAUSE NAME:** Named Individuals   B. **CLAUSE NO.:** 10-19

C. **CONTRACT TYPES USED IN:** Personal services or   D. **RISK RATING:** 2
                                 consulting contracts

E. **INTENT AND SCOPE**

To require the vendor of personal services to name the people who will be assigned to the project.

H. **IDEAL COVERAGE**

The vendor shall assign the following individuals to the project herein described, on a full time basis and in the capacities set forth below:

Project Manager: _____

Project Staff: _____

                   _____

Project Assistant: _____

Resumes of these individuals are attached as Schedule A.

K. **COMMENTS**

The individuals who will perform the tasks are the key to the success and quality of any personal services project. It is necessary to stipulate which individuals will be involved since the user typically purchases services of this kind on the basis of specific individuals' capabilities. All too often, in the absence of such a provision users find that the very talented and insightful consultant, who put the deal together and induced the user to commit to the work, is fully occupied in marketing and that far less impressive individuals are assigned to the work.

L. **REFERENCES TO OTHER CLAUSES:** 6-20, 8-17, 10-20.

A. **CLAUSE NAME:** Rights to Approve Changes in Staff   B. **CLAUSE NO.:** 10-20

C. **CONTRACT TYPES USED IN:** Personal services—   D. **RISK RATING:** 2
consulting contract

E. **INTENT AND SCOPE**

To assure that the user has the right to approve any staff changes in a personal service contract.

G. **STANDARD CLAUSE PROVIDED BY MANUFACTURERS**

Personnel: In recognition of the fact that IBM personnel provided to the Customer under this Agreement may perform similar services from time to time for others, this Agreement shall not prevent IBM from performing such similar services or restrict IBM from using the personnel provided to the Customer under this Agreement. IBM will make every effort consistent with sound business practices to honor the specific requests of the Customer with regard to the assignment of its employees; however, IBM reserves the sole right to determine the assignment of its employees.

H. **IDEAL COVERAGE**

The user has the absolute right to approve or disapprove any proposed vendor changes in project staff from those listed in 10-19. The user, in each instance, will be provided with a resume of the proposed substitute and an opportunity to interview that person, prior to giving its approval or disapproval.

I. **FALL–BACK ALTERNATIVES**

A fallback would require the vendor to permit the user to select each substitute staff member from, say, three proposed substitutes.

L. **REFERENCES TO OTHER CLAUSES:** 6-20, 10-19.

A. **CLAUSE NAME:** Security Interest in Equipment   B. **CLAUSE NO.:** 10-21

C. **CONTRACT TYPES USED IN:** Installment purchase   D. **RISK RATING:** 2
contract

E. **INTENT AND SCOPE**

To protect the vendor's security in the equipment purchased on an installment basis.

G. **STANDARD CLAUSE PROVIDED BY MANUFACTURERS**

Security Interest:

(a) UNIVAC reserves title in the equipment sold as security for the performance of this agreement. Notwithstanding any other terms or provisions hereof, should the Purchaser default in the payment of the purchase price of equipment when due or fail to comply with any and all provisions of this agreement, UNIVAC shall have the right to remove and/or repossess such equipment after ten (10) days prior written notice as it may deem necessary to protect its interest.

(b) The equipment, accessories and devices furnished under this Agreement shall, at all times and for all purposes, be considered personal property, notwithstanding the manner or mode of its attachment to Purchaser's premises. Purchaser shall keep such equipment free from liens and encumbrances and shall not remove said equipment, accessories and devices, from Purchaser's installation site address set forth herein, without UNIVAC's prior written consent.

(c) Purchaser shall be fully responsible for the care and safekeeping of all equipment, accessories and devices covered hereby from the date of delivery to its premises and shall procure and maintain fire, extended coverage, vandalism and malicious mischief insurance thereon, during the term hereof, for the full insurable value thereof, naming UNIVAC as an additional insured and with loss Payable to UNIVAC and Purchaser, as their interests may appear. Evidence of such coverage shall be provided by a Certificate of Insurance, which is to be submitted to UNIVAC and shall be satisfactory to UNIVAC; such certificate to include the statement that "In the event of cancellation of, or material change in, the policy, 10 days prior written notice of such action shall be given to UNIVAC at the address stated below". In the event that such insurance shall be included under a policy covering Purchaser's own property, such policy shall contain a clause reading substantially as follows: ". . . including the property of others which the assured has agreed to insure prior to loss or damage or for which the assured may be liable in the event of loss or damage . . .".

(d) "Purchaser agrees to execute any financing statements and all other documents re-quested by UNIVAC to protect UNIVAC's security interest in the equipment, and to comply with state and local requirements for filing and/or recording. If Purchaser fails to execute any such documents, UNIVAC is hereby given power of attorney to execute same in Purchaser's name."

Security Interest and Location of Machines: IBM reserves a purchase money security interest in each of the machines and Purchaser hereby grants a security interest in any substitutions, replacements and additions thereto and the proceeds thereof. These interests will be satisfied by payment in full of the Total Time Sale Price. A copy of this Installment Payment Agreement may be filed with appropriate state authorities at any time after signature by the Purchaser as a financing statement in order to perfect IBM's security interest. Such filing does not constitute acceptance of this Installment Payment Agree-ment by IBM. The Purchaser also shall execute from time to time, alone or with IBM, any financing statements or other documents and do such other act or acts considered by IBM to be necessary or desirable to perfect or protect the security interests hereby created. The machines shall remain personal property, not become part of the freehold, and be kept at No. _____ (address)

Security Interest: UNIVAC reserves title in the equipment sold as security for the performance of this Agreement. Notwithstanding any other terms or provisions hereof, should the Purchaser default in the payment of the purchase price of equipment when due or fail to comply with any and all provisions of this Agreement, UNIVAC shall have the right to remove and/or repossess such equipment after ten (10) days prior written notice and to take such other action as it may deem necessary to protect its interest, it being understood that the remedies contained in this Section 4 are cumulative and in addition to all other rights and remedies of UNIVAC under this Agreement, by operation of law or otherwise.

H. IDEAL COVERAGE

The user grants to vendor a security interest in the equipment and in any substitutions, replacements and additions thereto, pending the full payment of the purchase price. The security interest herein granted shall be governed by the Uniform Commercial Code of the State of _____ and the user shall have all the benefits accorded to debtors thereunder.

K. COMMENTS

User counsel should review all security interests in the context of state law and attempt to obtain as many user protections and the waiver of as many vendor UCC rights as are negotiable. For instance, many debtor's attorneys seek to require the vendor in foreclosure to have a public sale, with notice to the user and with specified advertising.

L. REFERENCES TO OTHER CLAUSES: 10-22.

A. **CLAUSE NAME:** No Liens or Encumbrances   B. **CLAUSE NO.:** 10-22

C. **CONTRACT TYPES USED IN:** Installment purchase contract   D. **RISK RATING:** 3

E. **INTENT AND SCOPE**

To protect the vendor against second encumbrances on the equipment.

G. **STANDARD CLAUSE PROVIDED BY MANUFACTURERS**

Purchaser's Covenants: The Purchaser covenants and agrees that: (a) it will not create, assume, or voluntarily suffer to exist, without giving IBM at least 15 calendar days prior written notice, any mortgage, pledge, encumbrance, security interest, lien or charge of any kind upon the machines, or any of them; (b) it will keep the machines in good repair and operating condition; (c) it will pay promptly all taxes, interest and other charges when levied or assessed upon the machines or their operation or use in connection with this Installment Payment Agreement; and (d) it will promptly satisfy all liens against the machines. (IBM)

H. **IDEAL COVERAGE**

The purchaser agrees to maintain the equipment free from any liens, encumbrances or security interests (other than the within security interest in favor of vendor) until the purchase price shall have been fully paid.

K. **COMMENTS**

Vendors like this clause and believe it simplifies their lives. Users should resist it if at all possible, since its existence can sometimes hinder or prohibit valuable financing arrangements. For example, if a user has an encumbered computer, on which there is a very small balance owing, the user equity in which constitutes a significant part of its net worth, institutional financing may be unavailable unless the computer can be mortgaged to the lender; sometimes, the lender will simply advance the additional amount necessary to pay off the manufacturer thereby freeing the equipment as collateral to the lender. This may increase aggregate user interest costs and may not be possible unless the user has a right of prepayment. See 10-25.

L. **REFERENCES TO OTHER CLAUSES:** 10-21, 10-25.

A. **CLAUSE NAME:** Right to Cure Default	B. **CLAUSE NO.:** 10-23
C. **CONTRACT TYPES USED IN:** Installment purchase contract	D. **RISK RATING:** 2

E. INTENT AND SCOPE

To provide for notice to the user of any default and opportunity to cure it.

G. STANDARD CLAUSE PROVIDED BY MANUFACTURERS

Defaults: In the event that any one or more of the following events of default shall occur and be continuing: (a) the Purchaser shall fail to pay in full any sum payable by the Purchaser when payment thereof shall be due hereunder; or (b) the Purchaser shall, for more than 30 days after IBM shall have demanded in writing performance or observance thereof, fail or refuse to comply with any other covenant, agreement, term or provision of this Installment Payment Agreement on its part to be kept or performed; or (c) any information furnished by the Purchaser to IBM in its Application for Credit or in its financial information for the purpose of inducing IBM to enter into this Installment Payment Agreement was inaccurate and IBM would not have entered into this Installment Payment Agreement on the basis of the correct information; or (d) any obligation of the Purchaser (other than any obligation secured hereby) for the payment of borrowed money becomes or is declared to be due and payable prior to the expressed maturity thereof; or (e) a substantial portion of the machines suffer a Casualty Occurrence; or (f) the Purchaser makes an assignment for the benefit of creditors, files a petition in Bankruptcy, is adjudicated insolvent or bankrupt, petitions or applies to any tribunal for any receiver or any trustee of Purchaser or any substantial part of its property, commences any proceeding relating to the Purchaser under any reorganization, arrangement, re-adjustment of debt, dissolution or liquidation law or statute of any jurisdiction, whether now or hereafter in effect, or if there is commenced against the Purchaser any such proceeding which remains undismissed for a period of 60 days, or the Purchaser by any act indicates its consent to, approval of or acquiescence in any such proceeding or the appointment of any receiver of or any trustee for it or any substantial part of its property, or suffers any such receivership or trusteeship to continue undischarged for a period of 60 days; then at any time after the occurrence of such an event of default IBM may declare all unpaid installments immediately due and payable.

H. IDEAL COVERAGE

The non-payment or non-performance of any obligation of user hereunder shall not be deemed a default unless the same shall not have been cured within _____ days after written notice to user of such non-payment or non-performance; any non-performance which, in the exercise of due diligence, cannot be cured within such _____ day period shall not be deemed a default so long as user shall within such period commence and thereafter continue diligently to cure such non-performance.

K. COMMENTS

In the event that user fails in some way to perform, the user should have the opportunity to cure prior to repossession of the equipment, or acceleration of the purchase price. Notice of claimed default is particularly necessary in these days of decentralization of operations, reliance on computers and administrative foul-ups.

L. REFERENCES TO OTHER CLAUSES: 5-23.

A. CLAUSE NAME: Disaster Protection   **B. CLAUSE NO.:** 10-24

C. CONTRACT TYPES USED IN: Installment purchase contract   **D. RISK RATING:** 3

E. INTENT AND SCOPE

To require that the equipment be insured both to protect the debt owing on the equipment and the user's equity in it.

G. STANDARD CLAUSE PROVIDED BY MANUFACTURERS

Insurance: The Purchaser further agrees to procure and maintain fire insurance with extended coverage on the machines for the full insurable value thereof for the life of this Installment Payment Agreement, the policy for such insurance being endorsed to show loss payable to IBM and assigns as respective interests may appear. Upon request a certificate of such insurance will be furnished to IBM or assigns. Any proceeds received directly by IBM under such insurance shall be credited to the payment required from the Purchaser pursuant to the next succeeding paragraph.

Destruction of Machines: In the event that any of the machines shall be lost, stolen, irreparably damaged or destroyed or otherwise rendered permanently unfit for use from any cause whatsoever (such occurrences being hereinafter called Casualty Occurrences) prior to the payment in full of the Total Time Sale Price and such Casualty Occurrences do not constitute an event of default, the Purchaser shall promptly pay to IBM a sum equal to the aggregate Casualty Value of such machines. Any money so paid shall be applied, on the installment date next following receipt by IBM of such payment, to reduce monthly installments thereafter falling due so that such installments represent only the payments due for the remaining machines.

    The Casualty Value of each machine suffering a Casualty Occurrence shall be the sum of the balances of the state and local taxes, Unpaid Principal Cash Balance and Time Price Differential unpaid at the time of such Casualty Occurrence and attributable to such machine, such Time Price Differential being adjusted to reflect the shorter payment period.

H. IDEAL COVERAGE

So long as any portion of the purchase price remains unpaid, user shall maintain and pay for fire (with extended coverage), _____ , and _____ insurance upon the equipment in an amount equal to at least $_____ , which amount may be decreased by not more than _____ percent for each year after installation, which insurance shall name the vendor and the user as co-insureds, as interests may appear and shall provide that the insurer may not cancel or terminate such insurance except upon _____ days notice to vendor.

K. COMMENTS

If the equipment is destroyed, the vendor has lost its security interest, but the user retains the obligation to continue the time payments, which are normally independent of the status of the equipment. As a result, insurance is mandatory from the viewpoint of both the user and the vendor.

L. REFERENCES TO OTHER CLAUSES: 6-50, 9-27.

A. **CLAUSE NAME:** Right to Prepayment   B. **CLAUSE NO.:** 10-25

C. **CONTRACT TYPES USED IN:** Installment purchase contract   D. **RISK RATING:** 1

E. **INTENT AND SCOPE**

To permit the user to prepay the deferred price whenever it is to the user's advantage to do so.

H. **IDEAL COVERAGE**

The user may, at any time, or from time to time, prepay all or any part of the outstanding installment obligation to vendor, without premium or penalty, but with interest to date of such prepayment. Any partial prepayment shall be applied against last maturing installments of the installment obligation in inverse order of maturity.

K. **COMMENTS**

An installment purchase agreement is for the convenience of the user, and vendors do not usually depend on the interest income as their primary source of revenues. Accordingly, the user should have the absolute right to prepay without penalty, if at any time the user can obtain better interest rates elsewhere or has obtained sufficient cash to enable it to avoid paying interest.

When the contract is fully prepaid, clauses 10-21, 10-22, and 10-24 should terminate.

L. **REFERENCES TO OTHER CLAUSES:** 10-21, 10-22, 10-24.

A. CLAUSE NAME: Advance Deposit Requirement   **B. CLAUSE NO.:** 10-26

C. CONTRACT TYPES USED IN: Advance deposit agreement **D. RISK RATING:** 3

E. INTENT AND SCOPE

The user with insufficient credit to obtain a machine can do so by providing an advance deposit.

H. IDEAL COVERAGE

Simultaneously herewith user has deposited with vendor the sum of $_____ representing _____ months equipment rental charges to secure the vendor against user default hereunder. Said deposit shall be applied by vendor against the last _____ months rental hereunder, unless such deposit shall have been applied upon user default or returned to user pursuant to 10-28. Said deposit shall, until application, be segregated by vendor in an interest bearing account and the interest shall be user's property and remitted to user at least semi-annually.

K. COMMENTS

Advance deposit agreements basically provide for prepayment of several months rental, as security for the user's obligations. The user should seek interest on the deposit and, if there is any cause for concern about the vendor's financial position, should require that the advance be placed in escrow.

L. REFERENCES TO OTHER CLAUSES: 10-27, 10-28, 10-29.

A. **CLAUSE NAME:** Refund Rights on Termination   B. **CLAUSE NO.:** 10-27

C. **CONTRACT TYPES USED IN:** Advance deposit   D. **RISK RATING:** 2
agreement

E. **INTENT AND SCOPE**

To assure the return of advance deposits upon contract termination.

G. **STANDARD CLAUSE PROVIDED BY MANUFACTURERS**

If, at any time after the commencement of this Agreement, all machines provided under
the Agreement for IBM Machine Service shall have been discontinued and all amounts due
to IBM shall have been paid, then IBM will refund to Customer all amounts paid to IBM
as Advance Deposits including the initial Advance Deposit and any additional Deposits
paid pursuant to paragraph 2 and this Agreement will be terminated.

Customer agrees to place with IBM additional Advance Deposits equivalent to a maximum of six months' rental, for any additional IBM machines to be installed during the
term of this Agreement if so requested by IBM. Such additional Advance Deposits shall
be merged with the initial Advance Deposit and the total shall be subject to the terms
of this Agreement.

If, at any time after the commencement of this Agreement, the total of Customer's unpaid and overdue IBM invoices equals or exceeds the total Advance Deposits being held
under this Agreement, then IBM may retain and apply such Deposits to the past due
indebtedness and initiate equipment removal procedures and this Agreement will be
terminated. IBM expressly reserves its rights to pursue all other remedies available to
it under the terms of the Agreement for IBM Machine Service and under the provisions
of the Uniform Commercial Code. Should this Agreement terminate under the provisions
of this paragraph, IBM shall have no obligation to furnish additional machines under the
Agreement for IBM Machine Service.

H. **IDEAL COVERAGE**

Upon the expiration of this agreement, or its earlier termination, except by reason of
user's default, the advance deposit shall forthwith be refunded to purchaser with all
accrued interest. If terminated by reason of user default, any excess remaining after
satisfaction of user's obligations hereunder shall likewise be returned to user.

K. **COMMENTS**

If the contract is for a fixed term the deposit can be applied against last rentals due as in
10-26.

L. **REFERENCES TO OTHER CLAUSES:** 10-26, 10-28.

A. **CLAUSE NAME:** Refund Rights on Establishment of Credit   B. **CLAUSE NO.:** 10-28

C. **CONTRACT TYPES USED IN:** Advance deposit agreement   D. **RISK RATING:** 2

E. **INTENT AND SCOPE**

To enable the user to recover the deposit upon establishment that its credit is satisfactory.

G. **STANDARD CLAUSE PROVIDED BY MANUFACTURERS**

If, at any time after the commencement of this Agreement, Customer (a) shall have paid **as due,** for any period of **12 consecutive** months, all IBM invoices and (b) meets at that time IBM's standard credit guidelines (which require a reasonable debt to tangible net worth ratio and a satisfactory cash flow) then IBM shall refund to Customer all Advance Deposits paid to IBM, both the initial Advance Deposit and any additional Advance Deposits which have been paid pursuant to paragraph 2, and this Agreement will be terminated.

H. **IDEAL COVERAGE**

If the user (a) shall have fully and timely paid the first _____ months of equipment rental hereunder, or (b) shall have attained a current asset/current liability ratio of _____ and a net worth of $_____ ; then, in either event, vendor shall forthwith return to user its deposit made hereunder.

K. **COMMENTS**

When proper credit has been established, either through a record of prompt payments or through improvement in user's balance sheet to meet defined standards, the advance deposit should be returned as well.

L. **REFERENCES TO OTHER CLAUSES:** 10-27.

A. CLAUSE NAME: Trust Funds　　　　　　　　　　**B. CLAUSE NO.:** 10-29

C. CONTRACT TYPES USED IN: Advance deposit agreement　**D. RISK RATING:** 2

E. INTENT AND SCOPE

To protect the advance deposit from the claims of vendor's creditors.

H. IDEAL COVERAGE

The vendor shall hold the user deposit in a separate, segregated interest-bearing account, as trust funds, with appropriate designation of their source and character and shall not comingle such funds with any funds of the vendor. Vendor shall notify user of the name of the bank and the account number of the account at which the funds are maintained.

K. COMMENTS

Funds held in an advance deposit agreement should be treated as trust funds and should not be comingled with other general funds of the vendor. This will protect the funds from claims of vendor's creditors. If the user is insecure about the vendor's financial strength, the deposit should be placed in escrow with a third party.

L. REFERENCES TO OTHER CLAUSES: 10-26.

A. **CLAUSE NAME:** Functions Performed During Relocation   B. **CLAUSE NO.:** 10-30

C. **CONTRACT TYPES USED IN:** Relocation agreement   D. **RISK RATING:** 3

E. **INTENT AND SCOPE**

To comprehensively define the obligations of the manufacturer in relocation of equipment.

G. **STANDARD CLAUSE PROVIDED BY MANUFACTURERS**

Discontinuance Service:

Pre-shipment Testing: The machine, including all active IBM features but excluding NON-IBM alterations, will be tested prior to disassembly to insure correct operation. Malfunctions of machines covered by an IBM Maintenance Agreement will be corrected at no charge prior to disassembly, if feasible, or at the next location. IBM Hourly Maintenance Service is available for machines not covered by an IBM Maintenance Agreement.

Disassembly: The machine will be disassembled to the extent necessary for shipment and assistance given to the customer in identifying cables, terminators and other items to be shipped with the machine. The customer is responsible for specifying the actual cable and terminator complements to be shipped. In the absence of specific instructions, IBM will identify the items which are normally shipped with the machine.

Packaging Materials: IBM will furnish, at the prevailing price, standard packaging materials. Requests should be made sufficiently in advance of the date the services are required so that the necessary materials may be obtained. These packaging materials and procedures are designed as precautionary measures to minimize likelihood of damage in transit, but do not guarantee against such damage.

Installation of Packaging Materials: The appropriate internal packaging materials will be installed to prepare the machine for shipment. Technical information will be provided, if required, to assist the customer in external packing of the machine, cables, terminators and other items. Arrangements for shipment of the machine are the customer's responsibility.

Documentation: At the conclusion of Discontinuance Service, IBM will provide an Equipment Relocation Activity Record itemizing the specific services performed, with comments as required. Copies will be included with the machine for use at the receiving location, mailed to the owner and given to the customer's representative on site.

Installation Service:

Installation Planning: IBM will assist in the physical planning of systems installations. This includes information on aspects of the physical environment such as floor layout planning, cable requirements, air conditioning, electrical requirements, instrumentation or communication facilities and safety considerations.

Assembly: Internal packing will be removed and the machine assembled including necessary interconnection of required IBM machine cables. Technical information will be provided, if required, to assist the customer in the unpacking of the machine, cables, terminators and other items.

Installation and Testing: IBM will install and fully test the machine including active IBM features and applicable IBM System Control Programming but excluding NON-IBM alterations. Diagnostics will be reconfigured if required.

H. IDEAL COVERAGE

In consideration of this relocation agreement, the vendor agrees to perform the following services:

a) testing of the equipment prior to shipment.

b) disassembling and disconnecting of the equipment.

c) packaging and crating all equipment components.

d) providing the necessary documentation and bills of lading.

e) planning the installation at the new site.

f) uncrating, unpacking and assembly.

g) installation and certification of readiness for use.

From commencement of disassembly until readiness for use at the new location, the vendor shall assume all risks of loss, damage or destruction of the equipment.

K. COMMENTS

A relocation agreement should require the manufacture to dismantle, crate, prepare, plan, uncrate and re-install the equipment. Normally, the manufacturer does not provide the actual shipment, since this must be done by licensed movers.

L. REFERENCES TO OTHER CLAUSES: 10-31.

A. **CLAUSE NAME:** Applicability of all Warranties   B. **CLAUSE NO.:** 10-31

C. **CONTRACT TYPES USED IN:** Relocation agreement   D. **RISK RATING:** 2

E. **INTENT AND SCOPE**

To assure the equipment, after relocation, remains in the same physical condition and subject to the same contractual advantages.

H. **IDEAL COVERAGE**

The vendor warrants that the equipment, after relocation, will operate in the same manner as it did prior to relocation, that all warranties applicable to the equipment prior to relocation will remain in full force and effect, all as if the equipment had not been relocated, and that the existing maintenance agreement will remain in full force and effect, in accordance with its terms.

K. **COMMENTS**

To the extent that the manufacturer is providing maintenance, and has warranted the equipment, the continuance of such warranties is desirable from the viewpoint of the user, even though the equipment has been relocated from one site to another.

L. **REFERENCES TO OTHER CLAUSES:** 10-30.

A. CLAUSE NAME: Time Required   **B. CLAUSE NO.:** 10-32

C. CONTRACT TYPES USED IN: Equipment relocation agreement   **D. RISK RATING:** 3

E. INTENT AND SCOPE

To define the schedule of relocation, and to require the vendor to perform it at a time convenient to the user.

H. IDEAL COVERAGE

The relocation shall be completed in a period of _____ days. The vendor agrees to schedule such _____ days in a contiguous period, selected by the user upon not less than _____ days notice to vendor. Such period may include a week-end, if feasible to the user, and no additional charges shall accrue by virtue of the time of day or time of week during which the relocation shall be carried out. The vendor recognizes that time is of the essence in the performance of this agreement.

K. COMMENTS

If the relocation is over an extended distance, the problems of scheduling become intensified and both lengthy notice and margin for error will probably have to be allowed to the vendor. If the vendor is not in control of the actual shipment, it will want exculpation from delays occasioned by the mover.

L. REFERENCES TO OTHER CLAUSES: 10-30.

A. **CLAUSE NAME:** Course Contents and Objectives   B. **CLAUSE NO.:** 10-33

C. **CONTRACT TYPES USED IN:** Training contract   D. **RISK RATING:** 2

E. **INTENT AND SCOPE**

To define the goals to be achieved by the training course.

H. **IDEAL COVERAGE**

The subject matter and detailed table of contents of the course is as follows:

The principal objective of the training program is to take entry level students and to teach them the following skills:

K. **COMMENTS**

As in most other personal services contracts, the principal problem is to define the contract and objectives to be achieved. The contract should include a statement of the substantive content of the course and its objectives in terms of the skills to be achieved by the attendees. The statement of objectives should where the user deems it important also have and describe the qualifications of the instructors. (See 10-19, 10-20)

Also review 6-21 through 6-27 for training course clauses with respect to hardware training.

L. **REFERENCES TO OTHER CLAUSES:** 8-01, 8-02, 10-18.

A. **CLAUSE NAME:** Course Schedule | B. **CLAUSE NO.:** 10-34

C. **CONTRACT TYPES USED IN:** Training contract | D. **RISK RATING:** 3

E. **INTENT AND SCOPE**

To describe the amount of time required to teach the course, and the specific schedule in which it will be taught.

H. **IDEAL COVERAGE**

The course will commence at 9 a.m. on _____ and end at 5 p.m. on _____ and will include _____ hours of lectures and _____ hours of workshop. At the option of the user, the course can be extended by up to an additional _____ hours of workshop time, without additional charge.

K. **COMMENTS**

If the course is complex, the time allocated to various subjects can be negotiated and recorded in the contract. It is wise for the user to examine the course breakdowns offered by the vendor and to select among them; if larger time segments are requested with respect to a specific area than are offered by the vendor, the vendor will be tempted to expand it by merely filling time.

L. **REFERENCES TO OTHER CLAUSES:** 10-33.

A. **CLAUSE NAME:** Attendee Characteristics   B. **CLAUSE NO.:** 10-35

C. **CONTRACT TYPES USED IN:** Training contract   D. **RISK RATING:** 4

E. **INTENT AND SCOPE**

To define the prerequisites for attendance, the course size and any other special characteristics of the course that could affect eligibility for attendance.

H. **IDEAL COVERAGE**

The course is designed to teach a maximum of _____ students. In order to attend, user employees should have the educational background, general and specific data processing experience and special characteristics set forth in Schedule A.

K. **COMMENTS**

The prerequisite characteristics of the attendees can be stipulated in the contract, to assure that the objectives can be properly achieved. The user, of course, should be permitted to send whomsoever it chooses. Defined characteristics should include the previous education and experience which may be required in order to properly absorb the training. In addition, the total number of attendees which will be admitted in a training program should be defined. Many vendors define charges by reference to numbers of attendees.

L. **REFERENCES TO OTHER CLAUSES:** 10-33.

A. **CLAUSE NAME:** Training Facilities   B. **CLAUSE NO.:** 10-36

C. **CONTRACT TYPES USED IN:** Training contracts   D. **RISK RATING:** 4

E. **INTENT AND SCOPE**

To avoid uncertainty as to the focus of responsibility for various necessary physical elements attendant to the training course.

G. **STANDARD CLAUSE PROVIDED BY MANUFACTURERS**

The Customer agrees to provide classroom space, facilities, and computer time for the listed course(s) and not exceed the stated student maximum per class. Course specifications and requirements are shown in the following table, and course description(s), objectives, and prerequisites are shown in the attachments. The course price includes the use of required materials and publications. (IBM)

Title and Course Code	Course Length	Computer Time	Price	Maximum No. of Students

H. **IDEAL COVERAGE**

The vendor will provide all necessary instructional equipment and materials, including audio visual equipment, specimen machinery, calculation equipment and student and instructor materials. The user will supply the classroom, lecterns and refreshments for attendees, if desired.

K. **COMMENTS**

The training contract should stipulate the facilities required to provide the training and the party responsible for their provision. Training facilities generally include audio-visual equipment, blackboards, the room, refreshments, and students' facilities such as physical equipment, materials, pencils, pads and workbooks for workshop participation. Training materials include course syllabi, agendas, tests, workbooks, instructor's guides, audio-visual material, and the like.

L. **REFERENCES TO OTHER CLAUSES:** 10-33.

APPENDIX B

CHECKLIST
FOR A
COMPUTER HARDWARE CONTRACT*

This material represents a checklist of items to be included in a typical computer hardware contract, from the view of the user. It is not complete, and all hardware contracts must be tailored to specific user and vendor situations. The material is deliberately in random sequence, to avoid any imputation of importance to any item or items.

1. Hardware Configuration
2. Software Configuration
3. Hardware Component Specification
4. Software Component Specification
5. Systems Performance—Batch
6. Systems Performance—On-Line
7. Attachment of Proposal
8. Attachment of Hardware Manuals
9. Attachment of Software Manuals
10. Attachment of Functional Specification
11. Hardware Component Prices
12. Software Component Prices
13. Other Charges
14. Total Price
15. Price Protection—Hardware and Software
16. Price Protection—Maintenance
17. Price Protection—Expansion or Future Equipment
18. Price Protection—Other Charges
19. Supplies Required—Specifications
20. Supply Sources
21. Supply Costs
22. Guarantee of Supply Availability
23. Upward/Downward Compatibility
24. Ability to Interface with Other Equipment
25. Ability to Interface with Standard Communications Equipment
26. Changes and Attachments
27. Ability to Modify in Field
28. Environmental Requirements
29. Power Requirements
30. Cabling Requirements
31. Staffing Supplied by Type and Amount
32. Reliance on Vendor Expertise
33. Staff Caliber
34. Education Available
35. Educational Allotment
36. Continuing Availability of Education
37. Availability of Instructors
38. Rights to All Training Materials

---

*For included software, see "Turnkey Systems Contract," "Software Package Contract," or "Software Development Contract." For processing services, see "Facilities Management Contract."

39. Rights to Future Courses
40. Rights to Teach Courses Internally
41. Price Protection—Software Enhancements
42. Rights to Future Software Enhancements
43. Test Time Supplied—Schedule/Site
44. Documentation Availability
45. Rights to Reproduce Documentation
46. Agreement Term
47. Method of Payment
48. Holdbacks for Contract Compliance
49. Taxes
50. Pass Through of Investment Tax Credit
51. Percentage of Property Tax Applicable
52. Warranty of New Equipment
53. Method of Charging by Types of Charges
54. Credits for Malfunction
55. Reliability Definitions
56. Guarantees of Reliability
57. Warranty Period
58. Free Maintenance Period
59. Right to Replace Components
60. Back Up Availability
61. Disaster Protection
62. Acceptance Procedures
63. Acceptance Test Data
64. Benchmarks
65. System Software Support
66. Business Terms
67. Hardware Maintenance Types
68. On-Site Maintenance
69. Off-Site Maintenance Response Time
70. Maintenance Access Needs
71. Spare Parts Availability
72. Space and Maintenance Facilities
73. Continuity and Rights to Renew Maintenance
74. Reconditioning on Resale
75. Rights to Maintenance Training
76. Rights to Purchase Spares in Future
77. Engineering Changes
78. No Subcontracts
79. Malfunction and Correction Reporting
80. Preventive Maintenance Schedule
81. Separation of Maintenance Costs in Rental Contract
82. Availability of Expansion Units
83. Installation Responsibility
84. Installation Costs
85. Transportation Costs
86. Risk of Loss at All Stages
87. Insurance Requirements
88. Delivery Schedule by Group or Component

89. Rights to Postpone Delivery
90. Rights to Advance Delivery
91. Delivery and Shipping Notices
92. Delivery Delays
93. Irreparability of Certain Delays
94. Site Preparation Responsibility
95. Cancellation of Components Prior to Delivery
96. Substitution of Components Prior to Delivery
97. Unrestricted Use and Function
98. Unrestricted Location
99. Future Hardware Upgrades
100. Future Software Upgrades
101. Trade-In
102. Title Transfer
103. License to Software
104. Purchase Option (If Rental Contract)
105. Rental Credit on Purchase Option
106. Purchase Price Protection
107. Termination Prior to Delivery
108. Liquidated Damages
109. User Costs of Delays
110. Arbitration
111. Continuity During Dispute
112. Most Favored Nations
113. Acceptance Test Failure Actions
114. Patent and Copyright Indemnity
115. User Confidentiality
116. Vendor Confidentiality
117. Force Majeure
118. Force Majeure Cancellation Rights
119. Vendor Bankruptcy
120. Notice of Default and Right to Cure
121. Non-Hire of Staff
122. Compliance with Client Security
123. Performance Bond
124. Non-Assignment of Contract
125. No Brokers or Intermediaries
126. Indemnities
127. Right of Offset
128. Survival Beyond Completion
129. No Partial Shipments
130. Limitations of Liability
131. Severability and Partial Invalidity
132. UCC Applicability
133. Notices
134. All Amendments in Writing
135. Order of Precedence
136. Headings not Controlling
137. Authority
138. Entire Agreement

139. Statute of Limitations
140. Governing Law and Forum
141. Breach not Waiver
142. Publication and Advertising
143. No Liens or Encumbrances

CHECKLIST
FOR A
SOFTWARE PACKAGE CONTRACT*

This material represents a checklist of items to be included in a typical software package contract, from the view of the user. It is not complete, and all software contracts must be tailored to specific user and vendor situations. The material is deliberately in random sequence, to avoid any imputation of importance to any item or items.

1. Attachment of Package Specification
2. Attachment of Package Documentation
3. Hardware Facility Requirements
4. Software Facility Requirements
5. Package Price
6. Package Lease Terms and Renewals
7. Rights to Future Enhancements
8. Performance (run time)
9. Freedom of Use
10. Freedom of Location
11. Warranty of Operation
12. Payment Terms
13. Other Charges
14. Price Protection—License Fee
15. Price Protection—Maintenance Fee
16. Ownership Warranty
17. Non-Taxability as Property
18. Business Termination
19. Vendor Financials
20. Access to Source Code
21. Source Code Escrow
22. Arbitration
23. Non-Assignment by Vendor
24. Assignment by User with Consent
25. Confidentiality
26. Protection of Vendor Rights by User
27. Delivery
28. Installation Support
29. Training Support
30. Maintenance Warranty
31. Force Majeure
32. Future Training Availability

---

*If equipment is included also, see "Turnkey Systems Contract." For included processing services, see "Facilities Management Contract."

33. Fixes
34. Upgrades
35. User Right to Modify Package
36. User Right to Modify Source Code
37. User Obligation to Identify Errors
38. Compliance with ANSI Standards
39. Quiet Enjoyment
40. UCC Applicability
41. Warranty of Functionality
42. Delivery Failure
43. Acceptance Method
44. Acceptance Test Procedures
45. Support Requirements
46. Non-Infringement
47. Patent and Copyright Indemnity
48. Rights of Rescission in Initial Period
49. Other Deliverables
50. Rights to Reproduce Documentation
51. Exclusion of Taxes
52. Inclusion of Expenses
53. Most Favored Nations
54. Installation Responsibility
55. Delivery Delay
56. Adaptation to Hardware Operating System Changes
57. Power and Authority to Grant Licenses
58. Continuity During Dispute
59. Cancellation Costs
60. Notice of Default and Right to Cure
61. Staff Caliber (installation-modification staff)
62. Rights to Change Staff
63. Staff Insurance
64. Non-Hire of Staff
65. Staff Execution of Non-Disclosure
66. Compliance with Client Security
67. Product Liability Insurance
68. Progress Reports
69. Access to Design by Auditor
70. Workmanship
71. No Brokers or Intermediaries
72. Indemnities
73. Limitation of Liabilities
74. Statute of Limitations
75. Survival Beyond Completion
76. Training Materials Supplied by Vendor
77. Location of Training
78. Payment Holdback
79. Severability
80. Partial Invalidity
81. Notices
82. Amendments in Writing

83. Headings not Controlling
84. Entire Agreement
85. Governing Law and Forum
86. Breach not Waiver
87. Publication and Advertising
88. Non-Competition
89. File Compatibility
90. Notice of Automatic Renewal

If Modifications are Tailored to User Requirements by the Vendor

91. Ownership Rights of Modification
92. Title Transfer
93. Non-Use for Other Clients
94. Fixed Price or Level of Effort
95. Specifications
96. Client Acceptance
97. Delivery Dates by Segment
98. Warranty of Original Development
99. Progress Reporting
100. Test Data to be Used
101. Integration with Package

CHECKLIST
FOR A
SOFTWARE DEVELOPMENT CONTRACT*

This material represents a checklist of items to be included in a typical software development contract, from the view of the user. It is not complete, and all software contracts must be tailored to specific user and vendor situations. The material is deliberately in random sequence, to avoid any imputation of importance to any item or items.

1. Definition of Project Scope
2. Attachment of Functional Specifications
3. Attachment of Proposal
4. Hardware Configuration Requirements
5. Software Configuration Requirements
6. Definition of Stages and Tasks
7. Deliverables by Stage
8. Standards/Methodology by Stage
9. Completion Percentages by Stage
10. Documentation Requirements
11. Documentation Standards
12. Progress Payments by Stage
13. Total Price
14. Expenses and Other Charges
15. Taxes

---

*For software packages, see "Software Package Contract." When software development is sold with the dedicated hardware see "Turnkey Systems Contract." For included processing services see "Facilities Management Contract."

16. Title Transfer by Stage
17. Progress Reports
18. Non-Competition
19. Vendor Confidentiality
20. User Confidentiality
21. Employee Agreements
22. Constraints on Resource Usage by Vendor
23. Guarantee of Original Development
24. Arbitration
25. Continuity During Dispute
26. Acceptance Responsibility
27. Acceptance Test Procedure by Stage
28. Test Data to be Used
29. Cancellation Rights by Stage
30. Cancellation Actions
31. Payment Holdback
32. Staff Qualifications
33. Staff Quantity
34. All Employees Full-Time, Assigned Full-Time
35. Right to Access Staff on Business Termination
36. Staff Insurance
37. Staff Compliance with Client Security
38. Workmanship
39. Client Ownership Rights
40. Client Freedom of Use
41. Performance (Run-Time/Response-Time)
42. Warranty
43. Corrections, Modifications, Upgrades
44. Maintenance Provisions After Acceptance
45. Operating Reliability Standards
46. Non-Taxability as Property
47. Vendor Financials Available
48. Change Procedure
49. Most Favored Nations
50. Business Terms
51. Delivery by Stage
52. Final Acceptance Date
53. Delays in Delivery
54. Material Delivery Failure
55. Patent and Copyright Indemnity
56. Warranty of Growth Capability
57. Force Majeure
58. Force Majeure Cancellation Rights
59. Events of Default
60. Rights to Cure
61. Training Supplied
62. Installation Supplied
63. Continuing Training Availability
64. Location of Training
65. Project Manager Designated

66. Right to Reject Staff
67. Non-Hire of Employees
68. Product Liability Insurance
69. Non-Assignment by Vendor
70. Assignment with Consent by Client
71. Auditor Access
72. Project Management Methodology
73. Data Conversion Programs
74. Data Conversion Responsibility
75. Language Used
76. Business Termination
77. UCC Applicability
78. Non-Infringement
79. Adaptation to Hardware Operating System Changes
80. No Brokers or Intermediaries
81. Limitation of Liabilities
82. Statute of Limitations
83. Survival Beyond Completion
84. Severability
85. Partial Invalidity
86. Notices
87. Amendments In Writing
88. Headings not Controlling
89. Entire Agreement
90. Governing Law and Forum
91. Breach not Waiver
92. Publication and Advertising
93. Cross-Guarantees
94. Consequential Damages
95. Rights to New Ideas
96. Client Site Access
97. No Subcontracting Without Consent
98. Client Information
99. Right of Offset
100. Order of Precedence
101. No Liens or Encumbrances
102. Client Ownership Marking

CHECKLIST
FOR A
THIRD PARTY COMPUTER LEASE*

This material represents a checklist of items to be included in a typical third party computer lease, from the view of the user. It is not complete, and all contracts must be tailored to specific user and vendor situations. The material is deliberately in random sequence, to avoid any imputation of importance to any item or items. The checklist presumes the existence of a separate computer hardware contract (see

---

*For included software, see "Turnkey Systems Contract," "Software Package Contract," or "Software Development Contract." For processing services, see "Facilities Management Contract."

"Checklist for a Computer Hardware Contract"), either directly between user and vendor, or between lessor and vendor.

1. Primary Lease Conditions—Type of Lease
2. Hardware Specification
3. Hardware Vendors by Component
4. Software Specifications
5. Software Vendors by Component
6. Attachment of Lease Proposal
7. Lessor Financial Statement
8. Prospectus or Financing Document
9. Lease Term
10. Payment Terms
11. Lease Termination Options
12. Lease Termination Values
13. Insurance Values
14. Other Charges
15. Taxes Applicable
16. Price Protection
17. Inclusion of Expansion Equipment
18. Substitution Prior to Delivery
19. Substitution After Delivery
20. Maintenance Responsibility
21. Maintenance Costs
22. Maintenance Price Protection
23. Attorney-in-Fact with Other Vendors
24. Treatment of Investment Tax Credit
25. Depreciation Treatment
26. Property Tax Responsibility
27. Rights to Dispute Taxes
28. Default Notice
29. Right to Cure Default
30. Arbitration
31. Continuity During Dispute
32. Disaster Alternatives
33. Business Terms
34. Rights to Purchase
35. Malfunction and Correction Reporting
36. Rebates for Serious Failures
37. Risk of Loss
38. Transportation Costs
39. Tasks on Lease Termination
40. Trade-in Rights
41. Termination Prior to Delivery
42. Acceptance Rights
43. Quiet Enjoyment
44. Right to Defend in Actions
45. Support to be Provided
46. Warranty of New Equipment
47. Warranty of Ownership and Title
48. Freedom of Use

49. Freedom of Location
50. Assistance in Relocation
51. Right of Assignment
52. Right of Sublease
53. Delivery Dates by Component
54. Invoicing Methods
55. Late Payment Remedies
56. Maximum Liability of User for Shipment on Termination
57. Maximum Liability of User for Reconditioning on Termination
58. Applicability of UCC
59. Indemnification by Lessor
60. Indemnification by Lessee
61. Patent and Copyright Indemnity
62. Installation Responsibility
63. Certification of Readiness for Use
64. Notice of Intent to Repossess
65. Lessor Bankruptcy
66. Lessee Bankruptcy
67. Limitations of User Liability
68. Attachment of Vendor Contracts
69. Remedies for Delivery Failure
70. Liquidated Damages
71. Vendor Failure to Raise Financing
72. Force Majeure
73. Force Majeure Termination Rights
74. Insurance Requirements
75. No Liens or Encumbrances
76. User Authority
77. User Rights to Make Changes
78. User Rights to Make Attachments
79. Field Modification
80. Engineering Changes
81. Pass-Through of Free Maintenance Period
82. Rights to Postpone Delivery
83. Rights to Advance Delivery
84. Shipping Notices
85. Method of Transportation
86. Treatment of Title
87. License for Software
88. Most Favored Nations
89. User Confidentiality
90. Vendor Confidentiality
91. Non-Hire of Staff
92. Compliance with Client Security
93. Bonding of Lessor Staff
94. No Brokers or Intermediaries
95. Right of Offset
96. No Partial Shipments
97. Survival Beyond Termination
98. Severability and Partial Invalidity

99. Notices
100. All Amendments in Writing
101. Performance Bond
102. Headings not Controlling
103. Order of Precedence
104. Entire Agreement
105. Statute of Limitations
106. Replacement Warranty
107. Industry Compatibility
108. Designation of Ownership
109. Attorneys Fees and Other Costs of Indemnity
110. Lease Extension Rights
111. Governing Law and Forum
112. Consent to Breach Not Waiver
113. Publication and Advertising
114. Percentage of Property Tax Applicable
115. Counterparts

CHECKLIST
FOR A
FACILITIES MANAGEMENT CONTRACT*

This material represents a checklist of items to be included in a typical facilities management contract, from the view of the user. It is not complete, and all such contracts should be tailored to the specific objectives of user and vendor. The list is deliberately in random sequence, to avoid any imputation of importance to any item or items.

1. Definition of Services Performed
2. Turnaround Time for Batch Work
3. Response Time for On-Line Work
4. Quality Standards
5. Costs and Charges
6. Term of the Agreement
7. Payment Method
8. Business Terms
9. Adjustments to Charges When Volume Changes
10. Adjustments to Charges Over Time
11. Price Protection
12. Change Procedure—Programming
13. Change Procedure—Processing
14. Reliability Parameters
15. Reliability Standards
16. Equipment Configuration to be Used
17. Site to be Used
18. List of Facilities and Furnishings at Site
19. File Ownership
20. Data Ownership
21. Media Ownership and Marking

---

*For hardware alone, see "Computer Hardware Checklist."

22. Program Ownership
23. Security Procedures
24. Staff Bonding
25. Contract Termination
26. Takeover on Termination
27. Assistance on Termination
28. Miscellaneous Charges—paper, supplies, messenger, reproduction, binding, etc.
29. Staff Expenses
30. Auditor Access
31. Site Access
32. Arbitration
33. User Access to Source Code
34. Miscellaneous Services to be Provided
35. Delivery of Programs and Changes
36. Title Transfer
37. Notice of Automatic Renewal
38. Protection from Levy by Creditors
39. Business Termination
40. Staff Transfer Rights
41. Destruction of Cartons, Intermediate Files, Rejects
42. Release of Information to Designated Personnel
43. Rights to Security Inspection
44. Evidence of Insurance
45. No Infringement of Software
46. Rights to All Programs
47. Available Facilities for Storage
48. Back-Up System Availability
49. Back-Up Files and Programs
50. Disaster Recovery Procedures
51. Equipment Lease Transfer on Termination
52. Pass-Through of Investment on Termination
53. Workmanship
54. Duty of Care
55. Attachment of Equipment Leases
56. Attachment of Space Leases
57. Attachment of Proposal
58. Attachment of Maintenance Contract
59. List of Systems Software Required
60. Most Favored Nations
61. Risk of Loss at all Stages
62. Start of Services
63. Impact of Delay
64. Liquidated Damages for Delay
65. Access to Client Information
66. License to Use Supplier Software
67. Acceptance Tests—Turnaround
68. Acceptance Tests—Reliability
69. Documentation Acceptance
70. Acceptance Failure Actions

71. Patent and Copyright Indemnity
72. License to Vendor Software
73. Power and Authority to Grant Licenses
74. User Confidentiality
75. Vendor Confidentiality
76. Force Majeure
77. Force Majeure Cancellation Rights
78. Other Events of Default
79. Reliance on Vendor Expertise
80. Subcontracts
81. Other Resources Supplied by User
82. Other Resources Supplied by Vendor
83. Exclusion of Specified Taxes
84. Equipment Adequacy at Volume Levels
85. Software Maintenance Responsibility
86. Continuity During Dispute
87. Costs of Termination/Cancellation
88. Rights to Disclose Data to Other Vendors
89. Non-Sale to User Competition
90. Notice of Default and Right to Cure
91. Standards to be Used
92. Errors, Modifications and Fixes
93. Assignment by Vendor
94. Assignment by User
95. Vendor Status as Independent Contractor
96. Progress Reports
97. Economic Reports
98. Breakdown of Charges
99. Staff to be Assigned
100. Staff Caliber
101. Project Manager
102. Right to Change Staff
103. Staff Insurance
104. Non-Hire of Staff
105. Staff Execution of Non-Disclosure/Non-Compete
106. Vendor Financials
107. Full-Time Employees
108. Performance Bond
109. Product Liability Insurance
110. Hardware Changes
111. Designation of Authorized Representatives
112. Maintenance of Time and Cost Records
113. Constraints on Vendor Use of User Resources
114. Supplies Specifications
115. Supply Sources
116. No Brokers or Intermediaries
117. Indemnification
118. Inclusion of Costs in Indemnity
119. Rights of Offset
120. Survival Beyond Completion

121. Reasonable Efficiency
122. Safeguarding of User Data and Property
123. Training of User Staff
124. Responsibility for the Supply of Communication Lines
125. Responsibility for Reruns Due to Errors
126. Liaison Representatives
127. Priority of Work
128. Order of Precedence for Attachments
129. Limitations of Liability
130. Rights to Teach Vendor Training Course
131. Rights to Reproduce Documentation and Materials
132. Payment Hold Backs
133. Severability and Partial Invalidity
134. UCC Applicability
135. Notices
136. All Amendments in Writing
137. Headings Not Controlling
138. Authority
139. Entire Agreement
140. Statute of Limitations
141. Governing Law and Forum
142. Breach not Waiver
143. Publication and Advertising
144. No Liens or Encumbrances

If Systems Are Owned by the User:

145. Ownership
146. Rights to Enhancements
147. Return of Systems on Termination
148. Non-Use for Other Clients of Vendor
149. Insurance or Protective Bond

If Systems Development Work is Included at the Outset:

150. Level of Effort Required
151. Fixed Price or Amortization of Costs
152. Payment Method
153. Client Acceptance
154. Functional Specification
155. Data and Program Compatibility
156. Conversion Responsibility
157. Delivery Dates by Application
158. Warranty of Original Development
159. Deliverables by Stage
160. Progress Reporting
161. Test Data to be Used

If the Facility is on the Client Site:

162. Site Specifications
163. Ambient Environment Requirements
164. Security Compliance

165. Staff Clearance and/or Bonding
166. Installation Responsibility
167. Transportation and Installation Costs
168. Installation Drawings
169. Vendor Access Procedures and Rights

If Terminals are Supplied to Client:

170. Terminal Costs
171. Terminal Maintenance
172. Title Transfer to Terminal
173. Rights to Use Terminals for Other Functions
174. Guarantee of Terminal Adequacy

CHECKLIST
FOR A
TURNKEY SYSTEMS CONTRACT*

This material represents a checklist of items to be included in a typical systems contract, from the view of the user. It is not complete, and all turnkey contracts must be tailored to specific user and vendor situations. The material is deliberately in random sequence, to avoid any imputation of importance to any item or items.

1. Attachment of Functional Specification
2. Attachment of Hardware Configuration and Price List
3. Attachment of Proposal
4. List of Systems Software Required
5. List of Vendors and Subcontracts
6. Reliance on Vendor Expertise
7. Vendor Review of User Documents
8. Responsibility for Development
9. Phases and Tasks of Development
10. Rights to Cancel at Phase Ends
11. Percentage Completion by Phase and Task
12. Deliverables by Phase
13. Equipment and Resource Requirements
14. Procedure for Changes
15. Performance and Operating Characteristics
16. Package Elements Used
17. Rights to Enhancements
18. Support for System Software
19. Price
20. Payment Terms
21. Inclusion of all Expenses
22. Exclusion of Specified Taxes
23. Business Terms
24. Price Protection—Current Prices
25. Price Protection—Future Hardware
26. Price Protection—Software Enhancements
27. Software Maintenance

*For hardware only, see "Computer Hardware" or "Third Party Lease" checklists.

28. Equipment Adequacy
29. Rights to Supplier Contracts
30. Hardware Maintenance Contract
31. Warranty of New Equipment
32. Availability of Expansion Units
33. Computation of Total Price
34. Most Favored Nations
35. Installation Responsibility
36. Installation Costs
37. Transportation Costs
38. Risk of Loss at All Stages
39. Pass-On of Price Reductions or Discounts
40. Delivery—Hardware
41. Delivery—Software
42. Shipping Notices
43. Responsibility for Trans-Shipment
44. Delivery Deferral Rights
45. Delivery Acceleration Rights
46. Delay Impact
47. Client Site Access
48. Site Preparation Requirements
49. Installation Timing
50. Site Inspection Rights
51. Installation Drawings
52. License to Use Supplier Software
53. License to Use Vendor Software
54. Acceptance Tests—Hardware
55. Acceptance Tests—Software
56. Performance Acceptance
57. Reliability Acceptance
58. Acceptance Rerun
59. Acceptance of Deliverables
60. Lemon Clause
61. Acceptance Test Failure Actions
62. Patent and Copyright Indemnity
63. Title Transfer
64. Warranty of Original Development
65. Warranty of System Conformance
66. Pass-Through of Supplier Warranties
67. Power and Authority to Grant Licenses
68. User Confidentiality
69. Vendor Confidentiality
70. Force Majeure
71. Force Majeure Cancellation Rights
72. Bankruptcy of Vendor
73. Other Events of Default
74. Termination Rights
75. Arbitration
76. Continuity During Dispute
77. Cancellation Costs

78. Right to Disclose Data to Other Vendors
79. Non-Sale to User Competition
80. Notice of Default and Right to Cure
81. Staff Caliber
82. Staff Quantity
83. Project Manager Assignment
84. Right to Change Staff
85. Staff Insurance
86. Non-Hire of Staff
87. Staff Execution of Non-Disclosure
88. Compliance with Client Security
89. Vendor Financials
90. Full-Time Employees
91. Staff Access on Business Termination
92. Facility Inspection Rights
93. Performance Bond
94. Product Liability Insurance
95. Other Insurance Requirements
96. Hardware Changes
97. User Right to Modify Software
98. User Access to all Source Codes
99. Contents of Documentation
100. Standards to be Used
101. Errors and Corrections
102. Assignment by Vendor
103. Assignment by User
104. Vendor Status as Independent Contractor
105. Progress Reports
106. Access by Auditors
107. Designation of Authorized Representatives
108. Time Records
109. Detailed Schedule and Status Availability
110. Workmanship
111. Rights to Reproduce Documentation
112. Rights to Use System Anywhere
113. Rights to Use System in Any Way
114. Rights to Provide Consulting Services to Others
115. Constraints on Vendor Use of User Resources
116. Facilities Limitations
117. Supplies Specification
118. Supply Sources
119. No Brokers or Intermediaries
120. No Subcontracting Without Consent
121. Indemnities
122. Inclusion of Costs in Indemnity
123. Data Conversion Specifications
124. Data Conversion Assistance
125. Right of Offset
126. Liquidated Damages for Delays
127. Survival Beyond Completion

INDEX

*Page numbers preceded by "A" are in appendix A.
Page numbers preceded by "B" are in appendix B.